Exploring Research

Third Edition

Neil J. Salkind

University of Kansas

Prentice Hall, Upper Saddle River, New Jersey 07458

Library of Congress Cataloging-in-Publication Data

Salkind, Neil, J.
      Exploring Research / Neil J. Salkind. —3rd ed.
        p. cm.
      Includes bibliographical references and index.
      ISBN 0–13–520636–7
        1. Psychology—Research—Methodology. 2. Education—
Research—Methodology. I. Title.
      BF76.5.S24 1997
      150'.72—dc20   96–5624
                                          CIP

Editor-in-Chief: Peter Janzow
Assistant Editor: Nicole Signoretti
Production Editor: Mary Rottino
Manufacturing Buyer: Tricia Kenny
Book Designer: Traci L. Bunkers
Cover Illustrator: Marianne Hughes
Cover Director: Jayne Conte

This book was set in New Century Schoolbook and Futura
by Traci L. Bunkers and was printed and bound by Quebecor/Semline.
The cover was printed by Lehigh.

 © 1997, 1994, 1991 by Prentice-Hall, Inc.
Simon & Schuster/A Viacom Company
Upper Saddle River, New Jersey 07458

Printed in the United States of America

10 9 8 7 6 5 4

ISBN 0-13-520636-7

Prentice–Hall International (UK) Limited, *London*
Prentice–Hall of Australia Pty. Limited, *Sydney*
Prentice–Hall Canada Inc., *Toronto*
Prentice–Hall Hispanoamericana, S. A., *Mexico*
Prentice–Hall of India Private Limited, *New Delhi*
Prentice–Hall of Japan, Inc., *Tokyo*
Simon & Schuster Asia Pte. Ltd., *Singapore*
Editora Prentice–Hall do Brasil, Ltda., *Rio de Janeiro*

Dedicated to the teaching enthusiasm of
James R. Raths
and to my colleagues at the University of Kansas

AT A

GLANCE

At a Glance

Contents

Chapter 3: Selecting a Problem and Reviewing the Research   51

Chapter 4: Sampling and Generalizability   95

Chapter 5: Measuring Behavior

Chapter 6: Methods of Measuring Behavior

Chapter 7: Data Collection and Descriptive Statistics   159

Chapter 8: Introducing Inferential Statistics   183

Chapter 9: Nonexperimental Research Methods   203

Chapter 10: Experimental Research

Chapter 11: Quasi-Experimental Research: A Close Cousin to Experimental Research

Chapter 12: Writing a Research Proposal   259

Chapter 13: Writing Research A Manuscript   275

Preface

One of the best things about any professor's job is working with students and helping them explore their ideas and reach their goals. For the past 20 years, I have been lucky enough to be part of this activity in my teaching of research methods courses at the University of Kansas.

What I have tried to do in this third edition of *Exploring Research* is to share some of those experiences with you, and I sincerely hope that I have succeeded in some part. This book is intended for upper-level undergraduate students and graduate students in their first research methods course in the social and behavioral sciences. It is intended to provide an introduction to the important topics in the general area of research methods and to do so in a non-intimidating and informative way. I am particularly thrilled about this third edition, since by its existence it appears that there is an audience for presenting this material in a way that is straightforward and unassuming.

What's New in This Edition

You will find several new things in this third edition of *Exploring Research*, many of them the result of suggestions from students and faculty.

- The contents have been reorganized to include two chapters on preparing professional materials, which are writing a research proposal (chapter 12) and writing a research manuscript (chapter 13). Both of these were added in response to professors who feel their students need to have basic skills in these areas, and the material is too important to be relegated to an appendix.
- Chapter 3 now includes extensive material on the use of the Internet for doing research in the behavioral and social sciences and new general information on doing research on-line. I assume that most students these days have basic computer skills and need no introduction to such tools as word processors, spreadsheets, and databases. Hence, that material has been removed from this edition.
- Appendix A covers the basic features of the Statistical Package for the Social Sciences (SPSS). The first and second editions of *Exploring Research* featured MYSTAT. SPSS, which is very powerful and becoming increasingly available, is the preferred tool for data analysis. This appendix can serve as an introduction to the basic features of SPSS including entering and analyzing data.
- New readings and additional exercises are offered at the end of each chapter.

How This Book Is Organized

Exploring Research is organized into 13 chapters and two appendices.

Chapter 1, *The Role and Importance of Research*, covers the basics about the scientific method and includes a brief description of the different types of research that are most common in the social and behavioral sciences.

The Research Process (chapter 2) focuses on some of the basic terms and concepts in research methods including variables, samples, populations, hypotheses, and the concept of significance. It also includes a section on ethical concerns and ethical practices.

The first step for any researcher is the selection of a problem, which is what chapter 3 (*Reviewing the Research and Selecting a Problem*) is all about. Here you will learn how to use the library and its vast resources to help you focus your interests and actually turn them into something you want to know more about! You will also be introduced to the use of electronic sources of reference material such as on-line searches, CD-ROM, and how the use of the Internet can enhance your research skills considerably.

The content of chapter 4, *Sampling and Generalizability*, is critical to understanding the research process. How you select the group of participants and how and when the results of an experiment can be generalized from this group to others is a fundamental premise of all scientific research. In this chapter you will read all about this process.

What is research without measuring outcomes? Not much, I'm afraid. Chapter 5, *Measuring Behavior*, introduces you to the measurement process and the important concepts of reliability and validity. Not only do you need to understand the principles of measurement, but the methods used to measure behavior need to be understood as well. That is what you will learn about in chapter 6, *Methods of Measuring Behavior*, where different types and the importance of tests are discussed.

Once you understand what you want to study and the importance of measuring it, the only thing left to do is to go out and collect data! Chapter 7, *Data Collection and Descriptive Statistics*, takes you through the process step-by-step and includes a summary of important descriptive statistics and how they can be used.

One of the reasons data is collected is to make inferences from a smaller group of people to a larger one. In chapter 8, *Introducing Inferential Statistics*, you will find an introduction to the discipline of the same name and how results based on small groups are inferred to larger ones.

Chapter 9 is the first of three chapters that deal with different types of research methods. In this chapter, *Nonexperimental Research Methods*, you will learn about various research methods including historical research, the case study approach, and correlational methodologies.

Chapters 10 and 11 (*Experimental Research Methods* and *Quasi-Experimental Research Methods*) continue this overview of research methods by introducing you to the different types of research designs that explore the questions of cause and effect.

Chapter 12, *Writing a Research Proposal*, goes through the steps involved in planning and writing a proposal and includes an extensive set of questions that can be used to evaluate the proposal.

Exploring Research ends with chapter 13, *Writing a Research Manuscript*, a step-by-step discussion of how to prepare a manuscript for submission to a journal for publication using the format prescribed by the American Psychological Association.

Appendix A takes you through the basic features of SPSS, and using the data in Appendix B shows how to complete both simple and complex data analytic skills including entering data, using the Output Navigator, creating charts, and doing inferential analysis. Appendix B contains a data set you can work with.

What's Special About This Book

I have included several features in each of these 13 chapters and appendices that I hope will help make this book more useful and the learning of the material more interesting.

- *What You Will Learn About in This Chapter* is a listing of the major points that will be covered in the chapter. This listing acts not only as a set of advanced organizers but also as a summary of the primary topics covered in the chapter.
- You will find *marginal notes* on each page that highlight important points contained in the text. These can be used for review purposes and help to emphasize especially important points.
- At the end of each chapter, you will also find *Exercises* that help reinforce the content of the chapter. Some of these have answers, but many are there to stimulate thinking, discussion, and further investigation of a particular topic or point covered in the chapter.
- Each chapter ends with *Want to Know More?*, your chance to read through a summary of resources that include more information about the content of the chapter. These annotated listings are organized into two groups. First, *Further Readings* deal directly with the chapter material. This section includes summaries of well-known articles or books that can give you a more advanced picture of what you have just read about.

    Second, *Readings of Other Interest* include readings that might be related to the topic but are of a more informal nature, such as works of fiction, and resources that you might not think would be found in a book like this one.
- Last, but not least, is a glossary of important terms found at the end of the book. The terms that you find in the glossary appear in **bold type like this**.

How to Use This Book

I have tried to write this book so that it is (you guessed it) user-friendly. Basically, what I think this means is that you can pick it up, understand what it says, and do what it suggests. One reviewer and user of the second edition was put off at first by the easy-going way in which the book is written. My philosophy is that important and interesting ideas and concepts need not be written about in an obtuse and convoluted fashion. Simple is best. You see, your mother was right.

Whether you are using this book as the main resource in a research methods course or as a supplemental text, here are some hints on how to go about using the book to make the most out of the experience.

- Read through the *At a Glance* Table of Contents so you can get an idea of what is in the book.
- If you find a chapter that seems particularly interesting, turn to that page, and take a look at *What You'll Learn About in this Chapter*.
- Take your time, and do not try to read too much in any one sitting. You will probably be assigned one chapter per week. While it is not an enormous task to read the 20 to 30 pages that each chapter contains in one sitting, breaking your reading up by main chapter sections might make things a little easier. Too much too soon leads to fatigue, which leads to frustration, and then no one is happy!
- Do the exercises at the end of each chapter. They will give you further insight into the materials that you just read and some direct experience with the techniques and topics that were covered.

- Write down questions you might have in the margins of pages where things seem unclear. When you can, ask your professor to clarify the information or bring your questions to your study group for discussion.

BIG Thanks

All textbooks have the author's name on the cover, but no book is the work of a single person. Such is also the case with *Exploring Research*. Many people helped make this book what it is, and they deserve the thanks that I am offering here. First, thanks to copy editor and friend Janet Majure who made this book as readable and accurate as it is, and graphic designer Traci Bunkers, who made a bunch of pages, figures and tables into a book. At Prentice-Hall, sincere thanks to Nicole Signoretti, assistant editor and Mary Rottino, assistant managing editor, for their support, encouragement and professionalism. If this book is successful, it is to them that much the credit should be given.

Second, I would like to thank the people who acted as outside reviewers and offered invaluable suggestions, all of which improved the quality of the finished manuscript. They are Kenneth A. Weaver, Emporia State University and Andrew Kinney, Mohawk Valley Community College.

Third, several students, especially Lisa Kerwin, read drafts of this book, offered constructive suggestions as to how it might be improved, and helped with the exercises and readings at the end of each chapter. Other students in my research methods classes pointed out typos and such that were overlooked in the second edition.

I take full responsibility for the errors and apologize to those students and faculty who might have used the book and had difficulty because of the mistakes. As many of those screw–ups (that is exactly the phrase) have been removed as humanly possible.

Finally, as always, it is to Leni and Sara and Micah (and now Pepper) that I look for the support and love that see projects like this through to the end. My love to them all.

So, now it is to you. Use the book well. Enjoy it, and I hope that your learning experience is one filled with new discoveries about your area of interest as well as about your own potential. I would love to hear from you about the book, including what you like and do not like, suggestions for change, or whatever. You can reach me through snail mail (the regular postal service) or one of the e-mail addresses below.

Neil J. Salkind
Bailey Hall
University of Kansas
Lawrence, KS 66045
njs@falcon.cc.ukans.edu
70404.365@compuserve.com

Knowing is not enough; we must apply.
Willing is not enough; we must do.
—Goethe

CHAPTER 1 ONE

The Role and Importance of Research

What You'll Learn About in this Chapter

- Who does research and why
- How research is defined, and what some of its purposes are
- What a model of scientific inquiry is, and how it guides research activities
- Some of the things that research is, and some of the things it isn't
- What researchers do, and how they do it
- The characteristics of good research
- How a method of scientific inquiry guides research activity
- The different types of research methods and examples of each

Say Hello to Research!

Walk down the hall in any building on your campus where social science professors have their offices, to such departments as psychology, sociology, and human development. Do you see any bearded, disheveled, white-coated men wearing rumpled pants and smoking pipes, hunched over their computers and mumbling to themselves? How about disheveled, white-coated women wearing rumpled skirts, smoking pipes, hunched over their computers and mumbling to themselves?

Researchers hard at work? No. Stereotypes of what scientists look like and do? Yes. What you are more likely to see in the halls of your classroom building or in your adviser's office are men and women of all ages who are hard at work. They are committed to finding the answer to just one more piece of the great puzzle that helps us understand human behavior just a little better than the previous generation of scientists.

Research is a process of constant exploration and discovery.

Just as everyone else, these people go to work in the morning, but unlike many others these researchers have an almost undying passion for understanding what they study and for coming as close as possible to finding the "truth." While elusive and sometimes even unobtainable, researchers work toward these truths for the satisfaction of answering important questions and then using this new information to help others. Early intervention programs, treatments of psychopathology, conflict resolution techniques, effective drug programs, and even changes in policy and the law as to when people should retire have resulted from evidence that researchers like your professors collected. While not always perfect, each little bit of evidence from a new study or a new idea for a study contributes to a vast legacy of knowledge for the next generation of researchers, such as yourself.

You might already know and appreciate something about the world of research. The purpose of this book is to provide the tools you need to do even more, such as to

- develop an understanding of the research process,
- prepare you to conduct research of your own,
- learn how to judge the quality of research,
- learn how to read, search through, and summarize other research,
- learn what the Internet is all about and how it can be used in everyday research activities,
- reveal the mysteries of basic statistics, and show you how easy they can actually be,
- measure the behaviors, traits, or attributes that interest you,
- collect the type of data that relate to your area of interest,
- use one of the leading statistical packages (Statistical Package for the Social Sciences, or SPSS) to analyze data,
- design research studies that answer the question you want answered, and
- write the type of research proposal that puts you in control, one that shows you have command of the content of the research as well as command of the way that the research should be done.

Sound ambitious? A bit terrifying? Exciting? Maybe those and more, but boring is one thing this research endeavor is not. That statement is especially true when you consider that the work you might be doing in this class as well as the research proposal that you might write could hold the key to expanding our knowledge and understanding of human behavior.

So here you are, beginning what is probably your first course in the area of research methods and wondering about everything from what researchers do to what your topic will be for your thesis. Relax. Thousands of students have been here before you, and almost all of them have left with a working knowledge of what **research** is, how you do it, and what distinguishes a good research project from one that is doomed. Hold on, and let's go. This trip will be exciting.

What Research Is, and What It Isn't

Perhaps it is best to begin by looking at what researchers really do for a living. To do so, why not look at some of the best? Here are some researchers, the awards they won, and the focus of their work. These various awards were given by the American Psychological Association in recognition of outstanding work. All these people started out in a class just like the one you are in, reading a book similar to the one you are reading. Their interest in research and a particular issue continued to grow until it became their life's work.

Leonard D. Eron received the Gold Medal Award for Life Contributions by a Psychologist in the Public Interest in 1995 for his contributions to the theory and understanding of psychological measurement. Specifically, his work has focused on describing and understanding the role of aggression by children and its prevention. Frances K. Graham received the Gold Medal for Life Achievement in Psychological Science in 1995 for her work in psychophysiology and her insights into the working of the neonatal (newly born child's) mind. Peter J. Lang received a Distinguished Scientific Contribution award in 1995 for his research in emotion, particularly fear and anxiety.

What all these people have in common is that at one time or another during their professional careers they were active participants in the process of doing research. Research is a process through which new knowledge is discovered. A **theory** of motivation or development, for example, helps us organize new information into a coherent body, a set of related ideas that explain events that have occurred and predict events that will happen. Theories are an important part of science. It is at the ground-floor level, however, that the researcher works to get the ball rolling, adding a bit of new insight here and a new speculation there, until it comes together to form a corpus of knowledge.

High-quality research is characterized by many different attributes:

1. It is based on the work of others.
2. It can be replicated.
3. It is generalizable to other settings.
4. It is based on some logical rationale and tied to theory.
5. It is doable!
6. It generates new questions or is cyclical in nature.
7. It is incremental.
8. It is an apolitical activity that should be undertaken for the betterment of society.

Good research has as its ultimate aim the benefit of society.

First, *research is an activity based on the work of others.* No, this does not mean that you copy the work of others (that's plagiarism), but you always look to the work that has already been done to provide a basis for what and how you might conduct your own work. For example, if there have been 200 studies on the relationship between the number of children in a family and the average level of IQ scores, those studies should not be ignored. You may not want to replicate any one of these studies, but you certainly should take methodologies that were used and the results into consideration when you plan your own research in that area.

A good example of this principle is the tremendous intellectual and scientific effort that went into the creation of the atomic bomb. Although a horrific weapon, hundreds of top-flight scientists from all over the world were organized at different locations in an intense and highly charged effort to combine their knowledge. What was unique about this effort is that it was compressed in time; many people who would probably share each other's work in any case did so in days rather than months because of the military and political urgency of the times. What was discovered one day literally became the basis for the next day's experiments.

When the results of research can be replicated, the researcher's arguments are stronger.

Second, while we're talking about other studies, *research is an activity that can be replicated*. If someone conducts a research study that examines the relationship between problem solving ability and musical talent, the results of the experiment should be replicable for two reasons. First, one of the hallmarks of any credible scientific finding is that it can be replicated. If you can spin gold from straw, you should be able to do it every time, right? How about using a new method to teach children to read? Or developing early intervention programs that produce similar results when repeated? Second, if the results of an experiment can be replicated, this means they serve as a basis for further research in the same area.

Third, *good research is generalizable to other settings*. This means, for example, that if adolescent boys are found to be particularly susceptible to peer pressure in one setting, the results would probably stand up in a different, but related, setting. While some research has limited generalizability, since it is difficult to replicate the exact conditions under which the research was carried out, the results of most research can lend at least something to another setting.

Fourth, *research is based on some logical rationale and tied to theory*. Research ideas do not stand alone as just an interesting question. Rather, research activity provides answers to questions that help fill in pieces to what can be a large and complicated puzzle. No one could be expected to understand, through one grand research project, the entire process of intellectual development in children or the reason why adolescents form cliques or what actually happens during a mid-life crisis. All these major areas of research need to be broken into smaller elements, and all these elements need to be tied together with a common theme, which more often than not is some underlying, guiding theory.

Fifth, and by all means, *research is doable*! Too often, especially for the young or inexperienced scientist (such as yourself), the challenge to come up with a feasible idea is so pressing that almost anything will do as a research topic. So your professor sometimes sees statements from students such as, "The purpose of this research is to see if the use of drugs can be reduced through exposure to television commercials."

This level of ambiguity and lack of a conceptual framework makes the statement almost useless and certainly not doable. Good research poses a question that can be answered, and then does so in a timely fashion.

Sixth, *research generates new questions or is cyclical in nature*. Yes, "what goes around comes around." The answers to today's research questions provide the foundation for research questions that will be asked tomorrow. You will learn more about this process later in this chapter when a method of scientific inquiry is described.

Seventh, *research is incremental*. No one scientist stands alone but instead on the shoulders of others. Contributions that are made usually take place in small, easily definable chunks. The first study ever done on the development of language did not answer all the questions about language acquisition, nor did the last study that was done put the icing on the cake. Rather, all the studies in a particular area come together to produce a body of knowledge shared by different researchers and providing the basis for further research. The whole, or all the knowledge about a particular area, is more than the sum of the parts, because each new research advance not only informs us, but it also helps to place other findings in a different and often fruitful perspective.

Finally, at its best, *research is an apolitical activity that should be undertaken for the betterment of society*. I'm stressing *at its best*, since too often this or that special interest group dictates how research funding should be spent. Finding a vaccine for AIDS should not depend upon one's attitudes toward individual lifestyles. Similarly, whether early intervention programs should be supported is independent of one's personal views.

While being apolitical, research should have as its ultimate goal the betterment of society. Researchers or practitioners do not withhold food from pregnant women to study the effects of malnutrition on children. To examine the stress-nutrition link, researchers do not force adults to eat particular diets that might be unhealthy. These unethical practices would not lead to a greater end, especially since there are other ways to answer such questions without resorting to possibly harmful practices.

If these attributes make for good research, what is bad research? It takes the opposite approach of all the things stated above and even more. In sum, bad research is the fishing trip you take looking for something important when it simply is not to be found. It is plagiarizing other people's work. Falsifying data to prove a point. Misrepresenting information, and misleading participants. Unfortunately, there are researchers whose work is characterized by these practices, but they are in the minority.

A Model of Scientific Inquiry

In the past 20 years, the public has been exposed to the trials and tribulations of the research process as described through hundreds of books by and about the everyday work of scientists around the world. Some of the best of these books are listed in the *Want to Know More?* section at the end of this chapter.

Regardless of the specific content of these stories, they all have one thing in common. The work was accomplished through adherence to guidelines that allowed these researchers to progress from Point A to Point Z while remaining confident that they were on the trail of finding (what they hoped was) an adequate answer to the questions they had posed.

Their methods and their conclusions are not helter-skelter because of one important practice: They share the same general philosophy about how questions about human behavior should be answered. In addition, for scientists to be able to trust their colleagues, in the sense of having confidence in the results produced by their studies, scientists must have something in common besides good intentions. As it turns out, what they share is a standard sequence of steps in formulating and answering a question. That sequence is often referred to as the **scientific method**.

When you read in a journal article that Method A is more effective than Method B for improving retention or memory, you can be pretty sure that the steps described below were followed, in one form or another. Because there is agreement about the general method used to answer the question, the results of this comparison of Method A and Method B can be applied to the next study. It perhaps would investigate variations of Method A and how and why they work. The research efforts of developmental psychologists, gerontologists (specialists in aging), linguists, and psychophysiologists all depend upon the integrity of the process.

Here is a set of such steps (shown in Figure 1.1) as part of a model of scientific inquiry. The goal of this model is to find "the truth" (whatever that means!) or, in other words, to use a method that results in a reasonable and sound answer to important questions that will further our understanding of human behavior.

An interesting and exciting topic, the effects of television on children, will be used as an example of the different steps in this model.

Many ideas for research come from everyday experiences.

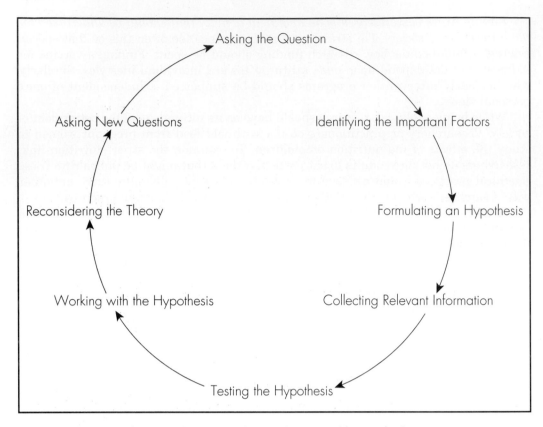

Figure 1.1 The steps in the research process, where each step sets the stage for the next.

Asking the Question

Remember the story of the Wizard of Oz? When Dorothy realized her need to get to the Emerald City, she asked Glinda, the good witch, "But, where do I begin?" Glinda's response: "Most people begin at the beginning, my dear," as is the case in almost any scientific endeavor.

Our first and most important step is asking a question (*I wonder what would happen if...*) or identifying a need (*We have to find a way to...*) that arises as the result of curiosity, and it becomes necessary to find an answer. For example, you might be curious about how watching television affects the development of children's language skills. You also might feel an urgency to find out how to use television most effectively for educating children and adults about the dangers of drugs.

Questions can be very broad or quite narrow.

Such questions are informally stated and often intended as a source of discussion and stimulation about what direction the specific research topic should take. Where do such questions come from? They rarely come from the confines of a classroom or a laboratory. Rather, questions spring (in the fullest sense of the word) from our imagination and our own experiences, enriched by the worlds of science, art, music, and literature. It is no coincidence that many works of fiction have a basis in fact (such as science fiction). The truly creative scientist is always thinking about everything from solutions to existing questions to the next important question to ask. When Louis Pasteur said that "chance favors the prepared mind," he was really saying, take advantage of all the experiences you can, both in and out of school. Only then can you be well prepared to recognize the importance of certain events which will act as a stimulus for more rigorous research activity.

Questions can be as broad as inquiring about the effects of television on language development, or as specific as the relationship between the content of certain television commercials and teenagers' buying habits. Whatever their content or depth of inquiry, questions are the first step in any scientific endeavor.

Identifying the Important Factors

Once the question has been asked, the next step is to identify the factors that would have to be examined to answer the question. They might range from the most simple, such as the child's age or socioeconomic status, to more complicated measures of the effects of violent cartoons on the child's behavior.

Just look at this list of factors that have been investigated over the past 10 years by various researchers who have been interested in the effects of televisio.n on children:

- age of the child
- degree of violence in programs
- stage of the child's cognitive growth
- producer's attitude
- facial expression
- decision-making
- mother's description of viewing patterns
- emotional arousal
- ethnic differences in response to television programs
- family communication patterns

And that is only 10 of hundreds of topics that could be explored with each topic defining important factors. But of all the factors that could be important and that help us understand more about the effects of television, which ones should be selected as a focus? In general, you want to select factors that

- have not been investigated before,
- will contribute to the understanding of the question you are asking,
- are available to investigate,
- hold some interest for you personally or professionally, and
- lead to another question!

It is hard enough to define the nature of the problem you want to study, let alone generate questions that lead to more questions, but once you begin the journey of becoming a scientist, you are a member of an elite group who has the responsibility to contribute to the scientific literature not only by what you do, but by what you see that needs to be done as well.

Formulating an Hypothesis

When asked what she thought an **hypothesis** was, a 9-year-old girl said it best: an educated guess. An hypothesis results when the questions are transformed into statements that express the relationships between variables as an "if... then..." statement.

For example, if the question is, "What effects does viewing violence on television have on boys?", then the hypothesis could be, *Boys who view aggressive acts during*

Hypotheses pose "questions" that the researcher attempts to answer.

prime time cartoon shows are more likely to exhibit aggressive behaviors right after the television viewing session than boys who watch nonaggressive acts during prime time shows. Several characteristics make some hypotheses better than others, and we will talk about those in the next chapter.

For now, you should realize that an hypothesis is an objective extension of the question that was originally posed. While all questions might not be answerable because of the way they are posed, which is fine for the question stage, a good hypothesis poses a question in a *testable* form. Good questions lead to good hypotheses, which in turn lead to good studies.

Collecting Relevant Information

Hypotheses should posit a clear relationship between different factors such as television viewing and aggressive behavior in males. That is hypotheses' job. Once an hypothesis is formulated, the next step is the collection of information or empirical data that will confirm or refute the hypothesis. So if you are interested in whether or not viewing aggressive television programs leads to aggressive behavior, the kind of data that allow the hypothesis to be tested needs to be collected.

For example, you might collect two types of data to test the hypothesis mentioned above. The first might be the number of violent acts in a 1-hour segment of prime time television. The second would be the number of aggressive behaviors observed in children who watched the program and the number of such acts in children who did not watch the program.

An important point about testing hypotheses is that a good scientist sets out to *test* them, not necessarily to *prove* them. As a good scientist, you should be intent on collecting data that reveal as much of the truth about the world as is possible and letting the chips fall where they may, whether "right" or "wrong" or whether you agree or disagree with the outcomes. Setting out to prove an hypothesis can place scientists in the unattractive position of biasing the methods for collecting data or the way in which results are interpreted. If bias occurs, then the entire sequence of steps can fall apart. Besides, there really is no being "wrong" in science. Not having hypotheses supported means only that there are additional questions to ask or that the ones asked need to be reformulated. That is the beauty of good science—there is always another question to ask on the same topic that can shed just a bit more light. And who can tell? That bit more light might be just the amount needed to uncover an entirely new and significant finding.

Testing the Hypothesis

Is it enough to simply collect data that relate to the phenomena being studied? Not quite. What if you have finished collecting data and find that boys who watched aggressive prime time television programs show 4.8 aggressive acts in the 1-hour period following exposure and that boys who watched a nonaggressive program exhibited an average of 2.2 acts? What would your conclusion be?

On the one hand, you could say that the boys who watched the aggressive programs were more than twice as aggressive. On the other hand, you might argue that the difference between the two averages is not large enough for you to reach any conclusion. To be able to say that watching the aggressive television segment really made a difference, you would have to see a much bigger difference, you might say. An unsolvable dilemma? Not at all.

Say hello to *inferential statistics* (and see chapter 8 for more!), a set of tools that allows researchers to separate the effects of an isolated factor (such as aggressive or nonaggressive television viewing) from differences between groups that might be due to some other factor or to nothing other than **chance**. Yes, luck, fate, destiny, the wheels of fortune, or whatever you want to call what you cannot control, sometimes can be responsible for differences between groups. For example, what if one of the boys who did not watch the aggressive segment feels a bit crabby that day and decides to whack his playmate? Or if one of the boys who did watch the aggressive segment is tired and just does not feel like playing at all? The job of these tools is to help you separate the effects of the factors being studied from other, unrelated factors. What these statistical tools do is assign a probability level to an outcome so you can decide whether what you see is really due to what you think it is or to something else that you will have to leave for the next study.

Chance is always an attractive explanation for any outcome.

Working with the Hypothesis

Once you have collected the data that your question requires and have tested the hypothesis, as a good scientist you sit down, put up the old feet, look intellectual, and examine the results. The results may confirm or refute the hypothesis. In either case, it is off to the races. If it is a confirmation, then the factors that were hypothesized to be related and conceptually important were borne out, and you can go your merry way as the next scientific experiment is planned. If the hypothesis is not confirmed, it can very well be a time for learning something that was not known previously. In the example used earlier, it would mean that watching television segments with aggressive models does not alone result in aggressive behavior on the part of the boy. Although the researcher might be a bit disappointed that the initial hunch (formally called a hypothesis) was not supported, the results of a well-run study always provide valuable information, regardless of the outcome.

Reconsidering the Theory

Finally, it is time to take stock and relate all these research efforts to what guides our work in the first place: theory. Earlier in this chapter, a theory was defined as a set of statements that predict things that will occur in the future and explain things that have occurred in the past. But the very nature of theories is that they can be modified according to the results of research based on the same assumptions on which the theory is based.

In general, theories help guide what researchers do.

For example, a particular approach to understanding the development of children and adults is known as social learning theory, which places special importance on the role of modeling and vicarious, or indirect, learning. According to this theory, exposure to aggressive behavior would lead to aggressive behavior, once the environment contains the same kinds of cues that were present when the initial aggressive model (such as aggressive cartoon characters) was observed.

If the hypothesis that observing such models increases aggression is confirmed, another building block, or piece of evidence, has been added to the house called social learning theory. Good scientists are always trying to see what type of brick (new information) fits where, or if it fits at all. In this way, new knowledge can change or modify the way the theory (or the house) appears or has to say about human behavior. In this way, new questions might be generated from the theory that will help contribute further to the way the house is structured.

In any case, the last step in this simplified model of scientific inquiry is to ask a new question. It might be a simple variation on a theme (*Do males react differently than females to aggressive models?*), or a refinement of the original question (*How much exposure to aggressive models is necessary before children begin modeling the behavior?*). No matter if the hypothesis is supported or not, good research leaves you farther along the trail to answering the original question. You just might be at a different place than you thought or intended to be.

Different Types of Research

By now, you have a good idea what research is and how the research process works. Now it is time to turn your attention to a description and examples of different types of research methods and the type of questions they pose.

Interestingly, the types of research methods that will be discussed differ mostly on two dimensions: the nature of the question asked and the method used to answer it. One way in which these methods do not necessarily differ, however, is in the content or the focus of the research. In other words, if you are interested in the effects of television on children, your research can be nonexperimental, where you survey watching habits, or experimental, where you expose children to certain models and look at the effect of the exposure on their behavior.

A summary of the three general categories of research methods that will be discussed in *Exploring Research* is shown in Table 1.1. In this table you can see the purpose of each, the time frame that each encompasses, the degree of control the different method has over competing factors, and an example of each. Chapters 9, 10, and 11 go into greater detail about each of these research methods.

Nonexperimental Research

Nonexperimental research includes a variety of different methods that describe relationships between variables. The important distinction between nonexperimental methods and the others you will learn about later is that nonexperimental research methods do not set out, nor can they test, any causal relationships between variables. For example, if you wanted to survey the television watching behavior of adolescents, you could do so by having them maintain a diary where they record what they watch and whom they watch it with. This descriptive study provides information about their TV watching habits but says nothing about why they watch what they do. You are not in any way trying to have an impact on their television watching behavior or investigate why they might watch particular shows. This is nonexperimental in nature since no cause-and-effect relationships of any type are being hypothesized.

Nonexperimental research methods that will be covered in *Exploring Research* are descriptive, historical, and correlational. All three will be covered in chapter 9. Here is a brief overview of each.

Type of Research	Nonexperimental (Descriptive)	Nonexperimental (Historical)	Nonexperimental (Correlational)	Experimental	Quasi-Experimental
Purpose	Describe the characteristics of an existing phenomenon	Relate events that have occurred in the past to current events	Examine the relationships between variables	To test for true cause and effect relationships	To test for causal relationships without having full control
Time Frame	Current	Past	Current or past (correlation) Future (prediction)	Current	Current or past
Degree of Control over Factors	None or low	None or low	Low to medium	High	Moderate to high
Example	A survey of dating practices of adolescent females	An analysis of Freud's use of hypnosis as it relates to current psychotherapy practices	An investigation that focuses on the relationship between the number of hours of television watching and grade point average	The effect of a preschool language program on the language skills of inner city children	Gender differences in spatial and verbal abilities

Table 1.1 Here are the different types of research you will read about in *Exploring Research*.

Descriptive Research

Descriptive research describes the characteristics of an existing phenomenon. The U.S. Census is descriptive research as is any survey that assesses the current status of anything from the number of faucets in a house to the number of adults over the age of 60 who have grandchildren.

What can be done with this information? First, it provides a broad picture of a phenomenon you might be interested exploring. For example, if you are interested in learning more about the reading process in children, you might want to consult *The Reading Report Card*, published by the Educational Testing Service in Princeton, New Jersey. This annual publication summarizes information about the reading achievement of children 9, 13, and 17 years of age. Or you might want to consult a publication of the Center for Disease Control, the *Morbidity and Mortality Weekly*, to find out what the current rate of measles cases might be in the Midwest, or the Bureau of Labor Statistics to determine the current unemployment rate and how many working single parents there are who have children under the age of 5 years (about 60%). If you want to know it, there is a place to find it. Descriptive research demands this type of information.

Another example is where Peter O. Peretti and Kris G. Majecen (1991) interviewed 58 elderly individuals, from 68 to 87 years of age, using a structured

Descriptive research describes the status of things in the present.

interview to investigate the variables that affect emotional abuse among the elderly. As a result of the interviews (a type of survey research), they found nine variables are common to elderly abuse, including lack of affection, threats of violence, and confinement.

Not only can descriptive research stand on its own as the examples show, but it can also serve as a basis for other types of research in that a group's characteristics often need to be described before the meaningfulness of any differences can be addressed.

Historical Research

Historical research relates past events to one another or to current events. Basically, historical research (or **historiography**) answers the question, *What is the nature of events that have happened in the past?* For example, one might want to examine trends in the way mental illness has been treated or how attitudes toward work and families have changed. All these require the detective work of a historian, finding and collecting relevant data and then, just as with any other research endeavor, testing an hypothesis. In fact, like any other researcher, the historian collects data, analyzes them, and then comes to conclusions about the tenability of his or her hypothesis. One significant difference between historical research and other types of research is the *type* of data collected and the method of collection.

Researchers who do historical research often accomplish this goal through the use of *primary sources* (original documents or people who have personally experienced an event) and *secondary sources* (secondhand documents or people who may have some knowledge about the event but did not experience it firsthand). Even if these sources are readily available, however, one of the greatest challenges in doing such research is in knowing how much faith the researcher can put in the accuracy of the sources.

An example of historical research is where Nancy Burton and Lyle Jones (1982) examined trends in achievement levels of black and white children. Burton and Jones examined high school graduation rates for blacks and whites who were born before 1913, between 1913 and 1922, 1923 and 1932, 1933 and 1942, 1943 and 1947, and 1948 and 1952 for people who were 25 years or older in 1977. They also examined a variety of other historical indicators in more recent groups of white and black children and concluded that differences in achievement between white and black students are decreasing. To complete their analysis, Burton and Jones obtained data from the National Assessment of Educational Progress. With today's sophisticated data retrieval tools, historical researchers can use their computers (see chapter 3) to tap into almost any database they need and save trips to the library.

Correlational Research

Descriptive and historical research provide a picture of events that are currently happening or have occurred in the past. Researchers often want to go beyond mere description and begin discussing the relationship that certain events might have to one another. The most likely type of research to answer questions about the relationship among variables or events is called correlational research.

Correlational research examines relationships among outcomes.

What **correlational research** does, which neither descriptive nor historical research does, is provide some indication as to how two or more things are related to one another, or how well a specific outcome might be predicted by one or more pieces of information. Correlational research uses a numerical index called the correlation coefficient (see chapter 9 for a complete discussion) as a measure of the strength of this relationship. Most correlational studies report such an index.

If you were interested in finding out the *relationship* between number of hours that freshmen study and their grade-point averages, you would be doing correlational research since you are interested in the relationship between these two factors. If you were interested in finding out the best set of *predictors* of success in graduate school, you would be doing a type of correlational research that includes prediction.

For example, in a study of the relationship between temperament and attachment behavior in infants (Vaughn, Lefever, Seifer, and Barglow, 1989), researchers examined the correlation among different types of attachment behaviors, how securely attached the infants were to their mothers, and the infant's general temperament, a term often used to discuss an infant's personality. The researchers found that an infant's temperament does not predict how securely attached the child is to his or her mother.

One of the most important points about correlational research is that it examines relationships between variables but in no way implies that one causes another. In other words, correlation and prediction examine associations but not causal relationships, where a change in one factor directly influences a change in another. For example, it is a well established fact that as the number of crimes in a community increases, so does the level of ice cream consumption! What is going on? Certainly, no thinking person would conclude that the two are causally related such that if you banned ice cream, there would be no more crimes. Rather, another variable, temperature, better explains the amount of ice cream consumed and crime rate (they both go up when it gets warm). It might seem ridiculous that people would identify causality just because events are related, but you do not have to read far in the daily newspaper to see politicians reaching such unwise conclusions.

Experimental Research

You already know that correlational research can help establish the presence of a relationship among variables but not give us any reason to believe that variables are causally related to one another. How does one find out if characteristics or behaviors or events are related in such a way that the relationship is a causal one? There are two types of research that can answer that question for us. The first is quasi-experimental research, and the second is experimental research. For now, let's briefly discuss experimental research.

The only way to establish a true cause-and-effect relationship in any study is to isolate and eliminate all the factors that might be responsible for a particular outcome and test only those that you directly want to measure.

Experimental research is where participants are assigned to groups based on some selected criterion often called the treatment variable. For example, let us say that you are interested in comparing the effects of two different techniques for reducing obsessive compulsive disorder behavior in adults. The first technique includes behavioral therapy, and the second does not. Once adults are assigned to groups and the programs are completed, you will want to look for any differences between the two groups as to the effects of the therapy on the number of obsessive compulsive behaviors. Since assignment to the groups is determined by the researcher, he or she has complete control over what the adults are exposed to.

Experimental research investigates cause-and-effect relationships.

This is the ideal setting for establishing a cause-and-effect relationship since you have clearly defined the possible cause (if indeed it results in some effect) and can keep very close tabs on what is happening. Most important, however, you have complete control over the treatment. In a quasi–experimental study, you do not have such a high degree of control since people have already been indirectly assigned to those groups (such as social class, abuse, gender, and type of injury) for which you are testing the effects.

The distinction between experimental and other methods of research does boil down to a matter of control. True experimental research designs, of which you will learn about in chapter 10, isolate and control all the factors that could be responsible for any effects except the one of most interest.

For example, Fleming, Klein, and Corter (1992) examined the effects of participation in a social support group on depression, maternal attitudes, and behavior in new mothers. As part of the experimental design, the researchers divided a total of 142 mothers into three groups. Group 1 received the intervention, Group 2 received the no-intervention condition, and Group 3 received a special group-by-mail intervention. The key point here is the *manipulation* (the key word in experimental designs) of the condition for each of the three groups.

This research is experimental, since the researcher determined group membership participation in the social support group as a function of the treatment itself. As you will learn, in a quasi-experimental study the researcher has no control over group membership.

The primary difference between quasi-experimental and experimental research is that in **quasi-experimental research** the researcher does not have complete control over the criterion used to assign participants to groups, but in experimental research he or she does have that control, and what a difference that makes.

Quasi-experimental research is where participants are assigned to groups based on some characteristic or quality these people bring to the study. Differences in sex, race, age, class in school, neighborhood of residence, type of job, and even experiences are examples. These group assignments have already taken place *before* the experiment begins, and the researcher has no control as to what people will belong to each group.

Let us say you are interested in examining voting patterns as a function of neighborhood. You can't change the neighborhood people live in, but you can use the quasi-experimental method to establish a causal relationship between residence and voting patterns. In other words, if you find that voting pattern and residence are related, you can say with some degree of confidence (but not as much as with an experimental study) that where one resides has some causal relationship as to how one votes.

The most important use of the quasi-experimental method is where researchers cannot, in good conscience, assign people to groups and test the effects of group membership on some other outcome. For example, researchers interested in the effects of unemployment on children could not very well encourage mothers or fathers to quit work. Rather, they would seek out families where parents are already unemployed and then conduct the research. Norma Radin and Rena Harold-Goldsmith (1989) did exactly that. They compared the involvement of 17 jobless fathers and 31 employed fathers with their children. They also looked at other factors, including the father's view of the male role in the family, maternal employment, and the child's age.

Quasi-experimental research is also called **post hoc** research or after-the-fact research since the actual research takes place after the assignment of groups such as employed versus unemployed, malnourished versus nonmalnourished, male versus female. Because assignment has already taken place, the researcher has a high degree, but not the highest degree, of control over the cause of whatever effects are being examined. For the highest degree of control to occur, the experimental method needs to be used.

Applied Versus Basic Research

Sometimes in the research world, distinctions need to be made not only about the type of research but also about the most general category into which the implications or utility of the research might fall. This is where the distinction between basic and applied research comes in. But beware! This distinction is sometimes used as a convenient way to classify research activity rather than to shed light on the intent or purpose of the researcher and the importance of the study.

The most basic distinction between the two is that **basic research** (sometimes called pure research) is research that has no immediate application at the time it is completed, whereas **applied research** does. If this appears to be a somewhat ambiguous distinction, it is, because almost all basic research eventually results in some worthwhile application over the long range.

For example, for every 1 dollar spent on the basic research that supported the lunar missions during the 1960s and 1970s, 6 dollars were returned in economic impact. Data from basic research that hypothesizes a relationship between Alzheimer's disease in older people and Down's syndrome (a genetic disorder) in younger people in time could prove to be the critical finding that leads to a cure for both diseases. Another example: Who cares if some children have a more difficult time than others in distinguishing between two very similar stimuli? You do, if you want to teach them how to read. Many different reading programs have grown directly from such basic research efforts.

Therefore, do not judge the quality of either the finished product or the worth of supporting a research project by branding it as basic or applied research. Rather, look closely at its content, and judge it on its merit. This approach obviously has been happening, since more and more reports about basic research (at one time beyond the interests of everyday practitioners) show up in such practitioner-oriented professional journals as *Phi Delta Kappan* and the *American Psychological Association Monitor* as well as the Sunday *New York Times Magazine*, *Newsweek*, and *Science News*.

Great! You have finished the first chapter of Exploring Research, *and I hope you have a good idea as to what research is (and isn't), what the purpose of research is, and some of the different ways in which research can be carried out. With this new information under your belt, let's turn to the next chapter, which focuses on some "researcheese," or the language that researchers use, and how these new terms fit together with what you have learned here.*

Exercises

1. The process of research never stands independently from the content of what the research is about. As a student new to the field of research, and perhaps even to your own discipline (such as psychology or sociology or nursing), answer the following questions:
   a. What areas within your discipline especially interest you?
   b. Who are some of the outstanding researchers in your field, and what is the focus of their work?
   c. Of the different types of research described and discussed in this chapter, which one do you think best fits the type of research that is done in your discipline?

2. Visit your college or university library, and locate an article from a professional journal that describes a research study. From the description of how scientific inquiry takes place (which you read about in this chapter), answer the following:
   a. What is the primary question posed by the study?
   b. What important factors are identified?
   c. Is there an hypothesis stated? If so, what is it?
   d. Describe the way the information was collected.
   e. How could the results of the study affect the originally posed hypothesis?

3. Interview an active researcher on your campus, and ask about his or her research activities including
   a. the focus of his or her research interests,
   b. why he or she is interested in this area,
   c. what the most exciting part of the research is,
   d. what the least exciting part of the research is, and
   e. what impact the results of the research may have on his or her particular discipline.

4. Select a discipline within the social and behavioral sciences, such as child development, social psychology, higher education, or health psychology. For the discipline you select, find a representative study that is quasi-experimental or experimental in nature. Write a one-paragraph description of the study. Do the same for a historical study as well.

5. In a fictitious correlational study, the results showed that age was related to strength. That is, as children get older, their strength increases. What is the problem with the statement that *increased strength is caused by increasing age* or that *the stronger you get the older you get?*

6. What do you think a good definition of science is? How would your definition of science differ from a student's in a similar class 25 years ago? How would your definition differ from that put forth by a physical (e.g., physics, chemistry) scientist, if it differs at all?

7. Look for examples of editorials or research articles that present correlational evidence. Do the authors infer a cause-and-effect relationship in the correlation? Why might it be difficult for even seasoned researchers to keep from making this mistake?

8. Research often replicates findings made by others. What is the value in this process?

9. Identify five attributes that characterize high quality research.

10. Restate the following question as a hypothesis:

   What social impact does day care have on a child who attends during his preschool and primary grade school years?

11. Explain the difference between historical, correlational, and quasi-experimental research.

Want to Know More?

Further Readings

Bond, D. (1990). Economics and critical thinking. *Social Studies Review, 29(3)*, 42-46.
   Advocates the critical thinking approach including problem-solving and hypothesis testing to help secondary teachers teach economic concepts to secondary students.

Dillenger, A. M. (1983). Experimentation in the classroom: Use of public school students as research subjects. *Journal of Law and Education, 12(3)*, 347-78.
   Reviews the history of research using students as subjects in public schools and the legal responsibilities involved in the approval and supervision of such research.

Dormen, L., and Edidin, P. (1989, July/August). Original spin. *Psychology Today, 23,* 47–51.
   Discusses ways to stimulate your creative thought processes, including brainstorming by computer. Has some excellent suggestions for you to use to find ideas for research that may be personally interesting to you.

Kuhn, T. S. (1970). *The structure of the scientific revolution*. Chicago: The University of Chicago Press.
   The book to read if you want to know more about how science is done and how different cultural and political forces influence the creation and revision of theories.

Wallen, N. E. (1989). A comparison of quantitative and qualitative research. *School of Education Review, 1(1)*, 6-10.
   Discusses important differences in the theory and practice of quantitative and qualitative research methodologies and suggests that each of these methodologies can be improved by utilizing key ingredients of the other.

Readings of Other Interest

Burke, J. (1978). *Connections*. Boston: Little Brown.
   A companion book to the acclaimed PBS television series. Traces the development of modern technology back thousands of years. Shows how scientific innovation, need, and coincidence often work together to advance civilization.

Downey, M. T., & Levstik, L. S. (1988). Teaching and learning history: The research base. *Social Education, 52(5)*, 336-338.
   Presents a review of research literature that was undertaken to determine the extent to which research about teaching and learning history supports the current reform movement.

Evered, D., and Harnett, S. (Eds.). (1989). *The evaluation of scientific research*. New York: Wiley.

> An accumulation of presentations at the Ciba Foundation Conference held in London in 1988 that discuss research trends, problems, methods, and evaluations. An overview for the new student to see how professionals in the research field view the techniques currently used.

Jackson, D., and Philippe, R. J. (Ed.). (1987). *Scientific excellence: origins and assessment*. Newbury Park, CA: Sage.

> Presentation of a group of papers that define the qualities of competent, successful scientists. Spends a great deal of time describing the behavior of psychologists. Gives the reader a flavor of what science is, and how it relates to research.

CHAPTER

2

TWO

The Research Process

What You'll Learn About in this Chapter

- The path from formulating questions to seeking and finding solutions
- The difference between dependent and independent variables
- What an hypothesis is, and how it works
- The importance of the null hypothesis
- The difference between the null and the research hypothesis
- The characteristics of a good hypothesis
- The importance of samples and populations in the research process
- What statistical significance means
- What criteria you should use to evaluate a research article
- How ethical research practices are the responsibility of all researchers
- Why confidentiality is among the most important of ethical criteria to maintain
- The standards of ethics published by different professional organizations
- The importance of internal research practice review committees

From Problem to Solution

How a study is conducted is often the most creative part of any research project.

All you need is an interesting question, collect some data, and poof! Instant research! Not quite. The model of scientific inquiry discussed in chapter 1 does a nice job of specifying the steps in the research process, but there is quite a bit more to the process than that.

At the beginning of this chapter, we will provide a "real-life" example of how the process actually takes place and how researchers begin with what they see as a problem (to be solved) and end up with a solution (or the results) to that problem. Keep in mind, however, that the meanings of the words *problem* and *solution* go beyond solving a simple problem of the 2 + 2 variety. Rather, the questions that researchers ask often reflect a more pressing social concern or economic issue. In addition, the results from a research study like this one provide the foundation for the next research endeavor.

We will look at an interesting study titled *Maternal Employment and Young Adolescents' Daily Experiences in Single-Mother Families* (Duckett and Richards, 1989) that examines the impact of maternal employment on adolescent development. One of the most creative things about this study is the way these researchers went about collecting the data they needed. They did not sit down and ask adolescents how they felt about this or that but instead tried to get an overall picture of their feelings outside the laboratory setting.

The researchers who conducted this study with 436 fifth- through ninth-graders and their mothers were interested in a combination of issues that have received considerable attention in the print and electronic media. The general goal of the research (and the problem) was to better understand some of the factors and consequences that surround the increasingly large number of working mothers with adolescent children.

To narrow their investigation, they set out to learn about the general nature of the children's experiences as a function of having a mother who works as well as about the quality of time that the adolescents spent with their mothers. Given that so many mothers, both in single- and dual-parent families, are now working outside the home, answers to such questions like those posed by this study are becoming increasingly important in the formation of social and economic policies.

To get the answers they wanted, the researchers had to compare adolescents living with two parents (382, or 88% of the total) with those adolescents who live with only their mothers (54, or 12% of the total). But to fully reach their goal of better understanding the effects of maternal employment, the researchers had to break down the group of children and parents even further, into those children whose mothers worked part-time, full-time, or were unemployed. When separated into groups based on these factors (family configuration and employment status), the researchers can make a comparison within and between the six groups (all combinations of single- and two-parent families, with employed part-time, employed full-time, and unemployed mothers) and get the information they need to answer the general questions posed above.

Now comes the really creative part of the study. They used a method called the *Experience Sampling Method* first developed by two other researchers (Csikszentmihalyi and Larson, 1987). According to this method, the adolescents participating in the study would carry electronic beepers. On an unpredictable schedule they would receive a beep from beep central(!) and would then stop what they were doing and complete a self-report form. They would do this for one week.

A signal telling the participant to stop and complete the form was sent on the average of every two hours between the hours of 7:30 a.m. and 9:30 p.m., with a total of 49 signals sent for the week for each participant. This means that in the course of one week, 49 separate forms were completed providing lots of information about how participants felt at any particular moment. For 436 participants at 49 forms each, a total of 21,364 forms was completed, which is a hefty sample of kids' behavior!

What was contained on these self-report forms? The adolescents had to report on what the researchers call *affect* (happy-sad, cheerful-irritable, friendly-angry) and *arousal* (alert-drowsy, strong-weak, excited-bored). Each of these six items was rated along a 1-to-7 scale. For example, they might indicate a 4, meaning they feel "right in the middle of happy and sad at that moment in time." These six items could be completed in a short period of time, and an accurate picture of the adolescent's daily life could then be formed. Adolescents also had to respond to "What were you doing?" and "Whom were you with?" as well as to some questions about their perceptions of their parents' friendliness and their feelings while with their parents.

Duckett and Richards have an interesting comparison (single-parent versus dual-parent moms, who are unemployed or employed part-time or full-time) and a nice size set of reactions from adolescents on which to base the researchers' analysis and discussion. To make sense of all this information, they compiled and then applied some statistical tests (you will learn more about these later) to reach their conclusions. Among the conclusions were

- Children of working single mothers benefit in ways other than just in the provision of income.
- Maternal employment is related to positive parent-child interactions.
- Children of single mothers employed full-time felt friendliest toward their fathers.

Most researchers recognize that they can study only a small part of a much larger question.

This was a nice, straightforward study that examined a question that bears on many issues that everyone from schoolteachers to employers needs answered. The study was done with a more than adequate group of participants and used methods that directly get at the type of information the researchers wanted. Although they did not answer every question about the relationship between employment and adolescent development, the researchers did provide an important piece to the puzzle of understanding employment's effects on growing children and changing families. The researchers seemed to take a logical approach of going from a question that has some import for many groups in today's society and articulating it in such a way that it can be answered in a reasonable and efficient manner. The issue of how children are affected by working parents is certainly still here, but the results of research such as that summarized bring us closer to a solution to some of the questions posed by such work arrangements. To be the kind of researcher you want to be, you need to know the rules of the game and follow them as did Duckett and Richards. This knowledge begins with an understanding of some basic vocabulary and ideas.

The Language of Research

Significance levels? Null hypotheses? Independent variables? Factorial designs? Research hypotheses? Samples? Populations?

These and other new words and terms form the basis for much of the communication that takes place in the research world. As with any endeavor, it is difficult to play the game unless you learn the rules. The rules begin here, with a basic understanding of the terminology that researchers use in their everyday activities. This chapter offers a language lesson of sorts. Once you become familiar with these terms, everything that follows in *Exploring Research* will be easier to understand and more useful. Each of the terms described and defined here will be used again throughout the book.

All About Variables

Variables are what is studied by researchers.

The word **variable** has several synonyms, such as changeable or unsteady. Our set of rules tells us that a variable is a noun, not an adjective, and represents a class of outcomes that can take on more than one value.

For example, hair color is a variable that can take on the values of red, brown, black, blond, and these days green, orange, and (I swear) puce. (I saw it outside my office this morning!) Other variables would be height (tall or short), weight (128 pounds or 150 pounds), age at immunization (6 weeks or 18 months), number of words remembered, time off work, party affiliation, and so on. The one thing these traits have in common is that the variable (such as party affiliation) can take on any one of several values (such as Republican, Democrat, or Independent).

Interestingly, variables that might go by the same name can not only take on different values—you could measure height in inches (60 inches) or in rank (the tallest), for example—but be defined differently as well, depending upon a host of factors such as the purpose of the research or the characteristics of the participants. For example, consider the variable called intelligence. For one researcher the definition might be scores on the Stanford-Binet Intelligence Test, while for another it might be scores on the Kaufmann Assessment Battery. For one such as Howard Gardner (1983) who believes in the existence of multiple intelligences, the definition might be performance in mathematics, music, or some physical activity. All these variables represent the same general construct of intelligence, assessed in different ways.

In the following few paragraphs, I describe several types of variables and summarize these types and what they do in Table 2.1.

Type of Variables	Definition	Synonym
Dependent	A variable that indicates whether the treatment or manipulation of the independent variable had an effect.	▪ Outcome variable ▪ Results variable ▪ Effect ▪ Criterion Variable
Independent	A variable that is manipulated to examine it's impact on a dependent variable or outcome variable.	▪ Treatment ▪ Factor ▪ Predictor variable
Control	A variable that is related to the dependent variable, the influence of which needs to be removed.	▪ Restricting variable
Extraneous	A variable that is related to the dependent or independent variable that is not part of the experiment.	▪ Threatening variable
Moderator	A variable that is related to the independent and dependent variable and has an impact on the dependent variable.	▪ Interacting variable

Table 2.1 Different types of variables, their definitions and examples

Dependent Variables

A **dependent variable** is a variable that reflects outcomes of a research study. For example, if you measure the difference between two groups of adults on how well they can remember a set of 10 single digits after a 5-hour period, then the number of digits remembered is the dependent variable. A final example: If you are looking at the effect of parental involvement in school on children's grades, the grades that the children received would be considered a dependent variable.

You can think of a dependent variable as the outcome that may depend on the experimental treatment or on what the researcher changes or manipulates.

Dependent variables are those outcome variables of your research.

Independent Variables

An **independent variable** represents the treatments or conditions that the researcher controls to test their effects on some outcome. An independent variable is also known as a *treatment variable*, and perhaps it is within this context that the term is most often used. An independent variable is manipulated in the course of an experiment to understand the effects of this manipulation on dependent variable.

For example, you might want to test the effectiveness of three different reading programs on children's reading skills. This design is illustrated in Figure 2.1. Method A includes tutoring. Method B includes tutoring and rewards, and Method C includes neither tutoring nor rewards (these kids just spend some time with the teacher). In this example, method of reading instruction is manipulated, and it is the independent variable. Reading scores are the outcome, or dependent, variable. This experiment includes three levels of one independent variable and one dependent variable.

Independent variables are under the control of the investigator.

Method of Teaching Reading (Independent Variable)		
Method A (with tutoring)	Method B (with tutoring and rewards)	Method C (no tutoring and no rewards)
Reading Scores (dependent variable)	Reading Scores (dependent variable)	Reading Scores (dependent variable)

Figure 2.1 Research designs can take on many different forms. Here, the researcher is examining the effects of three different methods of teaching reading on reading scores. Notice that in Method C, neither treatment is implemented. This is the control condition.

What if you wanted to investigate whether there is a difference between males and females in their mathematics scores on some standardized test? In this example, the independent variable is gender (male or female) and the outcome or dependent variable is mathematics score. Or, you could look at the effects of the number of hours of weekly TV watching time (less than 25 for group A or 25 or more for group B) on language skills. Here, the amount of time watching television is the independent variable, and language skills is the dependent variable.

The general rule to follow is that when the researcher is manipulating anything or assigning participants to groups based on some characteristic, such as age or ethnicity or treatment, that variable is the independent variable. When the researcher looks to some outcome to determine if the grouping had an effect, he or she looks to the dependent variable. In some cases, when researchers are not interested in looking at the effects of one thing on another, but only in how variables may be related, there are no independent variables. For example, if you are interested only in the relationship between the amount of time a father spends with his children and his job performance, nothing is manipulated.

Since independent variables must take on more than one value (since they are variables), they each must have at least two levels, or values. For example, if a researcher was studying the effects of gender differences (the independent variable) on language development (the dependent variable), the independent variable has two levels, male and female. Similarly, if a researcher was investigating age differences in stress for people ages 30-39, 40-49, and 50-59 years, the independent variable would be age, and it would have three levels.

What happens if you have more than one independent variable? Look at Figure 2.2, which represents a **factorial design** where gender, age, and social class are independent variables. Factorial designs are experiments that include more than one independent variable. Here are two levels of gender, three levels of age, and three levels of social class, accounting for a 2 by 3 by 3 design for a total of 18 (!) separate combinations, or **cells**, of levels of independent variables. You can see that as independent variables are added to a research design, the total number of cells can increase rapidly.

Gender →		Male			Female		
Age ↓	Social Class →	Low	Middle	High	Low	Middle	High
30-39							
40-49							
50-59							

Figure 2.2 Many experiments use more than one independent variable. In this example, there are three: gender, social class, and age.

The Relationship Between Independent and Dependent Variables

What are independent variables independent of? The best independent variable is independent of any other variable in the same study. In this way the independent variable can contribute the maximum amount of understanding beyond what other independent variables can offer.

What are dependent variables dependent on? The best dependent variable is one that is sensitive to changes in the different levels of the independent variable. Otherwise, even if the treatment had an effect, you would never know it.

The following equation summarizes the relationship between independent and dependent variables.

Independent and dependent variables have a specific relationship to one another.

$$DV = \int(IV_1, IV_2, \ldots IV_k)$$

where DV = the dependent variable
$\int$ = function of
IV = the independent variable(s)

For example, if one wants to investigate the effects of different screening techniques and years of experience on job satisfaction, the independent variables are screening technique (IV_1) and years of experience (IV_2). The dependent variable (DV) is job satisfaction.

Other Important Types of Variables

Independent and dependent variables are the two kinds that you will deal with most often throughout *Exploring Research*. There are other variables that it is important for you to know about as well, however, because an understanding of what they are and how they fit into the research process is essential for you to be an intelligent consumer and to have a good foundation as a beginning producer of research. Here are three more types of variables that you should be familiar with. Remember to look at Table 2.1 to get a summary of all the variables covered in this section, including a definition and an example of each one.

A **control variable** is a variable that has a potential influence on the dependent variable. Consequently, the influence has to be removed or controlled. For example, if you are interested in examining the relationship between reading speed and reading comprehension, you may want to control for differences in intelligence since intelligence is related to both reading speed and reading comprehension. Intelligence, then, needs to be held constant for you to get a good idea of the nature of the relationship between the variables of interest.

An **extraneous variable** is a variable that has an unpredictable impact upon the dependent variable. For example, if you are interested in examining the effects of television watching on achievement, you might find that the type of television programs watched is an extraneous variable that might affect achievement, since such programs as "Discovery," "Nova," "Sesame Street," and "3-2-1 Contact" might have a positive impact on achievement, and other programs might have a negative impact.

A **moderator variable** is a variable that is related to the variables of interest (such as the dependent and independent variable), masking the true relationship between the independent and dependent variable. For example, if you are examining the relationship between crime rate and ice cream consumption, you had better include temperature which moderates between that relationship. Otherwise, your conclusions will be inaccurate.

Hypotheses

In the last chapter, an hypothesis was defined as "an educated guess." While an hypothesis reflects many other things, perhaps its most important role is to reflect the general problem statement or question that was the motivation for undertaking the research study. That is why taking care and time with that initial question is so important. It can guide you through the creation of an hypothesis which in turn helps you determine the types of techniques you will use to test the hypothesis and answer the original question.

For example, the "I wonder..." stage becomes the problem statement stage, which then leads to the study's hypothesis. Here is an example of each of these.

The Stage	An Example
"I Wonder..."	It seems to me that several things could be done to help our employees lower their high absentee rate. Talking with some of them tells me that they are concerned about after school care for their children. I wonder what would happen if a program were started right here in the factory that could provide child supervision and activities?
The hypothesis	Parents who enroll their children in after school programs will miss fewer days of work in one year and will have a more positive attitude toward work as measured by the Attitude Toward Work survey (ATW) than parents who do not enroll their children in such programs.

So, a good hypothesis provides a translation from a problem statement into a form that is more amenable to testing using the research methods discussed in this book. We will talk about what makes a good hypothesis after defining the two types of hypotheses, the null hypothesis and research hypothesis, and how they are used.

The Null Hypothesis

The null hypothesis is an interesting little creature. If it could talk, it would say something like, "I represent no relationship between the variables that you are studying." In other words, **null hypotheses** are statements of *equality* such as the following null hypotheses demonstrate:

A null hypothesis is always a statement of equality.

- There will be no difference in the average score of ninth-graders and the average score of 12th-graders on the ABC memory test.
- There is no relationship between personality type and job success.
- There is no difference in voting patterns as a function of political party.
- The brand of ice cream preferred is independent of the buyer's age, gender, and income.

What these four null hypotheses have in common is that they all contain a statement of two or more things being equal or unrelated to each other.

What are the basic purposes of the null hypothesis? It acts as both a *starting point* and as a *benchmark* against which the actual outcomes of a study will be measured. Let's examine each of these purposes.

First, the null hypothesis acts as a starting point since it is the state of affairs that is accepted as true in the absence of other information. For example, let's look at the first null hypothesis stated above: *There will be no difference in the average score of ninth-graders and the average score of 12th-graders on the ABC memory test.* Given no other knowledge of ninth- and 12th-graders' memory skills, you have no reason to believe there will be differences between the two groups. You might speculate as to why one group might outperform another, but if you have no evidence *a priori* (before the fact), then what choice do you have but to assume that they are equal? This lack of a relationship, unless proved otherwise, is a hallmark of the method being discussed. In other words, until you prove that there is a difference, you have to assume that there is no difference.

Furthermore, if there are any differences between these two groups, you have to assume that the differences are due to the most attractive explanation for differences between any groups on any variable, *chance*! That is right; given no other information, chance is always the most likely explanation for differences between two groups. And what is chance? It is the random variability introduced into every study as a function of the individuals participating as well as many unforeseen factors, such as the way behavior is measured. For example, you could take a group of soccer players and a group of football players and compare their running speeds. But who is to know whether some soccer players practice more, or if some football players are stronger, or if both groups are receiving additional training? What is more, perhaps the way their speed is being measured leaves room for chance; a faulty stopwatch or a windy day can contribute to differences unrelated to true running speed. As good researchers, our job is to eliminate chance as a factor and to evaluate other factors that might contribute to group differences such as those that are identified as independent variables.

The second purpose of the null hypothesis is to provide a *benchmark* against which observed outcomes can be compared to see if these differences are due to chance or some other factor. The null hypothesis helps to define a range within which any observed differences between groups can be attributed to chance (which is the null hypothesis's contention) or due to something other than chance (which perhaps would be the result of the manipulation of the independent variable).

Most correlational, quasi-experimental, and experimental studies have an implied null hypothesis. Historical and descriptive studies do not. For example, if you are interested in the growth of immunization during the last 70 years (historical) or how people feel about school vouchers (descriptive) you are probably not concerned with group differences.

The Research Hypothesis

While a null hypothesis is a statement of no relationship between variables, a **research hypothesis** is a definite statement of the relationship between two variables. For example, for each of the null hypotheses stated earlier, here is a corresponding research hypothesis. Notice that I said "a" and not "the" corresponding research hypothesis, since there can certainly be more than one research hypotheses for any one null hypothesis. Here are some research hypotheses that correspond with the null hypotheses mentioned earlier.

- The average score of ninth-graders is different from the average score of 12th-graders on the ABC memory test.
- There is a relationship between personality type and job success.
- Voting patterns are a function of political party.
- The brand of ice cream preferred is related to the buyer's age, gender, and income.

Each of these four research hypotheses has one thing in common. They are all statements of *inequality*. They posit a relationship between variables and not an equality, as the null hypothesis does. The nature of this inequality can take two different forms—*directional* and *nondirectional*. If the research hypothesis posits no direction to the inequality (such as different from), the research hypothesis is a nondirectional research hypothesis. If the research hypothesis posits a direction to the inequality (such as more than or less than), the research hypothesis is a directional research hypothesis.

The Nondirectional Research Hypothesis

Nondirectional research hypotheses reflect a difference between groups, but the direction of the difference is not specified. For example, the research hypothesis *The average score of ninth-graders is different from the average score of 12th-graders on the ABC memory test* is nondirectional in that the direction of the difference between the two groups is not specified. The hypothesis only states that there is a difference and says nothing about the direction of that difference. It is a research hypothesis because a difference is hypothesized, but the nature of the difference is not specified.

A nondirectional research hypothesis such as the one described here would be represented by the following equation.

$$H_1: \overline{X}_9 \neq \overline{X}_{12}$$

where H_1: represents the symbol for the first (of possible several) research hypothesis
        $\overline{X}_9$ = represents the average memory score for the sample of ninth-graders
        $\overline{X}_{12}$ = represents the average memory score for the sample of twelfth-graders
        $\neq$ = not equal

The Directional Research Hypothesis

Directional research hypotheses reflect a difference between groups, and the direction of the difference is specified.

For example, the research hypothesis *The average score of 12th-graders is greater than the average score of ninth-graders on the ABC memory test* is directional, since the direction of the difference between the two groups is specified. One is hypothesized to be greater than the other.

Directional hypotheses can take the form of

- A greater than B (or A > B), or
- B greater than A (or A < B).

> A research hypothesis is always a statement of inequality.

These all represent inequalities. A directional research hypothesis such as the one described above, where 12th-graders are hypothesized to score better than ninth-graders, would be represented by the following equation.

$$H_1: \overline{X}_9 < \overline{X}_{12}$$

where H_1: represents the symbol for the first (of possible several) research hypothesis
        $\overline{X}_9$ = represents the average memory score for the sample of ninth-graders
        $\overline{X}_{12}$ = represents the average memory score for the sample of twelfth-graders
        $<$ = less than

What is the purpose of the research hypothesis? It is this hypothesis that is tested directly as one step in the research process. The results of this test are compared with what you expect by chance alone (reflecting the null hypothesis) to see which of the two is the more attractive explanation for any differences between groups you might observe.

Differences Between the Null Hypothesis and the Research Hypothesis

Besides the null hypothesis representing an equality and the research hypothesis representing an inequality, there are several other important differences between the two types of hypotheses. First, the two differ in that one (the null hypothesis) states there is no relationship between variables (an equality) while the other (the research hypothesis) states there is a relationship (an inequality). This is the primary difference.

Second, null hypotheses always refer to the *population* whereas research hypotheses always refer to the *sample*. As you will read later in this chapter, researchers select a sample of participants from a much larger population. One reason for this method is that it is too expensive and often impossible to work with the entire population.

Third, since the entire population cannot be directly tested (again, it is impractical, uneconomical, and often impossible), you can never really say that there is *actually* no difference between groups on a specified dependent variable (if you accept the null hypothesis). Rather, you have to infer it (indirectly) from the results of the test of the research hypothesis, which is based on the sample. Hence, the null hypothesis must be indirectly tested while the research hypothesis is directly tested.

Fourth, null hypotheses are always stated using Greek symbols, and research hypotheses are always stated using Roman symbols. For example, the null hypothesis that the average score for ninth-graders is equal to that of 12th-graders is represented as:

$$H_0: \mu_9 = \mu_{12}$$

where H_0: represents the null hypothesis
μ_9 = represents the theoretical average for the population of ninth-graders
μ_{12} = represents the theoretical average for the population of twelfth-graders

Research hypotheses are stated using Roman symbols such as $\overline{X}$ to represent the average of a sample.

For example, the research hypothesis that the average score for a sample of ninth-graders is less than the average score for a sample of 12th-graders would be represented by the following equation:

$$H_1: \overline{X}_9 < \overline{X}_{12}$$

where H_1: represents the symbol for the research hypothesis
$\overline{X}_9$ = represents the average for a sample of ninth-graders
$\overline{X}_{12}$ = represents the average for a sample of twelfth-grader

Finally, because you cannot directly test the null hypothesis, it is an *implied* hypothesis. The research hypothesis is *explicit*. It is for this reason that you rarely see null hypotheses stated in research reports, whereas you almost always see a statement of the research hypothesis.

What Makes a Good Hypothesis?

You now know that hypotheses are educated guesses. As with any guess, some are better than others right from the start. I cannot stress enough how important it is to ask the question you want answered and to keep in mind that any hypothesis you present is a direct extension of the original question you asked. This question will reflect your own personal interests and what research has been previously done.

With that in mind, here are some criteria you might use to decide whether an hypothesis you read in a research report or the ones you formulate are acceptable.

To illustrate, let's use an example of a study that examines the effects of after school child care programs for employees who work late on the parents' adjustment to work. Here is a well written hypothesis:

> *Parents who enroll their children in after school programs will miss fewer days of work in one year and will have a more positive attitude toward work as measured by the Attitude Toward Work survey (ATW) than parents who do not enroll their children in such programs.*

Good hypotheses are clearly stated and tell the reader exactly what is being investigated.

Here are the criteria.

First, *a good hypothesis is stated in declarative form and not as a question*. In the above example, the question, "Do you think parents and the companies they work for will be better..." was not posed, since hypotheses are most effective when they make a clear and forceful statement.

Second, a good hypothesis *posits an expected relationship between variables*. The hypothesis that is being used as an example clearly describes the relationship between after school child care, parents' attitude, and absentee rate. These variables are being tested to see if one (enrollment in the after school program) has an effect upon the others (absentee rate and attitude).

Notice the word *expected* in the above criterion? Defining an expected relationship is intended to prevent the fishing trip (sometimes called the "shotgun" approach) that may be tempting to take but is not very productive. The fishing trip approach is where you throw out your line and take anything that bites. You collect data on as many things as you can regardless of your interest or even whether collecting the data is a reasonable part of a scientific investigation. Or you load up them guns and blast away at anything that moves. You are bound to hit something. The problem is you may not want what you hit, and, worse, you may miss what you want to hit, and even worse (if possible) you may not know what you hit!

Good researchers do not want just anything they can catch or shoot. They want specific results. To get them, researchers need their opening questions and hypotheses to be clear, forceful, and easily understood.

Third, *hypotheses reflect the theory or literature they are based on*. As you read in chapter 1, the accomplishments of scientists can rarely be attributed to their hard work alone. Their accomplishments also are due to many other researchers who have come before them and laid a framework for later explorations. A good hypothesis reflects this, in that it has a substantive link to existing literature and theory. In the above example, let's assume there is literature indicating that parents are more comfortable knowing their children are being cared for in a structured environment, and parents then can be more productive at work. Knowing this would allow one to hypothesize that an after school program would provide parents the security they are looking for, which in turn allows them to concentrate on work rather than on the telephone to find out whether Rachel or Gregory got home safely.

Fourth, *an hypothesis should be brief and to the point*. You want your hypothesis to describe the relationship between variables in a declarative form and to be as to the point as possible. The more to the point, the easier it will be for others (such as your master's thesis committee members!) to read your research and understand exactly what you are hypothesizing and what the important variables are. In fact, when people read and evaluate research (as you will learn more about later in this chapter), the first thing many of them do is find the hypotheses to get a good idea as to the general purpose of the research and how things will be done. A good hypothesis tells you both these things.

Fifth, *good hypotheses are testable hypotheses*. This means that you can actually carry out the intent of the question reflected in the hypothesis. You can see from the sample hypothesis that the important comparison is between parents who have enrolled their child in an after school program with those who have not. Then, such things as attitude and work days missed will be measured. These are both reasonable objectives. Attitude is measured by the Attitude Toward Work survey (a fictitious title, but you get the idea), and absenteeism (the number of days away from work) is an easily recorded and unambiguous measure. Think how much harder things would be if the hypothesis were stated as *Parents who enroll their children in after school care feel better about their job*. While you might get the same message, the results might be more difficult to interpret given the ambiguous nature of words such as *feel better*.

In sum, hypotheses should

- be stated in declarative form,
- posit a relationship between variables,
- reflect a theory or a body of literature that they are based on,
- be brief and to the point, and
- be testable.

When an hypothesis meets each of these five criteria, you know that it is good enough to continue with a study that will accurately test the general question from which the hypothesis was derived.

Samples and Populations

As a good scientist, you would like to be able to say that if *Method A is better than Method B,* this is true *forever and always and for all people*. Indeed, if you do enough research on the relative merits of Methods A and B and test enough people, you may someday be able to say that, but it is unlikely. It takes too much money ($$$) and too much time (all those people!) to do all that research.

However, given the constraints of never enough time and never enough research funds that almost all scientists live with, the next best strategy is to take a *portion* of a larger group of participants and do the research with that smaller group. In this context, the larger group is referred to as a **population**, and the smaller group selected from a population is referred to as a **sample**.

A sample is representative of only part of a population but is used to generalize back to the population.

Samples should be selected from populations in such a way that the likelihood that the sample represents the population as closely as possible is maximized. The goal is to have the sample as much like the population as possible. The most important implication of ensuring similarity between the two is that once the research is finished the results based on the sample can be generalized to the population. When the sample does represent the population, the results of the study are said to be **generalizable** or to have generalizability.

I will talk more about the various types of sampling procedures in chapter 4.

The Concept of Significance

There is probably no term or concept that represents more confusion for the beginning student than that of statistical significance. It is explained in detail in chapter 8, but it is important to be exposed to the term early in *Exploring Research* since it is a basic and major component of understanding the research process.

At the beginning of this chapter, you read a simple overview of a study where two researchers examined the differences between adolescents whose mothers work and adolescents whose mothers do not (as well as family status, but for this example let's stick with the work and don't work groups).

Let's modify the meaning of the word *differences* to include the adjective, *significant*. What I mean by *significant differences* is that the differences observed between adolescents of mothers who work and of those who do not are due to some influence and do not appear just by chance. In this example, that factor is whether mothers work. Let's assume that other factors that might account for any differences were controlled for. Thus, the only thing left to account for the differences between adolescents is whether or not mothers work. Right? Yes. Finished? Not quite.

Since the world and you and I and the research process are not perfect, one must allow for some leeway. In other words, you need to be able to say that while you are pretty sure the difference between the two groups of adolescents is due to mothers' working, you cannot be absolutely, 100%, positively, unequivocally, indisputably (get the picture?) sure.

Why? For many different reasons. For example, you could just be (horrors!) wrong. Maybe during this one experiment, differences were not due to the group the adolescents were in but to some other factor that was inadvertently not accounted for, such as out-of-home experiences. How about if the people in one group were mostly adolescent males and reacted quite differently than the people in the other group, mostly adolescent females? If you are a good researcher and do your homework, such differences between groups are unlikely outcomes but possible nonetheless. This factor (gender) and others could certainly have an impact on the outcome or dependent variable and in turn have an impact on the final results and conclusion you reach.

Significance level is a probability assigned to an outcome.

So what to do? In most scientific endeavors that involve proposing hypotheses and examining differences between groups, there is bound to be a certain amount of error that cannot be controlled. **Significance level** is the risk associated with not being 100% confident that the difference is due to what you think and may be due to some unforeseen factor. If you see that a study resulted in *significant* findings at the .05 level, the translation is that a chance of 1 in 20 (or .05 or 5%) exists that any differences found were not due to the hypothesized reason (the independent variable) but to some other, unknown reason or reasons. Your job as a good scientist is to reduce this likelihood as much as possible by removing all the competing reasons, other than the one you are testing, for any differences that you observed. Since you cannot *fully* eliminate the likelihood, you deal with it by assigning a level of probability and report your results with that caveat. There is a technical side to determining specific levels of significance, and you will read more about that in chapter 8.

OK, that should wrap up some vocabulary and provide you a basic knowledge for understanding most of the basic terms used in the research process. Being familiar with them will provide a foundation to continue to the next section of this chapter, which deals with how to read and evaluate research articles.

Reading and Evaluating Research

Like anything else, understanding research articles takes practice.

Almost any research activity that you participate in involves the reading of research articles that appear in journals and textbooks. In fact, one of the most common faults of beginning researchers is not being sufficiently familiar with the wealth of research reports in their specific area of interest. It is indeed rare to find a research topic where nothing or nothing related has been done. You may not be able to find something that is exactly on the topic you wish to pursue (such as changes in adolescent behavior in Australian children who live in the outback), but there is plenty of information on adolescent behavior and plenty on children who live in Australia. Part of your job as a good scientist is to make the argument why these factors might be important to study. You can do that by reading and evaluating research that has been done in various disciplines on the same topic.

What Does a Research Article Look Like?

The only way to gain expertise in understanding the results of research studies is to read and practice understanding what they mean. Begin with one of the journals in your own area. Don't know of any? Then do one of two things.

- Visit your adviser or some faculty member in the area in which you are interested, and ask the question, "What is the best research journal in my area?"
- Visit the library and look through the index of periodicals. You are bound to find tens if not hundreds of journals.

For example, for those of you interested in education and psychology and related areas, here is a sample of 10 research journals that were rated by 700 people as those they would most like to publish in and those that they would find the most useful for reporting important research findings (Terrance and Johnson, 1978). If these 700 other accomplished researchers find these valuable as sources of information, wouldn't they be a great place for you to start?

- *American Educational Research Journal*
- *American Psychologist*
- *Educational Researcher*
- *Educational and Psychological Measurement*
- *Harvard Educational Review*
- *Journal of Educational Research*
- *Journal of Educational Psychology*
- *Journal of Educational Measurement*
- *Phi Delta Kappan*
- *Review of Educational Research*

Here are 10 more that focus primarily on psychology:

- *Child Development*
- *Cognition*
- *Human Development*
- *Journal of Experimental Psychology*
- *Journal of Personality and Social Psychology*
- *Journal of Applied Developmental Psychology*
- *Pediatrics*
- *Perceptual and Motor Skills*
- *Psychological Bulletin*
- *Sex Roles*

You will find a much more extensive list in the next chapter.

Criteria for Judging a Research Study

Judging anyone else's work is never an easy task. A good place to start might be the following checklist organized to help you focus on the most important characteristics of any journal article. These eight areas can give you a good start in better understanding the general format of such a report and how well the author(s) communicated to you what they did, why they did it, how they did it, and what it all means.

1. The Review of Previous Research

How closely is the literature cited in the study related to previous literature?
Is the review recent?
Are there any seminal or outstanding references you know of that were left out?

2. The Problem and Purpose

Can you understand the statement of the problem?
Is the purpose of the study clearly stated?
Does the purpose seem to be tied to the literature that is reviewed?
Is the objective of the study clearly stated?
Is there a conceptual rationale to which the hypotheses are grounded?
Is there a rationale for why the study is an important one to do?

3. The Hypothesis

Are the research hypotheses clearly stated?
Are the research hypotheses explicitly stated?
Do the hypotheses state a clear association between variables?
Are the hypotheses grounded in theory or in a review and presentation of relevant literature?
Are the hypotheses testable?

4. The Method

Are both the independent and dependent variables clearly defined?
Are the definition and description of the variables complete?
Is it clear how the study was conducted?

5. The Sample

Was the sample selected in such a way that you think it is representative of the population?
Is it clear where the sample comes from and how it was selected?
How similar are the participants in the study to those that have been used in similar studies?

6. Results and Discussion

Does the author relate the results to the review of literature?
Are the results related to the hypothesis?
Is the discussion of the results consistent with the results?
Does the discussion provide closure to the initial hypothesis that the author presents?

7. References

Is the list of references current?
Are they consistent in their format?
Are the references complete?
Does the list of references reflect some of the most important reference sources in the field?

8. General Comments About the Report

Is it clearly written and understandable?
Is the language biased?
What are the strengths and weaknesses of the research?
What are the primary implications of the research?
What would you do to improve the research?

Basic Principles of Ethical Research

Although researchers should be excited and enthusiastic about their work, the most important thing to remember is that human beings are serving as participants. These individuals need to be treated so that their dignity is maintained in spite of the research or the outcomes. Easier said than done? You bet.

The challenges that ethical behavioral research demands have created a whole field of study, called (not to your surprise) ethics. As long as researchers continue to use humans and animals as participants, the way these people and animals are treated and how they benefit, even indirectly, from participation are critical issues that must kept in the forefront of all our considerations.

Later in this chapter, the specific guidelines published by professional groups for their members are listed. But first, let's address the general issues that arise in any discussion of ethical behavior.

Maintenance of Privacy

Maintenance of privacy speaks to several concerns, but most directly to anonymity. Being anonymous within a research context means that there is no way that anyone except the principal investigator (usually the director) can match the results of an experiment with the individual associated with these results.

Anonymity is most often maintained through the use of a single master sheet that contains both the names of the participants and their subject number. Then, on scoring sheets, code sheets, or other testing materials, only the number is placed. The list of corresponding names and numbers is kept in a secure place out of the public eye and often under lock and key.

A second concern regarding privacy is that one does not invade another's private spaces to observe behavior and collect data. For example, it would be unethical to secretly record the verbal interaction between therapists and their clients. While this might be a rich source of information, it would not be legitimate unless the client and therapist agree.

Coercion

People should not be forced, for whatever reason, into participation. As you well know, college students and especially those in introductory psychology classes are often the most used population for many different research studies. Is it always ethical to require these students to participate in an experiment? Probably not, yet many students must participate as a course requirement. Similarly, people in the workplace are often required to complete surveys, answer questionnaires, and provide other types of information for research purposes as a part of their job-related duties.

The key here is not to force people to participate. If they do not want to participate, an alternative way to fulfill a course or job requirement should be provided.

Informed Consent

This may be the most important requirement, and the informed consent form might be the one tool to ensure ethical behavior. Without question, every research project that uses human participants should have an informed consent form read and signed by each participant or the person granting participation (in the case of a child with the parent signing off).

What does such a consent form look like? You can see one in Figure 2.3. These are not just invitations to participate (although they may be that as well), but a description of what will happen throughout the course of the research. As you can see, such a letter contains at least the following information:

- the purpose of the research
- who you are
- what you are doing
- how long the participant will be involved
- an offer to withdraw from the experiment at any time for any reason
- potential benefits to the individual as well as to society
- potential harm or risks for discomfort to the individual
- an assurance that the results will be kept in strictest confidence
- how to get a copy of the results
- how you can be reached should anyone have questions
- a place for prospective subjects (or parent of) to sign indicating that they agree to participate and that they understand the purpose of the research

The letter is printed on official stationery and illustrates all the above points. It is not written in scientific mumbo-jumbo, but it is as straightforward as possible. The goal here is to inform, not to coerce or cajole people into participating.

Department of Educational Psychology & Research

University of Kansas • Lawrence, KS 66045

November 13, 1995

Dear Mr. and Mrs. Eisner:

The Department of Educational Psychology & Research at the University of Kansas supports the practice of informed consent and protection for human subjects participating in research. The following information is provided for you to decide whether you will allow Nikki and Alexandra to participate in the present study. You are free to withdraw either or both of them at any time.

Your child will be asked to play a game with another child with a disability in a room that has toys and books, and your child's behavior will be recorded on videotape. One session will last approximately 25 minutes. We are interested in studying the interaction between children who have a disability and children who do not. This information is important since it will help us develop methods for increasing the effectiveness of efforts to integrate children with disabilities into the regular education classroom.

Your child's participation is solicited but strictly voluntary. We assure you that your child's name will not in any way be associated with the research findings. The information will be identified only through a code number.

If you would like additional information concerning this study before or after it is completed, please contact one of us by phone or mail. Thank you very much for your time, and we appreciate your interest and cooperation.

Sincerely,

Bruce Saxon   Sam Fine
Graduate Student   Professor
(913) 123-4567   (913) 123-4567

_____
Signature of parent or legal guardian

Figure 2.3 A typical consent form including all the important information so potential subjects know exactly what is going on.

Informed Consent with Children

There is an obvious problem when it comes to ensuring informed consent with children. An example is an investigation of visual development in young children, where the child is too young to give consent of any kind. It is left to the judgment of the parents whether they will allow their child to participate.

But there are issues galore when it comes to ethics and children, far beyond the difficult process of ensuring that children will not be placed in any danger, either of a physical or psychological nature. For example, are 12-year-old children old enough to make a decision about withdrawing as the consent form should clearly state is an option for them? Can they understand the long-range implications of the research in which they are participating? The potential risks? This has to be where the good judgment of the researcher comes into play. If a child feels strongly about not participating, you may lose that subject and those data, but his or her wishes need to be respected just as those of any adult would be. Additionally, forcing participation may result in an unhappy or angry child and untrustworthy data.

As children grow older, however, the issue becomes more complex. For example, what about the 12-year-old who is old enough to understand the purpose of the experiment? Should he or she sign the consent form as well as the parent(s)? No researcher in his or her right mind would not first obtain permission from the parent(s). Additionally, when school-age children are used in research, more and more school districts require that the proposal be reviewed by a school-wide research committee. To top it all off, more researchers than ever now have liability insurance to cover themselves if an angry parent sues or some unintended injury occurs.

The best advice? Make any experimental session or treatment with children as pleasant as possible. One way to do that is to encourage them, make the activities pleasant, and reward them when you have finished (as long as the promise of a reward does not interfere with what you are studying). But above all, remember that children are physically, emotionally, and socially different from adults, and those differences must be taken into account when they are used as subjects.

Confidentiality

Whereas anonymity means that records cannot be linked with names, confidentiality is maintained when anything that is learned about the participant is held in the strictest of confidence. This means that information is disguised when necessary (which touches on anonymity as well), but, more important, all the data are kept in a controlled situation.

The best way to maintain confidentiality is by minimizing the number of people who see or get to handle the data. There is no better example of this than recent concerns about AIDS and the results of screening tests. People are reluctant to be tested for HIV (the virus associated with AIDS) since they are concerned that insurance companies and potential employers will have access to the results of the tests and use them against the individual when he or she applies for a job or health or life insurance.

Protection from Harm

Above all, subjects must be prevented from physical or psychological harm. If there is any doubt at the onset that there is a significant risk involved (relative to the payoffs), then the experiment should not be approved. Notice risks and benefits are the focus. In the case of a terminally ill child, the most dramatic and even unconfirmed techniques that may save the child's life (but may also hasten his or her death) may have a high risk, but the potential benefits may be just as important to consider.

Sharing Results

Scientific knowledge belongs in the public domain, and, although there have been some heated arguments about when to tell whom, most researchers agree that it is important to bring new discoveries to the public as soon as practical and possible. When you complete your research and write up a final report, you should be willing to share your results with others.

Some of the most important of these others are the people who participated in your experiment. In practical terms you can offer to send them a summary of the final report or have a meeting where they can be informed as to the outcomes.

Debriefing

Another component of sharing the results of an experiment is when a particular group of subjects needs to be debriefed.

For example, you design an experiment where you tell one group of subjects a lie as part of the experiment. You might tell young children not to play with a particularly attractive toy and then videotape their behavior without their knowledge.

Once the experiment is completed, it is your responsibility to inform them that they have been deceived to some extent for the purposes of the experiment. Most people will take that just fine (as do the contestants on "Candid Camera!"), but some will get upset when they learn that they have been manipulated. If they remain angry, it is difficult to do anything other than apologize and try to set the record straight. The easiest way to debrief participants is to talk with them immediately following the session or to send a newsletter telling participants the general intent and results of the study but leaving out specifics such as names.

Sharing Benefits

The last principle may be the most often violated. Here is the scenario. In an experiment a treatment was used to increase the memory of older people in the early stages of Alzheimer's disease, a devastating and almost always fatal illness. Let's say that the researcher uses two groups, one that receives the training (the experimental group) and one that does not (the control group). Much to the researcher's pleasure, the treatment group learns faster and remembers much more for much longer. Success!

What is the concern? Simply that the group that did not receive the treatment should now be exposed to it. It is the right thing to do. When one group benefits from participation in a study, any other groups that participated in the study should benefit as well. This does not mean that it is possible that all elderly people can be helped. That may not be feasible. But all direct participants in the experiment should benefit equally.

All these ethical issues apply to the different types of research methods described in chapters 9, 10, and 11 with differing degrees of importance. For example, one need not be concerned about debriefings when conducting a case study since no treatment and no deception is involved. Nor would one be concerned with sharing of benefits in that situation.

Ensuring High Ethical Standards

There are several steps that even the beginning researcher can take to ensure that ethical principles, such as those described above, are maintained. Here are some of the most important.

1. Do a computer simulation, where data are constructed and subjected to the effects of various treatments. For example, mathematical psychologists and statisticians often use Monte Carlo studies to examine the effects of a change in one variable (such as sample size) upon another (such as accuracy of measurement). Elaborate models of human behavior can be constructed, and different assumptions can be tested and conclusions drawn about human behavior. While this is somewhat advanced work, it does give you an idea of how certain experiments can be conducted with the "participants" being nothing more than values generated by a computer.

2. When the treatment is deemed harmful, do not give up. Rather, try to locate a population that has already been exposed to the harmful effects of some variable. For example, the thousands of children and pregnant women who were malnourished during World War II provided an invaluable sample for estimating the effects of malnourishment on fetal and neonatal development as well as the long-range effects of malnourishment on young children. While not pleasant, this is about the only way that such research is possible. This type of research is called quasi-experimental and will be covered in greater detail in chapter 11.

3. Always secure informed consent. If the treatment includes risk, be absolutely sure that the risks are clear to the participant and other interested parties (parents, other family members).

4. Publish all reports using group rather than individual data. This measure maintains confidentiality.

5. If you suspect that the treatment may have negative side effects, use a small, well-informed sample until you can expand the sample size and the ambitiousness of the project. Also, be sure to check with your institutional review board (more about that in a moment).

6. Use your colleagues to review your proposal and especially your experimental procedures before you begin. Ask them the question, "Would you participate without any fear of being harmed?" If they say "no," go back to the drawing board.

7. Almost every public institution (such as public universities) and every private agency (such as some hospitals and private universities) have what is called an **institutional review board**. Such boards consist of a group of people from several disciplines (including representatives from the community) who render a judgment as to whether participation in the experiment is free from harm. At the University of Kansas, the group is called the Advisory Committee on Human Experimentation (ACHE). There is a separate review board for experiments using animals.

The groups usually meet and then approve or disapprove the procedure (but not necessarily the content of research) and take into consideration the issues already discussed. These committees usually meet about once a month, and if a proposal that they review is not acceptable, they invite the researcher to resubmit according to their recommendations. In Figure 2.4, you can see a sample of the form used by the ACHE at the University of Kansas.

The Role of Professional Organizations

It is unquestionably the role of the researcher to ensure that the ethical standards discussed above are always kept in mind when conducting any type of research.

There are more formalized sets of guidelines published by professional organizations such as the American Psychological Association (APA), the Society for Research in Child Development (SRCD), the American Sociological Association (ASA),

#_____

APPLICATION FOR PROJECT APPROVAL
ADVISORY COMMITTEE ON HUMAN EXPERIMENTATION

Please use a typewriter to complete this form

1. Name of Investigator(s) _____

2. Department Affiliation _____

3. Campus Mailing Address _____

4. Phone Number(s): (a)Campus _____(b)Home_____

5. Name of Faculty Member Responsible for Project_____

6. Type of investigator and nature of activity. (Check appropriate categories.)

_____ Faculty or staff of Kansas University

       _____ Project to be submitted for extramural funding; Agency _____

       _____ Project to be submitted for intramural funding; Source _____

       _____ Project unfunded

       _____ Other

_____ Student at Kansas University

       _____ Graduate   _____ Undergraduate   _____ Special

       _____ Thesis   _____ Dissertation

       _____ Class project (number & title of class) _____

       _____ Independent study (name of faculty supervisor) _____

       _____ Other (please explain) _____

7. Title of investigation _____
_____

All student applications submitted to the ACHE for review must be signed by all investigators including the faculty member supervising the research activity.

8. _____ Individuals other than faculty, staff, or students at Kansas University. Please identify investigators and research group _____
_____

9. Certifications

I am familiar with the policies and procedures of the University of Kansas regarding human subjects in research. I subscribe to the standards and will adhere to the policies and procedures of the ACHE.

and

I am familiar with the published guidelines for the ethical treatment of subjects associated with my particular field of study (e.g., as published by the American Psychological Association, American Sociological Association, etc.).

Date_____   Date_____

Signature_____   Signature_____
       First Investigator   Faculty Supervisor

Figure 2.4 A sample institutional review form.

Date_____   Date_____

Signature_____   Signature_____
               Second Investigator   Third Investigator

Principal Investigator_____
ACHE#_____

Title_____

10. Please answer the following questions with regard to the research activity proposed:
Does the research involve:

                                                          Yes   No

a.   drugs or other controlled substances?   _____ _____
b.   payment of subjects for participation?   _____ _____
c.   Access to subjects through a cooperating institution?   _____ _____
d.   substances taken internally by or applied externally
      to the subjects?   _____ _____
e.   mechanical or electrical devices (e.g.electrodes) applied
      to the subjects?   _____ _____
f.   fluids (e.g., blood) or tissues removed from the subjects? _____ _____
g.   subjects experiencing stress (physiological or psychological)? _____ _____
h.   deception of subjects concerning any aspect of purposes
      or procedures?   _____ _____
i.   subjects who would be judged to have limited freedom of
      consent? (mentally retarded, ill, or aged)?   _____ _____
j.   any procedure or activities that might place the subjects at
      risk (psychological, physical, or social)?   _____ _____
k.   use of interviews, survey, questionnaires, audio or
      video recordings?   _____ _____
l.   data collection over a period greater than one year? _____ _____
m.   a copy of the consent form will be given to the subjects _____ _____

11. Approximate number of subjects to be involved in research   _____

Complete the following questions on this page. Please do not use continuation sheets. ACHE will not process applications which do not stay within the page limitations. See instructions.

12. Project Purpose(s)

13. Describe the proposed subjects (age, sex, race, or other special characteristics).

14. Describe how the subjects are to be selected.

Figure 2.4 Continued.

the American Educational Research Association (AERA), and just about every other social or behavioral science professional group. To illustrate just what these guidelines suggest, here is a summary of those presented by the American Psychological Association (a group of about 25,000 professionals) and the Society for Research in Children Development (a group of about 6,000 professionals).

APA Ethical Guidelines

The set of guidelines formulated by an APA committee was first presented in 1953. Here is a summary of the latest.

1. When a study is planned, the researcher must be the first and most important judge of its ethical acceptability.
2. Subjects must be judged to be "at no risk" or "at minimal risk."
3. The researcher is responsible for ensuring ethical practices, including the behavior of assistants, students, employees, collaborators, and anyone else involved in the process.
4. A fair and reasonable agreement must be reached between the researcher and the subjects, prior to the beginning of the research.
5. If deception is necessary, the researcher must be sure it is justified and a mechanism must be built in to ensure that subjects are debriefed when the research is concluded.
6. Researchers must respect the subject's choice to withdraw and must not practice coercion to get the subject back into participating.
7. Every possible effort should be made to protect participants from physical and psychological harm.
8. Once the research is complete, should the participant so indicate, the results should be shared and the participant should be given a chance to clarify any discrepancies she or he might be aware of.
9. If the research should result in harm of any kind, the researcher has the responsibility to correct the harm.
10. All the information obtained in a research study is confidential.

SRCD Ethical Guidelines

Because this is a group committed to learning more about the development of children, you will notice how precisely these guidelines are written to consider children's well-being.

1. The rights of the child supersede the rights of the investigator no matter what the age of the child.
2. All ethical issues surrounding the research project are the responsibility of the head investigator.
3. If there are changes in approved procedures that might affect the ethical conduct of the research, consultation with colleagues or experts should be undertaken.
4. The child should be fully informed as to the research process, and all questions should be answered in a way that can be understood.
5. Children are free to withdraw from the research at any time.

6. Informed consent from parents, teachers, or whoever is legally responsible for the child's welfare must be obtained in writing.
7. Informed consent must also be obtained from others who are involved in the experiment (such as parents, etc.), besides the individual child.
8. The responsibilities of the child and of the investigator must be made clear.
9. When the potential for harm is present, the investigator must either find an alternative way to collect the necessary information or abandon the research.
10. When deception is necessary, a committee of the investigator's peers should approve the planned methods.
11. All information is confidential.
12. If institutional records are to be used as a source of information, permission must be obtained from all affected parties.
13. The findings from any study should be reported to the participants in a way that is comprehensible to them.
14. Investigators should be especially careful about the way they report results to children and should not present the results in the form of advice.
15. If during the course of the investigation information arises that is important to the child's welfare, the investigator has an obligation to report the information to parents, teachers, or other appropriate parties.
16. All undesirable consequences should be corrected.
17. Investigators should be aware that research can have political, social, and human implications, and they should be mindful of this when results are reported and shared.
18. If treatments are effective, control groups should be offered similar opportunities to receive the treatment.
19. These ethical standards should be presented to students in the course of their training.
20. All investigators have the responsibility of maintaining their own ethical conduct and that of their colleagues as well.
21. Editors of journals that report investigations of children should provide authors space to summarize the steps they took to ensure these standards. If it is not clear such standards were followed, editors should request additional information.
22. These standards are always open to discussion and amendment.

Do the ethical standards of the APA and the SRCD work? In general, the answer is probably yes, but since it is up to each individual to practice such guidelines, it is difficult to gain any objective picture.

In order to play the research game, you have to know the rules. This chapter introduced you to some of the most important terms and concepts about the research process and those that will be mentioned again and again throughout this book. As you begin to review literature either in preparation of a proposal or for some related research activity, you will see these terms being used and see how helpful it is to know how they should be used and what they mean. You will also want to keep those important basic principles of ethics foremost in your mind as you plan your research activities.

Exercises

1. In the following examples, identify the independent and dependent variable(s).
   a. Two groups of children were given different types of physical fitness programs to see if the programs had an effect on their strength.
   b. A group of 100 heavy smokers was divided into five groups, and each group participated in a different stop-smoking program. After six months of program participation, the number of cigarettes each participant smoked each day was counted.
   c. A university professor was interested in determining the best way to teach introductory psychology and assure that his students learn the material.

2. Why is the null hypothesis always a statement of equality? Why can the research hypothesis take on many different forms?

3. Write the null and research hypotheses for the following paragraph:

   A group of middle-aged men was asked to complete a questionnaire on their attitudes toward work and family. These men are married and have at least two children each. Another group of men, who have no children, also completed the same survey.

4. No one would argue that defining variables clearly and in an unambiguous manner is critical to good research. With that in mind, work as a group and define the following variables. Keep track of how different people's definitions reflect their personal view of what the variable represents, and note how easy it is to define some variables and how difficult it is to define others.
   a. intelligence
   b. height
   c. social skills
   d. age
   e. aggressiveness
   f. conservatism
   g. alcohol consumption
   h. street smarts
   i. personality

   Be sure to note that even those that appear to be easy to define, such as height, can take on different meanings and definitions (tall, 5' 1", awesome) as well.

5. A researcher spent five years on a project, and the majority of the results were not significant. How can the lack of significant results still make an important contribution to the field?

6. Indicate which of the following are variables and which are constants:
   a. Lew's hair color
   b. age in years
   c. number of windows in your residence
   d. the color of a late-model car
   e. current time of day
   f. number of correct answers on this week's quiz
   g. the number of signers of the Declaration of Independence

h. the name of the fifth girl in the third row
i. today's date
j. number of words remembered

7. Go to the library and locate three journal articles in your area of interest. Do the following:
    a. Identify the independent and dependent variables.
    b. For each dependent variable, specify how it is going to be measured and whether it is clearly defined.
    c. For each independent variable, identify the number of levels of that variable. What other independent variables would you find of interest to study?

8. What makes a good hypothesis?

9. What purpose does reading and evaluating research articles serve?

10. Name three of the five criteria of an acceptable hypothesis.

11. What are two of the basic principles of ethical research? Why are they important?

Want to Know More?

Further Readings

Hoskisson, K., & Garrison, J. (1988). Predictive reading and scientific enquiry. *Reading, 22*, 118-125.
> Discusses the skills in predictive reading and how they correlate with students' learning to make informed guesses in a story, then later being able to develop hypotheses. Argues that predictive reading skills are valuable in developing students' scientific attitudes and thought habits.

Jones, P. (1988). On-line research at the secondary level: Access to a world of information. *Tech Trends, 33(3)*, 22-23.
> Discusses the development of research skills through on-line searching by secondary students and compares on-line and optical data disk systems. Compares factors including cost, currency, subject areas, number of uses, search time, preparation needed, search methods, help needed, and alternative use of the equipment.

Keith, T. Z. (1995). Best practice in applied research. In A. Thomas & J. Grimes (Eds.), *Best Practice in School Psychology* (3rd ed.). Washington, DC: NASP, 153-143.
> Looks into the factors of becoming an effective consumer of research. Investigates issues such as the quality of research questions, the appropriateness of the research sample, the statistical analysis used, and the generalizability of the research. Uses good examples to aid the reader in becoming a better consumer of research.

St. James, J. D. (1989). The MEL library in the undergraduate research methods course. *Behavior Research Methods, 21*, 245-247.
> A library reference teaching tool for undergraduates to learn how to do research. Provides practical experiences in experimental design, data representation, and integration of results.

Readings of Other Interest

Callahan, D. (1989). *What kind of life*. New York: Simon and Schuster.
> Discusses problems with our health care system from both a cultural and moral view. A good example of how to use a source to discover relevant and current potential research problems.

Cordell, B. J. (1991). A study of learning styles and computer assisted instruction. *Computers and Education, 16(2)*, 175-183.
> Investigates whether learning styles affect outcomes of learning with two computer assisted instruction design strategies, linear and branching.

James, P. D. (1990). *Devices and Desires*. New York: Knopf.

> A good example of the process of research used in detective work. Shows how problems are identified and how they lead to other problems until finally a solution is determined. Adam Dalgliesh, Scotland Yard commander, once again shows his intellectual abilities through sleuthing the solution by observation and interview techniques.

Winn. W. et al. (1991). Diagrams as aids to problem solving: Their role in facilitating search and computation. *Educational Technology, Research and Development, 39(1)*, 17-29.

> Views two experiments conducted with graduate students to test hypotheses regarding the effectiveness of diagrams in which concepts were shown spatially. Compares response latencies for problems applying kinship rules to information presented in family trees and in lists of statements, and examines the use of rules to computer responses.

CHAPTER

3

THREE

Selecting a Problem and Reviewing the Research

What You'll Learn About in this Chapter

- How to select a research problem
- Sorting out idea after idea until one fits your interests
- The importance of personal experience in selecting a problem
- The steps in reviewing the literature
- Different sources of information, and how to use them
- How to use journals, abstracts, and indexes
- The difference between primary and secondary resources
- Using a synthesis of literature
- How scholarly journals work
- All about computerized literature searches

So here you are, in the early part of a course that focuses on research methods, and all of a sudden you have to come up with a problem that you are supposed to be interested in! You are probably so anxious about learning the material contained in your professor's lectures and what is in *Exploring Research* that you barely have time to think about anything else.

But if you stop for a moment and let your mind explore some of the issues in the behavioral and social sciences that have piqued your interest, you will surely find something that you want to know more about. That is what the research process is all about — finding out more about something that is, in part, already known.

Once you select an area of interest, you are only part of the way there. Next comes the statement of this interest in the form of a research question and then a formal hypothesis. Then it is on to reviewing the literature, a sort of fancy phrase that sounds like you will be very busy! A literature review involves library time and note taking and organizational skills, but it provides a perspective on your question that you cannot get without knowing what other work has been done as well as what new work needs to be done.

But hold on a minute! How is someone supposed to have a broad enough understanding of the field and spew forth well-formed hypotheses before the literature is reviewed and then become familiar with what is out there? As poet John Ciardi said, therein "lies the rub."

The traditional philosophers and historians of science would have us believe that the sequence of events leading up to a review of what has been done before (as revealed in the literature) is as shown in Figure 3.1a.

idea →research question →research hypothesis →literature review

Figure 3.1a From idea to literature review (with the research hypothesis on the way).

This sequence of steps as shown here is fine in theory. As you will find out, the actual process does not go as smoothly as indicated. The research question and research hypothesis are more an outgrowth of an *interaction* between the scientist's original idea and an ongoing, thorough review of the literature (good scientists are always reading!) as you see in Figure 3.1b. This means that once you formulate an hypothesis, it is not carved in stone but can be altered to fit what the review of literature may reflect, as well as any change in ideas you may have.

Figure 3.1b From idea and literature review to hypothesis.

For example, you might be interested in the effects of extended after school care programs on the socialization skills of children. That is the kernel of the idea you want to investigate. A research question might ask what the effects of after school programs are on how well children get along with one another. As an hypothesis, you predict that

Children who participate in extended after school programs will have an increased level of social skills as measured by the XYZ test of socialization.

You might consider the hypothesis to be finished at this point, but in reality your ongoing review of the literature and your changing ideas about the relationship between the variables influences the direction your research will take. For example, what if you find out that a similar study has been done suggesting you add an interesting dimension (such as single- or dual-parent families) to your study, since the addition is consistent with the intent of the study? You should not have to restrict your creative thinking or your efforts to help you understand the effects of these after school programs just because you have already formulated an hypothesis and completed a literature review. Indeed, the reason for completing the review is to see what new directions your work might take. The literature review and the idea play off one another to help you form a relevant and conceptually sound research question and research hypothesis.

Use the results of previous studies to fine-tune your research ideas and hypotheses.

In sum, you will almost always find that your first shot at an hypothesis might need revision, given the content of the literature you review. Remember, it is your idea that you will pursue. The way that you execute it as a research study will be determined by the way you state the research question and the way you test the research hypothesis. It is doubtful that a review of the relevant literature would not shed some light on this matter.

This chapter begins with some pointers on selecting a problem worth studying, and then the focus moves on to a description of the tools and the steps involved in preparing a review of the literature.

Selecting a Problem

People go to undergraduate and graduate school for a variety of reasons, including preparing for a career, the financial advantages that an education can ensure, and even to expand their personal horizons and experience the sheer joy of learning (what a radical thought!). Many of you are in this specific course for one or more of these reasons.

Select a problem that you are genuinely interested in.

The great commonality among your course work and activities is that you are exposed to a wealth of information you would not otherwise experience. That is the primary purpose of taking the time to select a research problem that makes sense to you and that interests you, while at the same time the project can make a contribution to your specific discipline. The selection of the problem you want to work on is terribly important for two reasons. First, research takes a great deal of time and energy, and you want to be sure the problem you select interests you. You will work so hard throughout this project that continuing to work on it, even if its the most interesting project, may at times become too much. Just think of what it would be like if you were not interested! Second, the problem you select is only the first step in the research process. If this goes well the remaining steps, which are no more or less important, have a good chance of going well also.

Just as there are many different ways to go about selecting a research problem, there are also some hazards you can run into. To start you off on the right foot, here is a brief review of some of these almost fatal errors.

It is not hard to do, but *falling in love with your idea can be fatal*. This happens when you become so infatuated with an idea and the project and invest so much energy in it that you cannot bear to change anything about it. Right away someone is going to say, "What's wrong with being enthusiastic about your project?" My response is a strong "Nothing at all." As does your professor, most researchers encourage and look for enthusiasm in students (and scientists) as an important and essential quality.

But enthusiasm is not incompatible with being objective and dispassionate about the actual research process (*not* the content). Sometimes, and this is especially true for beginning research students, researchers see their question as one of such magnitude and importance that they fail to listen to those around them, including their adviser, who are trying to help them formulate their problem in such a way as to make it more precise and, in the long run, easier to address. Be committed to your ideas and really like your topic a lot but not so much that it clouds your judgment as to the practical and right way to do things.

Next, *sticking with the first idea that comes to mind isn't always wise*. Some of you might remember the cartoon character Betty Boop and her inventor grandfather. Every time Betty had a problem, Grandpa would sit on his stool, cross his legs (taking a Rodin-like pose) and think about a solution. Like a bolt from the blue, the light bulb above his head would go on, and he would exclaim, "I've got it!", but it wouldn't be it quite yet. Another flash would occur, but once again not perfect. Invariably, it was the third time the light went on that he struck gold. Do you like your first idea for a research study? Great, but don't run out and place an advertisement for research subjects in the paper quite yet. Give it a few days to rest and think about, and by no means should you stop talking to other students and your adviser during this thinking stage. Second and third ideas are usually much more refined, easier to do, and more manageable than first ones. As you work, rewrite and rethink your work...constantly.

Want to guarantee an unsuccessful project that excites no one (but perhaps yourself)? *Doing something trivial* by selecting a problem that has no conceptual basis or has no apparent importance in the field can lead to a frustrating experience and one that provides no closure. Beginning students who make this mistake sometimes overintellectualize the importance of their research plans and don't stop for the moment it takes to ask themselves, "Where does this study fit in with all that has been done before?" Any scientific endeavor has as its highest goal the contribution of information that will help us better understand the world in general and the specific topic being studied in particular. If you find what has been done by reading previous studies and use that information as a foundation, you will surely come up with a research problem of significance and value.

Ah, then there is the *bites off more than he or she can chew* researcher. Silly? Not to the thousands of advisers who sit day after day in their offices trying to convince very well-intentioned beginning students that their ideas are interesting but that (for example) asking all the adults in New York City their attitudes toward increasing taxes for education may be a bit ambitious. Grand schemes are fine, but unless you can reduce a question to a manageable size, you might as well forget about starting. If these giant studies by first-timers ever do get done (most of the time they don't in their original form), it is usually a more negative than positive experience. Sometimes these students end up as ABDs (all but dissertation). While you may not be seeking a doctorate right now, the lesson is still a good one. Give yourself a break from the beginning, and choose a research question that is doable.

Finally, *do something that has already been done*, and you could be wasting your time. There is a fine line between what has been done and what is important to do next based on what has been done. Part of your job is to learn how to build and elaborate on the results of previous research without duplicating previous efforts. You might remember from the beginning of this chapter that we stressed how replication is an important component of the scientific process and good research? Your adviser can clearly guide you as to what is redundant (doing the same thing over without any sound rationale) and what is an important contribution (doing the same thing over but exploring an aspect of the previous research or even asking the same question while eliminating possibly confounding sources of variance present in the first study).

Be realistic and attempt only what you can finish, given other demands on your time and energy.

Defining Your Interests

It might be easy for an accomplished researcher to come up with additional ideas for research, but that is what he or she gets paid for (in part, anyway). Besides, experienced researchers can put all that experience to work for themselves and one thing (a study) usually leads to another (another study).

But what about the beginning student like yourself? Where do you get your ideas for research? Even if you have a burning desire to be an experimental psychologist, a teacher, a counselor, or a clinical social worker, where do you begin to find hints about ideas that you might want to pursue?

In some relatively rare cases, students know from the beginning what they want to select as a research area and what research questions they want to ask. But for many others, there is more anxiety and doubt than confidence. Before you begin the all-important literature review, first take a look at these suggestions for where you might find interesting questions that are well worth considering as research topics.

First, *personal experiences and firsthand knowledge* more often than not can be the catalyst for starting research. For example, perhaps you worked at a summer camp with disabled children and are interested in knowing more about the most effective way to teach these children. Or, through your own personal reading you have become curious about the aging process and how the process of learning changes with aging. At least three of my colleagues are special educators because they have siblings who were not offered the special services they needed as children to reach their potential. Your own experiences shape the type of person you are. It would be a shame to ignore your past when considering the general area and content of a research question, even if you cannot see an immediate link between these experiences and possible research activities. Keep reading, and you will see ways that you can create that link.

You may want to take complete responsibility for coming up with a research question. On the other hand, there is absolutely nothing wrong with going to your adviser or some other faculty member who is working on some interesting topic and asking, "What's next?" *Using ideas from your mentor or instructor* will probably make you very current with whatever is happening in your field. Doing so also will help to establish and nurture the important relationship between you and your adviser (or some other faculty member) that is necessary for an enjoyable and successful experience. These are the people doing the research, and it would be surprising not to find that they have more ideas than time to do them and would welcome an energetic and bright student (like you) who wants to help extend their research activities.

Next, you might *look for a research question that reflects the next step in the research process.* Perhaps A, B, and C have already been done, and D is next in line. For example, your special interest might be understanding the lifestyle factors that contribute to heart disease, and you already know that factors such as personality type (for example, Type A and Type B) and health habits (for example, social drinking) have been well studied and their effects documented. The next logical step might be to look at such factors as work habits (including occupation and attitude) or some component of family life (such as relationships with a spouse). As with research activities in almost all disciplines and within almost all topics, there is always that next logical step that needs to be taken.

Last, but never least, is that *you may have to come up with a research question because of this class.* Now that is not all bad either, if you look at it this way: People who come up with ideas on their own are all set and need not worry about coming up with an idea by the deadline. Those people who have trouble coming up with ideas need a deadline, otherwise they would not get anything done. So while there are

Don't disregard personal experience as an important source of ideas.

loftier reasons for coming up with research questions, sometimes it is just required by the powers that be. Even so, work very hard at selecting a topic that you can formulate as a research question so that your interest is held throughout the duration of the activity.

Ideas, Ideas, Ideas (and What to Do with Them)

Even if you are sure what your interest might be, it is still difficult sometimes to come up with a specific idea for a research project. For better or worse, you are really the only one who can do this for yourself, but here is a list of possible research topics. For each of these topics there is a wealth of associated literature. So if one topic piques your interest, go to that literature (described in the second part of this chapter) and start reading. Here are 61 topics, one of which might strike a chord!

aggression	development of drawing	mediation
AIDS	diets	memory
bilingual education	divorce	menarche
biofeedback	dreams	mental sets
biology of memory	drug abuse	middle adulthood
birth control	early intervention	motivation
body image	egocentrism	narcolepsy
central nervous system	endocrine system	neural development
child care	epilepsy	nightmares
circadian rhythms	ethics	nutrition
classical conditioning	fat	optimism
cognitive development	fetal alcohol syndrome	pain
color vision	fluid intelligence	parenting
competition	gender differences	perception
compliance	Head Start	prejudice
computer applications	identity	racial integration
conflict	imagery	reinforcement
creativity	intelligence	relaxation
déjà vu	language development	REM sleep
delusions	learning disabilities	self-esteem
depression		

From Idea to Research Question to Hypothesis

Once you have determined what your specific interest might be, you should move as quickly as possible to formulate a research question that you want to investigate and begin your review of literature.

There is a major, important difference between your expressing an interest in a particular idea and the statement of a research question. Ideas are full of those products of luxurious thinking; beliefs, conceptions, suppositions, assumptions, what if's, guesses, and more. Research questions are the articulation, best done in writing, of those ideas that at the least imply a relationship between variables. Why is it best done in writing? Because it is too easy to "get away" with spoken words. It is only when one has to write things down and live with them (spoken words seem to mysteriously vanish) that you face up to what has been said, make a commitment, and work to make sense out of the statement.

A research question is not a declarative statement like a hypothesis, but a clearly stated expression of interest and intent.

In the pay-me-now or pay-me-later tradition, the more easily understood and clearer the research question, the easier your statement of an hypothesis and review of the literature will be. Why? Because from the beginning, a clear idea of what you want to do allows you to make much more efficient use of your time when it comes to searching for references and doing other literature review activities.

Finally, it is time to formulate an hypothesis or a set of hypotheses that reflects the research question. Remember in chapter 2 how a set of five criteria that apply to the statement of any hypothesis was documented? To refresh your memory, here they are again. A well written hypothesis

- is stated in declarative form.
- posits a relationship between variables.
- reflects a theory or body of literature that they are based on.
- is brief and to the point.
- is testable.

In fact, when you derive your hypothesis from the research question, you should look to these criteria as a test of whether what you are saying is easily communicated to others and easily understood.

Remember, the sources for ideas can be anything from a passage that you read in a novel last night to your own unique and creative thoughts. When you get to the research question stage, however, you need to be more scientific and clearly state what your interest is and what variables will be considered.

In Table 3.1, you can see five research interests, the research questions that were generated from those ideas, and the final hypotheses. These hypotheses are only final in the sense that they more or less fit the five criteria stated above. But, clearly, your literature review and more detailed discussion may mean that variables have to be further defined and perhaps even that new ones will need to be introduced. A good hypothesis tells what you are going to do, not how you will do it.

Reviewing the Literature

Here it comes again. Today's research is built on a foundation of the hard work and dedication of past researchers and their productive efforts. Where does one find the actual results of these efforts? In scholarly journals and books, which are located (that is right) in the library.

While all stages in the research process are important, a logical and systematic review of the literature often sets the stage for the completion of a successful research proposal and a successful study. Remember one of the fatal mistakes mentioned at the beginning of the chapter about selecting a research question that has been done before? Or one that is trivial? You find out about all these things and more when you see what has already been done and how it has been done. A complete review provides a framework within which you can answer the important question(s) that you pose. A review takes you chronologically through the development of ideas, shows how some ideas were left by the wayside for lack of support, and how some were confirmed as being truths. Extensive and complete reviews of the literature give you that important perspective to see what has been done and where you are going—crucial to a well-written, well-documented, and well-planned report.

Research questions lead the way to hypotheses.

The review of literature provides a framework for the research proposal.

Research Interest or Ideas	Research Problem or Question	Hypothesis
Open classroom and academic success	What is the effect of open versus traditional classrooms on reading?	Children taught reading in open classroom settings will read at a higher grade level than children taught reading in a traditional setting.
Test-taking skills and grades	Will students who know how to "take" a test improve their scores?	Students who receive training in the "Here Today, Gone Tomorrow" method will score higher on the SATs than students who do not receive any training.
Television and consumer behavior	How does watching television commercials affect the buying behavior of adolescents?	Adolescent boys buy more of the products advertised on television than adolescent girls.
Drug abuse and child abuse	Is drug abuse related to child abuse?	There is a positive relationship between drug abuse among adults and their physical and psychological abuse as children.
Adult Care	How have many adults adjusted to the responsibility of caring for their aged parents?	The number of children who are caring for their parents in the child's own home has increased over the past 10 years.

Table 3.1 Ideas, questions, and hypotheses. You never know where they will come from, so read widely, and keep an open mind.

So get your yellow (or recyclable white) pads, index cards, #2 pencil, and maybe your laptop computer ready, and let's get started. Also, don't forget your school ID card so you can check out books.

The literature review process consists of the steps that you see in Figure 3.2. You begin with as clear an idea as possible about what you want to do, either in the form of a clear and general statement about the variables you want to study or as a research hypothesis. You should end with a well written and clear document that details the rationale for why you chose the topic you did, how it fits into what has been done before, what needs to be done in the future, and its relative importance to the discipline.

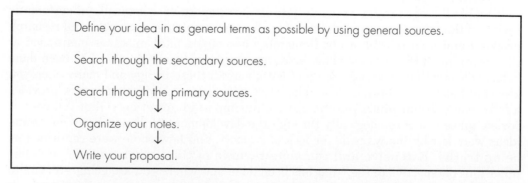

Figure 3.2 The steps in reviewing the literature. It is a formidable task, but when broken down step by step, it is well within your reach.

There are basically three types of sources that you will consult throughout your review of the literature (as you can see in Table 3.2). The first are **general sources**, which provide clues to the location of references of a general nature on a topic. While they certainly have their limitations (which you will get to in a moment), they can be a real asset because they provide a general overview of, and introduction to, a topic. For example, let's say you are interested in the general area of sports psychology but have absolutely no idea where to turn to find more information. You could start with the recent article that appeared in the *New York Times* and find the name of the foremost sports psychologist and then go to more detailed secondary or primary sources to find more about his or her work.

The second source type is called **secondary sources**. These sources are "once removed" from the actual research and are review papers, anthologies of readings, syntheses of other work in the area, textbooks, and encyclopedias.

Finally, the last and most important sources are **primary sources**. These are accounts of the actual research that has been done. They appear as journal articles or as other original works including abstracts. You can see a summary of what general, secondary, and primary resources do and some examples in Table 3.2.

Information Source	What It Does	Examples
General sources	Provides an overview of a certain topic and acts us a lead to where more information can be found.	Daily newspapers, news weeklies, popular magazines, trade books, *Reader's Guide to Periodical Literature, New York Times Index*
Secondary sources	Provides a level of information "once removed" from the original work.	Books on specific subjects, reviews of research
Primary sources	The original reports of the original work.	Journals, abstracts, and scholarly books, ERIC

Table 3.2 Different sources of information, what they do, and some examples. General sources are especially valuable as a starting point.

Using General Sources

General sources of information provide two things: a general introduction to areas in which you might be interested and some clues as to where you should go for the more valuable or useful (in a scientific sense, anyway) information about your topic. They are also just great browsing material.

Any of the references below, especially the indexes of national newspapers and such, can offer you 5, 10, or 50 articles in a specific area. In these articles you will often find a nice introduction to the subject area and a mention of some of the people doing research and where they are located. From there, you can look through other reference materials to find out what other work that person has done or even contact him or her directly.

There are loads of general sources in your college or university library as well as in the public library. Here is a brief description of just a few of the most often used sources and a listing of several others you might want to consult. Remember, use general sources only to orient yourself to what is out there and to familiarize yourself

General, primary, and secondary sources can all add valuable information to your review.

with the topic. While the articles in the *New York Times* are always interesting, well written, and informative, they do not take the place of reading and understanding the original research.

The Reader's Guide to Periodical Literature is far and away the most comprehensive available guide to general literature. It is organized by topic and is published monthly, covering hundreds of journals (such as the *New England Journal of Medicine*) and periodicals or magazines (such as *Scientific American*). Since the topics are alphabetically listed, you are bound to be able to find reading sources on a selected topic easily and quickly. Part of a page from *The Reader's Guide* is shown in Figure 3.3. As you can see, this page shows available entries on the topic of teenage pregnancy. Notice that there is a general heading, Teenage Pregnancy, and underneath is a listing of specific articles by title and where they appear.

TEENAGE PREGNANCY

See *also*

Teenage mothers

The baby trap [cover story] E. Gleick and others. il *People Weekly* v42 p38-55 O 24 '94

The best contraceptive [M. Carrera's Adolescent Pregnancy Prevention Program in Harlem] E. Gleick and others, il por *People Weekly* v42 p56 O 24 '94

I had my rapist's baby. *Sassy* v7 p35 N '94

Lifelike dolls that can make you cry [Baby Think It Over crack-addicted doll] il *Newsweek* v124 p68 D 5 '94

The name of the game is shame [morally wrong for unmarried teens to bear children] J. Alter. il *Newsweek* v124 p41 D 12 '94

Wake-up call [R. Jurmain, inventor of Baby Think It Over doll] S. K. Reed, il por *People Weekly* v42 p103-4 O 10 '94

What to do when your teenage daughter tells you she's pregnant. K. A. Haynes. il *Ebony* v42 p 100+ S '94

Figure 3.3 An entry from *The Reader's Guide to Periodical Literature.*

Another valuable general source is *Facts on File*, published in New York since 1941. FOF summarizes news that is reported in more than 50 foreign and domestic newspapers and magazines, a great place to find out whether anything has appeared in these outlets in your particular area of interest. FOF is published weekly, and its index is cumulative for the current year, so it should not take you more than a few minutes to find out if there is information available.

The *New York Times Index* goes back to 1851 and lists all the articles published in the *Times* by subject. Once you find reference to an article that might be of interest (as you see in Figure 3.4), you then go to the stacks and select a copy of the actual issue or view it on microfilm. The originals are seldom available because they are printed on thin paper designed to hold up only for the few days that a newspaper might be passed around.

Instead, contents are recorded on microfilm or some other medium and are available through your library. Many libraries now offer microfilm readers that allow

```
CHILDREN AND YOUTH.  See also
Accidents and Safety, S 20
Acquired Immune Deficiency Syndrome (AIDS), Ja 5,6,8,10,11,12, F
        10,13,21,24,25, Mr 9,21,25, Ap 1,24, 29, My 6,8, Je 7,8,17,26,27,
        Jl 2,11, Ag 17,19, S 26, O 22,24, N 3,21,D4
Adoptions
Advertising, Jl 25
Afghanistan, F 21,22
Africa, Je 18, 19
Agriculture, Jl 6
Airlines and Airplanes, Ap 6,28,29, My 1, Jl 13, S 28,D25
Alcohol Abuse, Je 12
Alcoholic Beverages, Mr 6, Ag 24, S 28
Amusement Parks, Ag 31, S 1
Animals, Mr 1
Apparel, F 16, Ag 22,28
Architecture, Ja 20, My 5
Art, Ja 6, Mr 23, Je 3, S 4, O 26,23
Assaults, Ja 29,30, Mr 9, My 14, Je 11, S 8,30, O 24, N 30, D 14,15
Asthma, Ja 4, My 8
```

Figure 3.4 An entry from the *New York Times Index*. This newspaper is the premier daily in the United States and usually covers many important developments in all fields.

you to copy directly from the microfilm image and make a print or hard copy of what you are viewing. The full text of many newspapers is also now available electronically, which you will read about later in this chapter.

Nobody should take what is printed as the absolute gospel, but weekly news magazines such as *Time*, *Newsweek*, and *U.S. News and World Report* offer general information and keep you well informed about other related events as well. You may not even know that you have an interest in a particular topic (such as ethical questions in research). A story on that topic might be in this week's issue, catch your eye, and before you know it you will be using that information to seek out other sources.

There are also some specialty magazines that you might want to know about. *Science News* (published weekly) and *Science Digest* (a monthly publication) provide summaries of important news from the world of science. They are current and informative.

Finally, there is the wealth of information you can dig out of everyday sources such as your local newspaper, company newsletters, and other publications. Local newspapers often carry the same *Associated Press* articles as major papers such as the *New York Times* and the *Washington Post*. And, please, do not forget the U.S. Government and U.S. Government Printing Office (GPO). They regularly publish thousands of documents on everything from baseball to bees, and a large majority of them are free. (Don't worry – your parents have already paid.)

One especially useful source that you should not overlook is *The Statistical Abstract of the United States*, published yearly by the U.S. Department of Commerce. This is the national data book about the United States, including valuable and easily accessible information on demographics and much more. Want to know more about the GPO? Write to Government Printing Office, North Capitol and H Streets, NW, Washington, DC 20401 for a catalog of what is available.

Using Secondary Sources

Secondary sources are those that you seek out if you are looking for a scholarly summary of the research that has been done in a particular area or if you are looking for further sources of references.

Reviews and Syntheses of Literature

These are the BIG books you often find in the reference section of the library (not on the stack shelves). Since so many people want to use them, they always have to be available. Here is a summary of some of the most useful.

The Review of Educational Research first appeared in 1973 and is still published by the American Educational Research Association on a quarterly basis. The *Review* offers a collection of critical reviews of research in a specific area such as minimum competency testing (1983) or changing conceptions of intelligence (1983). While the *Review* might not offer exactly what you want, it will give you a very good perspective on that subject if you hit upon the topic you are interested in.

There is also *The Encyclopedia of Educational Research*, last published in 1992, that consists of four volumes including articles written by experts. Each of these articles contains an extensive bibliography, so it is a good place to start finding information about a particular topic.

A general secondary source of literature reviews is the *Annual Reviews of Psychology* (published by Annual Reviews) containing about 20 chapters and focusing on a wide range of topics. Just think of it; you can go through the last 10 years of these volumes and be very up to date on a wide range of general topics in psychology. If you happen to find one chapter on exactly what you want to do, you are way ahead of the game.

Another annual review that is well worth considering is *The National Society for the Study of Education* (or NSSE) *Yearbooks*. Each year since 1902, this society has published a two-volume annual that focuses on a particular topic such as adolescence, microcomputers in the classroom, gifted and talented children, or classroom management. The area of focus is usually some contemporary topic, and if you are interested in what is being covered, the information can be invaluable to you.

Interested in child development? Seek out the four-volume *Handbook of Child Psychology* (published in 1983 by John Wiley). The fourth edition of this work is the starting point for developmental and child psychology students, early childhood education students, medical and nursing students, and others across a wide field. The four individual volumes are

- History, Theory, and Methods
- Infancy and Developmental Psychobiology
- Cognitive Development
- Socialization, Personality, and Social Development

The fifth edition of the *Handbook* is due out in 1997.

Don't overlook major syntheses of information.

A more life-span approach is offered by the series of reviews in *Life Span Developmental Psychology* (published by Academic Press). These various volumes deal with such topics as research and theory, cognition, and normative life crises.

Also, do not forget the large number of scholarly books that sometimes have multiple authors and are edited by one individual or that are written entirely by one person (which in the latter case is sometimes considered a primary resource, depending upon its content). Use the good old card catalog (or your library's computerized search system) to find the title or author you need.

Using Primary Sources

Primary sources are the meat and potatoes of the literature review. While you will get some good ideas and a good deal of information from reading the secondary sources, you have to go to the real thing to get the specific information to make your points and to make your points stick!

In fact, your best bet is to include mostly primary sources in your literature review, with some secondary sources to help make your case, and do not even think about including general sources. It is not that the information in *Redbook* or the *St. Louis Dispatch* is not useful or valuable. It is secondhand, and you do not want to build an argument based on someone else's interpretation of a concept.

Using Journals

Journals? You want journals? Just take a look at the list in Table 3.3 arranged by category. This should be enough for you to answer your professor when he asks, "Who can tell me some of the important journals in your own field?" This list is only a small selection of what is out there.

Journals are by far the most important and valuable primary sources of information about a topic since they represent the most direct link between the researcher, the work of other researchers, and your own interests.

What actually is a journal, and how does it work? A journal is a collection (most often) of research articles published in a particular area by some professional group. For example, the American Psychological Association publishes journals including *The Journal of Experimental Psychology, Psychology, Public Policy and Law*, and the *Journal of Counseling Psychology* (and many others). The Society for Research in Child Development publishes *Child Development* and *Child Development Monographs*. Membership in these groups gets you the journals as part of the package, or you can subscribe separately for just the journals.

Most respectable journals work something like this.

First, a researcher writes an article according to a specific format (such as the one shown in Appendix A) and then sends in as many copies as the journal editor requires (usually three). Guidelines for preparing manuscripts are usually found in the beginning of each issue.

Second, once the article has been received by the editor, who is usually an acknowledged expert in that particular field, the article is sent to at least three reviewers who are also experts in the field. These reviewers participate in a process called blind review, where they do not know the author(s) of the paper. The authors'

Get to know your library and where you can find journals in your field—they are the sources for what has already been done.

Education

Administrative Science Quarterly
Administrator's Notebook
Adult Education
Alberta Journal of Educational Research
American Biology Teacher
American Education
American Educational Research Journal
American Journal of Education
American School Board Journal
Arithmetic Teacher
Art Education
Black Scholar
Bulletin of the National Association of
    Secondary Schools Principals
Business Education Forum
Business Education World
Career Education
Clearing House
College Board Review
Community/Junior College Quarterly of
    Research and Practice
Community/Junior College Research
    Quarterly
Computers and Education
Educational Administration Quarterly
Educational Communication and
    Technology: A Journal of Theory,
    Research, and Development
Educational Evaluation and Policy
    Analysis
Educational Gerontology
Educational Leadership
Educational Record
Educational Research Quarterly
Educational Researcher
Elementary School Journal
Evaluation Review
High School Journal
Home Economics Research Journal
Integrated Education
Journal for Research in Mathematics
    Education
Journal of Aesthetic Education
Journal of Biological Education
Journal of Black Studies
Journal of Business Education
Journal of Career Education
Journal of Computer-Based Instruction
Journal of Computers in Mathematics
    and Science Teaching
Journal of Drug Education
Journal of Economics Education
Journal of Educational Measurement
Journal of Educational Research
Journal of Educational Statistics
Journal of Experimental Education
Journal of Instructional Development
Journal of Negro Education

Journal of Research and Development in
    Education
Journal of Research in Mathematics
    Education
Journal of Research in Music Education
Journal of Research in Science Teaching
Journal of Social Studies Research
Journal of Teacher Education
Journal of Vocational Educational
    Research
Kappa Delta Pi Record
Library Quarterly
Library Research
Lifelong Learning: The Adult Years
Mathematics and Computer Education
Mathematics Teacher
Modern Language Journal
Music Education Journal
National Education Association
    Research Bulletin
National Elementary Principal
Negro Education Review
Peabody Journal of Education
Phi Delta Kappan
Review of Educational Research
School Library Media Quarterly
School Psychology Review
School Science and Mathematics
School Science Review
Science and Children
Science Education
Science Teacher
Secondary School Theatre Journal
Social Education
Studies in Art Education
Studies in Educational Evaluation
Teachers College Record
Theory and Research in Social
    Education
Theory into Practice
Today's Education
Voc Ed
Young Children

Sociology and Anthropology

American Anthropologist
American Behavioral Scientist
American Journal of Sociology
American Sociological Review
Anthropology and Education Quarterly
Child Welfare
Family Relations
Group and Organization Studies
Human Organization
Human Services in the Rural Environment
Journal of Correctional Education
Journal of Marriage and the Family
Rural Sociology

Sex Roles: A Journal of Research
Social Work
Sociology and Social Research
Sociology of Education
Urban Anthropology
Urban Education
Urban Review
Youth and Society

Analytical Research

Administration and Society
American Historical Review
American Political Science Review
Annals of the American Academy of
    Political and Social Science
Comparative Education Review
Daedalus
Economics of Education Review
Education and Urban Society
Educational Forum
Educational Studies
Educational Theory
Harvard Civil Rights-Civil Liberties Law
    Review
Harvard Educational Review
History of Education Quarterly
Journal of Collective Negotiations in the
    Public Sector
Journal of Educational Finance
Journal of Educational Equity and
    Leadership
Journal of Law and Education
Journal of Thought
Negro History Bulletin
NOLPE School Law Journal
Paedagogica Historica
Political Science Quarterly
School Law Bulletin
School Law Reporter
School Review
Social Policy
Urban Affairs Quarterly
Western Journal of Black Studies

Psychology

Adolescence
American Journal of Family Therapy
American Journal of Orthopsychiatry
American Psychologist
Behavioral Disorders
Child Development
Child Study Journal
Developmental Psychology
Contemporary Educational Psychology
Educational and Psychological
    Measurement

Table 3.3 Thousands of journals are regularly published. Because many different journals may report on the same topic, you have to look far and wide to be sure you have found all the important references you need.

Journal of Abnormal Child Psychology	Exceptional Parent	Journal of Sport History
Journal of Applied Behavioral Analysis	Focus on Exceptional Child	Physical Educator
Journal of Autism and Developmental	Gifted Child Quarterly	Research Quarterly of the American
Disorders	Hearing and Speech Action	Alliance for Health, Physical
Journal of Child Psychology and	International Journal for the Education of	Education, Recreation and Dance
Psychiatry and Allied Disciplines	the Blind	School Health Review
Journal of Consulting and Clinical	Journal for the Education of the Gifted	
Psychology	Journal of The Association for the	
Journal of Counseling Psychology	Severely Handicapped	**Guidance and Counseling**
Journal of Educational Psychology	Journal of Learning Disabilities	
Journal of Experimental Child	Journal of Mental Deficiency Research	American Mental Health Counselors
Psychology	Journal of Special Education	Association Journal
Journal of Experimental Psychology:	Journal of Special Education Technology	Counselor Education and Supervision
Human Perception and Performance	Journal of Speech and Hearing	Elementary School Guidance and
Journal of Experimental Psychology:	Disorders	Counseling
Learning, Memory, and Cognition	Journal of Speech and Hearing	Humanistic Education and Development
Journal of Genetic Psychology	Research	Measurement and Evaluation in
Journal of Humanistic Psychology	Journal of Visual Impairment and	Guidance
Journal of Personality and Social	Blindness	Personnel and Guidance Journal
Psychology	Learning Disability Quarterly	School Counselor
Journal of Psychology	Mental Retardation	School Guidance Worker
Journal of Research in Personality	Sightsaving Review	Vocational Guidance Quarterly
Journal of School Psychology	Teaching Exceptional Children	
Perceptual and Motor Skills	Teacher Education and Special	
Psychological Bulletin	Education	**Reading, Language Arts, English**
Psychological Review	Teacher of the Blind	
Psychology in the Schools	Topics in Early Childhood Special	English Education
Psychology of Women Quarterly	Education	English Journal
Small Group Behavior	Volta Review	Journal of Linguistics
Transactional Analysis Journal		Journal of Reading
		Journal of Reading Behavior
		Journal of Research in Reading
Special Education and Exceptional Children	**Health and Physical Education**	Language Arts
		Language Learning
Academic Therapy	Health and Educational Journal	Reading Horizons
American Annals of the Deaf	Health Education	Reading Improvement
American Journal of Mental Deficiency	Journal of Alcohol and Drug Education	Reading Psychology
Behavioral Disorders	Journal of Leisure Research	Reading Research Quarterly
Education and Training of the Mentally	Journal of Motor Learning	Reading Teacher
Retarded	Journal of Nutrition Education	Reading World
Education of the Visually Handicapped	Journal of Outdoor Education	Research in the Teaching of English
Exceptional Children	Journal of Physical Education, Recreation	
Exceptional Education Quarterly	and Dance	
	Journal of School Health	

Table 3.3 continued.

names appear only on a cover sheet that is torn off by the editor, and the social security number or some other coded number is used for identification. This makes the process quite fair where there is no possibility that personalities get in the way of what can be a highly competitive goal: publishing in the best journals. The reviewers each make a recommendation. The options from which the reviewers can select are usually something like

- *accept outright*, meaning that this is an outstanding article and can be accepted for publication as is,
- *accept with revisions*, meaning that some changes need to be made by the authors before it is accepted,
- *reject with suggestions for revisions*, meaning that the article is not acceptable as of now, but after changes are made the author(s) should be invited to resubmit it, and
- *reject outright*, meaning that the article is completely unacceptable.

Finally, if a consensus is reached by the reviewers, the editor of the journal conveys that decision to the author(s). If not, it is the editor's job to make a decision or to send the article to another reviewer for additional comments. Editors work very hard to ensure that the review process and the journal publication process are fair. Editors' terms usually are four to six years.

By the way, you might be interested to know that the average rejection rate for the top journals is about 80%. Yes, 80% of the articles submitted never get in, but those rejected by the top journals usually find their way into other journals. Just because they are not accepted by the journals with the highest rejection rate does not mean they are not useful reports. In fact, several studies have shown that there is little consistency among reviewers, and what one might rank high, another might rank quite low.

One more note about primary sources in general. If you know of a journal or a book that you might need and your library does not have it, do not despair. First, check other libraries within driving distance or check with some of the professors in your department. They might have it available for loan. If all else fails, use the *interlibrary loan system*, which your reference librarian will be glad to help you with. This service helps you locate and physically secure the reference materials you want for a limited amount of time from another library. The system usually works fast and is efficient.

Using Abstracts

If journals are the workhorses of the literature review, collections of abstracts cannot be very far behind in their convenience and usefulness. An **abstract** is a one- (or at most two-) paragraph summary of a journal article. It contains all the information readers should need to decide whether to read the entire journal article.

By perusing collections of abstracts, researchers can save a significant amount of time compared with leafing through the journals that these abstracts are drawn from. Most abstracts also include subject and author indexes to help readers find what they are looking for, and abstracts of articles routinely appear in more than one abstract resource. For example, a study on how to deal with disruptive children might appear in *Psychological Abstracts* (from a journal such as *Perceptual and Motor Skills*) as well as in the *Current Index to Journals in Education* (from a journal such as *Psychology in the Schools*). Do not be concerned if there is overlap. Actually, it means you are covering all the bases.

Here is a brief description of some abstract collections you might find useful.

The granddaddy (grandmommy?) of all the abstracts is *Psychological Abstracts*, published by the American Psychological Association. *Psychological Abstracts* regularly reviews and abstracts over 1,000 (count 'em) journals in the following 16 different areas:

- General psychology
- Psychometrics
- Human experimental psychology
- Animal experimental and comparative psychology
- Physiological psychology
- Physiological intervention
- Communications systems
- Developmental psychology
- Social processes and social issues
- Social psychology
- Physical and psychological disorders

The peer review process of reviewing journals ensures that experts see the research report before it is published.

Abstracts help save you the time it would take to look through every individual journal in your discipline.

- Treatment and prevention
- Professional personnel and professional issues
- Educational psychology
- Applied psychology
- Sport psychology and leisure

There is so much information in *Psychological Abstracts* that a more efficient method of finding information had to be devised beyond a simple subject index. That is where the *Thesaurus of Psychological Index Terms* comes in, as shown in Figure 3.5. Before you begin to use *Psychological Abstracts*, you first use the thesaurus to select key words for your search, then go to the actual abstracts, and look under the key words you identified. For example, if your interest is in pregnancy, you would find the following key words (or related terms) in the thesaurus: birth, childbirth training, fertilization, obstetrical complications, placenta, and more.

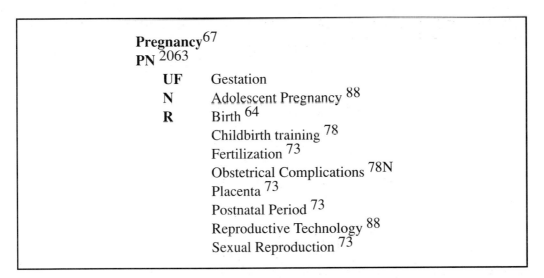

Pregnancy[67]
PN 2063

UF	Gestation
N	Adolescent Pregnancy [88]
R	Birth [64]
	Childbirth training [78]
	Fertilization [73]
	Obstetrical Complications [78N]
	Placenta [73]
	Postnatal Period [73]
	Reproductive Technology [88]
	Sexual Reproduction [73]

Figure 3.5 A *Psychological Abstracts* thesaurus entry.

One other way to use *Psychological Abstracts* is by looking up the key word *bibliography*. Under this heading you will find a list of bibliographies that have already been published. Maybe you will be lucky and find the one that focuses on your area of interest. Two indexes that are especially useful (published by the Educational Resources Information Center or ERIC) are *Resources in Education* and *Current Index to Journals in Education*, each of which performs a separate function.

Resources in Education (RIE) presents the abstracts of papers that have been presented at conferences, the results of "in-house" investigations including progress reports while a project continues, and other documents that do not readily appear in formal journals. Many of these papers are eventually published and are then contained in abstracts such as *Psychological Abstracts*.

Current Index to Journals in Education (CIJE) is not really an index but a set of abstracts from more than 750 journals focusing on the broadly defined field of education. Once again, you can expect these journal abstracts to appear elsewhere as well.

As with *Psychological Abstracts*, the ERIC system works with a set of descriptive terms found in a thesaurus, the *Thesaurus of ERIC Descriptors*, which is always your first stop on the way to using *RIE* or *CIJE*. Once you find the search words or descriptors, you then use the subject index (published monthly) until you find the number of a reference that sounds like what you want. Finally, you are off to the actual description of the reference. If you want a copy of the entire document represented by this abstract (ERIC calls abstracts resumes), you can order either a hard copy or a microfilm copy (smaller and cheaper) through the ERIC Document Reproduction Service using forms available at your library. It usually takes about two weeks to receive the document. But you may not need to order a copy. If you have a government documents department in your library, it might already have the document on hand. Also, you might be able to contact the original author as listed in the resume.

ERIC has been in business since 1981 and has 19 regional clearinghouses that archive, abstract, and disseminate educational articles and documents. Education is broadly defined, so many disciplines in the social and behavioral sciences are covered quite adequately. You can see how broad is ERIC's reach by examining the list of subject areas covered by these 19 clearinghouses:

- adult, career, and vocational development
- art education
- counseling and personnel services
- educational management
- elementary and early childhood education
- handicapped and gifted children
- higher education
- information resources
- junior colleges
- languages and linguistics
- literacy education
- reading and communication skills
- rural education and small schools
- science, mathematics, and environmental education
- social studies/social science education
- teacher education
- tests, measurements, and evaluation
- United States–Japan studies
- urban education

Think that is enough to get started?

Psychological Abstracts and the ERIC sets of abstracts are major resources, but there are others that are a bit more specialized and also very useful.

Figure 3.6 shows you an abstract from a recent issue of *Child Development Abstracts & Bibliography*. You can see that it contains the complete reference for the article and a one-paragraph summary of the article's contents including

- an introductory sentence about the article's contents,
- a description of the participants by age and other factors of interest, and
- a statement of the results.

Child Development Abstracts & Bibliography abstracts more than 300 journals and provides reviews of books about children and families including coverage in six different areas:

- biology, health, and medicine
- cognition, learning, and perception
- social psychology and personality studies
- education
- psychiatry and clinical psychology
- history, theory, and methodology

356. Olson, Heather Carmichael; Sampson, Paul D.; Barr, Helen; Streissguth, Ann P. & Bookstein, Fred L. (1992). **Prenatal exposure to alcohol and school problems in late childhood: A longitudinal prospective study.** Development and Psychopathology, 4, 341-359.

This follow-up study of 458 singletons assesses the degree to which children's classroom behavior and achievement difficulties at age 11 are predicted by prenatal alcohol exposure across the full spectrum of maternal use. Analyses reveal a significant and subtle dose-response relationship between prenatal alcohol exposure and children's school performance a decade later. Maternal binge drinking and drinking during very early pregnancy are particularly salient for children's poorer school performance. A wide variety of problematic classroom behaviors, including attentional, activity, information-processing, and academic difficulties, are salient for prenatal alcohol exposure.

Figure 3.6 An entry from *Child Development Abstracts & Bibliography*, which surveys more than 300 different journals.

Titles of other abstracts such as *Sociological Abstracts*, *Exceptional Child Education Resources*, *Research Related to Children*, and *Dissertation Abstracts* reveal the wide variety of available reference material.

Using Indexes

Journals and abstracts provide the substance of an article, a conference presentation, or a report. If you want a quick overview of where things might be located, turn to an index, an alphabetical listing of entries by topic, author, or both.

A good starting point in any literature review is to look at the work of people in the same position as you are in, master's or doctoral students. First, there is the *Comprehensive Dissertation Index*, published by the University of Michigan (and, of course, in your library), listing dissertations for which abstracts are available.

Other similar indexes are *American Doctoral Dissertations* and *Master's Abstracts: A Catalog of Selected Masters Theses on Microfilm*, also published by the University of Michigan. While not as current as the *Comprehensive Dissertation Index* mentioned above, *American Doctoral Dissertations* lists dissertation titles by subject and year as gleaned from commencement programs. *Master's Abstracts* provides abstracts of master's theses.

> Indexes help you locate the source of important information.

The widely used and popular *Social Sciences Citation Index (SSCI)* and *Science Citation Index (SCI)* work in an interesting and creative way. *SCI* deals with the fields of medicine, agriculture, and technology. *SSCI* deals with the fields of social and behavioral sciences. Let's say you read an article that you find to be very relevant to your research proposal and want to know what else the author has done. You might want to search by subject through abstracts as we have talked about, but you might also want to find other articles by the same author or on the same general topic. Tools like *SSCI* allow you to focus on your specific topic and access as much of the available information as possible. For example, do you want to find out who has mentioned the classic article "Mental and Physical Traits of a Thousand Gifted Children" (written by Louis Terman and published in 1925)? Look up Terman, L., in *SSCI* year by year, and you will find more references than you may know what to do with.

Finally, you can consult the *Bibliographic Index*, a compilation of bibliographies that results from a search of about 2,600 periodicals. Just think of the time you can save if you locate a relatively recent bibliography on whatever you are interested in.

Using the Computer for Literature Searches

The future may find us using computers to access literature more often than going to the library.

Imagine this if you will: You are in your apartment, and it is late at night. You find that you need one more reference on the development of adolescent self-esteem to complete your literature review. You are tired. It is snowing. The library is about to close, and they might not have what you need anyway.

Zoom, your on-line computer search service to the rescue. Pop in the software (or call it up on your hard disk), dial up the number, log onto the service, locate the database, and search for the reference. In 20 seconds you have got the reference to read or to print. Is this for real? You bet, and there is a good chance your professor already uses a service that provides this capability. You can also bet that by the time you are finished with your undergraduate or graduate training, you will be zooming around databases and information providers using your personal computer and some simple, inexpensive hardware and software.

At home, in your office, or in the confines of the library, the use of computers for completing literature searches and reviews is booming and blooming with new databases to search becoming available each day.

Searching Off-Line using a CD-ROM

At the University of Kansas, you can walk into Watson Library (the main research library), sit down at a $500 computer, insert one of the CD-ROM (compact disk read only memory) disks containing ERIC documents, and search through them in seconds for the reference you want. Not bad. You can also access centrally stored CD-ROMs

For example, here is what happened during a search for references on teacher burnout in elementary schools. First, the characters *teacher-burnout* were entered. The hyphen represents the ERIC instruction to seek records that are related to both words. In three seconds, 366 records were found.

Second, the characters *elementary-school-teachers* were entered, and 559 records were reported as available.

Finally, to see how many records contain both types of information, the characters 1! and 2! were entered, telling ERIC to look for records containing both teacher-burnout and elementary-school-teacher references, for which 15 were made available and listed on the screen. You can then print this information, read it off the screen, or save it to disk. Easy? Definitely. Expensive? In this case, it is free (read: taxes pay for it!). As additional disks and computers need to be purchased, there is sure to be a real dollar cost associated with search.

Another incredibly useful source of reference information that you can access through your personal computer on a CD-ROM is Microsoft's Bookshelf, a set of reference works including an encyclopedia, a dictionary, a compilation of quotations, an atlas, an almanac, a thesaurus, and a timetable. You can see in Figure 3.7 how we found information on Sir Francis Galton, the famous geneticist. While this is not enough to write your term paper, it is certainly enough to give you a clue as to who this person is and even to get information on what he did. At $70 (for the Windows 95 version) it is a steal, and you can even get it bundled with other Microsoft products.

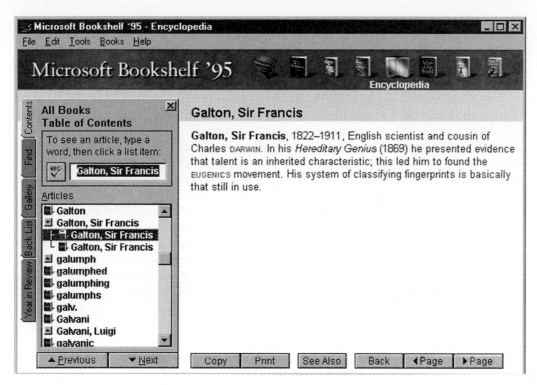

Figure 3.7 Using Microsoft Bookshelf for general information.

Searching On-Line

Your library offers you some incredible resources for accessing information through the use of personal computers either acting alone (as with ERIC) or connected to some other computer on campus or in another city.

Researchers in universities, businesses, and the government are turning to on-line information providers more and more to find the key information they need, whether a specific reference or fact, such as the number of bicycles produced by Japan or the number of young adults who live in urban areas.

The Value of On-Line Searches

Why conduct an on-line search if you can just as well let your fingers do the walking through the stacks, books, journals, abstracts, and indexes (tired yet?) discussed earlier in this chapter?

I am sure you guessed by now...*time*. You can do a search using one of the services described below in one quarter of the time it takes to do it manually. Just schlepping to the library can take 30 minutes. If you drive, you spend 15 minutes more looking for a parking space, and the list goes on.

Another important advantage of on-line searches, if your search skills are anywhere near competent, is that you are not likely to miss very much. The information providers (such as Compuserve and America Online) provide access to tens of thousands of documents, either in their own databases, or others they can tap into. Keep in mind also that most colleges and universities now allow access to their libraries from off campus, another good reason to become proficient in this area. At

On-line searches look expensive but can be very economical if you know what you want and how to use the service.

the least, you can work through a catalog of holdings on-line. At best, you can actually access the holdings.

Finally, and this may be the most attractive advantage, it is the way of the future. There is so much information out there that soon it will be close to impossible to search intelligently without the aid of a computer.

But there is a down side to the use of on-line services as well: cost. There is no free lunch, and there is no free searching of the literature either. For example, NewsNet, a service that provides on-line copy from hundreds of newspapers (before they hit the streets) is $60 per hour! That is a lot of money for an individual. CompuServe charges $2.95 per hour (beyond the $9.95 monthly charge that gets you 5 free hours) and with practice (and they have a free practice forum) you can be on and off and get what you need quickly. Most information providers have local phone numbers, so telephone charges are minimized, and you pay only for extra services such as specialized searches. So if you want to play Zaxxon against your college buddy in San Francisco and you are in Russell, Kansas, go right ahead and have fun. There is probably no extra charge. But if you want to search through *Dissertation Abstracts*, be prepared to pay extra. As you become more familiar with the systems, you will find yourself able to search more efficiently, which costs you less money.

What You Need to Search On-Line

You need four things to get started in the telecommunications business.

- a computer (almost any kind will do)
- a modem
- communications software
- an open phone line

The first is a computer, which you may already have. In any telecommunications activity the computer acts as a sender and recipient of information.

Second is a **modem**. A modem is a device that *mo*dulates and *dem*odulates electronic signals (representing information) and transforms data (whether an abstract of an article or an entire manuscript) into signals that can be transmitted over a telephone line. The modem converts digital information into sound. The modem is located between your computer and the telephone line. It sits there (and another modem sits on the other end of the phone line) acting as the grand translator and when working well, you do not even know it is operating. No matter how sophisticated any part of your telecommunications system is, if your modem is cheap and does not do the job, the fanciest hardware in the world will not help at all. For example, some modems have filters that screen out some of the telephone junk noise that invades every line. When you are talking, this interference is just a nuisance. When you are telecommunicating, line noise can be a disaster since it corrupts transmissions and what you send either does not get there at all or is different from what you sent. The quality of the software (which usually comes with the modem) is critical as well, since some programs (such as ProComm from DataStorm in Columbia, Missouri) make it simple and fast to connect, while others can be so frustrating that it is no wonder people give up and never try again.

Third, to make all this work, you need **communications software**. This is the software that translates the information as it appears to you into the form of the information as it is actually sent. Most modems come with some communications software, and now many operating systems, such as Windows 95, also do. In addition, you can buy communications software, usually offering far more features than what is packaged with a modem.

Modems translate information to sounds, which they send over the telephone lines.

Exploring Research

Finally, you need a connection through a telephone line to where you want to send (or from where you want to receive) information. In other words, you need a phone line. It may mean a line dedicated just for telecommunications or a regular line that you also use for voice. If you have only one line for both voice and data, then you cannot talk on the telephone when you are transmitting. Most people who become really serious about telecommunications end up with two phone lines.

A Look at Some On-Line Services

While many people use telecommunications to share information directly with other people, the focus here is on gaining access to *information providers*, such as CompuServe, America Online, Prodigy, or the relatively new Microsoft Network and Wow! These are basically gateways to proprietary forums or discussion groups and huge on-line databases that you tap into through your telecommunications hardware and software, or the software that the information provider distributes. You can also use a ton of other services with these providers including electronic mail, newsgroups, forums, and more (all of which we will talk about later in this chapter).

Here is a brief rundown of some of the bigger services and what they offer. Most cost nothing to join and just a call to their 800 number gets you a nice startup kit.

CompuServe (800/848-8990) gets you right into on-line activities with 10 hours of free time when you sign up. With over 4 million subscribers, CompuServe offers news, weather, sports, travel, shopping, electronic mail, financial information, and access to other information services, including more than 900 bibliographic databases (need to find that article?). CompuServe is by far the most in-depth, research-oriented service. In Figure 3.8, you can see a sample of its opening screen and what is available.

Figure 3.8 The CompuServe opening screen and some of what is available.

If you are a Macintosh user, CompuServe offers Navigator, a software tool that greatly increases the speed and power of search activities. You can select your destination (for example, the database you want to go and key words you want to search for) before you go on line, and then run that script through Navigator to arrive where you want at a greatly decreased cost. For DOS users and Windows, CompuServe offers the CompuServe Information Manager, a similar tool that lets you do the same. As with most services, CompuServe offers database searches at an extra cost.

As information services become more popular, innovative people are designing software to help users spend less time on line and be more efficient. For CompuServe, there is TAPCIS (a DOS utility available from Support Group, Inc., at 800/872–4768). TAPCIS lets you create and read mail off line (at no cost), and it also allows you to set up your searches before you go on line, which can create quite a savings.

America Online (AOL, 800/827–3338), the most popular and subscribed to on–line service, has more than 6 million members and is the place to go if you want quick access to a host of daily newspapers (such as *The New York Times*) as well as a large number (but smaller than CompuServe) of databases. AOL is well known for its special forums dealing with entertainment and sports. More of the energy behind the design and execution of AOL is devoted to general consumer needs than to those of the researcher. You can still certainly access databases and find information, though, and AOL might be the ultimate general source!

Finally, there is the relatively new *Microsoft Network* (800/426–9400). Microsoft has limited their subscriber base to 500,000 for the time being. As you can see in Figure 3.9, it offers current news plus a host of other connections for information on everything from the Arts to Business and Finance.

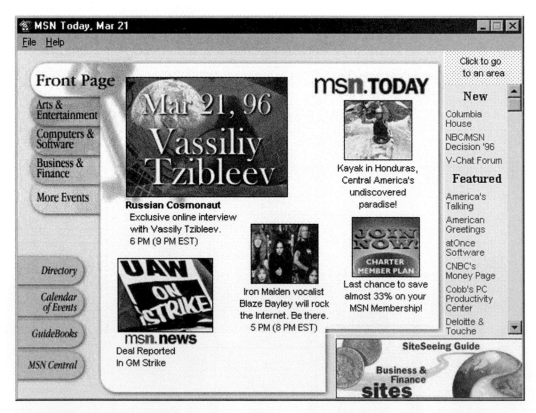

Figure 3.9 The Microsoft Network Infocenter.

Any of these on–line information providers contains more information than you could ever get through and probably lots of information related to exactly your interest. Which one for you? I would guess that CompuServe is the best for sheer volumes of information and access to different databases. The other two certainly have a lot to offer. If you are interested, perhaps the best step is to join each one for its trial offer of 10 hours. Try to find information through each service about a topic in which you are interested, and see which is most complete. Just be sure that it is easy to "unsubscribe," since the service providers ask you for a credit card (which is used in billing) when you first sign up. For example, you cannot unsubscribe from AOL any other way than by calling their 800 number. You cannot even unsubscribe on–line!

Using the Internet for Research

You have heard about it and maybe even seen it, but here it is, the Internet! Mysterious beyond description, it has gotten its fair share of hype and more. It has gotten bashed as well. Is it for you? I think I can show you the answer is "yes." Here is why.

What is the Internet?

In the most basic of terms, the **Internet** (also commonly referred to as the **Net**), is a **network** of networks. What is a network? A collection of computers that are connected to one another and that can communicate with each other.

Imagine if all these networks were connected to one another. Imagine hundreds of networks and thousands of computers of all different types attached to one another and millions of people using those computers. Now you have some idea how large the Internet is. In fact, it is growing by more than 10% each month, with some 30,000 connections (and potentially hundreds of people using each connection) now active.

Research Activities on the Net

If you are talking about information in all shapes and sizes, there is not much that you cannot do on the Net. Here is a brief overview of how the Net can be used for research purposes, whether it is contacting an expert in your field via e-mail, or finding the home page of the university (more on home pages later) where you would like to apply for graduate school, or getting a bibliography on a particular topic.

- The Internet is probably used most often for electronic mail or **e-mail**. Just as you exchange mail with a colleague across the United States or the world, so you can do the same without ever placing pen to paper. You create a message and send it to your correspondent's electronic address. It is fast, easy, and fun. For example, if you would like a reprint of an article that you find interesting, you could e-mail the author. Increasingly, faculty and staff members at large and small educational institutions have e-mail.
- Information, information, information—all available in millions of files on the Net. Using **file transfer protocol** or **ftp**, you can download or transfer files from other locations to your computer. With a little practice, you can surf the net for anything from the University of Kansas' history collection to the lyrics of '60s rock and roll hits. For example, many researchers make their data available as a file, which can then easily be transferred from the researcher's computer to any one else's computer so access to the data is quick and easy.

- There are thousands of electronic **newsgroups** available to you on the Internet. These are places where information can be posted and shared among Internet users, with topics that range from space exploration to the authenticity of a Civil War era land deed. You can drop in and contribute to any of these newsgroups. For example, if you are interested in K–12 math curriculum, try the k12.ed.math newsgroups. How about pathological behavior? Try the sci.psychology.psychotherapy newsgroup.

- When you **telnet**, or connect to a remote site, it is as if you were using a computer at another location. With an Internet connection, you can control computers from thousands of miles away and get the information that those computers have access to. For example, wanting to know what other works a particular author had completed, I telneted to the Library of Congress and entered the author's full name. In a second, there was a list of his 40 other titles.

- Finally, there is the **World Wide Web** or **WWW**, which everyone has been talking about. Here you can use a browser to make a connection to these graphical stops on the information highway. You can access the National Institutes of Health home page and see what types of funding programs are available or go to the latest timetable at the University of Kansas to find out when Statistics 1 is being offered and who is teaching it.

This chapter will limit its comments to e-mail, newsgroups, and an exploration of the World Wide Web. It will also provide examples of how these various Internet features can be used. The system to connect and use the Internet at your school is probably different from what you will see here, but the principles are exactly the same.

Electronic Mail for Everyone

Imagine it is 1925, and you are sitting at your desk at college, writing a letter to a friend in England. You stamp the letter, mail it, and three weeks later an answer comes back. You are amazed at how fast the mail is and sit down to answer your friend's new questions about how much you like college and what you will do after you graduate.

Now imagine it is 1996, and you are writing to a friend in England. Only this time, you use **electronic mail** or **e-mail**. From your home, you compose the message, press the send key, and your friend has it on her desk in less than 30 minutes. The message back to you arrives within 20 minutes more, and you are amazed. In this chapter, we will show you how easy it is to send mail via the Windows and Mac based program named Eudora.

E-mail works much like conventional mail. You write a message and send it to an address. The big difference is that there is no paper involved. Rather, the messages you send travel from one computer to another in a matter of minutes or hours, rather than in days or weeks, as fast as your voice travels in a telephone conversation.

Eudora and E-Mail

It takes a fully featured mail program like Eudora to really manage all your mail activities.

Here is a sample Eudora session where I mail a researcher who I know is doing work in my area of interest, dissemination of public information. Here is a demonstration where I write to a colleague and request a reprint.

As you can see in Figure 3.10, I have composed a message to a colleague requesting a copy of an article. The Eudora screen is like many other mail program screens where you compose a letter.

- It has a location for the Internet address to whom the message is being sent (Judy Turner).
- It shows who the message is from (njs@falcon.cc.ukans.edu, who in real life is Neil J. Salkind).
- It shows the topic or subject of the message (Copy of article).
- It has room for a copy to someone else (Cc:).
- It has room for a blind carbon copy (Bcc:).
- It has room for an attachment (such as a file or some other document).

The content of the message is shown in the main message area starting with "Dear Dr. Turner." Once the message is complete, I click the Send button at the top of the screen, and the message is sent to Judy Turner.

Usually, when any kind of mail is sent, be it e–mail or snail mail, the recipient answers. Eudora automatically checks my mailbox every 30 minutes and lets me know if I have mail to read. If I do have mail, a chime sounds, and I can to go the option in Eudora that allows me to see what mail is there, such as shown in Figure 3.11.

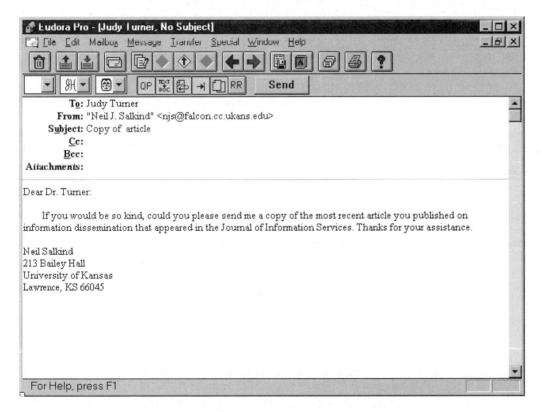

Figure 3.10 Composing a message in Eudora.

As you can see in Figure 3.11, I have a message from Judy Turner waiting to be read (which is what the dot (•) to the left of the message indicates).

To read the mail, I double–click on the message, and I see its content as shown in Figure 3.12.

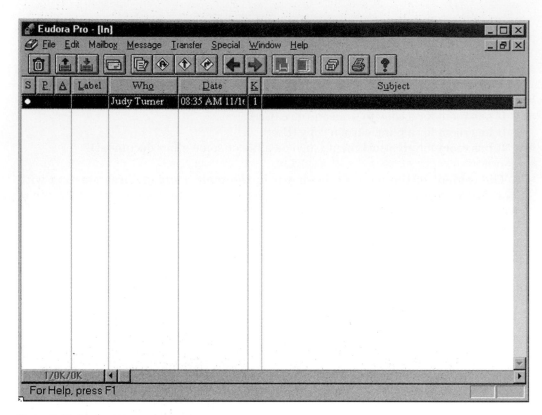

Figure 3.11 Mail waiting to be read.

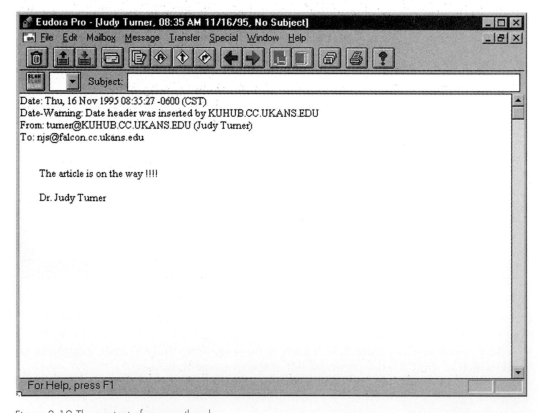

Figure 3.12 The content of an e-mail reply.

You can see in any of the Eudora screens shown that there are many different buttons that can be clicked and lots of menus with lots of options from which you can select. We are not going into any of those since our purpose is not to teach you how to use Eudora but only to show you how e-mail works. However, it would be useful for you to have some idea what any good e-mail program can do, and Eudora is one of the best.

Its features allow you to

- save and print mail messages.
- forward mail to one or 100 other people.
- include your "signature" with every mail message you send. This can be a quote or your e-mail address or whatever you feel works best. For example, here is the signature of a student of mine. It automatically appears at the end of every e-mail message he sends.

```
*****************************************************************
*Jim Williams          | phone: (817) 555-4532                 *
*Summit High School    | voice mail: (817) 255-4399 ext. 52    *
*2318 Blue Pkwy        | fax: (817) 555-3419                    *
*Webster, MO 64063                                              *
*              www: http://www.place.k12.mo.us/                 *
*****************************************************************
```

- have as many mailboxes as you want.
- check spelling.
- use nicknames (instead of "jt@kuhub.cc.ukans.edu" I can use "Judy Turner").
- store mail for later reading.

An Introduction to Newsgroups

Imagine being able to find information about 30,000 topics ranging from stereo systems to jokes (censored and otherwise) to the ethics of law to college football to astronomy. Where in the world would you be able to find a collection of such diverse information that can be easily accessed? You guessed it. The Internet and the various **USENET** sites that ship news each day around the world. The news that fits in one category, such as college football or the ethics of law, forms a newsgroup (also called a group). A newsgroup is simply a collection of information about one topic.

To help manage the flow of articles, news sites are managed, moderated, administered, and censored by system administrators who work for institutions such as universities and corporations. Not all newsgroups reach each potential site or everyone who has access to an Internet site. The newsgroups from which you can select news are those that the system administrator makes available.

What's in the News?

Newsgroups are named and organized following a set of rules. The most general of these rules has to do with the name of the group itself. There is a hierarchical structure to a newsgroup name, with the highest level of the hierarchy appearing in the left-most position. For example, the newsgroup name *k12.ed.tech* means that within *k12* (the general name for the kindergarten through 12th grade newsgroup), there is a subset named *ed (for education)* and within that another subset named *tech* (for technology).

Newsgroup Name	General Area of Focus	Example Newsgroups
comp	Information about computers, computer science, software, and general interest computer topics.	<ul><li>comp.champ (artificial intelligence)</li><li>comp.lang.c (the C programming language)</li><li>comp.bbs.misc (bulletin boards)</li></ul>
news	Information about news, newsgroups, and the newsgroup network.	<ul><li>news.adm (administering news)</li><li>news.ao.members (members of a particular newsgroup)</li></ul>
rec	Information about recreation, hobbies, the performing arts, and fun stuff.	<ul><li>rec.sports.football (for those football nuts among us)</li><li>rec.arts.movies (movie reviews and discussion)</li><li>rec.audio (high fidelity audio)</li></ul>
sci	Information about science, scientific research and discoveries, engineering, and some social science stuff	<ul><li>sci.astro (astronomy)</li><li>sci.med (medicine)</li><li>sci.skeptic (UFOs and other neat speculation)</li></ul>
soc	Information about the social sciences.	<ul><li>soc.history (history)</li><li>soc.roots (genealogy)</li><li>soc.women (topics related to women)</li></ul>
talk	Forums on controversial topics and issues of debate	<ul><li>talk.abortion (abortion)</li><li>talk.rumors (rumor control)</li><li>talk.religion (religious topics)</li></ul>
misc	Everything else that does not easily fit into one of the above categories.	<ul><li>misc.taxes (taxes)</li><li>misc.jobs (employment)</li><li>misc.fitness (physical fitness)</li></ul>

Table 3.4 The names of the main newsgroups, their general areas of focus, and examples.

There are seven major newsgroups, each using a specific label for the first level of the hierarchy. You can see in Table 3.4 what these groups are named and examples of what is in each of these categories.

What you see in Table 3.4 is a listing of all the major newsgroups. There is also an alternative set of newsgroups, some of which are even more popular than main newsgroups. These alternative groups, shown in Table 3.5, are very active and can provide valuable information as well.

Now you know what to expect based on the label used at the beginning of a newsgroup name.

To see how a newsgroup works, let's follow an example of someone interested in educational technology using NewsXpress, a popular Windows-based news reader.

Alternative Newsgroup	General Area of Focus
alt	anything somewhat out of the ordinary
bionet	biology
bit	the BITNET e-mail network
biz	business
clari	newsgroup specific category not covered by any others
de	information in German
fj	information in Japanese
gnu	a project run by the Free Software Foundation
ieee	electrical engineering
k12	kindergarten through 12 subjects of interest
relcom	Russian language
umsnet	the VMS computer system

Table 3.5 The names of the alternative newsgroups, their general areas of focus, and examples.

Using NewsXpress for News

NewsXpress is a shareware news reader that offers a comprehensive set of tools for easily reading and participating in newsgroups. The tools also let you see all those thousands of newsgroups, so you can make any selection you want.

Figure 3.13, the opening NewsXpress window, shows the news groups to which I have already subscribed. In NewsXpress and other newsgroup readers, you can usually see all the newsgroups that your site administrator allows access to. From those, you can select the ones you want to subscribe to. Each time you start your news reader, you will get the updated version of those newsgroups including all the news that has been added to that group since the last time you opened it. Newer versions of world wide web browsers, such as Netscape, also allow you to access and participate in newsgroups.

The next step would be to open the k12.ed.tech newsgroup and examine the contents, as you see in Figure 3.14. Within newsgroups, you will see a listing of topics (in this case 12), each one started by an individual as a source for more information, a place to meet electronically, discuss issues, and so forth.

If someone wants to participate in a certain newsgroup, they can add a new topic at this level, or go into an existing newsgroup and make their own contribution.

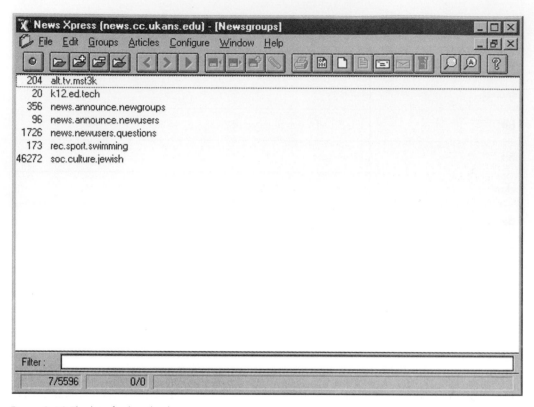

Figure 3.13 The list of subscribed newsgroups.

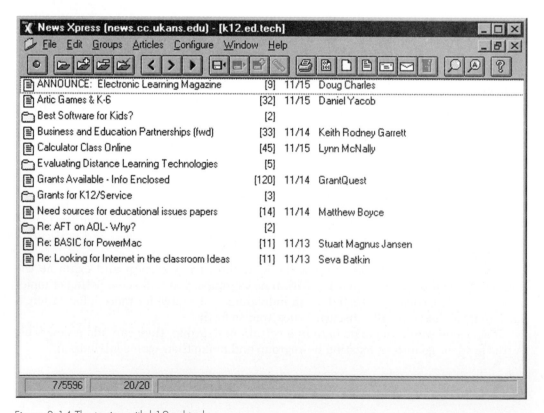

Figure 3.14 The topics with k12.ed.tech.

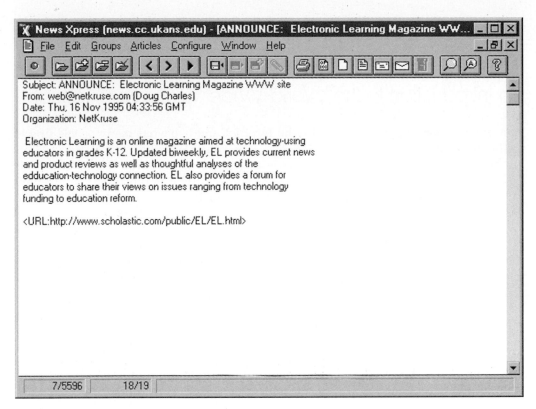

Figure 3.15 A message within the ANNOUNCE... group.

In Figure 3.15, you can see the contents of the ANNOUNCE: Electronic Learning Magazine, showing the first of nine contributions that have been made. At this level as well, someone can respond to this contribution by posting a message that would join the other nine or by writing directly to the author of this message (in which case the response would not be posted).

Using Mailing Lists

There is another really neat way to use newsgroups, and it is a great source of information. You can sign up for a **listserv discussion group**. A listserv discussion group is an automatic depository for information. If you subscribe to it, you receive everything that the list receives. A mail list is also known as a **listserv mailing list**.

For example, if you belong to the kindergarten through 12th grade educational technology mailing list, then each time someone sends mail to that list, you will receive it as well. There are more mail servers than you can imagine, and it will take some exploration to find out which ones fit your needs.

To subscribe to a mailing list, you need to send a message to the list's administrator. As soon as you do that, a constant stream of messages will come your way. But be careful; if a list is very active you can receive hundreds of messages in one day. If you go even a day without checking your mail, your electronic mailbox is likely to get so full of messages that you won't be able to read anything! Imagine your real mailbox outside your apartment or home. When it gets stuffed full, it is very difficult to pull out any one piece because the mail is packed so tightly. You need a bigger box, or you needed to empty the box before it gets so full. Such is the case with an Internet mailing list. Either get a larger e–mail box (ask for more storage space from the system administrator), or check your mail more than once a day.

An Introduction to the World Wide Web and Netscape

Now we are ready to actually explore the Internet and use what many people find to be the most attractive aspect of the Internet—the World Wide Web.

You already know that the Internet is a network of networks. The World Wide Web (or WWW) is a collection of documents representing different locations that are linked to one another, such that clicking on a particular word or picture or sound in one can quickly take you to another. On the Web, you will find what are called **distributed hypertext documents**. These documents, also called **home pages**, contain **hot links**. These links connect one home page to another. To see and use these home pages and hot links, you need a viewer, and that is where Netscape comes in. Netscape is a browser that can be used for exploring the WWW. There are other viewers, such as Mosaic and Cello, and they all work pretty well. The reason I selected Netscape for this book is that it is available on-line, which means you can try it for free before you pay and register. It is widely available, and it is being used by more people than any other type of viewer. But the best reason for using Netscape is that it is so easy to use and more fun than you might think possible. So get ready to browse and meet the World Wide Web.

All About Home Pages

A home page is a collection of information, with each home page having some very similar characteristics. You can get to different home pages in a variety of ways, which I will explain more about in this chapter. For now let's explore one of the opening home pages for the Library of Congress as shown in Figure 3.16. This home page has to do with the exhibits at the Library of Congress.

First, at the top of the page, you see the title "Library of Congress World Wide Web Home Page." The title tells you what the current home page is. The *Location* text box shows you the address of the active home page. This is an address on the WWW and is also called a **URL** for **universal resource locator**. Once you know the URL for a particular home page, you can just enter the URL in the Location text box, press Enter, and Netscape will take you there. By their nature, URLs are cryptic, and it is tough to tell where one is physically located or what institution is sponsoring the home page. That means it is handy to keep a running list of URLs you like and want to visit once again. That is exactly what the *Bookmark* pull-down menu does.

Then, the main portion of the screen shows the contents of the home page, which starts with a nice graphic showing the Library of Congress main building. As you can also see in Figure 3.16, this Library of Congress home page contains the graphic, plus underlined words that are links to other pages (such as what's new or search). When you click on one of these highlighted words, Netscape takes you to a new page.

In Figure 3.17, you can see a home page from "Yahoo!," one of the great Web sites. It contains almost nothing but links to other home pages. Click on any one of these links, and you will be connected to another home page with other links. The Web just goes on and on.

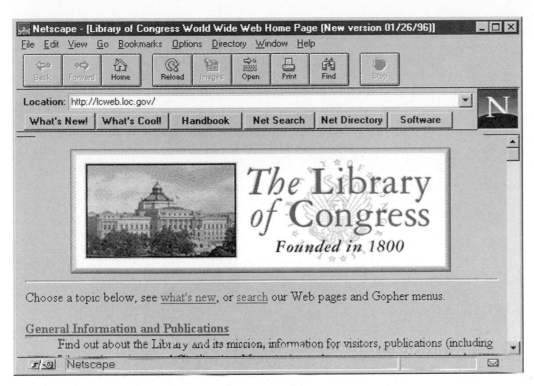

Figure 3.16 The home page for the Library of Congress Exhibits.

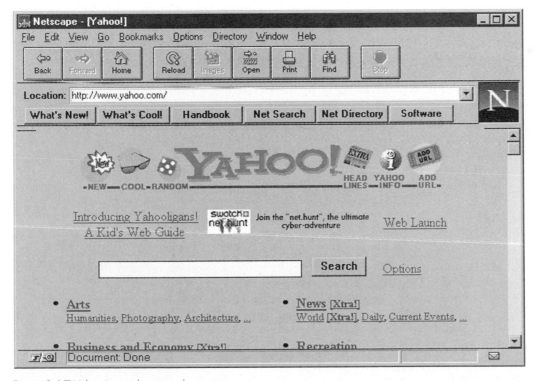

Figure 3.17 Yahoo! search engine home page.

This is *the* $64,000 question. There is no central listing of home pages, so you cannot go to a directory or some other source and find something like "All the Home Pages on the Word Wide Web." You cannot do this because the Web and the number of pages on it are changing rapidly. Many books offer different listings, but some of those books are out of date before they are published. Nonetheless, such a book may be a good place to start.

The best way to find home pages, however, is to explore the Web. Talk with your colleagues to find out what they are discovering, and use some kind of a search tool. When you find a terrific home page, save its location as a bookmark, and share that information with a friend. Now, if you have the time, there is one terrific home page, named URouLette, you should explore. This home page, created at the University of Kansas, allows you to click on a roulette wheel (what else?) and go to a home page. Which one? It selects home pages at random, so you might find yourself at a home page on X rays in Uganda, or solar and stellar physics at Harvard (http://CFA–www.harvard.edu/CFA/ssp.html) or Point Grey Mini School in Vancouver, British Columbia (http://trinculo.educ.sfu.ca/pgm/pgmhome.html), or "Gleanings from the Writings of Baha'u'llah" (http//:www.cs.cornell.edu/Information/ People/kalantar/ Writings/ Bahaullah/GWB/sec–24.html).

By now you probably want the URL for URouLette, right? Here is how to get to it, and we will talk more about this URL later.

http://www.uroulette.com:8000/

Try it. You'll like it.

Searching on the Web

While there is no central listing of Web sites, there are search engines, which help you find what you are interested in. For example, a very popular search engine I showed you earlier is Yahoo! which has a URL of http://www.yahoo.com/. That address gets you an opening page with hundreds of links to topics in every area imaginable. Another search engine is WebCrawler, which regularly searches over 250,000 Web pages. Its URL is http://www.webcrawler.com/. Just enter that address, and you will be able to search.

For example, let's say we are interested in finding information on learning styles. Figure 3.18 shows the term learning styles entered in the WebCrawler section of the All-In-One page. A click on the Search button yields the links you see in Figure 3.19. Now you can go to wherever you want to follow up on the initial query given the 1460 that WebCrawler found. Now, a lot of these links may not be relevant to your search, but many will be. Besides, the other links will take you places and introduce you to information that may prompt new ideas and direction for your own work.

Yahoo is one of many different search engines which helps you find information that may be contained in a home page on the web. Wouldn't you know it, but some ambitious webmeister placed all these search engines on one page. You can locate the All-In-One search page by pointing your world wide web browser at http://www.albany.net/allinone and then search by people, subjects, and even the news and weather.

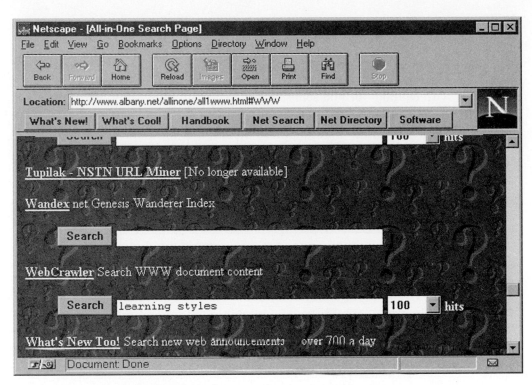

Figure 3.18 Using WebCrawler to find information about learning styles.

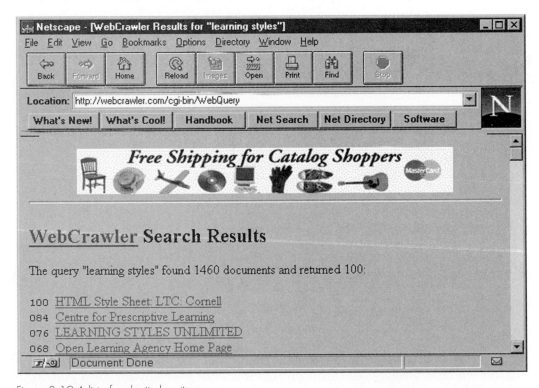

Figure 3.19 A list of web site locations.

Some Interesting Starting Points

Table 3.6 shows some interesting Web sites you might want to explore to give you a flavor of what is out there. If you are even a little bit of a Web fan, read this section of the chapter with caution—or find someone else to do your homework, job, chores, and other obligations. Once you get connected and start exploring, you will find it more than easy to spend hour after hour on the Web. And the best way to get started is through some special sites such as Yahoo! and a site that gives you access to Web servers (that contain access to thousands of home pages).

World Wide Web Site	URL
Yahoo! at Stanford University	http://akebono.stanford.edu/yahoo
URouLette at the University of Kansas	http://www.uroulette.com:8000/
A Virtual Library (The WWW Virtual Library home page)	http://info.cern.ch/hypertext/DataSources/bySubject/Overview.html
Visit the Louvre (The Louvre Home Page)	http://mistral.enst.fr/~pioch/Louvre
Maps and More (Map Viewer Home Page)	http://pubweb.parc.xerox.com/map/
Free Stuff (Windows Shareware Archive home page)	http://coyote.csum.edu/cwis/winword/winword.html
More Really Free Stuff (Free Stuff from the Internet home page)	http://power.globalnews.com/articles/txt/freestuf/contents.htm
All You Need to Know (AskERIC Virtual Library home page)	http://eryx.syr.edu/COWSHome.html
All the People, All the Time (The Constitution of the United States home page)	http://www.law.cornell.edu/constitution/constitution.overview.html

Table 3.6 Interesting Web sites.

Writing the Literature Review

It is now time to take all the information you have collected and organize it somehow so it begins to make sense. This is your review of literature, and now you need to actually write it (horrors!). Here are some writing hints.

First, *read other literature reviews*. There is no arguing with success. Ask a student who has already been through this course or your adviser for a successful proposal. Look carefully at the format as well as the content of the literature review. Also, look at some of the sources mentioned earlier in this chapter, especially sources that are reviews of literature, journal articles, and other review papers.

Second, *create a unified theme*, or a line of thought, throughout the review. Your review of literature is not supposed to be a novel, but most good literature reviews build from a very general argument to a more specific one and set the stage for the purpose of the research. You should bring the reader "into the fold" and create some interest in where you will be going with this research that other people have not gone.

Third, *use a system to organize your materials*.

Writing the literature review helps you to solidify the purpose of your research.

Most reviews of the literature will be organized chronologically within topics. For example, if you are studying gender differences among adults in anxiety and verbal ability, you would organize all the references by topic area (anxiety and verbal ability) and then within each of these topics begin your review with the earliest dated reference. This way you move from the earliest to the latest and provide some historical perspective.

Fourth, *work from an outline*. If you are an accomplished and skilled writer, you can ignore this suggestion. But if you are just starting out, it is a good idea to use this tool to help organize the main thought in your proposal before you begin the actual writing process.

Fifth, *build bridges between the different areas that you review*. For example, if you are conducting a cross-cultural study comparing the way that East Indian and American parents discipline their children, you might not find a great deal of literature on that specific topic. But there is certainly voluminous literature on child rearing in America and in India and tons of references on discipline. Part of the creative effort in writing a proposal is being able to show where these two come together in an interesting and potentially fruitful way.

Sixth, *practice may not always make perfect but it certainly doesn't hurt*. For some reason, most people believe a person is born with or without a talent for writing. Any successful writer would admit that to be a class A basketball player or an accomplished violinist you have to practice. Should it be any different for a writer? Should you have any doubts about this question, find a serious writer and ask him (or her) how many hours a day or week he or she practices that craft. More often than not, you will see it is the equivalent of the ball player or the musician. In fact, a writing friend of mine gives this advice to people who want to write but don't have a good idea about the level of involvement it requires. She says, "Just sit down at your typewriter or word processor, and open a vein." That is how easy it is.

So the last (but really the first) hint is to practice your writing. As you work at it and find out where you need to improve (get feedback from other students and professors), you will indeed see a change for the better.

Everyone who does research starts somewhere, and most of the time a review of the literature puts ideas and goals into perspective. The literature, and all the tools available to work with the literature, is your first and best ally in putting together a well-researched and comprehensive discussion of what has occurred in the past. Once important variables are identified, you need to turn your attention to how these variables can be measured, the focus of the next chapter.

Exercises

1. Make a list of 10 topics you would find interesting to pursue research in. These can be any topics dealing with education or psychology that you might glean from newspapers, radio, and television news, magazines, research journals, and even overheard conversations. Rank these various ideas by level of interest, and for each of the top five write one sentence explaining why it appeals to you.

2. Take the idea that you ranked #1 above and do the following:
   a. Write a one-paragraph description of a study that incorporates that idea.
   b. List the steps you could take in reviewing the specific literature relevant to this topic.
   c. From this idea, generate three more questions derived from the original question or idea.

3. Use the idea that you ranked #2 above and do the following:
   a. Locate a reference from a journal, and write out the complete citation.
   b. Locate an abstract from a study that focuses on the topic.

4. Find 10 other sources of information about any of the topics you listed in #1 above, and write out the complete citation for each. Try to complete a set of other sources that is as diverse as possible.

5. Go to your library and find five journals in your field of study. If you need to, use the list of journals in this chapter. After you have located the journals, examine them to determine
   a. what type of articles are published (reviews of literature, empirical studies, etc.).
   b. whether the journal is published by a professional organization (such as the American Psychological Association) or by a private group (such as Sage Press).
   c. the number of articles in each journal and if there is any similarity in the topic areas covered within each issue of the journal.
   d. how often the journal is published and other information about its editorial policies (e.g., guidelines, features, etc.).

6. Find an article of particular interest in a research journal and do the following:
   a. Provide the complete citation for the article.
   b. Identify the theoretical rationale on which the research is based, and summarize the rationale that the author(s) present for doing the research.
   c. State any assumptions that might be made by the researcher(s) or author(s).
   d. Critique how well you think the author presents his or her argument as a justification for the content of the research study as reported in the article.

7. Go to the *Reader's Guide to Periodical Literature* and see what information is contained for the last three months for the topic depression. Now go to *Psychological Abstracts* (either the hard copy or on line), and look up the same general area.
   a. Which source has more information?
   b. What is the primary difference between the type or quality of information that each contains?
   c. Which was the easier to use, and why?
   d. What are advantages and disadvantages of using the *Reader's Guide*? What are the advantages and disadvantages of *Psychological Abstracts*?

8. Find three abstracts from recent research journals. For each abstract identify the following:
   a. the purpose
   b. the hypothesis
   c. the type of study (correlational, experimental, etc.)
   d. the conclusion

9. What are the steps in writing a review of the literature?

10. What is the purpose of a review of the literature?

11. You have been assigned the topic of gender differences in adolescent development of independence for a research study. Formulate five research questions that address this topic.

12. Use ERIC or PSYCHLIT (another on-line database) to find five references on any of the topics in which you have an interest (as you defined in earlier questions).

13. State the difference between a research question and a research hypothesis.

Want to Know More?

Further Readings

Collins, M. E. (1988). Search strategies: Teaching research in children's literature to graduate education students using ERIC. *Research Strategies, 6*, 127–132.
> Shows how to use ERIC databases to research children's literature materials using both thesaurus and subject indexes. Also lists advantages of using on-line searching to retrieve citations.

Kahn, P. (1988). Making a difference: A review of the user interface features in six CD-ROM databases products. *Optical Information Systems, 8*, 169–183.
> Reviews BRS MEDLINE, Wilson disk Cumulative Book index, MLA International Bibliography, Dialog OnDisc, ERIC, SilverPlatter Sociofile, CCOHS, and Knowledge Finder MEDLINE. Describes each as to how to browse, use menus, search, access on-line versions, print, and save.

Stewart, L., & Olsen, J. (1988). Compact disk databases: Are they good for users? *Online, 12*, 48–52.
> Looks at four groups of undergraduate students researching assigned topics with use of printed and CD-ROM versions of ERIC. One group was given formal instruction with the CD-ROM, one group used CD-ROM without instruction, a third group used the printed version with instruction, and the last group used the printed version without instruction. Results illustrate the advantages of using CD-ROM for searches.

Maclay, V. (1989). Selected sources of United States agency decisions. *Government Publications Review, 16(3)*, 271-301.
> Discusses frequently used sources of U.S. agency decisions, including computer, assisted legal research systems and the availability of on-line research systems.

Strunk, W., & White, E. B. (1959). The elements of style. New York: Macmillan.
> THE book containing simple and straightforward rules and tips on how to improve your writing. A must for anyone who writes anything!

Readings of Other Interest

Edelman, G. M. (1989). *The remembered present.* New York: Basic Books.
> After stating the problem, presents author's theory of the brain (neural Darwinism) with supportive logic, past information, and opinion. You see how a problem can be connected to a theory and the logic used.

Goldberg, F. S. (1988). Telecommunications and the classroom: Where we've been and where we should be going. *Computing Teacher, 15(8)*, 26-30.

> Discusses the use of telecommunications, and highlights projects designed by the New York City Board of Education to investigate telecommunications alternatives for the classroom. Some of the models described are on-line research, user-supported libraries, and computer mediated dialogues.

Huntington, R. B. (1993). Networks for success: Using the BITNET and Internet in institutional research. *Journal of Maryland Association for Institutional Research, 2*, 78-87.

> Discusses the advantages of using on-line database searches' availability to investigate research issues in greater depth prior to conducting research. Overall, covers various issues of using on-line searches and this technology's impact on institutional research.

Sampling and Generalizability

What You'll Learn About in this Chapter

- Why good sampling may be the most important step in any research project
- The importance of generalizability
- The difference between a sample and a population
- What the word random means
- How to use a table of random numbers in selecting a sample
- The difference between simple random sampling and stratified sampling
- How probability and nonprobability sampling strategies differ
- What sampling error is and why it is important
- How to reduce sampling error
- How to estimate sample size

Imagine this. You are assigned the task of measuring the general attitude of high school students toward unrestricted searches of their lockers for drugs. You are already enough of a research expert to know you will have to develop some kind of questionnaire and be sure it covers the important content areas and is easy to administer and score. After all that preliminary work has been done, you are faced with the most important question: Whom will you ask to complete the questionnaire? All 4,500 students in all the high schools throughout the district? You cannot do that, it is too expensive. Ask students at only those schools where there is reportedly a drug problem? Cannot do that either. It is too likely there also are drugs in schools that have not been identified as problem schools. How about asking only seniors, since they are supposed to know what is going on about town? Cannot do that since freshmen, sophomores, and juniors use drugs as well. What do you do?

Hmm. Decisions, decisions, decisions—ones that are not to be taken lightly. The success of your project depends on the way you select the people who will participate in your study, whether you will be distributing a questionnaire or administering a memory task. This chapter discusses various ways of selecting people to participate in research projects and the importance of the selection process to the research outcomes. It is all about samples and sampling.

Populations and Samples

A sample is a subset of a population.

In several places throughout the first four chapters of *Exploring Research*, you read about the importance of inferring the results of an experiment from a sample to a population. This is the basis of the inferential method. If everyone in the population cannot be tested, the only other choice is to select a **sample**, a subset of the population. Good sampling technique includes maximizing the degree to which this selected group represents the population.

A **population** is a group of potential participants to whom you want to generalize the results of a study. And **generalizability** is the name of the game. For it is only if the results can be generalized from a sample to a population that research results have meaning beyond the limited setting in which they were originally obtained. When results are generalizable, they can be applied to different populations with the same characteristics in different settings. When results are not generalizable (when the sample selected is not an accurate representation of the population), the results are applicable only to the people in the same sample who participated in the original research and to no others.

Generalizability is often the key to a successful study.

For example, if you want to find out about high school students' attitudes toward locker searches, one class of senior chemistry students could be given the questionnaire. But how much are they like the general population of students who attend all the high schools in the district? Probably not much. Or 10% of female freshman and sophomore girls from all the high schools could be asked the same questions. This selection encompasses a far larger group than just the 30 or so students in the chemistry class, but how representative are they? Once again, not much.

The task before us then is to devise a plan to ensure that the sample of students selected is representative of *all* students throughout the district. If this goal is reached, the results can be generalized to the entire population with a high degree of confidence, even when using a small percentage of the 4,500 high school students. In other words, if you do the job (selecting a sample) right, the results can be generalized. How will you know if you "do the job right?" Well, some guidelines are discussed throughout this chapter, but one way to do a self-check of sorts is to ask yourself the question: *Does the sample I selected from the population appear to have all the characteristics of the population, in the same proportion?* Is the sample, in effect, a *mini population*?

To understand sampling, you need to first distinguish between two general types: probability and nonprobability sampling strategies. **Probability sampling** is a type of sampling where the likelihood of any one member of the population being selected is known. If there are 4,500 students in all the high schools, and if there are 1,000 seniors, the odds of selecting one senior as part of the sample is 1,000:4,500 or 0.22.

Nonprobability sampling is where the likelihood of selecting any one member from the population is not known. For example, if you do not know how many children are enrolled in the district's high schools, the likelihood of any one being selected cannot be computed.

You often do not know the probability of selecting any one member from the population.

Probability Sampling Strategies

Probability sampling strategies are the most commonly used because the selection of participants is determined by chance. Since the determination of who will end up in the sample is determined by nonsystematic and random rules, the chance that the sample will truly represent the population is high.

Simple Random Sampling

The most common type of probability sampling procedure is **simple random sampling**. Here, each member of the population has an *equal* and *independent* chance of being selected to be part of the sample. *Equal* and *independent* are the key words here. *Equal*, since there is no bias that one person will be chosen rather than another. *Independent* because the choice of one person does not bias the researcher for or against the choice of another. When randomly sampling, the characteristics of the sample should be very close to that of the population.

For example, would it be simple random sampling if you were to choose every fifth name from the phone book? No, since both the criteria of equal and independent are being violated. First, if you begin with name 5 on page 234 of the phone book, then names 1, 2, 3, and 4 never had an equal chance of being selected. Second, if you chose 5 on the list and then every fifth name from there on, only names 10, 15, 20, and so on have any chance of being selected. In other words, the selection process is no longer independent.

The process of simple random sampling consists of four steps.

1. The definition of the population from which you want to select the sample.
2. The listing of all the members of the population.
3. The assignment of numbers to each member of the population.
4. The use of a criterion to select the sample you want.

For example, Table 4.1 shows a list of 50 names, with numbers already assigned (steps 1, 2, and 3 above). It is not a very large population but fine to work with for illustrative purposes. From this population, a sample of 10 individuals will be selected using what is called a **table of random numbers**. Here is how it works.

1. Jane	**11.** Susie	**21.** Ed T.	**31.** Dana	**41.** Nathan
2. Bill	**12.** Nona	**22.** Jerry	**32.** Bruce	**42.** Peggy
3. Harriet	**13.** Doug	**23.** Chitra	**33.** Daphne	**43.** Heather
4. Leni	**14.** John S.	**24.** Glenna	**34.** Phil	**44.** Debbie
5. Micah	**15.** Bruce	**25.** Misty	**35.** Fred	**45.** Cheryl
6. Sara	**16.** Larry	**26.** Cindy	**36.** Mike	**46.** Wes
7. Terri	**17.** Bob	**27.** Sy	**37.** Doug	**47.** Genna
8. Joan	**18.** Steve	**28.** Phyllis	**38.** Ed M.	**48.** Ellie
9. Jim	**19.** Sam	**29.** Jerry	**39.** Tom	**49.** Alex
10. Terrill	**20.** Marvin	**30.** Harry	**40.** Mike G.	**50.** John D.

Table 4.1 Here is a group of 50 names that constitutes a "population" for our purposes. Notice that each one is numbered and is ready to be selected.

Using a Table of Random Numbers

A table of random numbers is a terrific criterion, since the basis on which the numbers in the table are generated is totally unbiased. For example, in Table 4.2 there are nearly equal numbers of 1's, 2's, 3's, 4's, 5's, and so on. As a result, the likelihood of selecting a number ending in a 1 or a 2 or a 3 or a 4 or a 5 is equal. This means that when names are attached to the numbers the likelihood of selecting any particular name is equal as well.

23157	48559	01837	25993
05545	50430	10537	43508
14871	03650	32404	36223
38976	49751	94051	75853
97312	17618	99755	30870
11742	69183	44339	47512
43361	82859	11016	45623
93806	04338	38268	04491
49540	31181	08429	84187
36768	76233	37948	21569

Table 4.2 A partial table of random numbers. In a table of random numbers, you can expect there to be an equal number of single digits, randomly distributed throughout all the numbers.

With that fact in mind, let's select one group of 10 names using the table of random numbers in Table 4.2. Follow these steps.

1. Select a starting point somewhere in the table by closing your eyes and placing your finger (or a pencil point) anywhere in the table. Selecting your starting point in this way ensures that no particular starting point (or no name) is selected.

For this example, the starting point was the first column of numbers, last row (36768), with the pencil point falling on the fourth digit, the number 6.

2. The first two-digit number, then, is 68 (in boldface type in Table 4.3). Since the population goes up to 50, and there is no name 68, this number is skipped and the next two-digit number is considered. Since you cannot go down in the table, go to the top of the next column, and read down, once again selecting the first two digits. For your convenience, Table 4.3 has each pair of two-digit numbers separated.

23157	48 55 9	01837	25993
05545	50 43 0	10537	43508
14871	03 65 0	32404	36223
38976	49 75 1	94051	75853
97312	17 61 8	99755	30870
11742	69 18 3	44339	47512
43361	82 85 9	11016	45623
93806	04 33 8	38268	04491
49540	31 18 1	08429	84187
36**68**	76 23 3	37948	21569

Table 4.3 The starting point in the selection of 10 cases using the table of random numbers. You can begin anywhere, as long as the place you begin is determined by chance and not intentionally chosen.

3. 48! Success! Person 48 on the list is Ellie, and she becomes the first of the 10-member sample.
4. If you continue to select two-digit numbers until 10 values between 01 and 50 are found, the names of the people that correspond in Table 4.2 with the numbers in boldface type in Table 4.4 are selected. Here is a breakdown of which numbers worked and which did not for the purposes of selecting a random sample of 10 people from the population of 50.

- Reading down the first column of two-digit numbers, 48, 50, 03, 49, and 17 are fine because they fall within the range of 50 (the size of the population), and they have not been selected before,
- 69 and 82 are out of the range,
- 04 and 31 are fine, and
- 76 is out of the range.

Since you cannot read farther down the column, it is time to go up to the next set of two digits (in the same five-digit column) at the top of the column, which begins with the number 55.

- 55 is not within the range,
- 43 is fine,
- 65, 75, and 61 are not acceptable,
- 18 is,
- 85 is not, and (finally!)
- 33 is, and there you have the 10 people.

Using any criterion for
selecting a sample
assumes that the criterion
is unrelated to what you
are studying.

Here they are:

Number	Name
48	Ellie
50	John D.
03	Harriet
49	Alex
17	Bob
04	Leni
31	Dana
43	Heather
18	Steve
33	Daphne

Now you have a sample of 10 names from a population of 50 selected entirely by chance. Your sample is selected by chance because the distribution of the numbers in the partial table of random numbers in Table 4.2 was generated by chance. Is it just a coincidence that three of the first five numbers (48, 50, 03, 49, 17) in the partial table of random numbers are grouped together? Absolutely yes. This group of five is the best approximation and the most representative of any sample of five from the entire population, given that each member of the population has an equal and independent likelihood of being chosen.

23157	**48** 55 9	01837	25993
05545	**50 43** 0	10537	43508
14871	**03** 65 0	32404	36223
38976	**49** 75 1	94051	75853
97312	**17** 61 8	99755	30870
11742	69 **18** 3	44339	47512
43361	82 85 9	11016	45623
93806	**04 33** 8	38268	04491
49540	**31** 18 1	08429	84187
36768	76 23 3	37948	21569

Table 4.4 The selection of the numbers in the random number table that correspond to the 10 names selected as a sample group. Notice how the individual pairs of numbers are in boldface type so you can see them separated from those that were not selected.

The big assumption, of course, is that the names in the population (Table 4.1) were listed in a random fashion. In others words, names 01 through 20 were not listed as the first 20 of 50 because they come from a different neighborhood, are very wealthy, or have no siblings or any other characteristic that might get in the way of an unbiased selection.

The general rule is to use a criterion that is unrelated to that which you are studying. For example, if you are doing a study on volunteering, you do not want to ask for volunteers!

Systematic Sampling

Another type of random sampling is called **systematic sampling**, where every *kth* name on the list is chosen. The term *kth* stands for a number between 0 and the size of the sample that you want to select. For example, here is how to use systematic sampling to select 10 names from the list of 50 shown in Table 4.1. To do this, follow these steps.

1. Divide the size of the population by the size of the desired sample. In this case, 50 divided by 10 is 5. Therefore, you will select every fifth name from the list.
2. As the starting point, choose one name from the list at random. Do this by the "eyes closed pointing method" or, if they are numbered, use any one or two digits from the serial number on a dollar bill. The dollar bill used in this example has as its first two digits 43, which will be the starting point.
3. Once the starting point has been determined, select every fifth name. In this example, using the names in Table 4.1 and starting with Heather (#43), the sample will consist of Ellie (#48), Harriet (#3), Joan (#8), Doug (#13), Steve (#18), Chitra (#23), Phyllis (#28), Daphne (#33), and Ed M. (#38).

Systematic sampling is easier and less trouble than random sampling, and that is one reason it is often preferred. It is also a bit less desirable. Clearly, the assumption of each member of the population having an equal chance to be selected is violated. For example, given that the starting point is Heather (#43), it would be impossible to select Debbie (#44).

Systematic sampling does reduce the chances of certain participants being selected.

Stratified Sampling

The two types of random sampling that were just discussed work fine if specific characteristics of the population (such as age, sex, ethnicity, ability group, and so on) are of no concern. In other words, if another set of 10 names was selected, one would assume that since both groups were chosen at random, they are in effect, equal. But what if the individuals in the population are not "equal" to begin with? In that case, you want to assure that the profile of the sample matches the profile of the population, and this is done by creating what is referred to as a **stratified sample**.

Strata are like different levels, representing characteristics.

The theory behind sampling (and the entire process of inference) goes something like this: If you can select a sample that is as close as possible to being representative of a population, then any observations you can make regarding that sample should also hold true for the population. So far so good. Sometimes, though, random sampling leaves too much to chance, especially if you have no assurance of equal distributions of population members throughout the sample. In that case, stratified sampling is used.

For example, if the population is 82% Methodists, 14% Catholics, and 4% Jews, the sample should have the same characteristics *if religion is an important variable in the first place*. Understanding the last part of the preceding sentence is critical. If this or that characteristic of the population is not related to what is being studied, there is no reason to be concerned about creating a sample patterned after the population and stratifying on one of those variables.

Let's assume that the list of names in Table 4.1 represents a *stratified* population (males and females), and attitudes toward abortion is the topic of study. Since sex or gender differences may be important, you want a sample that reflects gender differences in the population. The list of 50 names consists of 20 females and 30 males, or 40% female and 60% male. The sample of 10 should mirror that distribution and have 4 females and 6 males. Here is how you would select such a sample using stratified random sampling.

1. All the males and all the females are listed separately.
2. Each member in each group receives a number. In this case, the males would be numbered 01 through 30 and the females 01 through 20.

3. From a table of random numbers, 4 females are selected at random from the list of 20.
4. From a table of random numbers, 6 males are selected at random from the list of 30.

Although simple examples (with only one stratum or layer) such as this might occur, you may often have to stratify on more than one variable. For example, in Figure 4.1, a population of 10,000 children is stratified on the variables of grade (40% first grade, 40% third grade, 20% fifth grade) and location of residence (30% rural, 70% urban). The same strategy is used: select 10% (since 1,000 is 10% of 10,000) of each of the stratified layers to produce the sample size in Figure 4.1. For example, of the 1,200 rural children in the first grade, 10%, or 120, were randomly selected. Likewise 140 urban children in fifth grade were selected.

Location	Grade			Total
	1	2	3	
Rural	1,200 (120)	1,200 (120)	600 (60)	3,000 (300)
Urban	2,800 (280)	2,800 (280)	1,400 (140)	7,000 (700)
Total	4,000 (400)	4,000 (400)	2,000 (200)	10,000 (1,000)

Figure 4.1 Selecting a sample when there is more than one stratum consists of taking a proportion of each level. Here, the sample size is shown in ( ) below the size of each group in the population.

Cluster Sampling

Clusters are groups that appear together.

The last type of probability sampling is **cluster sampling**, where *units* of individuals are selected rather than individuals themselves. For example, you might be doing a survey of parents' attitudes toward immunization. Rather than randomly assign individual parents to two groups (say, for example, those who will be sent informational material and those who will not), you could just identify 30 pediatricians' offices in the city and then, using a table of random numbers, select 15 for one group and designate 15 for the second group.

Cluster sampling is a great timesaver, but you must be sure that the "units" (in this case the people who use each pediatrician) are homogeneous enough that any differences in the unit itself might not contribute to a bias. For example, if one pediatrician refuses to immunize children before a certain age, that would introduce a bias you want to stay clear of.

Nonprobability Sampling Strategies

The second general category of sampling strategies, nonprobability sampling, is those where the probability of selecting a single individual is not known. Since this is the case, you have to assume that potential members of the sample do not have an equal and independent chance of being selected. Let's look at some of these sampling methods.

Convenience Sampling

Convenience sampling is just what it says. A football coach gives each team member a questionnaire. The audience (the team) is a captive one, and it is a very convenient way to generate a sample. Easy? Yes. Random? No. Representative? Perhaps, but to a limited extent. You might recognize this method of sampling as the reason why so many experiments in psychology are based on results using college sophomores; these students are a captive audience and often must participate for credit.

Quota Sampling

You might be in a situation where you need to create a sample that is stratified on certain variables, yet for some reason proportional stratified sampling is not possible. In this case, quota sampling is what you might want.

Quota sampling selects people with the characteristics you want (such as first-grade rural children) but does not randomly select from the population a subset of all such children, as would occur in proportional stratified sampling. Rather, the researcher would continue to enlist children until the quota of 120 is reached. The 176th rural kid in first grade never has a chance, and that is primarily why this is a nonprobability sampling technique.

Here is another example of a quota system. Let's say you have to interview 20 freshmen of both genders. First you might interview 10 males, and, knowing that the distribution of males and females is approximately a 50/50 split, you interview the next 10 females who come along, and then you call it quits. While quota sampling is by far easier than stratified sampling, it is also less precise. Imagine how much easier it is to find 10 freshman males than a specific 10 males, which is what you would have to do in the case of stratified sampling.

Table 4.5 lists the different types of probability and nonprobability strategies that have been discussed, when they should be used, and some of the advantages and disadvantages.

Samples and Sampling Error

No matter how hard a researcher tries, it is impossible to select a sample that *perfectly* represents the population. He or she could, of course, select the entire population as the sample, but that defeats the purpose of sampling—making an inference to a population based on a smaller sample.

Reducing sampling error is a major goal of any selection procedure.

One way that the lack of fit between the sample and the population is expressed is as **sampling error**. Sampling error is the difference between the characteristics of the sample and the characteristics of the population from which the sample was selected. For example, the average height of 10,000 fifth-graders is 40 inches. If you take 25 samples of 100 fifth-graders and compute the average height for each set of 100 children, you will end up with an average height for each group, or 25 averages. If all those averages are exactly 40 inches, there is no sampling error at all. This result, however, is surely not to be the case. Life is not that easy nor the selection of samples that perfect. Instead, you find the values something like 40.3 inches, 41.2, 39.7, 38.9, and so on. The amount of variability or the spread of these values gives you some idea of the amount of sampling error. The larger the diversity of sample values, the larger the error.

Think for a moment what would happen if the entire population of 10,000 fifth-graders was the sample. You would find the average height to be 40! Perfect! No error! The

Type of Sampling	When It Should Be Used	Advantages	Disadvantages
Probability strategies			
Simple random sampling	When the population's members are similar to one another	Ensures a high degree of representativeness	Time consuming and tedious
Systematic sampling	When the population's members are similar to one another	Ensures a high degree of representativeness; no need to use a table of random numbers	Less truly random than simple random sampling
Stratified random sampling	When the population is heterogeneous in nature and contains several different groups.	Ensures a high degree of representativeness of all the strata in the population	Time consuming and tedious
Cluster sampling	When the population consist of units rather than individuals	Easy and convenient	Possibility that members of units are different from one another, decreasing the sampling's effectiveness
Nonprobability sampling strategies			
Convenience sampling	When the sample is captive	Convenient and inexpensive	Results in questionable representativeness
Quota sampling	When strata are present, and stratified, sampling is not possible	Ensures some degree of representativeness of all the strata in the population	Results in questionable representativeness

Table 4.5 A summary of different sampling techniques. When you begin considering the selection of a sample, you need to take into account many factors, all of which will affect the type and size of sample you select.

lesson? The larger the sample, the smaller the sampling error, because larger samples approach the size of the population and are more representative of the population.

The exact process for computing the sampling error, which is expressed as a numerical value, is beyond the scope of this book, but you should recognize that your purpose in selecting a good sample is to minimize that value. The smaller the value, the less discrepancy there is between the sample and the population.

But there is more. You already know that the larger a sample is, the more representative the sample is of the population. Let's say it comes time to test whether there is a difference between samples. It turns out that the better the samples represent their respective population, the more accurate the test of differences will be. In other words, better sampling leads to more accurate and truer tests of population differences.

How do you minimize sampling error? Simple. Use good selection procedures as described earlier in this chapter, and increase sample size as much as possible and reasonable. The next question you are ready to ask (I hope) is, "How big should the sample size be?" Glad you asked. Let's look at the last section in this chapter for more insight into the answer to that question.

How Big Is Big?

Now that you know something about sampling, just how many of those high school students do you need to select from the population of 4,500? If 50 is good, is not 500 better? And why not 1,500 if you have the time and resources to commit to the project?

You already know that too small a sample is not representative of the population, and too large is overkill. Sampling too many high school students would be self-defeating since you no longer are taking advantage of the power of inference. Some people believe that the larger the sample the better, but this strategy does not make economical or scientific sense. Too big a sample does not increase the precision of testing your question beyond the costs and trouble incurred in getting that size sample. You want a method for computing the actual *number* of high school students you should select for the sample. Remember, the less representative the sample is of the population, the more sampling error is present. In addition, the higher the sampling error, the less generalizable the results will be to the population and the less precise your test of the null hypothesis.

Samples should be big enough to show any differences if they are there but not so big that the samples are uneconomical.

Estimating Sample Size

The sample size you need to most accurately represent the population can be estimated, but it will take some faith on your part for two reasons. First, it involves concepts that are a little beyond the level of *Exploring Research*. Since you are bright and enthusiastic, however, you can probably understand the basics of this material. Second, and more important, you have to estimate certain values, which is often difficult even for the experts.

Here are the components that go into the estimating of the sample sizes for two groups being compared with one another.

s = the standard deviation of the dependent variable or how much variability there is in the scores on this variable

t = the critical value needed for rejection of the null hypothesis

D = your estimate of the average difference between the two groups

Let's take the case of a research study where you are trying to determine if one reading program is more effective than another. The dependent variable is average reading score.

The way you estimate the standard deviation for a sample before members of the sample are tested is by looking at scores and descriptive statistics for the dependent variable when the dependent variable was used in other studies. For example, let's say this reading test has a manual, and the manual shows that the standard deviation for 10th-graders in the past has been 15.

Next, you enter the critical value that reflects the difference you would expect if chance alone (and not any treatment) was the only factor operating. Critical values can be found in specialized tables. You will learn more about this in Chapter 8.

Finally, you need to provide some idea of what you think the difference between the two groups will be. If the possible score on the reading test can range from 20 to 50, you certainly do not expect the difference between the two averages to be more than 30. Be reasonable.

For this example,

You can (and should) estimate the needed sample size before you begin selecting participants.

- the standard deviation equals 15 (supposedly reported from an earlier study),
- the t value is 2 (the value found in our special table), and
- the estimated difference between the groups is 6, which is also a ballpark figure.

Given these values, the following formula can be used to compute n, which is the estimated sample size necessary for each group under the constraints that have been established:

$$n = \frac{2s^2 \times t^2}{D^2}$$

where n = estimated sample size for each group
s = standard deviation based on earlier studies
t = critical value
D = your estimate of the difference between each group

Substituting values, the formula now looks like this:

$$n = \frac{(2 \times 15^2) \times 2.00^2}{6^2}$$

It reveals that, given these constraints, you need about 50 people in each of the groups.

What is interesting to examine is the effects of changing certain values (such as standard deviation and estimated difference) on the estimated size of n, the sample size you need. Look what happens in Table 4.6 as the estimated difference between the two groups changes.

The effect on sample size when you change the amount of estimated error			
s	t	d	n
15	2	6	50
10	2	6	22
5	2	6	6
The effect on sample size when you change the amount of estimated difference			
s	t	d	n
10	2	2	200
10	2	4	50
10	2	6	22

Table 4.6 You can see how dramatic the effect can be when you change the estimated difference between groups.

The larger the estimated difference (from 2 to 4 to 6), the smaller the size the group needs to be. Why? Because the larger the difference between the groups, the less representative the groups have to be of the population for you to see any effect, if it exists. It is as if a large difference between two things is easier to notice than a small one. You can see in Table 4.6 how dramatic the change can be. If you double the estimated size of the difference (from 2 to 4), you dramatically decrease the estimated sample size needed from 200 in each group to 50.

What is the real scoop on sample size? Keep the following considerations in mind.

- In general, the larger the sample (within reason), the smaller the sampling error and the better job you can do.
- If you are going to use several subgroups in your work (such as males and females, who are both 10 years of age, and healthy and unhealthy rural residents), be sure your initial selection of subjects is large enough to account for the eventual breaking down of subject groups.
- If you are mailing out surveys or questionnaires (and you know what can happen to many of them), count on increasing your sample size by 40%-50% to account for lost mail and uncooperative subjects.
- Finally, remember that big is good, but appropriate is better. Do not waste your hard-earned money or valuable time generating samples that are larger than you need.

Although some people might differ with you on your selection of topics to study, what you choose is your business as long as you can provide a reasonable rationale for what you are doing. Your selection of a sample, however, is another story entirely. There really is a whole bunch of right ways, and then there is the wrong way. If you choose the wrong way (where you are arbitrary and follow no plan), you could very well end up sabotaging your entire research effort since your results might have no generalizability and, therefore, no usefulness to the scientific community.

Exercises

1. You are the head researcher on a longitudinal research study that is tracking vocational preferences from high school through middle adulthood. List the steps you would take in selecting the sample to be used in the study.

2. What is the reason a table of random numbers is so useful as a tool for assigning people to different groups?

3. What is the difference between a probability and a nonprobability sampling strategy? Provide an example of each. Also, what are the advantages and disadvantages of each type of sample?

4. What is the easiest way to reduce sampling error? What is the relationship between sampling error and the generalizability of the results of a study? Finally, what happens to sampling error as the size of the sample increases? Why?

5. From a population of 10,000 children (50% male and 50% female, 70% white and 30% nonwhite, and 57% single-parent family and 43% dual-parent family), what are the steps you would use to select a representative sample size 150?

6. Using a table of random numbers, select six names from the following list of 10.

   Michael
   Susan
   Sara
   Herman
   Selma
   Harriet
   Bill
   David
   Sharon
   Ed

   How many of the six would you expect to be males, and how many would you expect to be females? Why?

7. What are the implications if using a sample that is too big or a sample that is too small?

8. You are interested in the difference among children receiving creative instruction versus traditional instruction regarding the child's creativity. A creativity scale is used which yields a possible score falling between 70 and 100. From previous research you estimate the standard deviation to be 15. You have access to 60 individuals (30 for each group). You estimate that the difference between the creatively instructed children and traditionally instructed children on the creativity scale will be 10 points. With the constraints listed above, what sample size is necessary for each group?

9. What are the risks of increasing a sample size too much?

10. When should cluster sampling and simple random sampling be used?

11. What is sampling error?

Want to Know More?

Further Readings

Brewer, J. K., & Sindelar, P. (1988). Adequate sample size: A priori and post hoc considerations. *Journal of Special Education, 21,* 74-84.
> Discusses the relationships among power, alpha, effect size, and sample size for hypothesis testing. It further describes the interrelationships of the previous factors to precision, confidence, and sample size for interval estimation.

Klitzner, M., & Stewart, K. (1990). *Evaluating faculty development and clinical training programs in substance abuse: A guide book.* Rockville, MD: National Institute on Drug Abuse.
> Discusses the issues surrounding evaluation and training programs. Looks into research methods of sampling, such as random, stratified, simple random, systematic, stratified cluster, and sequential sampling and the potential sampling errors that can occur with them. Also discusses issues surrounding sample size and generalizability in the evaluation process.

Kraemer, H. C., & Thiemann, S. (1987). *How many subjects? Statistical power analysis in research.* Newbury Park, CA: Sage.
> Want to know all about how many subjects you need in your research given the type of question you are asking? Get this book at your library.

Wampold, B. E. (1990). Hypothesis validity of clinical research. *Journal of Consulting and Clinical Psychology, 58(3),* 360-367.
> Describes hypothesis validity as the extent to which research results reflect theoretically derived predictions about relations between or among constructs. Discusses the role of hypotheses in theory testing and presents some of the threats to hypothesis validity.

Readings of Other Interest

Hershey, R. D., Jr. (1988, November 4). Counting the Jobless a Job in Itself. *New York Times,* p. D1.
> Describes the work as a field interviewer for the Census Bureau's Current Population Survey. The factors looked at in this job are good ideas for researchers in examining their selected sample.

Hill, E. (1987). What is the effect of random variation in state unemployment rates? *Monthly Labor Review, 110(12),* 41-46.
> Examines the population survey data to indicate the impact of sample size on the standard error of subpopulations in the sample and how these errors can influence policy decisions.

Newlin, B. (1985). *Answers online: Your guide to informational data bases.* Berkeley, CA: Osborne McGraw-Hill.
> A good resource to list and describe different information sources that you can use on a library computer.

Measuring Behavior

What You'll Learn About in this Chapter

- Why measurement is an important part of the research process
- What the process of measurement includes
- What different levels of measurement are, and how they are applied
- What reliability is
- The different types of reliability, and how they are used
- How to increase the reliability of a test
- What validity is
- The different types of validity, and how they are used
- How to increase the validity of a test
- The relationship between reliability and validity

The Measurement Process

Even without knowing it, you probably spend a good deal of time making judgments about the things that go on around you. In many cases, these judgments are informal ("I really like the way he presented that material"), but at times they are as formal as possible ("Eighty-five percent of her responses were correct").

Measurement is the assignment of values to outcomes.

In both these examples, a judgment is being made about a particular outcome. That is what the process of measurement is all about, and its importance in the research process cannot be overestimated. All your hard work and efforts at trying to answer this or that interesting question are for naught if what you are interested in cannot be assessed, measured, gauged, appraised, evaluated, classified, ranked, graded, ordered, sorted, arranged, estimated, rated, surveyed, or weighed (get the idea?).

The classic definition of measurement was offered more than 45 years ago by experimental psychologist S. S. Stevens (1951), as the "assignment of numerals to objects or events according to rules." With all due respect to Professor Stevens, this definition can be broadened such that **measurement** is the *assignment of values to outcomes*. Numbers (such as 34.89 and $54,980) are values, but so are outcomes such as hair color (red or black) and social class (low or high). In fact, any variable by its very definition can take on more than one value and can be measured. It is these values that you want to examine as part of the measurement process.

This chapter introduces you to some of the important concepts in the measurement process including levels of measurement, a classification system to help assess what is measured, and the two primary qualities that any assessment tool must possess: reliability and validity.

Levels of Measurement

The level of measurement you use depends on how you want to measure an outcome.

Stevens is owed credit not only for the definition of measurement on which much of the content of this chapter is based but also for a method of classifying different outcomes into what he called levels of measurement. A **level of measurement** is the scale representing a hierarchy of precision on which a variable might be assessed. For example, let's take the variable height, which can be defined in a variety of ways with each definition corresponding to a particular level of measurement.

One way to measure height is to simply place people in categories such as A and B, without any reference to their actual size in inches, meters, or feet. Here, the level of measurement is *nominal* since people are assigned to groups based on the category to which they belong.

A second strategy would be to place people in groups that are labeled along some dimension such as Tall and Short ("this" or "that"). People are still placed in groups, but at least there is some distinction beyond a simple categorical label. In other words, the labels "tall" and "short" have some meaning in the context they are used, where Category A and Category B tell us just that the groups are different, but the nature of the difference is not known. Here, the level of measurement is *ordinal*.

A third strategy is where Rachel is found to be 5 inches taller than Gregory. We know not only that there is a difference between the two measurements but also the precise extent of that difference (5 inches). Here, the level of measurement is *interval*.

Finally, the height of an object or a person could even be measured on a scale that can have a true zero. While there can be problems in the social and behavioral sciences with this *ratio* level of measurement, it has its advantages, as you shall read later in this chapter.

Keep in mind two things about this idea of level of measurement. First, the qualities of one level of measurement (such as nominal) are characteristic of the next level up as well. In other words, variables measured at the ordinal level also contain the qualities of variables measured at the nominal level. Likewise, variables measured at the interval level contain the qualities of variables measured at both the nominal and ordinal level. For example, if you know that Lew is 60 inches tall and Linda is 54 inches tall (interval or possibly ratio level of measurement), then Lew is taller than Linda (ordinal level of measurement), and Lew and Linda differ in height (nominal level of measurement). Second, in any research project an outcome variable belongs to one of these four levels of measurement. The key, of course, is how the variable is measured.

Here is a more detailed discussion of each of these different levels of measurement, with examples and applications. You can find a summary of these four levels, and what you can and cannot say about them in Table 5.1.

Level	Qualities	Example	What You Can Say	What You Can't Say
Nominal (categories)	Assignment of labels	• Gender (male or female) • Preference (like or dislike) • Voting record (for or against)	Each observation belongs to its own category.	An observation represents "more" or "less" than another observation.
Ordinal (categories and orders)	Assignment of values along some underlying dimension	• Rank in college • Order of finishing a race	One observation is ranked above or below another.	The amount that one variable is more or less than another.
Interval (categories and orders and has equal intervals)	Equal distances between points	• Number of spelling words correct • Intelligence test scores • Temperature	One score differs from another on some measure that has equally appearing intervals.	The amount of difference is an exact representation of differences on the variable being studied.
Ratio (categories and orders and has equal intervals and has a zero point)	Meaningful and non-arbitrary zero	• Age • Weight • Time	One value is twice as much as another or no quantity of that variable can exist.	Not much!

Table 5.1 The levels of measurement.

Nominal

The **nominal level of measurement**, from the Latin word *nomin* (name), describes variables that are categorical in nature and that differ in quality rather than quantity. That is, the variable you are examining characterizes your observations such that

Nominal level variables are categorical.

they can be placed into one (and only one) category. And these categories can be labeled as you see fit. All nominal levels of measurement are solely qualitative.

For example, hair color (blond, red, black), race (black or African-American, white or Anglo-European, Native American), and political affiliation (Republican, Democrat, Independent) are examples of nominal-level variables. Even numbers can be used in the measurement of nominal-level variables, although the numbers have no intrinsic value. For example, assigning males as Group 1 and females as Group 2 or giving all offensive linemen on a football team jerseys with the numbers 40 through 50 are all examples of nominal or categorical measurement. There is no intrinsic meaning to the number, but it is a label that identifies items being measured.

An example of a study that uses a nominal-level variable is one that examined the merits of two school-based programs that attempted to facilitate the integration of "normal" children with children who have severe mental handicaps (Cole, Vandercook, and Rynders, 1988). The nominal or categorical variable here is the type of arrangement that children participated in, the Special Friend or the Peer Tutor program. They could participate in one or the other program but not both. The researchers examined how interaction between the child with the handicap and the nonhandicapped child was different as a function of the type of program they participated in. Differences in social interaction during the program, during free play, and during a tutorial session were examined.

A few things to remember about the nominal level of measurement. First, the categories are mutually exclusive, one cannot be in more than one category at the same time. You cannot be both Jewish and Catholic (even if you do celebrate both Hanukkah and Christmas!). Second, if numbers are used as values, they are meaningless beyond simple classification. You simply cannot tell if someone in Category 3 is less or more smart than someone in Category 11.

Ordinal

The **ordinal level of measurement** describes variables that can be ordered along some type of continuum. Not only can they be placed in categories, but they can be ordered as well. For this reason, the ordinal level of measurement often refers to variables as rankings of various outcomes, even if there are only two categories involved such as *big* and *little*.

For example, you already saw that *tall* and *short* are two possible outcomes when measuring height. These are ordinal because they reflect ranking along the continuum of height. So would your rank in your high school graduating class be based (probably) on grade-point average. You can be first of 300, or 150th of 300. You will notice that you cannot tell anything about the absolute GPA score from that ranking but only the position relative to others. You could be ranked first of 300 and have a GPA of 3.75 or be ranked 150th of 300 and have a GPA of 3.90.

From *tall* and *short* or *first* and *150th* you cannot tell anything about how tall or how short or how smart or good a student, because ordinal levels of measurement do not include this information. But you can tell that if Donna is shorter than Joan and Joan is shorter than Leni, then Donna is shorter than Leni as well. So while absolute judgments (such as how much taller Leni is than Donna) cannot be made, relative ones can. You can only assign the value *graduate with honors* as well as *honors with distinction* and *highest honors with distinction* to even further distinguish among those graduating with honors. This scale is ordinal in nature.

Interval

The **interval level of measurement**, from the Latin *intervalum* (meaning spaces between walls) describes variables that have equal intervals between them (just as did the walls built by Roman soldiers). Interval level variables allow us to determine the difference between points along the same type of continuum that we mentioned in the description of ordinal information.

Interval level variables have equidistant points along some continuum.

For example, the difference between 30 and 40 degrees is the same as the difference between 70 and 80 degrees. There is a 10-degree difference. Similarly, if you get 20 words correct on a spelling test and someone else gets 10 words correct, you can accurately say that you got 10 more words correct than the other person. In other words, a degree is a degree is a degree and a correct spelling word is a correct spelling word is a correct spelling word.

A review by Wigfield and Eccles (1989) of test anxiety in elementary and secondary school units illustrates how a construct such as anxiety can be measured by interval level variables. For example, the Test Anxiety Scale for Children (Sarason, Davidson, Lighthall, Waite, and Ruebush, 1960) is a 30-item scale that assesses various aspects of anxiety and that yields an overall measure. Items such as

> *If you are absent from school and miss an assignment, how much do you worry that you will be behind the other students when you come back to school?*

provide an accurate measure of the child's anxiety level in this widely used measure of this fascinating construct.

To contrast interval with ordinal levels of measurement, consider the variable age where the ranking in age is as follows.

Oldest . . . . Youngest
Bill   Harriet   Joshua   Rachel   Jessica

We know that Bill is older than Harriet, but not by how much. In reality he could be 2 years older than Harriet, while Harriet is 20 years older than Joshua. Interval level variables give us that difference while ordinal scales cannot. Put simply, with an interval scale we can tell the difference between points along a continuum (and the exact difference between the ages of Bill, Harriet, Joshua, Rachel, and Jessica), but with ordinal scales we cannot.

Although an interval-level scale is more precise and conveys more information than a nominal- or ordinal-level scale, you must be cautious how you interpret the actual values along the scale. Eighty degrees might be 10 more than 70, and 40 might be the same distance from 30, but what a difference those 10 can make. The 10 degrees between 80 and 70 might make water a bit cooler, but in the 10 degrees between 40 degrees to 30 degrees water freezes. Similarly, just because you got 10 more words correct than a classmate does not mean you can spell twice as well (2 times 10) since we have no idea about the difficulty of the words or whether those 20 words sample the entire universe of all spelling words. More important, if you get no words right, does that mean you have no spelling ability? Of course not. It does mean, however, that on this test, you did not do very well.

Ratio

The **ratio level of measurement**, from the Latin *ratio* (meaning calculation), describes variables that have equal intervals between them but also have an absolute zero. In its simplest terms, this means they are variables for which one possible value is zero or the actual absence of the variable or trait is possible.

For example, a study on techniques to enhance prosocial behavior in the classroom (Solomon et al., 1988) measured prosocial behavior with behavior tallies. The five categories of behavior that were measured over a 5-year (that is long!) period were cooperative activities, developmental discipline, activities promoting social understanding, highlighting prosocial values, and helping activities. These researchers spent a great deal of time developing systems that could consistently (or "reliably," as we will call it later) measure these types of behaviors. The scales they designed are ratio in nature since they have a true zero point. For example, it is easily conceivable that a child could demonstrate no prosocial behaviors.

This is indeed an interesting level of measurement. It is by far the most precise. To be able to say that Scott (who is 8 years old) is twice as old as Erin (who is 4) is a very accurate, if not the most accurate, way to talk about differences between people on some variable. Imagine being able to say that response rate using method A is one-half that using method B, rather than just saying that response rate is faster (which is ordinal) or faster by 10 seconds (which is interval).

This is the most interesting scale of the four, for other reasons as well. First, the zero value is not an arbitrary one. For example, you might think that since temperature (in Celsius units) has a zero (brr!) point, it is ratio in nature. True, it does have a zero point, but that zero is arbitrary. A temperature of zero does not represent the absence of molecules bumping off one another creating heat (the nontechnical definition of temperature, and my apologies to Lord Kelvin). But the Kelvin scale of temperature does have a theoretical absolute zero (about -275 degrees Fahrenheit), where there is no molecular activity, and here is a true zero or an absence of whatever is being measured (molecular activity).

What is All the Fuss?

Let's be practical. In a research study, you want to measure the variable of interest in as precise a way as possible. There is just no advantage in saying that Group A is weaker than Group B when you can say that Group A averaged 100 sit-ups while Group B averaged 75. More information increases the power and general usefulness of your conclusions. Imagine being a school superintendent with $100,000 to spend on an early intervention program. Wouldn't you want to know which programs are best and by what margin rather than just that one is "better" than the other?

But sometimes you will be limited to the amount of information that is available. For example, what if you wanted to study the relationship between age in adulthood and strength, and all you know is which group an adult belongs to (strong or not strong) and not his or her strength score? Such limitations are one of the constraints of doing research in the real world; you have to make do with what you have. Those limitations also provide one of the creative sides of research, defining your variables in such a way that the definition maximizes the usefulness of the information.

At what level of measurement do we find most variables in the behavioral and social sciences? Probably nominal or ordinal, with most test scores (such as achievement) yielding interval-level data. It is highly questionable, however, whether scores from such measures as intelligence and personality tests provide anything more than ordinal levels of measurement. A child with an IQ of 110 is not 10 points smarter than a child with an IQ of 100 but might have scored 10 points more. Likewise, Chris might prefer the chocolate chips from Package A to the chocolate chips from Package B twice as often but not necessarily like them twice as much. Therein lies an important point: How you choose to measure an outcome defines the outcome's level of measurement. Twice as often is a ratio level variable, where how much Chris likes them is attitudinal and ordinal in nature.

Most researchers take some liberty in treating ordinal variables (such as scores on a personality test) as interval level variables, and that is OK as long as they remember that the intervals may not be (and probably are not) equal. Their interpretation of the data needs to take that inequality into account.

Also, you should keep in mind that Stevens' typology of measurement levels has not gone unchallenged. In the 50 years that this methodology has been around, various questions have been raised about the utility of this system and how well it actually reflects the real world variables that researchers have to assess (Velleman and Wilkonson, 1993).

Primarily, these criticisms focus on the fact that a variable might not conveniently fit into any one of the four classifications but be valuable nonetheless. For example, while intelligence may not be ratio level in nature (no one has none), it is certainly beyond interval in its real life applications. In other words, the taxonomy might be too strict to apply to real-world data. As with so many things in the world of research, this four-level taxonomy is a starting point to be worked with but not to be followed as law.

Reliability and Validity: Why They Are Important

You can have the sexiest-looking car on the road, but if the tires are out of round, you can forget good handling and a comfortable ride. The tires, or where "the rubber meets the road," are crucial.

In the same way, you can have the most imaginative research question with a well-defined and clearly articulated hypothesis, but if the tools you use to measure the behavior you want to study are faulty, forget your plans for success. The reliability (or the *consistency*) and validity (or the *does-what-it-should* qualities) of a measurement instrument are essential, since the absence of these qualities could explain why you act incorrectly in accepting or rejecting your research hypothesis.

For example, you may be studying the effect of a particular training program on the verbal skills of mildly retarded children, and you are using a test of questionable reliability and validity. Let's assume for the moment that the treatment truly works well and can be the reason for significant differences in the verbal skills of groups that receive the treatment when compared with groups that do not. Since the instrument you are using to assess verbal skills is not consistently sensitive enough to pick up changes in the children's verbal behavior, you can forget seeing any differences in your results no matter how good the treatment (and how sound your hypothesis). With that in mind, remember: Assessment tools must be reliable and valid, otherwise the research hypothesis you reject may be correct but you will never know it!

Reliability and validity are your first line of defense against spurious and incorrect conclusions. If the instrument fails, then everything else down the line fails as well. Now on to a more detailed discussion of reliability and validity, what they are, and how they work.

Reliability and validity are the hallmarks of good measurement.

A Conceptual Definition of Reliability

Here we go again with another set of synonyms. How about dependable, consistent, stable, trustworthy, predictable, and faithful? Get the picture? Something that is reliable will perform in the future as it has in the past. A reliable test or a measure of behavior can measure the same thing more than once and will result in the same outcome.

You can use any of the synonyms for the word *reliability* listed above as a starting definition, but it is important to first understand the theory behind reliability. So, let's begin at the beginning.

When we talk of reliability, we talk of scores. Performance for any one person on any variable consists of one score composed of three clearly defined components, as shown in Figure 5.1.

Observed score = True Score + Error Score

Method Error

Trait Error

Figure 5.1 The components of reliability. True score and error score are the primary components.

First is the **observed score**. This is the score that you would actually record (or observe) in a research setting. It is the number of correct words on a test, the number of memorized syllables, the time it takes to read four paragraphs of prose, or the speed of a response. It can be the dependent variable in your study or any other variable being measured. Any observed score consists of the two other components, true score and error score.

The second component, **true score**, is a perfect reflection of the true value of that variable, given no other internal or external influences. In other words, any one person has only one "real score" on a particular variable. Upon repeated measurements, there may be several values for a particular measurement, but there is only one true one. But one can never ascertain what that true value is. Why? First, because most variables, such as memory, intelligence, aggression, and even height (we are taller in the morning since our spine compresses as the day goes on), cannot be directly measured, and, second, because the process of measurement is imperfect.

Yet, the measurement process always assumes a true score is there. For example, on a variable such as intelligence, each person has a true score that accurately (and theoretically) reflects that person's level of intelligence. Suppose that by some magic, your true intelligence score is 110. If you are then given a test of intelligence and your observed score comes out to be 113, the test overestimates your intelligence quotient. But since the true score is a theoretical concept, there is no way to know that.

The third component in Figure 5.1 is the **error score**, which is all of those reasons why the true score and the observed score differ. For example, Mike might get 85 out of 100 words correct on a spelling test. Does this mean that Mike is an "85% correct speller" all days on all tests of spelling? Not quite. It means that on this day, for this test, Mike got 85 words out of 100 correct. Perhaps tomorrow, on a different set of 100 words, Mike would get 87 or 90 or even 100 correct. Perhaps, if his *true* spelling ability could be measured, it would be 88. Why the differences between his true score (88) and his observed score (85)? In a word, error. Perhaps he did not study as much as he should have, or perhaps he did not feel well. Perhaps he could not hear the teacher's reading of each word. Perhaps the directions where he was supposed to write the words on the test form were unclear. Perhaps his pencil broke. Perhaps, perhaps, perhaps…. All sources of error.

All these possible explanations make the point that repeated scores on almost any variable are almost always different from one another since the trait being assessed changes from moment to moment and the instrument being used can change (albeit ever so slightly) and is not perfect (which no measurement device is).

What Makes Up Error Scores?

Let's go beyond the catchall of error scores. You will also see in Figure 5.1 that error scores are made up of two elements that help to explain why true and observed scores differ.

The first component of error scores is called **method error**. This is the difference between true and observed score due to the testing situation. For example, let's say you are about to take an exam in your introductory psychology class. You have studied well, attended reviews, and feel confident that you know the material. When you sit down to take the test, however, there are matching items (which one in Column A goes with Column B) and crossword puzzle-like items, and you were expecting multiple choice! In addition, the directions as to how to do the matching are unclear. Instead of reaching your full potential on the test (or achieving as close to your true score as possible), you score lower. The error between the two is due to the method of measurement, the unclear instructions, and so on.

The second component is **trait error**. Here, the reason for the difference between the true and observed scores is characteristic of the person taking the test. For example, if you forgot your glasses and cannot read the problems, or you did not study, or you just do not understand the material, the source of the difference between the true score (what you really know if nothing else interferes) and what you get on the test (the observed score) is a result of trait errors.

Table 5.2 lists some examples of major sources of error that can affect test scores from one testing to the next. The more influential these various factors, the less accurate the measurement will be. That is, the more influential these factors the less likely the obtained score will be as close as possible to the true score, the ultimate goal.

OK, you have been a good sport and stayed with this stuff, but what do the components of error have to do with reliability? Quite simply, the closer a test or measurement instrument can get to the true score, the more reliable that instrument is. How do we get closer? By reducing the error portions of the equation you see in Figure 5.1. So conceptually, reliability is a ratio, as shown in Figure 5.2. Here you can see that as the error score gets smaller, the degree of reliability increases and approaches 1. In a perfect world, there would be no error and the reliability would be 1 since the true score would equal the observed score. Similarly, as error increases, the reliability decreases since more of what you observe is due to something that cannot be predicted very accurately: the changing contributions of trait and method error.

Both trait and method error contribute to the unreliability of a test.

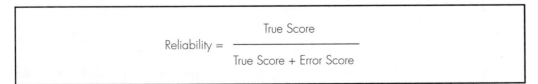

$$\text{Reliability} = \frac{\text{True Score}}{\text{True Score} + \text{Error Score}}$$

Figure 5.2 A conceptual formula for reliability.

Source of Error	Example
General characteristics of the individual	• Level of ability • Test-taking skills • Ability to understand instructions
Lasting characteristics of the individual	• Level of ability related to the trait being assessed • Test-taking skills specific to the type of items on the test
Temporary individual factors	• Health • Fatigue • Motivation • Emotional strain • Test environment
Factors affecting test administration	• Conditions of testing • Interaction between examiner and test taker • Bias in grading
Other factors	• Luck (no kidding!)

Table 5.2 Sources of error in reliability. Error can be part of the method used to assess behavior or the person or trait being assessed.

Increasing Reliability

Reliability is closely related to true and error score. Given a fixed true score (which is always the case, right?), reliability decreases as the error component increases. Thus, if you want a reliable instrument, decrease error. You cannot affect true score directly, so minimize those external sources of error (have clear, standardized instructions, bring more than one pencil in case one breaks, make sure the room is comfortable) you can control. Strive to minimize trait sources as well (have subjects get a good night's sleep, put off the assessment if someone does not feel well, and so forth).

Here is a summary of some important ways to increase reliability.

1. *Increase the number of items or observations.* The larger the sample from the universe of behaviors you are investigating, the more likely the sample is representative and reliable.
2. *Eliminate items that are unclear.* An item that is unclear is unreliable since some people will respond to it in one way and others will respond to it in a different fashion.
3. *Standardize the conditions under which the test is taken.* If the fourth grade has to take its achievement test with snow blowers running right outside the window or the heat turned up too high, you can certainly expect these conditions to affect performance, and, therefore, reliability.
4. *Moderate the easiness and difficulty of tests.* Any test that is too difficult or too easy does not reflect an accurate picture of one's performance.
5. *Minimize the effects of external events.* If a particularly important event—be it spring vacation, the signing of a peace treaty, the retirement of a major faculty

member, or such—occurs near the time of testing, postpone any assessment. These events are too likely to take center stage at the expense of true performance.

6. *Standardize instructions.* Bill in one class and Kelly in another class should be reading identical instructions and should take the test under the exact same conditions.

7. *Maintain consistent scoring procedures.* Anyone who has graded a stack of essay tests will tell you that reading the first one is much different from reading the last. Strive for consistency in grading, even if it means using a sheet that has scores down one column and criteria down the other.

How Reliability Is Measured

You know scientists; they love numbers. It is no surprise, then, that a very useful and easy to understand statistical concept called correlation (and the measure of correlation, the correlation coefficient) is used in the measurement of reliability. You will learn how to compute the correlation coefficient in Chapter 9. Correlations are expressed as a numerical value, represented by a lowercase r. For example, the correlation between test 1 and test 2 would be represented as

Reliability is often measured using correlation coefficients.

$$r_{test1 \bullet test2}$$

For now, all you need to know about correlation and reliability is that the more similar the scores in terms of change from one time to another (from one test to another), the higher the correlation and the higher the reliability. Reliability is a concern of the instrument not of the individual.

For example, as you will soon see, one way to measure the reliability of a test is to give the test to a group of people at one point in time and then give the same test to the same group of people at a second point in time, say, four months later.

Now, several things can happen when you have these two sets of scores. Everyone's score can go down from time 1 to time 2. Or everyone's score can go up from time 1 to time 2. In both these cases, when the scores tend to change similarly and in the same direction, the correlation will tend to be positive and the reliability high.

However, what if the people who score high at time 1 score low at time 2, or the people who score low at time 1 score high at time 2? Then the reliability would not be high. Instead it might be low or none at all since there is no consistency in performance between time 1 and time 2. In general, when the scores on the first administration remain in the same *relative* position on the second (high on test 1 and high on test 2, for example), the reliability of the test will be substantial. Reliability coefficients (which are roughly the same as correlation coefficients) range in value from -1.00 to +1.00. A value of 1.00 would be perfect reliability, where there is no error whatsoever in the measurement process. The standardized tests used in most research projects that you will learn about in the next chapter usually have reliability coefficients in the 0.80 to 0.90 range.

Types of Reliability

Reliability is a concept, but it is also a practical measure of how consistent and stable a measurement instrument or a test might be. There are several types of reliability, each one used for a different purpose. A discussion of what these types are and how they are used follows. A comparison and summary of the information is shown in Table 5.3.

Type of Reliability	What It Is	How You Do It	What the Reliability Value Looks Like
Test-retest	A measure of stability	Administer the same test at two different points in time to the same group of people.	$r_{time1} \cdot r_{time2}$
Parallel forms	A measure of equivalence	Administer two different forms to the same group of people.	$r_{form1} \cdot r_{form2}$
Inter-rater	A measure of agreement	Have two people rate behaviors and determine the amount of agreement between them.	Number of agreements/number of total observations
Internal Consistency	A measure of how consistently each item measures the same underlying construct.	Correlate performance on each item with total test score.	

Table 5.3 Different types of reliability. No matter what type of instrument you want to use, there is a type of reliability measure that will work for you.

Test-retest reliability examines reliability over time.

Test-Retest Reliability

Two synonyms for reliability used earlier in this section were consistency or stability. *Test-retest reliability* is a measure of how stable a test is over time. Here, the same test is given to the same group of people at two different points in time. In other words, if you administer a test at time 1 and then administer it again at time 2, will the test scores be stable over time? Will Jack's score at time 1 change or be the same as Jack's score at time 2, *relative* to the rest of the group?

An important question in the establishment of test-retest reliability is how long a time you wait between testings. The answer to this question depends on how you intend to use the results of the test as well as the purpose of your study. For example, let's say you are measuring changes in social interaction in young adults during their first year in college. You want to take a measure of social interaction in September and then another in May, and you would like to know whether the test you use has test-retest reliability. To determine this, you would have to test the same students at time 1 (September) and time 2 (May) and then correlate the set of scores. Since you are not interested in change in social interaction over a two-week period, establishing test-retest reliability over such a short period of time, given your intent, is not useful.

Parallel Forms Reliability

Parallel forms reliability examines reliability between forms.

A second common form of reliability is **parallel forms** or equivalence. Here, different forms of the same test are given to the same group of people. Then the two sets of scores are correlated with each other. The tests are said to be equivalent if the correlation is statistically significant.

When would you want to use parallel forms reliability, assuming you have created (or have) two forms of the same test? The most common example is when you need to administer two tests of the same construct within a relatively short time and you want to eliminate the influence of practice effects on participants' scores.

For example, let's say you are studying short-term memory. You read a list of words to people, and you have them recite what they can remember 10 minutes later. You might need to repeat this type of test every day for seven days, but you certainly could not use the same list of 10 words each day. Otherwise, by the last day, the subjects surely would have a good deal of the list memorized as a result of repetition, and the test would provide little information about short-term memory. Instead, you could design several sets of words that you believe are equivalent to one another. Then, if you can establish that they are parallel forms of the same test, you can use them on any day and expect the results from Day 1 to be equivalent to the results from Day 2.

Inter-Rater Reliability

Test-retest and parallel forms reliability are measures of how consistent a test is over time (test-retest) and how consistent it is from form to form (parallel forms). Another type of reliability is inter-rater reliability.

Inter-rater reliability is a measure of the consistency from rater to rater rather than from time to time, or even from test to test. For example, let's say you are conducting a study that measures aggression in preschool children. As part of the study, you are training several of your colleagues to accurately collect data. You have developed a "rating scale" consisting of a list of different behaviors that preschool children participate in, numbered 1 through 5, each representing a different type of behavior, as shown in Table 5.4.

Behavior	Code	Definition
Talking	1	Verbal interaction with another child
Solitary Play	2	Playing alone and not interacting with other children
Parallel Play	3	Playing alongside other children in the same activity
Hitting 1	4	Physically striking another child without provocation
Hitting 2	5	Physically striking another child with provocation

Table 5.4 Behaviors can be categorized and then used to objectively record their frequency, but reliability is as important here as with any other kind of measure.

Inter-rater reliability examines reliability across raters.

As you can see, #1 on the list is labeled *talking* and is defined as "verbal interaction with another child." Behavior #4 on the list is labeled *hitting 1* and is defined as "physically striking another child without provocation." Nothing so complicated about these definitions, right? They seem to be fairly operational and objective. But who is to say that even with these definitions that Steven and Andrea (the two raters) will identically categorize the behaviors they observe? What if Andrea sees Jill hit Elizabeth and categorizes it as a #4 behavior, but Steven categorizes it as a #5 behavior because Steve saw Elizabeth hit Jill first? You are in trouble. Raters need to be able to rate and place events in the same category.

To be sure that all raters are in agreement with one another, inter-rater reliability needs to be established. This is done by having raters "rate" behavior and then examining the percent of agreement between them. Let's say you have Andrea and Steven rate the behaviors of one child every 10 seconds as you train them on the use of the rating scale. Their pattern of choices could look something like what you see in Table 5.5. To compute their inter-rater reliability, just take the number of agreements and divide it by the number of total periods of time rated (20 in this example). In their before-training rating, the inter-rater reliability comes out to 15 (the number of agreements) divided by 20 (the number of possible agreements), which is .75 or 75%. After training, as you can see, the value has increased to 18/20 or .90 or 90%, which is quite respectable.

Before Training																				
Period	1	2	3	4	5	6	7	8	9	10	11	12	13	14	15	16	17	18	19	20
Andrea	5	5	4	5	5	3	4	2	3	2	2	3	3	3	5	3	3	4	3	4
Steven	4	5	4	4	5	3	5	2	3	2	2	3	3	3	4	3	3	5	3	4
After Training																				
Period	1	2	3	4	5	6	7	8	9	10	11	12	13	14	15	16	17	18	19	20
Andrea	5	5	4	5	5	3	5	2	3	2	2	3	3	3	5	3	3	5	3	4
Steven	4	5	4	4	5	3	5	2	3	2	2	3	3	3	5	3	3	5	3	4

Table 5.5 Inter-rater reliability before and after training. Training is the key, if the important aspects of the observation are attended to.

What did the training consist of? The head of the project probably looked at where the problems in misclassification were and reviewed the definition of behaviors and discussed examples with the raters. In Table 5.5, you can see how the most frequent problems were disagreements between ratings of a #4 behavior and a #5 behavior, which are types of hitting behaviors. Here is where any differences between raters' judgments would be clarified.

The consequences of low inter-rater reliability can be serious. If one of your raters misclassified 20% of the occurrences, it means that 20% of your data might be wrong, which can throw everything into a tizzy!

Internal Consistency

While **internal consistency** is a less frequently established form of reliability, you need to know about it as a beginning researcher. Internal consistency examines how unified the items are in a test or assessment. For example, if you are administering a personality test that contains 100 different items, you want each of these items to be related to one another as long as the model or theory upon which the test is based considers each of the 100 items to reflect the same basic personality construct. Likewise, if you were to give a test of 100 items broken down into five different subscales consisting of 20 items each, then you would expect that test to have internal consistency if the 20 items within each subscale relate more to one another than they do to the items within any of the other four subscales. If they do, then each of the scales has internal consistency.

Internal consistency is evaluated by correlating performance on each of the items in a test or a scale with total performance on the test or scale and takes the form of a correlation coefficient.

Establishing Reliability: An Example

One of the best places to look for reliability studies is in *The Mental Measurements Yearbook* (Conoley & Kramer, 1989), a compendium of summaries and reviews of tests that are currently available. As part of these reviews, the way reliability was established is often described and discussed.

For example, the *Multidimensional Aptitude Battery* is an objectively scoreable general aptitude or intelligence test for adults in the form of five verbal and five performance subtest scores. The authors of the test computed several types of reliability including test-retest correlation coefficients that ranged from .83 to .97 for the verbal scale of the test and .87 to .94 for the performance scale. They also computed other reliability indexes that provide some indication of how homogeneous or unidimensional the various tests are. In other words, the tests were found to consistently assess only one dimension of aptitude or intelligence. While the results of these reliability studies are not terribly exciting for us (but they certainly were for the authors of the test), it is crucial information that a potential user needs to know and that the author of any test needs to establish for the test to be useful.

Validity

You remember earlier in this chapter that we mentioned two essential characteristics of a good test. The first is that it be reliable, which we just discussed. The second is that it be valid, or that the test does what it is supposed to do.

A Conceptual Definition of Validity

Validity is the quality of a test doing what it is designed to do.

Remember consistency, stability, and predictability (among other synonyms for reliability)? How about *truthfulness, accuracy, authenticity, genuineness,* and *soundness* as synonyms for validity? These terms describe what **validity** is all about: that the test or instrument you are using actually measures what you need to have measured.

When you see the term *validity*, one or more of three things should come to mind about the definition and the use of the term. Keep in mind that the validity of an instrument is often defined within the context of how the test is being used. Here are the three aspects of validity.

First, validity refers to the results of a test and not to the test itself. So if we have the ABC test of social skills, the results of the test may be valid for measuring social interaction in adolescents. We talk about validity only in light of the outcomes of a test.

Second, just as with reliability (although validity is not as easily quantified), validity is never a question of "all" or "none." The results of a test are not just "valid" or "invalid." This progression occurs in degrees from low validity to high validity.

Third, the validity of the results of a test must be interpreted within the context in which the test occurs. If this were not the case, everything could be deemed to be valid just by changing its name. For example, here is one item from a 100-item test.

$$2 + 2 = ?$$

Most of you would recognize this question to have validity as a measure of addition skills. If we use the question in an experiment focusing on multiplication skills, however, the item loses its validity immediately.

The way the validity of a test should be examined, then, is whether the test focuses on the results of a study and whether the results are understood within the context of the research's purpose.

Just as with reliability, there are several types of validity that you will come across in your research activities. And you will, of course, have to consider validity when it comes time to select the instruments you intend to use to measure the dependent variable of your interest.

A summary of different types of validity, what they mean, and how they are established is shown in Table 5.6.

Type of Validity	What is It?	How Do You Do It?
Content	A measure of how well the items **represent** the entire universe of items.	Ask an expert if the items assess what you want them to.
Criterion **Concurrent**	A measure of how well a test **estimates** a criterion.	Select a criterion and correlate scores on the test with scores on the criterion in the present.
Predictive	A measure of how well a test **predicts** a criterion.	Select a criterion and correlate scores on the test with scores on the criterion in the future.
Construct	A measure of how well a test **assesses** some underlying construct.	Assess the underlying construct on which the test is based and correlate these scores with the test scores.

Table 5.6 Types of validity. As with reliability, there is an appropriate one for your research endeavor.

Types of Validity

There are four types of validity, each of which is used to establish the trustworthiness of results from a test or an assessment tool.

Content Validity

The most straightforward and simple type of validity is **content validity**. Content validity is the extent to which a test represents the universe of items from which it is drawn and is especially useful when evaluating the usefulness of achievement tests or tests that sample a particular area of knowledge.

Why just a sample? Because it is impossible to create all the possible items that could be written. Just think of the magnitude of the task! Imagine writing all the possible multiple choice items you could on the material covered (not necessarily contained) in an introductory psychology book. There must be 1 million items that conceivably could be written on the domains of personality, perception, or personality alone. You could get tired just thinking about it! That is why you sample from all the possible items that could be written.

But back to the real world. Let's say you are dealing with eighth grade history, and the unit deals with the discovery of North America and the travels and travails of several great European explorers. If you were to develop a history test that asks questions about this period and wanted to establish the validity of the questions, you could show it to an expert in early American history and ask, "Do these questions fairly represent the universe or domain of early American history?" You don't have to use such 25-cent words as "universe" and "domain," but you need to know if you have covered what you need to cover.

If your questions do the job, the sample of questions you selected to test an eighth-grader's knowledge of early American history, for example, was done as well. Congratulations. That is content validity.

Expert opinion is often used to establish content validity.

Criterion Validity

Criterion validity is concerned with how well a test either estimates present performance (called **concurrent validity**) or how well it predicts future performance (called **predictive validity**). Criterion validity is a measure of the extent to which a test is related to some criterion. Presumably the criterion with which the test is being compared has some intrinsic value as a measure of some trait or characteristic. Criterion validity is used most often to evaluate the validity of ability tests (current skills) and aptitude tests (potential skills).

In both types of criterion validity, a criterion is used as a confirmatory measure. For example, let's say you want to investigate the use of graduate school grades in predicting which people in the clinical psychology program will become especially successful researchers. To that end, you locate a sample of "good" researchers (as defined by the number of journal articles they have published in the last 20 years). Then, you would find out how well those researchers did as graduate students and how well their school performance (or grades) predicted membership in the "good" group. You might also want to locate a group of "not good" researchers (or those who did not publish at all) and compare how well their graduate school grades predicted membership in the good or not good groups. In this case, graduate school grades would have predictive validity (of success as a researcher) if grades (the test) correlated highly with performance as a researcher (the criterion).

This sounds nice and neat and clean, but who is to judge the value of the criterion? Does the number of articles published constitute good research? What if 90% of one researcher's articles are published in journals that have a rejection rate of 50% while someone else has published only one article in one journal where the rejection rate is 90%? And what if the one article someone publishes has a significant

One type of criterion validity, predictive validity, lets us know how well a test predicts future performance.

and profound effect on the direction of future research in the discipline? As with any other building block in the research process, the criterion that you use to establish validity must be selected with some rationale. In this case, you would have to provide the rationale for assuming the number of articles published, regardless of their quality, is what is important (if that is what you believe).

Another problem that occurs with both concurrent and predictive validity is the serious concern for what the tests actually measure. One assumes that if the tests correlate with the criterion, then the relationship must be meaningful. So if the results of your intelligence test correlate with eye color or nose size or the shape of the bumps on your head, does that mean you have a test with criterion validity? The answer is yes, if you think that eye color and nose size and study of bumps on the head (called phrenology, by the way) are good indicators of intelligence. Do not laugh; the history of science is filled with such well-meaning (and some not so well-meaning), but mistaken, assumptions and conclusions.

Construct Validity

Intelligence tests have high levels of construct validity.

Construct validity is the big one. It is a time-consuming and often difficult type of validity to establish, yet it is also the most desirable. Why? First a definition: **Construct validity** is the extent to which the results of a test are related to underlying psychological constructs. It links the practical components of a test score to some underlying theory or model of behavior.

For example, construct validity allows one to say that a test labeled as an "intelligence test" actually measures intelligence. How is this validity established? Let's say that based on a theory of intelligence (which has undergone some scrutiny and testing and which stands the test of time), intelligence consists of such behaviors as memory, comprehension, logical thinking, spatial skills, and reasoning. That is, intelligence is a construct represented by a group of related variables. If you develop a set of test items based on the construct and if you can show that the items reflect the contents of the construct, then you are on your way to establishing the construct validity of the test.

The first step in the development of a test that has construct validity, therefore, is to establish the validity (in the most general scientific terms) of the underlying construct on which the test will be based. This step might take study after study and years of research. Once the evidence for the validity of the construct is there, you then could move on to the design of a test that reflects the construct.

There are a variety of ways in which construct validity can be established.

First, as with criterion validity, you can look for the correlation between the test you are developing and some established test that has already been shown to possess construct validity. This is a bit of a "chicken and egg" problem since there is always the question of how construct validity was first established.

Second, you can show that the scores on the newly designed test will differ between groups of people with and without certain traits or characteristics. For example, if you are developing a test of aggression, you might want to compare the results for people known to be aggressive with those who are not.

Third, you can analyze the task requirements of the items and see if these requirements are consistent with the theory underlying the development of the test. If your theory of intelligence says that memory is important, you would then expect to have items that tap this ability on your test.

Establishing Validity: An Example

Speaking of intelligence, here is how three researchers (Krohn, Lampl, and Phelps, 1988) went about exploring the construct validity of the relatively new Kaufman Assessment Battery for Children (K-ABC).

The issue these researchers attacked is a familiar one: Is a test that is valid for one group of people (white preschoolers) valid for another group as well (black preschoolers)? To answer this question, the researchers used perhaps the most common strategy for establishing construct validity. They examined the correlation between the test in question and some other established and valid measure of intelligence. In this case, it was the Stanford-Binet Intelligence Scale, the most widely used intelligence test for young children.

I hope you are asking yourself, "If a widely used and presumably good test of intelligence exists, why go through the trouble to create another?" Very good question. The answer is that the developers of the K-ABC (Kaufman and Kaufman, 1983) believe that intelligence should tap cognitive abilities more than previous tests have allowed. The K-ABC measures both intelligence and achievement and is based on a theoretical orientation that is tied less to culture than to tests such as the Stanford-Binet and the Wechsler Scale of Intelligence for Children (known as the WISC).

In the Krohn, Lampl, and Phelps study (1988), the researchers tested the same children using both the K-ABC and the Stanford-Binet and found that the K-ABC had substantial support as a measure of intelligence in the population of black preschool children from which the sample was selected.

A test can be reliable but not valid, but the reverse cannot be true.

The Relationship Between Reliability and Validity

The relationship between reliability and validity is straightforward and easy to understand. It goes like this: A test can be reliable, but not valid, but a test cannot be valid without first being reliable. In other words, reliability is a necessary, but not sufficient, condition of validity.

For example, let's go back to that 100-item test. Here is the same example we used before:

$$2 + 2 = ?$$

Now, we can guarantee that this is a reliable item because it is likely to result in a consistent assessment of whether the person taking the test knows simple addition. But what if we named it a spelling test? It is obviously not a test of spelling and would certainly be invalid as such. This lack of validity, though, does not affect its reliability.

This might be an extreme example, but it holds true throughout the assessment of behavior. A test may be reliable and consistently assess some outcome, but unless that outcome addresses the issue being studied it is not valid. End of argument!

A Closing Thought

The measurement process is incredibly important and, like so many of the other things that guide researchers' work, is not simple. It is an area of endeavor filled with its share of controversies and new ideas. Let me plant one idea in your thinking that illustrates how generative and filled with potential the study of measuring human behavior is.

In a recent article in the prestigious scientific journal *Science*, Michelle Lampl and her colleagues (Lampl, et al., 1992), undertook a study that was implicitly suggested by a friend's comment on how fast Lampl's young baby was growing (as in your mother's report to your grandmother, "he shot up overnight!"). Doctors usually check infants' height and weight every month in the beginning and then every few months as they get older. Well, these researchers decided to see if babies really do grow in particularly fast spurts. So, the researchers measured babies' growth over an extended period of time. What did they find? You will be amazed to learn that some infants grew as much as 1 whole inch in a 24-hour period! What is the big deal? Well, the average length of infants of that age is about 20 inches, and the change represents about a 5% increase. If you are an average male adult (about 5' 10") and you grew 5% in a day, you would be about 6' 2", and if you are an average female (about 5' 4") you would be about 5' 7". Now about those new pants you need...

The lesson is that there are undoubtedly thousands of things going on in the social and behavioral sciences that we either don't notice because we don't measure them appropriately (not intentionally but because that is the way X or Y has been measured before) or because we might be making the wrong assumptions (such as that infant's growth occurs in smooth fashion with no abrupt changes). Most important, what researchers know about human behavior depends ultimately on how they measure what they are interested in studying. In other words, the measurement technique used and the questions asked go hand and hand and are very closely related, both in substance and method.

Want to cut corners in your research? Don't, but if you have to, don't ignore anything about the measurement process.

There is no argument about it; the measurement process is a critical part of putting together a research project and seeing it through to fruition. This part of the research project is especially important, since a test without the appropriate levels of reliability or validity is no use to you or anybody else. Using poorly designed measurement tools leads you down the path of never knowing whether you are on the right track or you never really accurately measured what you want. Use your good sense, and look around for instruments that have already been shown to have respectable levels of reliability and validity. It will save you time, trouble, and endless headaches.

Exercises

1. Identify the level of measurement associated with each of the variables listed here:
   a. spelling test score
   b. neighborhood
   c. age in years
   d. color expressed as wavelength
   e. grade-point average
   f. color of stimulus objects
   g. time for 100-yard dash
   h. after school club choice
   i. IQ score
   j. grade

2. Indicate which of the sources of error in reliability are trait (t) and which are method (m).
   a. not enough sleep the night before the test
   b. poor test instructions
   c. a test proctor who walks around too much
   d. poorly printed and difficult to read instructions
   e. age

3. Describe two ways the reliability of a test can be established, and explain the purpose of each of them.

4. You have just developed the ABC Test of History, which contains 100 items and tests a student's knowledge of history. What kind of validity would you need for a test like this, and how would you establish it?

5. What are some tests you have taken that were assumed to have predictive validity?

6. Define the phrase *level of measurement*.

7. Name the four levels of measurement, and provide an example of each.

8. What is the relationship between reliability and validity?

Want to Know More?

Further Readings

Adrien, J. L., Barthelemy, C., Perro, A., & Roux, S. (1992). Validity and reliability of the infant behavioral summarized evaluation (IBSE): A rating scale for the assessment of young children with autism and developmental disorders. *Journal of Autism and Developmental Disorders 22(3),* 375-394.

> Investigates the reliability and validity of the IBSE comparing samples of children with autism, children with mental retardation, and normally developing children. The IBSE was developed the assess the behaviors of young children with autistic disorders.

Bers, T. H., & Smith, K. E. (1990). Assessing assessment programs: The theory and practice of examining reliability and validity of a writing placement test. *Community College Review, 18(3),* 17-27.

> Describes a study of the validity and reliability of a writing skills assessment test. Looks at inter-rater reliability and predictive validity.

Jordan, J. (1989). Effects of race on inter-rater reliability of peer ratings. *Psychological Reports, 64,* 1221-1222.

> Illustrates how to compute inter-rater reliability. Shows inter-rater reliability scores appeared to be influenced by ethnic background of the rater and of the people being rated.

Readings of Other Interest

Gould, S. J. (1981). *The mismeasure of man.* New York: Norton.

> What can go wrong with testing intelligence? This entertaining science writer, paleontologist, Harvard professor, and fan of baseball and dinosaurs recounts how the assessment of intelligence has been used and abused.

Huot, B. (1990). Reliability, validity, and holistic scoring: What we know and what we need to know. *College Composition and Communication, 41(2),* 201-213.

> Discusses the impact holistic scoring has had on writing assessments. Looks at the importance of high inter-rater reliability and discusses the need for greater concern with validity in this review of holistic scoring.

CHAPTER

6

SIX

Methods of Measuring Behavior

What You'll Learn About in this Chapter

- The use of different methods of measuring behavior and collecting data
- What a test is
- How different types of tests are designed to assess different types of behavior
- The use of achievement tests in the behavioral and social sciences
- The design of multiple choice items
- How to do an item analysis
- The application of attitude scales
- The difference between a Thurstone and a Likert attitude scale
- How questionnaires are designed, and how they work

In Chapter 5, you got a healthy dose of the theoretical issues that provide the foundation for the science of measurement, why measurement is crucial to the research process, how reliability and validity are defined, and how each of these can be established.

In this chapter, you will begin learning about the application of some of these principles as you read about different methods that can be used to measure behavior, including the ubiquitous "test," questionnaire, interview, and other techniques.

As you read this chapter, keep several things in mind. Your foremost concern in deciding what method you will use to measure the behavior of interest should be whether the tool you intend to use is a reliable and valid one. This goes for the best-designed test and for the most informal-appearing interview. If your test does not "work," then virtually nothing else will.

Second, the way you ask your question will determine the way you go about measuring the variables(s) you are interested in. If you want to know about how people feel toward a particular issue, then you are talking about attitudinal scales. If you want to know how much information people have about a particular subject, then you are talking about an achievement test or some other measure of knowledge. The focus of a study (such as the effects of day care) might be the same, whether you measure attitude or achievement, but what you use to assess your outcome variable depends on the question you ask. You need to decide the intent of your research activity, which in turn reflects your original research question and hypothesis.

Finally, keep in mind that methods vary widely in the time it takes to learn how to use them, in the measurement process itself, and in what you can do with the information once you have collected it. For example, an interview might be appropriate to determine how teachers feel about changes in the school administration, but interviewing would not be very useful if you were interested in assessing physical strength.

So here is an overview of a variety of measurement tools. Like any other tool, use the one you choose well, and you will be handsomely rewarded. Likewise, if you use the tool incorrectly, the job may not get done at all, and even if it does the quality and value of your finished report will be less than what you expected.

Where else would be better to start than with the measurement method that all of us have been exposed to time and again: the good ol' test.

Tests and Their Development

In the most general terms, the purpose of a **test** is to measure the nature and the extent of individual differences. For example, you might want to assess teenagers' knowledge of how AIDS is contracted. Or you may be interested in differences that exist on some measure of personality such as the Myers-Briggs Type Indicator or an intelligence test such as the Wechsler Adult Intelligence Scale. Tests also are instruments that distinguish among people on such measures as reaction time or physical strength and agility or the strategy someone selects to solve a problem. Not all tests use paper and pencil, and the technique that a researcher uses to assess a behavior often reflects his or her creativity.

A good test should be able to reliably differentiate people from one another based on their scores. Before going on, just a few words of clarification. The word *test* is being used throughout this chapter to indicate a tool or technique to assess behavior but should not be used synonymously with the term *dependent variable*. While you may use a test to assess some outcome, you may also use it for categorization purposes. For example, you want to investigate the effectiveness of behavior therapy and medication on compulsive disorders. You might use a test to categorize subjects into severe or mild categories and then use another test to evaluate the effectiveness of each treatment.

Why Use Tests?

Tests are highly popular in the assessment of social and behavioral outcomes because they serve a very specific purpose. They yield a score that reflects performance on some variable (such as intelligence, reaction time, or activity level), and they can fill a variety of the researcher's needs, as summarized in Table 6.1.

What They Do	How They Do It	An Example
Help researchers determine the outcome of a study	Tests are used as dependent variables	A researcher wants to know which of two training programs is more effective
Help provide diagnostic and screening information	Tests are usually administered at the beginning of a program to get some idea of the person's status	A teacher needs to know what type of reading program in which a particular child should be placed.
Help in the placement process	Tests are used to place people in different settings based on specified characteristics	A mental health worker needs to place a client into a drug rehabilitation program
Assist in selection	Tests are used to distinguish between people who are admitted to certain programs	A graduate school committee uses test scores to make decisions about admitting undergraduates
Help evaluate outcomes	Tests are used to determine if the goals of a program were met	A school superintendent uses a survey to measure whether the in-service programs had an impact on teacher's attitudes

Table 6.1 What tests do, and how they do it.

First and foremost, tests *help researchers determine the outcome of an experiment*. Quite simply, they are the measuring stick by which the effectiveness of a treatment is judged or the status of a variable such as height or voting preference in a sample is assessed. Since test results help us determine the value of an experiment, they can also be used to help us build and test hypotheses.

Second, tests can be used as *diagnostic and screening tools*, where they provide insight into an individual's strengths and weaknesses. For example, the Denver Developmental Screening Test (DDST) assesses young children's language, social, physical, and personal development. While it is a general screening test at best, it provides important information about a child's status and developmental areas that might need attention.

Third, tests assist in *placement*. For example, children who missed the date for kindergarten entrance in their school district could take a battery of tests to see if they have the skills to enter public school early. High school students often take advanced placement courses and then "test out" of basic required college courses. In these two cases, test scores assist when a recommendation is made as to where someone should be placed in a program.

Fourth, tests *assist in selection*. Who will get into graduate school is often determined at least in part by an applicant's score on such tests as the Graduate Record Examination or the Miller's Analogy Test. Businesses often conduct tests to screen individuals before they are hired to be sure they have the basic skills necessary to complete training and perform competently.

Finally, tests are used to *evaluate the outcomes* of a program. Until you collect information that relates to the question you asked and then act on that information, you never really know whether the program you are assessing had, for example, the impact you sought. If you are interested in evaluating the effectiveness of a psychotherapy program on depression, it is unlikely you can judge without some type of formal evaluation.

What Tests Look Like

You might be most familiar with achievement-type tests, which usually include multiple choice items such as

The cube root of 8 is
   a)   2
   b)   4
   c)   6
   d)   8

Tests can take many different forms depending upon their design and purpose.

Multiple choice questions are common items on many of the tests you will take throughout your college career. But tests can take on a variety of appearances, especially when you have to meet the needs of the people being tested and to sample the behavior you are interested in learning more about.

For example, you would not expect people who have a severe visual impairment to take a pencil and paper test where they have to darken small circles placed closely together. Similarly, if you want to know about children's social interactions with their peers, you are probably better served by observing them play than by asking them about playing.

With such considerations in mind, you need to decide on the form a test might take. Some of the questions that will arise in deciding how a test should appear and be administered are

- Is the test administered using paper and pencil, or is it administered some other way?
- What is the nature of the behavior being assessed (cognitive? social? physical?)?
- Do people report their own behavior (self-report), or is their behavior observed?
- Is the test timed, or is there no time limit?
- Are the responses to the items subjective in nature (where the scoring is somewhat arbitrary) or objective (where there are clearly defined rules for scoring)?
- Is the test given in a group or individually?
- Are the test takers required to recognize the correct response (such as in a multiple choice test) or to provide one (such as in a fill-in item or an open-ended question)?

Exploring Research

Types of Tests

Tests are designed for a particular purpose: to assess an outcome whose value distinguishes different individuals from one another. Since there are many different types of outcomes that might be measured, there are different types of tests that can do the job. For example, if you want to know how well a group of high school seniors understood a recent physics lesson, an achievement test would be appropriate.

On the other hand, if you are interested in better understanding the structure of an individual's personality, then a test such as the Minnesota Multiphasic Personality Inventory or the Thematic Apperception Test, two popular yet quite different tests of personality, would be more appropriate.

What follows is a discussion of some of the main types of tests you will run into in your research work, how they are different from one another, and how they can best be utilized.

Achievement Tests

Achievement tests are used to measure knowledge of a specific area. They are the most commonly used tests when the outcome being measured is learning. They are also used to measure the effectiveness of the instruction that accompanied the learning. For example, school districts sometimes use students' scores on achievement tests to evaluate teacher effectiveness.

Achievement tests are used to assess expertise in a content area.

The spelling test you took every Friday in fourth grade, your final exam in freshman English, and your midterm in chemistry were all achievement tests for the same reason: They were designed to evaluate how well you understood specific information. Achievement tests come in all flavors, from the common multiple choice test, to true-false and essay examinations. All have their strengths and weaknesses.

There are basically two types of achievement tests, those that are standardized and those that are researcher-made. **Standardized tests** are usually produced by commercial publishers and have broad application across a variety of different settings. What distinguishes a standardized test from others is that it comes with a set of instructions and scoring procedures that are standard. For example, the Kansas Minimum Competency Test is a standardized test that has been administered to more than 1 million children across the state of Kansas in rural and urban settings, from very different social classes, school sizes, and backgrounds. Or, take the California Achievement Test (CAT), a nationally standardized test of achievement in the areas of reading, language, and arithmetic.

Researcher-made tests, on the other hand, are designed for a much more specific purpose and are limited in their application to a much smaller number of people. For example, the test that you might take in this course would most likely be researcher (or teacher) made and designed specifically for the content of this course. Another example would be a test designed by a researcher to determine whether the use of teaching machines versus traditional teaching makes a difference in the learning of a foreign language.

Achievement tests can also be broken down into two other categories. Both standardized and researcher-made tests can be norm-referenced or criterion-referenced.

A **norm-referenced test** is one where you can compare an individual's test performance to the test performance of other individuals. For example, if an 8-year-old student receives a score of 56 on a mathematics test, you can use the norms that supplied with the test to determine that child's placement relative to other 8-year-olds. Standardized tests are usually accompanied by norms, but this is usually not the case for researcher-made tests nor is the existence of norms a necessary condition for a test to be considered standardized. Remember, a test is standardized only if it has a standard or common set of administration and scoring procedures.

A **criterion-referenced test** (a term coined by psychologist Robert Glaser in 1963) is one where a specific criterion or level of performance is defined, and the only thing of importance is the individual's performance regardless of where that performance might stand in comparison to others. In this case, performance is defined as a function of mastery of some content domain. For example, if you were to specify a set of objectives for 12th-grade history and specify that students must show command of 90% of those objectives to pass, then you would be implying that the criterion is 90% mastery. Because this type of test actually focuses on the mastery of content at a specific level, it is also referred to as content-referenced testing.

When to use which? First, you have to make this decision before you begin designing a test or searching for one to use in your research. The basic question you want to answer is whether you are interested in knowing how well an individual performs relative to others (for which you need norms to make the comparison) or how well the individual has mastered a particular area of content (for which the mastery is reflected in the criterion you use).

Second, any achievement test, regardless of its content, can fall into one of the four cells shown in Table 6.2, which illustrates the two dimensions just described: Does the test compare results to other individuals or to some criterion, and who designed or authored the test.

Does the test compare results to other individuals or to some criterion?		
Who designed the test?	**Norm-Referenced**	**Criterion-Referenced**
Standardized	This type of test comes with a standard set of instructions for administration and scoring and performance is compared to that of another similar group of individuals.	This type of test comes with a standard set of instructions for administration and scoring and is designed so that individual performance can be compared to a specified criterion.
Researcher Made	This type of test is used to assess performance across some relatively narrow knowledge domain as compared to that of other individuals.	This type of test is used to assess performance across some relatively narrow knowledge domain as compared to a predefined criterion.

Table 6.2 Classifying achievement tests as norm- or criterion-referenced and as standardized or researcher-designed.

Multiple Choice Achievement Items

Remember those endless hours filling in "bubbles" on optical-scanner scoring sheets or circling the A's, B's, C's, and D's, guessing which answer might be correct or not, and being told not to guess if you have no idea what the correct answer is? All these experiences are part of multiple choice questions, by far the most widely used type of question on achievement tests and a type that deserves special attention.

What a Multiple Choice Item Looks Like

A multiple choice question has its own special anatomy, as shown in Figure 6.1. First, there is the *stem* which has the purpose of setting the question or posing the problem. Second, there is the set of *alternatives* or *options*. One of these options must be the correct answer (alternative A in this example), while the three others (in this example) should act as *distracters*.

The stem of a multiple choice question should be clearly stated and well written.

---

12. Intelligence tests given to preschool children

    A.   favor middle class children.
    B.   have questionable construct validity.
    C.   are based on motor skills.
    D.   are no fun at all.

Figure 6.1 A sample multiple choice item.

A good distracter is one that is attractive enough that a person who does not know the right answer might find the distractor to be plausible. Distractors that are far removed from reality (such as alternative D in Figure 6.1) are easily ruled out by the test taker and contribute to the lack of validity and reliability of the test. Why? Because the presence of poor distractors makes it even more difficult for the test to be an accurate estimator of a test taker's true score.

To Use or Not to Use?

Multiple choice questions are ideal for assessing the level of knowledge that an individual has about a specific content domain such as home economics, child development, geology, chemistry, Latin, fiber optics, sewing, or volleyball. But whatever the content of the test, the items must be written with the original objectives in mind of the lessons, chapters, papers, lectures, and other instruction that the test takers were exposed to. If your Geology 1 professor did not have as an objective the distinction between different types of land forms, items on distinguishing land forms should not be on the test. In other words, the content of a multiple choice test should unequivocally reflect the content and objectives from which the items are drawn.

Multiple choice items have both clear advantages and disadvantages.

There are several advantages and disadvantages to using multiple choice items on an achievement test. These should be taken into consideration if you intend to use such a test to assess a knowledge-based outcome. Here are some advantages:

■ They can be used to assess almost any content domain.
■ They are relatively easy to score and can be easily machine-scored.
■ Test takers do not have to write out elaborate answers but just select one of the test item's alternatives.

- Since multiple choice items focus on knowledge and not writing, people who are not good writers are not necessarily penalized for being unable to show what they know.
- Good items are an investment in the future since they can be used over again, saving you preparation time.
- Good distractors can help a teacher diagnose the nature of the test taker's failure to get the answer correct.
- It is difficult to fake getting the answer correct, since the odds (such as .25 with four alternatives including one correct answer) are stacked against it.

But do not forget that there are some liabilities to multiple choice items as well:

- They limit students' options to generate creative answers.
- There is no opportunity to practice writing.
- Some people just do not like them and do not do well on them.
- A multiple choice type of question limits the kind of content that can be assessed.
- Items must be very well written, or bright students will detect poorly written alternatives and eliminate those as viable distractors.

Item Analysis: How to Tell If Your Items Work

A multiple choice item is a good one if it does one thing very well, and that is if it discriminates between those who know the information on the test and those who do not. For example, an item that everyone gets correct is of no use since it does not tell the examiner who knows the material and who does not. Similarly, an item that everyone gets wrong provides as little information about the test taker's understanding of the material. In other words, and in both cases, the item does not discriminate.

Wouldn't it be nice if there were some numerical indexes of how good a multiple choice item really is? Wait no longer! **Item analysis** generates two such indexes: difficulty level and discrimination level. Using these powerful tools, you can easily assess the value of an item and whether it should be kept in the item pool (the collection of multiple choice items in a specific content area), revised, or tossed in the can!

The two measures that *psychometricians* (now isn't that a fancy name for people who study measurement?) use are the difficulty index and discrimination index, two independent but complementary measures of an individual item's effectiveness. Before either of these indexes is computed, the total number of test scores has to be divided into a "high" group and a "low" group. To create these two groups, follow these steps:

1. Rank all the test scores from the highest to the lowest, so that the highest score is at the top of the list.
2. Call the high group the top 27% of the test scores.
3. Call the low group the bottom 27% of the test scores.

For example, if you have 150 adults in your sample, then the top 41 scores (or 27% of 150) would be in the high group, and the bottom 41 scores would be in the low group.

Why 27%? That number is magic, because it is the amount that maximizes the discrimination between the two groups. If you remember, you want to compute the difficulty and discrimination indexes to contrast groups of people who perform well with those who do not perform well.

4. For each item, examine the number of alternatives that were chosen by constructing the type of table you see in Table 6.3. For example, 23 people in the high group selected alternative item A (which is the correct response), and 6 people in the low group selected alternative D.

You can maximize discrimination by including items that are moderately difficult.

12. Intelligence tests given to preschool children					
A. favor middle class children.					
B. have questionable construct validity.					
C. are based on motor skills.					
D. are no fun at all.					
Alternative	***A**	**B**	**C**	**D**	**E**
High Group (n=41)	23	12	4	2	41
Low Group (n=41)	11	9	15	6	41
Total	34	21	19	8	82

Difficulty index = .41
Discrimination Index = .29

Table 6.3 Data for computing difficulty and discrimination indexes.

The **difficulty index** is simply the proportion of test takers who got the item correct. The formula is

$$D = \frac{NC_h + NC_l}{T}$$

where D = difficulty level
  NC_h = number of people in the high group who got the item correct
  NC_l = number of people in the low group who got the item correct
  T = total number of people in the low and high groups

In this example, the difficulty level is

$$D = \frac{23 + 11}{82} = .41$$

meaning that the average difficulty level for that item is .41 or 41%, a moderately difficult item. (If everyone got the item wrong, the difficulty level would be 0%.)

The **discrimination index** is a bit more complicated. It is the proportion of test takers in the upper group who got the item correct minus the proportion of test takers in the lower group who got the item correct. This value can range from -1.00 to +1.00. A discrimination index of +1.00 means that the item discriminates perfectly; all the people in the high group got the item correct while all the people in the low group got the item incorrect. Likewise, if the index is -1.00, this means that everyone in the low group got the item correct, while none of the high-scoring people got the item correct (not really the way it should be!).

To compute the discrimination index, use this formula:

$$d = \frac{NC_h - NC_l}{(.5)T}$$

where d = discrimination level
NC_h = number of people in the high group who got the item correct
NC_l = number of people in the low group who got the item correct
T = total number of people in the low and high groups

In this example, the discrimination level is

$$d = \frac{23 - 11}{(.5)\,82} = .29$$

or 29%. You want items that discriminate between the "knowing" and the "unknowing" but are not too easy or too hard. Figure 6.2 shows how items can discriminate perfectly only when the difficulty level is at 50%. As difficulty increases or decreases, discrimination is constrained. You can work on both the discrimination as well as the difficulty level in an effort to make your items better.

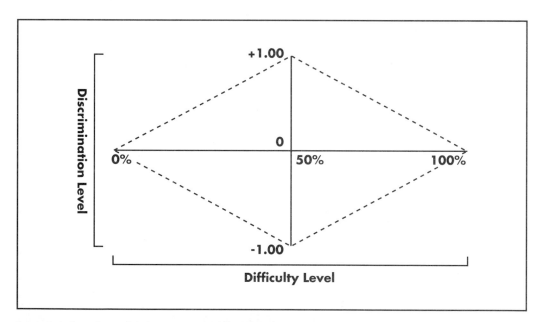

Figure 6.2 The relationship between item difficulty and item discrimination indexes.

Keep track of the discrimination and difficulty indexes in a file of index cards.

To change the difficulty level, try increasing or decreasing the attractiveness of the alternatives. If you change the attractiveness of the alternatives, you will also find that the value of the discrimination will change. For example, if an incorrect alternative becomes more attractive, it is likely that it will discriminate more effectively since it will fool those folks who almost—but not quite—know the right answer.

While computing these indexes can be a painstaking job, they are just about the only way you can tell whether an item is doing the job that it should. Many people who regularly use multiple choice items suggest that you do the following to help track your items.

Each time you write an item, do it on a 3" by 5" index card. On the back of the card enter the date of the test administration (and any other information you might deem important). Under the date add any comments you might have, and record the difficulty and discrimination indexes for that particular test item. Then, as you work with these test items in the future, you will develop a file of test items with varying degrees of difficulty and discrimination levels. These items can be reused or altered as needed.

In order for you to maximally discriminate between groups, try to adjust the difficulty level of the item (which to a large extent is under the control of the researcher) so that it comes as close as possible to the 50% mark.

Attitude Tests

Whereas achievement tests are probably the most used type of test in our society (think of all those Friday afternoon spelling tests!), other types are used in a variety of research applications.

Among these are **attitude tests**, which assess an individual's feelings about an object, person, or event. Attitude scales are used when you are interested in knowing how someone feels about a particular thing, whether it be preference for a brand of microwave popcorn or feelings about euthanasia legislation.

For example, Figure 6.3 illustrates the basic format of a simple attitude scale. A statement is presented, and then the individual indicates his or her attitude along some scale such as "Agree," "No Strong Feeling," and "Disagree." The selection of items to include and the design of the scale are tricky tasks that should not be undertaken lightly. Let's look at two of the standard methodologies used for creating two types of scales, the Thurstone and the Likert scales, and see how they are developed.

Item	Agree	No Strong Feeling	Disagree
The day before Thanksgiving should be a holiday.	_____	_____	_____
Final exams should be elective. The dining hall should serve gourmet food.	_____	_____	_____
My parents don't appreciate how smart I am.	_____	_____	_____
My professors don't appreciate how smart I am.	_____	_____	_____

Figure 6.3 A simple attitude scale.

Thurstone Scales

L. L. Thurstone was a famous psychometrician who developed the **Thurstone scale**, a method of measuring attitudes. He reasoned that if you could find out what value experts placed on a set of statements, then these statements could be scaled. People's

Thurstone scales come very close to an interval level of measurement.

responses to these statements would indicate their attitude about the item in question. Here are the steps involved in the development of such a scale:

1. As many statements as possible are written as potential test items. For example, if one was looking at parents' attitudes toward school, some of these items might be
   a. I like the way my child's teacher greets him/her in the morning.
   b. The principal does not communicate effectively with the teachers.
   c. My child's education and potential are at risk.
   d. School lunches are healthy and nutritious.
2. Judges, who are knowledgeable about the area of interest, place the statements into 11 (actual physically different) stacks, ranging from the least favorable statement to the most favorable statement. Stack 6 (being right in the middle), represents a neutral statement. For example, Item C above might be rated 1, 2, 3, 4, or 5 because it appears to be somewhat unfavorable.
3. Those statements rated consistently (with low variability) by judges are given the average score according to their placement. For example, if Item A were rated as being 9 or 10 (somewhere around very favorable), it could receive a scale value of 9.5.
4. A group of statements then is selected that covers the entire range from unfavorable to favorable. That is your attitude scale.

One of the major advantages of Thurstone-like scales is that they are as close to the interval level of measurement as one can get, since the judges who rated the items placed them in stacks that have (presumably) equal distances between points that reflect psychological differences. It is for this reason that a Thurstone scale is also referred to as the method of *equal-appearing intervals*.

Respondents are asked to check off items on which they agree. Since the scale value assigned to the items that were checked off is known, an attitude score can be easily computed. If a person checks off many different items with scale values that are not around the same, then either the individual's attitude is not consistent or not well formed, or the scale has not been developed properly.

For example, here are some items on attitudes toward church from Thurstone's classic work on attitude measurement, *The Measurement of Attitudes* (1929). Accompanying each item is its scale value.

> *I believe the church is the greatest institution in America today. (11)*
> *I believe in religion, but I seldom go to church. (9.6)*
> *I believe in sincerity and goodness without any church ceremonies. (6.7)*
> *I believe the church is a hindrance to religion for it still depends upon magic, superstition, and myth. (5.4)*
> *I think the church is a parasite on society. (.2)*

It should be clear that the item with a scale value of 5.4 is more neutral in content than any of the others.

Likert Scales

Likert scales are the most popular type of attitude scale.

The **Likert scale** (Likert, 1932) is simple to develop and widely used. Although its construction is similar to a Thurstone scale, its development is less time-consuming.

Here are the steps involved in the development of a Likert scale:

1. Statements are written that express an opinion or feeling about an event, object, or person. For example, if one was looking at attitude toward federal support for child care, items might look like this:
   a. The federal government has no business supporting day care.
   b. Day care is an issue that the federal government should fully support.
   c. Tax money should be used to fund day care programs.
2. Items that have clear positive and negative values (which is the developer's judgment) are selected.
3. The statements are listed, and to the right of each statement is a space for the respondent to indicate degree of agreement or disagreement, using a 5-point scale such as:

        SA Strongly Agree
        A   Agree
        U   Undecided
        D   Disagree
        SD Strongly Disagree

Respondents are asked to circle or check their level of agreement with each item, as you see in Figure 6.4.

Directions: Indicate to what extent you agree or disagree with each of the statements listed below by circling one of the following:

SA means you *strongly agree* with the statement
A   means you *agree* with the statement
U   means you are *undecided* about the statement
D   means you *disagree* with the statement
SD means you *strongly disagree* with the statement

Item	Rating				
The federal government has no business funding child care programs.	SA ○	A ✔	U ○	D ○	SD ○
Day care is an issue that the federal government should fully support.	SA ○	A ○	U ○	D ○	SD ✔
Tax money should be used to fund day care programs.	SA ○	A ○	U ○	D ○	SD ✔

Figure 6.4 A set of Likert items.

Likert scales are scored by assigning a weight to each point along the scale, and an individual's score is the average across all items. But it is not that simple. Since items can be "reversed" (such as where some are stated in the negative, for example, "I do not like school"), you have to be consistent and reverse the scale when you score these items. The rule is that favorable items ("I like school") are rated 5 through 1 with 5 representing Strongly Agree. Unfavorable items ("I do not like school") are rated 1 through 5 as well, with 1 representing Strongly Agree. This way, higher scores always reflect more positive attitudes.

In the example in Figure 6.4, the first item is written in the negative, and the last two are written as positive expressions. Given the choices you see in Figure 6.4, the scoring for these three figures would be

Item	Rating	Score
1	A	2
2	SD	1
3	SD	1

producing a score of (2 + 1 + 1)/3 or 1.3, indicating a relatively strong level of general disagreement. Remember, Item 1 was scored in reverse fashion because it is stated in the negative. Because you sum ratings, the development of a Likert scale is often referred to as the *method of summated ratings*.

Personality Tests

Personality tests assess stable individual behavior patterns and are the most common type of test listed in the *Buros Mental Measurement Yearbook* (Conoley & Kramer, 1989). While personality tests can be very valuable assessment tools, they are extremely time-consuming to develop and require training for the administration, scoring, and interpretation of the scores.

There are basically two types of personality tests, projective tests and structured tests.

Projective tests present the respondent a somewhat ambiguous stimulus and then ask the person to formulate some type of response. The assumption underlying these types of tests is that the person being tested will project (or impose) his or her own view of the world on the stimuli and that these responses will form a pattern that the trained person administering the test can evaluate.

Scoring these kinds of tests and reaching conclusions about personality patterns and behavior are not pie-in-the-sky stuff. Psychologists know that certain types of personalities respond in characteristic patterns. But to be able to recognize those patterns takes a great deal of time, training, and practice. Examples of these tests are the Thematic Apperception Test and the Rorschach Test.

Structured tests use a format that you might be familiar with, such as true-false, multiple choice, or yes-no. In these tests people are asked to agree or disagree with an item that describes their feelings toward themselves (such as, "I like myself"). Examples of these tests are the Sixteen Personality Factor Questionnaire and the Minnesota Multiphasic Personality Inventory. One of the major advantages of the structured over the projective test is that the structured test is objective in its item design and easy to score. In fact, the publishers of these (and many other types of tests for that matter) offer scoring services. However, the test's being easy to score has nothing to do with interpreting the results of the test. Have no doubts, personality tests are best left to the "big boys" and "big girls" who have the skills and who have had the training. In fact, most publishers of personality tests will not sell you the materials until you can show proof of training (such as a Ph.D.) or have a trained person (such as your adviser) vouch for you.

Observational Techniques

You may be most familiar with the type of test results that include a child or adult *taking* a test. That kind of test makes the respondent the active agent in the measurement process. In an entirely different class of behavior assessment methods the researcher, such as yourself, becomes the active agent. These are known as observational methods or observational techniques. It is where the researcher stands outside of the behavior being observed and creates a log, notes, or an audio or video record of the behavior.

Many terms are used to describe observational activity, several of which have been taken from the work done by anthropologists and ethologists such as *field work* or *naturalistic observation*. The most important point to remember about observational methods is why they have been so useful to scientists in other disciplines; that is, their primary goal is to record behavior without interfering with it. As an observer, you should make every effort to stay clear of the behavior you are observing so that you are nonobtrusive and do not interfere with it.

For example, if you are interested in studying play behavior among children with and without handicaps, you will be well served to observe them from afar rather than to become a part of their setting. Your being on top of them while they play can undoubtedly have an impact upon their behavior.

Techniques for Recording Behavior

There are several different techniques that can used to observe and record behavior in the field, and they fall into four general categories.

The first category is **duration recording**. Here, the researcher uses a device to keep track of time and measures the length of time that a behavior occurs. For example, the researcher might be interested in knowing how much physical activity occurs during kindergartner's morning recess. He or she might use a stopwatch to record the length of time that physical activity takes place for one child, then go on to another child, and so forth. He or she is recording the duration of a particular event.

The second major technique category for observing behavior is **frequency recording**, where the incidence or frequency of the occurrence of a particular behavior is charted. For example, a researcher might want to record the number of times that a shopper picks up and feels the fabric of which clothes are made or the number of comments made about a particular brand of soap.

Next on the list is **interval recording** or **time sampling**, where a particular subject is observed during a particular interval of time. For example, the researcher might observe each child in a play group for 15 seconds, record the target behaviors, and then move on to the next child for his or her 15 seconds. Here, the interval deals with the time the observer focuses on a particular subject, regardless of what the subject might be doing.

Finally, **continuous recording** is where all of the behavior of the target subject is recorded with little concern as to the specificity of its content. Often, people who complete case studies observe a child for a particular length of time and have no previously designated set of behaviors to look for. Rather, the behaviors that are recorded are those that occur in the natural stream of events. This is a rich and fruitful way of collecting information but has the major disadvantage that the little planning that goes into recording the information necessitates intensive sifting through of the records at analysis time.

In Table 6.4, you can find a summary of these four different kinds of techniques, what each kind does, and an example of each.

Why would these types of techniques not be attractive? The primary reason is that the very act of observing some behaviors interferes with the actual behavior researchers may want to study. For example, have you ever walked into an elementary school classroom and noticed that all the children look at you? Some children may even put on a bit of a show for you. Sooner or later that type of behavior on the part of the children would settle down, but you certainly are not going to get a view of what occurs there uninfluenced. The key word, then, is unobtrusive—observing behavior without changing the nature of what is being observed.

Technique	How it works	Example
Duration recording	The researcher records the length of time that a behavior occurs.	How much time is spent in verbal interaction between two children?
Frequency recording	The researcher records the number of times a behavior occurs.	How many times are questions asked?
Interval recording	The researcher observes a subject for a fixed amount of time.	Within a 60-second period, how many times do members of the group talk to another person?
Continuous recording	The researcher records everything that happens.	During a one-hour period, all the behavior of a six-year-old boy is recorded.

Table 6.4 Four different ways to observe behavior.

The use of four different techniques has been eased greatly by the introduction and availability of easy to use technology. For example, you need not sit and continuously observe a group of adults making a decision when you can videotape the group and then go back to do an in-depth analysis of their behaviors. Similarly, rather than using a pencil and paper to record behavior every 10 seconds, you can use your personal computer to beep every 10 seconds, and then you can just press a key to enter the category of the behavior.

The only caveat I have about the increasing role of technology (which makes data collection much easier and more reliable) is that the student of research techniques may never have the experience of using the technique to gather information. Time sampling, for example, is a good and useful technique that you should experience. Then you can use your fancy-shmancy personal computer to go from there.

Any such collection of data needs to be done with particular attention to such concerns as anonymity and respect for the person being observed (much of what was addressed in chapter 2). For example, you have to pick and choose where and how you do your observing. While it might be very interesting to listen in on the private talk of adolescents in the Restroom, it certainly might be violating their right to privacy. Recording phone conversations might be an effective way to assure anonymity, since you might not know the caller's name (if you solicit callers), but people need to be notified when conversations are being recorded.

Observational Techniques? Be Careful

No technique for assessing behavior is perfect, and all are fraught with potential problems that can sink your best efforts. Some particular problems that you should consider if you want to use observational techniques are as follows:

- Your very presence may affect the behavior being observed.
- Your own bias or viewpoints might affect the way in which you record behavior, from what you select to record to the way you do the recording.
- You may become fatigued or bored and miss important aspects of the behavior being recorded or miss the behavior itself.
- You may change the definition of those behaviors you want to observe, so what was defined as aggression at time 1 (touching without permission) is redefined at time 2 because you realize that all touching (even without permission) is not necessarily aggressive.

Questionnaires

Questionnaires are a paper-and-pencil set of structured and focused questions. Questionnaires save time since they allow individuals to complete them without any direct assistance or intervention from the researcher (many are self-administered). In fact, when you cannot be with participants directly, a questionnaire and the mail can produce the data you need.

There are other advantages to questionnaires besides their being self-administered:

- Because you can go through the mail, you can survey a broad geographic area.
- They are cheaper (even with increased mail costs) than one-on-one interviews.
- People may be more willing to be truthful because their anonymity is all but guaranteed.

Questionnaires can work very well, but their development demands time and attention to detail.

The objectivity of the data also makes it easy to share with other researchers and to use for additional analysis. Although the time that the data was collected may have passed, answers to new questions beyond those originally posed might just be waiting to be answered.

For example, in one study (Hanson and Ginsburg, 1988) researchers used the results of the "High School and Beyond" surveys originally collected in the spring of 1980 from more than 30,000 sophomore high school students. These researchers were interested in examining the relationships among high school students' values, test scores, grades, discipline problems, and drop-out status. With an original 84% response rate, these surveys provide a large, comprehensive database to work with. The response rate may have been unusually high since the students were probably part of a captive audience. In other words, they were given the questionnaires as part of regular school activities.

Keep in mind, however, that all these advantages are not a recommendation to go out and start collecting all your data using this method. One of the big disadvantages of questionnaires is that the completion and return rate is much lower than if you could personally ask the questions to each potential respondent through an interview, a technique you will get to shortly. While you would expect a high participation rate (up to 100%) if you visit people's homes and ask them questions, you can expect about a 35% return rate on a mail questionnaire even if you really do a good job.

What Makes Questionnaires Work

What is a good questionnaire? Several things go into a questionnaire that make it "work," or result in a high number of returns with all the items (or as many as possible) completed.

Always ask questions that the respondent can answer.

Now, you have surely completed questionnaires somewhere along the line, be they about your attitude toward the 1996 Democratic ticket or what you want in a stereo receiver. Whether the questionnaires work or not depends on a variety of factors that you have under your control. Let's look at a brief discussion of each of these factors, summarized in Table 6.5 and broken down into three general parts: basic assumptions on which the questionnaire is based, the questions themselves, and the format in which the items are presented.

Basic Assumptions

The questionnaire does not make unreasonable demands on the respondent.
The questionnaire does not have a "hidden agenda".
The questionnaire requests information that respondents presumably have.

The Questions
The questionnaire contains questions that can be answered.
The questionnaire contains questions that are straightforward.

Format
The items and the questionnaire are presented in an attractive, professional and easy-to-understand format.
All questions and pages are clearly numbered.
The questionnaire contains clear and explicit directions as to how it should be completed and how it should be returned.
The questions are objective.
The questions are ordered from easy to difficult and from general to specific.
Transitions are used from one topic to the next.
Examples are give when necessary.

Table 6.5 Some important things to remember about questionnaire design.

Basic Assumptions of the Questionnaire

There are five important points in Table 6.5 regarding the basic assumptions that one makes when designing a questionnaire. Possible respondents are probably quite willing to help you, but you must help them be the kind of respondent you want.

1. You do not want to ask respondents to complete a 40-page questionnaire or to take three hours on Saturday to do it. Your questionnaire must be designed in

such a way that its demands of time, expense, and effort are reasonable. You also want to avoid asking questions that are inappropriate (too personal) or asked in the wrong way. Anything that you find offensive will offend your potential respondents as well.

2. Your questionnaire must be designed to accomplish your goal and not to collect information on a related but implicit topic. If you are interested in racial attitudes, you should direct your questions to racial attitudes and not ask questions framed within a different context that is related, but not central to, your purpose.

3. If you want to find out about a respondent's knowledge of some area, you must assume that the person has the knowledge to share. Asking a first-semester freshman on the first day of classes about the benefits of college would probably not provide meaningful data. But on a student's last day of college, you would probably get a gold mine of information.

4. Encourage respondents by designing a questionnaire that contains interesting questions, that engages respondents in answering all your questions, and that prompts them to return the questionnaire to you. If you cannot make your questions interesting, perhaps you do not have enough knowledge or enthusiasm about the topic, and you should select another.

5. If you can get the same information through a source other than a questionnaire, by all means do so. If an interview gets you a better response and more accurate data, use an interview. If you can find out someone's grade point average through another source, better to take the extra time than to load the respondent with issues that are really secondary to your purpose.

What About the Questions?

Questions come in all shapes and sizes, and some are absolutely terrible. For example,

> *Do you often feel anxious about taking a test and getting a low grade?*

Can you see why it is not a good question? To begin with, the *and* makes it two questions rather than one, making it very difficult to know what the respondent was reacting to. Designing good questions is not impossible; it just takes some time and practice.

First, be sure the questions you ask can be answered. Do not ask about people's attitude toward political strife in some foreign country if they know nothing of the country's state of affairs.

Similarly, ask the question in a straightforward manner. This question,

> *Do you never not cheat on your exams?*

is convoluted, uses a double negative, and is just as easily asked as,

> *Do you ever cheat on your exams?*

It is also clearer and easier to answer accurately.

Finally, take into account the social desirability of questions. Will anyone graciously and positively answer the question,

> *Do you beat your children?*

Of course not, and information from such direct questions may be of questionable value.

The Format of the Questionnaire

As you can see in Table 6.5, several criteria can be applied to the format of a questionnaire, and each one of them is so important that glossing over it could sink your entire project.

For example, let's say that you design this terrific questionnaire with well-designed questions and allow just the right amount of time for completion, and you even call all the participants to see if they have any questions. Unfortunately, you forget to give them detailed instructions on how to return it to you! Or perhaps you include clear return instructions but forget to tell them how to answer the questions.

- If your questionnaire does not consist of items or questions that are easy to read (clearly printed, not physically bunched together, etc.), you will get nowhere fast. The items must be well arranged, and the entire questionnaire must be clearly duplicated. Photocopying produces a good copy, but so does printing the amount you need on a laser printer if you have one. If you can, get a friend who knows something about desktop publishing to help you with such considerations as white space, proportion, and balance.
- All questions and pages should be plainly numbered (e.g., 1, 2, 3, 4...). Do not use cumbersome combinations such as I-1.2 or II.4.
- Good questionnaires contain directions that are complete and to the point. They tell the respondent exactly *what* to do ("complete this section") and *how* to do it ("circle one answer," "check as many as apply"). These directions also offer explicit directions as to how the questionnaire should be returned, including preaddressed stamped envelopes and a phone number for calling for more information if necessary.

Cover letters can make or break the success of a project.

- Face it, your respondents are doing you a favor by completing the questionnaire. Your goal is to get as many as possible to do just that. One way to encourage responses is to show that your work is supported by a faculty member or your adviser, and you can do it through a cover letter like the one you saw in Figure 2.3.
- You want as honest an answer as possible from your respondents, and, consequently, you must be careful that your questions are not leading them to answer in a particular direction. Questions must be objective and forthright. Once again, be careful of socially undesirable statements.
- Early questions should warm up the respondent. In the beginning, relatively simple, non-threatening, and easy-to-answer questions ("How old were you on your last birthday?") should be presented so the respondent can feel comfortable. Then as the questions progress, more complicated (and personal) questions might be asked. For example, many questionnaires begin with questions about demographics such as age, gender, race, and so on, all information that most people find relatively nonintimidating to provide. Later questions could then deal with issues such as feelings toward prejudice, questions about religion, and the like.
- When your questionnaire changes gears (or topics), you have to let the respondent know. If there is a group of questions about demographics followed by a set of questions about race relations, you need a transition from one to the other, such as

  Thank you for answering these questions about yourself. Now we would like to ask you some questions about your experiences with people who are from the same ethnic group as you as well as from other groups.

- Finally, make every effort to design a questionnaire that is easy to score. When possible, provide answer options that are objective and close-ended, such as

27. *What is your annual income:*
   a. *below $20,000*
   b. *$20,000 to $24,999*
   c. *$25,000 to $29,999*

rather than

27. *Please tell us what your annual income is $*_____*.*

In the first example, you can enter a letter as the response to be used in the later analysis. In the second, you have to first take the number and then place it in some category, an extra step.

The Importance of the Cover Letter

An essential part of any questionnaire is the cover letter that accompanies it. This message is important since it helps set the scene for what is to come. A good cover letter is especially important for questionnaires that are mailed to respondents so that the sense of authority is established and importance of the project is conveyed.

Figure 6.5 shows an example of a such a cover letter used in the study of how parents use information they learn about children. You will notice that this cover letter (which also acts as a consent form which was talked about in chapter 2) contains certain features.

- It is done on university letterhead, which helps to favorably impress respondents and increases the likelihood that they will respond.
- It is dated recently, indicating there is some urgency to the request.
- The letter is personalized. It does not open by stating "Dear Participant" but "Dear Mr. and Mrs. Margolis."
- The purpose of the questionnaire and the importance of the study are clearly stated.
- A time estimate is given so they know when to return it.
- Confidentiality is clearly promised, and how confidentiality will be assured is indicated.
- Respondents are made part of the project in that a copy of the results will be sent to them when the study is complete. This can help respondents feel even more like an important part of the study.
- It has a clear, physically separate expression of thanks.
- It is signed by the big boss and by you. While you would like to stand on your own name and work, at this early point in your career this little bit of help from the boss can make an important difference.

In our society, tests for everything from selection to screening are everywhere, and their use has become one of the most controversial topics facing social and behavioral scientists. Tests definitely have their place, and in this chapter different kinds of measurement tools and how they can be used to reliably and validly assess behavior has been discussed. Remember, however, that careful formulation of hypotheses and attention to detail throughout the research project are also required for your measurement method to yield an accurate result.

Department of Educational Psychology & Research

University of Kansas • Lawrence, KS 66045

Dear Mr. and Mrs. Eisner:

The Department of Educational Psychology & Research at the University of Kansas supports the practice of informed consent and protection for human subjects participating in research. The following information is provided for you to decide whether you will allow Nikki and Alexandra to participate in the present study. You are free to withdraw either or both of them at any time.

Your child will be asked to play a game with another child with a disability in a room that has toys and books, and your child's behavior will be recorded on videotape. One session will last approximately 25 minutes. We are interested in studying the interaction between children who have a disability and children who do not. This information is important since it will help us develop methods for increasing the effectiveness of efforts to integrate children with disabilities into the regular education classroom.

Your child's participation is solicited but strictly voluntary. We assure you that your child's name will not in any way be associated with the research findings. The information will be identified only through a code number.

If you would like additional information concerning this study before or after it is completed, please contact one of us by phone or mail. Thank you very much for your time, and we appreciate your interest and cooperation.

Sincerely,

Bruce Saxon,   Sam Fine
Graduate Student Professor
(913) 123-4567   (913) 123-4567

_____

Signature of parent or legal guardian

Figure 6.5 A sample cover letter.

Exercises

1. For the following set of information about two achievement test scores, compute the difficulty and the discrimination indexes. The asterisk corresponds to the correct answer.

   Item 1

	Alternatives			
	*A	B	C	D
Upper 27%	28	15	7	20
Lower 27%	6	12	21	21

   Item 2

	Alternatives			
	*A	B	C	D
Upper 27%	10	7	28	15
Lower 27%	15	0	15	30

2. Write a 10-item questionnaire (using Likert type items) that measures attitude towards stealing. Be sure that you use both positive and negative statements and that all of the items are simply enough stated that they can be easily answered. Also, be sure to include a set of instructions.

3. Go to the latest edition of Buros' *Mental Measurements Yearbook*, and summarize a review of any test that is mentioned. What is the purpose of the test? Is the review positive or negative? How can the test be improved?

4. Interpret the following discrimination and difficulty scores.
   a. $D = .50$
      $d = -.90$
   b. $D = .90$
      $d = .25$

5. Describe three basic characteristics of a questionnaire.

6. What are three advantages of using a questionnaire?

Want to Know More?

Further Readings

Bracken, B. (1991). *Psychoeducational assessment of preschool children* (2nd ed.). Boston: Allyn & Bacon.

> Provides a thorough, in-depth analysis of major tests in the preschool assessment areas. There is also a balance between debates in the areas of ability and school readiness with a firm command of psychometric issues.

Kamphaus, R. (1993). *Clinical assessment of children's intelligence.* Boston: Allyn & Bacon.

> Shares an impressive knowledge of psychometrics and statistics. Covers references of all major intelligence tests for research and practice issues.

Lyman, H. B. (1991). *Test scores and what they mean.* Englewood Cliffs, NJ: Prentice-Hall.

> An easy to read and informative summary of all the things you wanted to know about test scores but were afraid to ask, including such areas as common sense and test scores and how to read test manuals.

Mitchell, J. V., Jr. (Ed.) (1985). *The ninth mental measurements yearbook (Vols. 1-2).* Lincoln, NE: The Buros Institute of Mental Measurements of the University of Nebraska-Lincoln.

> Large collections describing hundreds of published tests and providing critical reviews of these instruments.

Sattler, J. (1992). *Assessment of children* (Rev., Updated 3rd ed.). San Diego: Sattler.

> The standard in the field of children's assessment.

Wodrich, D. L. (1990). *Children's psychological testing* (2nd ed.). Baltimore: Paul H. Brookes.

> Discusses more than 50 commonly used children's tests that cover preschool through school-age development. Uses clear, jargon-free language to describe each instrument and three diagnosis categories.

Readings of Other Interest

Bulmer, M. (Ed.) (1982). *Social research ethics: An examination of the merits of covert participant observation.* London: Macmillan.

> Discusses the techniques that one needs to use in observation when the participants are not aware that they are being observed. Further details the ethics of such a technique and when it should and should not be used.

Gould, S. J. (1981). *The mismeasure of man*. New York: W.W. Norton.
    A wonderful account of the environmentalist and the hereditarian theories of intelligence.

Hernstein, R. J., & Murray, C. (1994). *The bell curve: Intelligence and class structure in American life*. New York: The Free Press.
    Controversial book that investigates the differences in intellectual capacity among people and groups and what those differences mean for America's future.

Data Collection and Descriptive Statistics

What You'll Learn About in this Chapter

- How to get started collecting your data
- How to begin "coding" your data
- All about constructing a data collection form
- The use and importance of descriptive statistics
- The difference between descriptive and inferential statistics
- What a distribution of scores is, and how distributions can differ among themselves
- Using measures of central tendency and variability to describe a set of scores
- How to compute the mean, median, and mode, and what they are used for
- How to compute the range, standard deviation, and variance, and what they are used for
- What the normal curve is, and why it is important to the research process

In every type of research endeavor, whether it be an historical examination of the role of medication in treating mental illness or the effects of using a computer mouse on children's eye-hand coordination, data about the topic needs to be collected and analyzed to test the viability of the hypotheses. You can speculate all you want on the relationship between certain variables or about why and how one might affect another, but until there is objective evidence to support your assertions, your work is no more accurate than drawing one of 10 possible answers at random out of a hat.

In the main part of this chapter, you will learn about data collection, beginning with the design of data collection forms and ending with a discussion of the actual process itself. Once you are familiar with these important first steps, you will move on to an introduction to the use of descriptive statistics — sets of tools to make sense out of these data you collected. You will continue learning about data analysis in the next chapter, titled "Inferential Statistics." Then you can learn about how to use your personal computer and software applications such as the Statistical Package for the Social Sciences (SPSS) to conduct data analysis.

On to the beginning of data collection and descriptive analysis.

Getting Ready for Data Collection

The data collection process consists of four steps.

After all that very hard thinking, going to the library, and formulating what you and your adviser feel is an important and (don't forget) interesting question, it is now time to begin the process of collecting your data.

The data collection process involves four steps:

- the construction of data collection forms used to organize the data you collect,
- the **coding** used to represent that data on a data collection form in the most efficient way possible,
- the collection of the actual data, and
- entry onto the data collection form.

Once you have completed these steps, you will be ready to begin analyzing your data.

Throughout this chapter we will use a sample data set representing 200 sets of scores collected during the testing of elementary and secondary school children as part of the Kansas Minimum Competency Testing Program funded by the Department of Education, State of Kansas. These tests in reading and mathematics are given to children in grades 2, 4, 6, 8, and 10 throughout the state. About 200,000 children are tested each year. This particular sample consists of 200 children, 95 boys and 105 girls. These data are shown in Appendix B, and your professor can get the set directly from the author of the *Exploring Research* (that's me!). As I go through specific, simple statistical procedures, use some of these data and follow along. Try it, you'll like it.

Here is a list of the information collected for each child.

- identification number
- gender
- grade
- building number
- reading score
- mathematics score

Six **data points** were gathered for each child. Figure 7.1 shows one way that the data might be organized using some basic demographic information (grade and gender). The information in Figure 7.1 was generated using SPSS and printed just as it appears using that program. You will learn all about using SPSS in Appendix A.

	GENDER	
	1	2
	GRADE	GRADE
	Count	Count
2	20	19
4	16	21
6	17	31
8	23	18
10	19	16

Figure 7.1 Grade and gender frequencies for the competency test sample.

The Data Collection Process

Now (I hope!) that you have your idea well in hand (and your professor or committee has approved your plans), it is time to start thinking about the process of collecting data. This involves everything from contacting and arranging data collection trips to the actual recording of the data on some type of form that will help you organize this information and facilitate the data analysis process.

Constructing Data Collection Forms

Once you know what information to collect and where you are going to get it (a critical part of your research), the next step is to develop an organizational scheme for collecting it so you can easily apply some techniques to analyze and make sense of your findings.

Think of your **raw** (that is, unorganized) **data** as the pieces to a jigsaw puzzle and the results of your data analysis as the strategy you use to put the pieces together. When you first open the box (ever try the pizza jigsaw puzzle?), the pieces look like a jumble of colors and shapes, which is just what they are. They are the raw data. The strategy you use to assemble them (such as "all the pieces with cheese on them in this pile") are just like the tools you use to analyze data.

When researchers collect data, their first step is to develop a **data collection form**. For example, Table 7.1 is an example of a data collection form that could be used to record scores and other information after the tests have been scored. Notice that the possible values (when known) for all the variables are included on the data collection form to make the recording easier. For example, males are to be coded as 1 and females as 2, and so on. More about coding later in this chapter.

One criterion to use in judging whether a data collection form is clear and easy to use is to show it to someone (such as another student in your class) who is unfamiliar with your project. Then ask that person to take data from the primary data source (such as the reading test itself) and enter it onto the data collection form. Would the individual know what to do and how to do it? Is it clear what goes where? What do the entries mean? These questions should all be answered with a clear "yes."

Test your data form with friends to be sure it works.

ID Number	Gender 1 = Male 2 = Female	Grade (2,4,6,8,10)	Building (1 through 6)	Reading Score	Math Score
001	2	8	1	55	60
002	2	2	6	41	44
003	1	8	6	39	37
004	2	4	6	56	59
005	2	10	6	32	32

Table 7.1 The first five of 200 cases in the set of competency scores.

The key to the design of an effective data collection form is the amount of planning that you invest in the process. You could use the test form itself as a data collection form if all the information you need is recorded in such a way that it is easily accessible for data analysis. Perhaps at the top of the test booklet or questionnaire you have spaces to record all the relevant information besides test results. That means you do not have to hunt to find all the data but can find them right at the top of the first page. Such a plan reduces the possibility of an error in the transfer from the original data to entry into the statistical program you use to analyze your data.

Table 7.1 shows the first five cases recorded on the completed data form. The columns are organized by variables, and the information on each student is entered as an individual row. These five cases are the first from the 200 cases (in Appendix B) that will be used in later sections of this chapter to demonstrate various data analysis techniques.

Remember, the data form you construct should be easy to understand and work with, because it is your main link between the original data and the first step in data analysis. Many researchers have two people work on the transfer of data from the original sheet to the data form to ensure that the number of errors is minimized. That is one reason why it is helpful to use graph paper or some other form that includes vertical and horizontal lines, as you see in Table 7.1.

Here are some general hints about constructing a data collection form. You can see how each is illustrated in Table 7.1.

- Use one line for each subject. If your data form needs lots of space, you may even need to use one page per subject.
- Use paper that has columns or grids like graph paper.
- Record actual subject's ID numbers as rows and scores or other variables as columns.

Make a copy of your data, and store it in a safe place.

- Include room for all the information that you want to record as well as information that you might anticipate recording in the future. For example, if you are doing a study where there will be a follow-up, leave room for the set of scores that will be entered later.
- As data collection forms are completed, make a copy of the form, and keep it in another location just in case the original data or your other data collection record gets lost.
- You may also want to date each form and initial it as it is completed.

Exploring Research

Collecting Data Using Optical Scanners

If you are collecting data where the subject's responses are recorded as one of several options (such as in multiple choice tests), you might want to consider scoring the test results using an **optical scoring sheet** scored on an **optical scanner**. You have probably taken tests using these (such as the College Boards or the SATs).

The responses on special scoring sheets are read by an optical scanner, and each response is compared with a key (which is another sheet that you also prepare). The scanner then records correct and incorrect responses, providing a total score at the top of the sheet. You can imagine the benefits that such a technique offers:

- It is very fast. Hand scoring of 50 multiple choice tests that have 100 items each can easily take hours.
- These scanners are more accurate than any of us can be. They (usually) do not make mistakes.
- Scanned responses can provide additional analysis of individual items on the test, such as the difficulty and discrimination indexes talked about in chapter 6. Are these machines expensive? At about $20,000 they will put a little dent in a budget, but the amount of time and money they save will more than cover the cost. Imagine having your data scored the day you finish collecting it.

So, when you can, use optical scoring sheets or, if appropriate, transfer the original data onto one of these sheets to make your work easier and more accurate. Optical scanning equipment is usually available at all major universities. Several companies also publish tests designed to use special answer sheets that are then returned to the company for scoring.

One word of caution, however. Just because this is an attractive methodology and may save you some time, do not fall victim to the trap of believing that an optical scoring sheet is the only way to collect and score data. If you do, you will end up trying to fit your objectives into a framework of assessment that may not fit the question you are asking.

Optical scanning is an accurate and quick way to score individual answer sheets.

Coding Data

Data are coded when they are transferred from the original collection form (such as a test booklet) into a format that lends itself to data analysis.

For example, a child may be a male or female. The actual letters that make up the words male or female would not be entered into the actual data form. Instead, the gender of the child will be coded with the value 1 representing male and the value 2 representing female as you saw in Figure 7.1 and Table 7.1. In this example, gender is coded as a 1 or a 2. Likewise, ethnicity or any other *categorical* variable can be entered as a single-digit number (as long as there are fewer than 10 categories using the numerals 0 through 9). In Table 7.2, you can see several different types of data and how they could be coded for the sample mathematics and reading scores.

The use of a single digit (rather than a word) not only saves space and entry time, but when it comes time for data analysis it also is much faster for the computer to look for all the entries under gender that are equal to *1* rather than *male*.

Use the simplest values available when coding data.

Variable	Range of Data Possible	Example
ID Number	001 through 200	138
Gender	1 or 2	2
Grade	1,2, 4, 6, 8, or 10	4
Building	1 through 6	1
Reading Score	1 through 100	78
Mathematics Score	1 through 100	69

Table 7.2 Coding data.

The one rule for coding data is to use codes that are as reduced in clutter and as unambiguous in meaning as possible, without losing the true meaning of the data themselves. For example, it is perfectly fine to code a fourth-grade boy as a 4 in grade and 1 for gender, but you would not be well served to use letters (such as F's and M's) since they are harder to work with. Also, do not combine categories, such as using 41 (for 4 and 1) for being in fourth grade (4) and a male (1). The problem here is that later on you will not be able to separate grade and gender as factors, and your data lose much of their value.

The rule here is always to record your data in elements that are as explicit and as discrete as possible. You can always combine data criteria during the analysis process. Do not do it right from the beginning.

The Ten Commandments of Data Collection

Do not let anyone fool you. The data collection process can be a long and rigorous one, even if it involves only a simple, one-page questionnaire given to a group of parents. The data collection process is probably the most time-consuming part of your project. If you are doing historical research, you are likely to find yourself spending most of your time in the library searching through books and journals or perhaps interviewing people about events that are important to your thesis. If you are actually collecting empirical data, other arrangements need to be made.

Well, here they are—your ten commandments for making sure your data get collected. Do not carve these in stone like the original Ten Commandments, but if you follow them you can avoid potentially fatal errors.

First, as you begin thinking about a research process, *begin thinking about the type of data you will have to collect* to answer your question.

Second, as you *think about the type of data you will be collecting, think about where you will be getting the data*. If you are using the library for historical data or accessing files of data that have already been collected (a great way to go!), you will have few logistical problems. But what if you want to assess the interaction between newborns and their parents? The attitude of teachers toward unionizing? The age at which people over 50 think they are old? All these questions involve needing people to provide the answers, and finding people can be tough. Start now.

Third, *make sure that the data collection form you are using is clear and easy to use*. Practice on a set of pilot or artificial data so you can make sure it is easy to go from the original scoring sheets to the data collection form.

Fourth, once you transfer scores to your data collection form, *make a duplicate copy of the data file*, and keep it in a separate location. This rule does not mean that you should duplicate the original data collection instrument for each participant, be it a competency test booklet or a set of figure drawings. Instead, once you have finished scoring and have transferred the information to the data collection sheets, keep a copy of those data collection sheets in a separate location. If you are recording your data as a computer file, such as a spreadsheet (more about this later), be sure to make a backup! Remember, there are two types of people: those who have lost their data and those who will.

Fifth, *do not rely on other people to collect or transfer your data* unless you have personally trained them and are confident that they understand the data collection process as well as you do. It is great to have people help you, and it helps keep the morale up during those long data collection sessions. But unless your helpers are competent beyond question, you could easily sabotage all your hard work and planning.

Sixth, *plan a detailed schedule of when and where you will be collecting your data*. If you need to visit three schools and each of 50 children needs to be tested for a total of 10 minutes at each school, that is 25 hours of testing. That does not mean you can allot 25 hours from your schedule for this activity. What about travel from one school to another? What about the child who is in the bathroom when it is his turn, and you have to wait 10 minutes until he comes back to the classroom? What about the day you show up and Cowboy Bob is the featured guest...and on and on. Be prepared for anything, and allocate 25%-50% more time in your schedule for unforeseen happenings.

Seventh, as soon as possible, *cultivate possible sources for your subject pool*. Since you already have some knowledge in your own discipline, you probably also know of people who work with the type of population you want or who might be able to help you gain access to these samples. If you are in a university community, it is likely that there are hundreds of other people competing for the same subject sample that you need. Instead of competing, why not try a more out-of-the-way (maybe 30 minutes away) school district or social group or civic organization or hospital where you might be able to obtain a sample with less competition.

Eighth, try to *follow up on subjects who missed their testing session or interview*. Call them back, and try to reschedule. Once you get in the habit of skipping possible participants, it becomes too easy to cut the sample down to too small a size.

Ninth, *never discard the original data*, such as the test booklets, interview notes, and so forth. Other researchers might want to use the same database, or you may have to return to the original materials for further information.

And number 10? Follow the previous 9. No kidding!

Supervise the data collection process if other people are helping you.

Getting Ready for Data Analysis

OK. You have spent many long, hard hours preparing a worthwhile proposal, a useful data collection form, and you have just spent six months collecting your data and entering it into a format that can be analyzed. What is next on the list?

First, through the use of **descriptive statistics**, you can describe some of the characteristics of the *distribution of scores* you have collected, such as the average score on one variable or the degree that one score varies from another. Finally, once the data are organized in a way that they can be closely examined, you will apply the set of tools called **inferential statistics** to help you make decisions about how the

Descriptive and inferential statistics are quite different from each other, but work hand in hand.

data you collected relates to your original hypotheses and how these results might be generalizable to a larger number of subjects than those who were tested.

The remainder of this chapter deals with descriptive statistics. Chapter 8 deals with inferential statistics.

Who would have ever thought that you would be enrolled in a class where that dreaded word *statistics* (sometimes called sadistics) comes up again and again? Well, here you will be learning about this intriguing part of the research process, and you may even gain some affection for the set of powerful tools that will be described. Since there is often so much anxiety and concern about this area of the research process, here are some pointers to make sure that you do not become a member of the group that suffers from the "I can't do it" complex before you even try:

- Read through the rest of this chapter without paying much attention to the examples. Just try to get a general feel for the organization and what material is covered.
- Start from the beginning of this section, and carefully follow each of the examples as they are presented, step by step. If you run into trouble, begin over with Step 1.
- If things get particularly difficult for you, take a short break and then come back to the part of the chapter or exercise that you clearly understood. Then, go on from there.
- Keep in mind that most of statistics is understanding and applying some simple and basic assumptions. Statistics is not high-powered, advanced mathematics.

Work through the exercises both by hand as well as with a calculator to be sure you understand the basic operations involved. When you learn about SPSS (Appendix A), work through the exercises again. The more you practice these techniques, the better you will be at using them as tools to understand your data.

Descriptive Statistics

The first step in the analysis of data is to describe them. Describing them usually means computing a set of descriptive statistics. These are called descriptive because they describe the general characteristics of a set or *distribution of scores*. In effect, they allow the researcher (or the reader of the research report) to get an accurate first impression of "what the data look like" (that's research talk!).

Before discussing different descriptive statistics, let's first turn to what a distribution of scores actually is and how it can help you better understand the data.

Distributions of Scores

Each score for any one individual represents a data point.

If you were to ask your best friend his or her age, you would have collected one piece of information or one data point for that individual. If you collect one piece of information for more than one individual, such as the ages of all the people in your class, you then have a set of scores and several data points. Two or more data points make up a distribution of scores. For example, in Figure 7.2, you see one way of representing a distribution of scores, using a special type of graph (called a histogram) of the distribution of mathematics scores for 200 children. By the way, this graph was created using SPSS.

The vertical axis corresponds to the frequency at which a particular score occurs. The horizontal, or X, axis corresponds to the value of the score. In this figure, each band represents 5 points along the scale. For example, approximately 12 children scored between 32.5 and 37.5. Judging from the shape of the distribution, you can make several judgments about this set of 200 scores just by a visual examination of the histogram.

- Most children score in the upper half of the distribution.
- The largest number of children scores around 55.

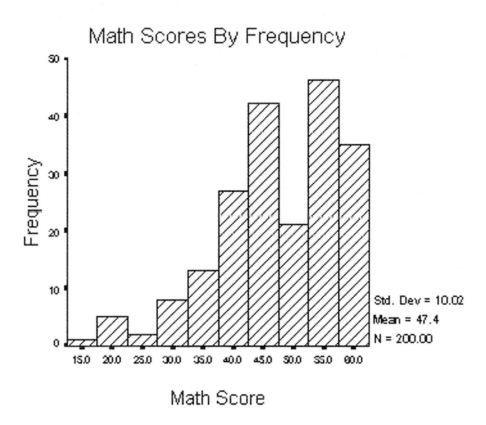

Figure 7.2 The distribution of mathematics scores for all children, grades 2 through 10.

Comparing Distributions of Scores

More than one distribution of scores can be viewed simultaneously and visually compared with one another. For example, in Figure 7.3 there are separate distributions for reading scores for second- and 10th-graders shown on the same graph. Here, you can see that the shapes of the curves are similar, but they are offset by the amount their most central point differs. That is just one difference in the characteristics of distributions. Let's turn to a discussion of how distributions can be compared.

Measures of Central Tendency

One property of a distribution of scores is that it has an average, or an individual value that is most representative of that distribution or set of scores. There are three types of **averages** or **measures of central tendency**: the mean, the median, and the mode.

The mean, the median, and the mode are all measures of central tendency.

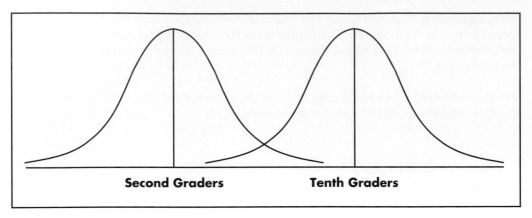

Second Graders　　　　**Tenth Graders**

Figure 7.3 Two different distributions for the same variable.

The Mean

The **mean** is the sum of a set of scores divided by the number of scores. You have probably computed several means over the years but referred to them as averages, such as the average amount of money you need to cover your expenses or to fill your car with gas or your average grade point average for the last three semesters.

There are several types of averages. The one explored here is the arithmetic mean, which is the most often used measure of central tendency. The formula for the mean is:

$$\bar{X} = \frac{\Sigma X}{n}$$

where　$\bar{X}$ = the mean
　　　　Σ = summation sign
　　　　X = individual scores
　　　　n = sample size

To compute the mean, follow these steps:

1. Add all the scores in the group to get a total.
2. Divide the total of all the scores by the number of observations.

For example, the mean reading test score for the first 10 students is 47.3. The first 10 scores are 55, 41, 46, 56, 45, 46, 58, 41, 50, and 35. Their total is 473, and when divided by 10 (the number of observations), the result is 47.3.

In this example, 47.3 is the value that best represents the most central location in the set of 10 scores. For the 200 reading test scores in Appendix B, the mean for reading is 48.6 and for math is 47.4. These values were computed the same way, by summing all 200 scores and dividing by the number of scores in the set, 200.

Likewise, the mean for any variable can be computed using the same method. As you learned in chapter 3, however, it makes no sense to add nominal-level values (such as those representing ID or gender) because the result is meaningless. (What do you get when you add a boy and a girl and divide by 2?)

The Median

The **median** is the score, or the point, in a distribution above which one-half of the scores lie. For example, in a simple set of scores such as 1, 3, and 5, the median is 3. If another score, say, 7, was added, the median would be the value that lies between 3 and 5, or 4. Here, 50% of the scores fall above the value 4 (and, of course, 50% fall below).

To compute the median when the number of scores in the set is odd, follow these steps.

1. Order the scores from lowest to highest.
2. Count the number of scores.
3. Select the middle score as the median.

For example, you can see here how the reading scores of 15 second-graders were ordered from lowest to highest in value. The eighth score (the score occupying the eighth position in the group) is the median. In this case, that value is 43.

31 33 35 38 40 41 42 43 44 46 47 48 49 50 51

To compute the median when the number (not the sum) of scores in the set is even, follow these steps.

1. Order the scores from lowest to highest.
2. Count the number of scores.
3. Find the mean of the two middle scores as the median.

For example, the following 14 scores were ordered from lowest to highest in value. The median was computed by adding the seventh and eighth scores (or the scores occupying the seventh and eighth positions in the group, 42 and 43), and dividing by 2, getting 42.5.

31 33 35 38 40 41 42 43 44 46 47 48 49 50

The Mode

The **mode** is the score that occurs most frequently. Caution! It is not the number of times that the score occurs but the score itself. If you have the following numbers

58 27 24 41 27 26 41 53 14 29 41 53 47 28 56

the mode is 41, not 3 (the number of times that the value 41 occurs).

The mode is best used with nominal data such as gender. In the set of competency data, the mode for gender is female since there are 105 females and 95 males. The mode is not how frequently the value "female" occurs, which is 105. The mode is an excellent choice if you want a general overview of which class or category occurs most frequently.

Which Measure When?

The mean, the median, and the mode give us different types of information and should be used in different ways. Table 7.3 summarizes when each of these should be used. As you can see, the use of one or the other measure of central tendency depends on the type of data you are describing.

What Measure of Central Tendency To Use?		
Measure	**Level of Measurement**	**Examples**
Mean	Ratio and Interval	speed of response, age in years
Median	Ordinal	class rank, order of finish
Mode	Nominal	party affiliation, eye color, ethnicity

Table 7.3 A comparison of the mean, the median, and the mode.

For example, describing data that are interval or ratio in nature (such as the number of correctly spelled words) calls for the use of the mean which provides relatively more information than the mode or the median. The golden rule is that when the data fit, and when you can, use the mean.

The median is often used with extreme scores.

The median is best suited to data that are ordinal or ranked. For example, the set of scores 7, 22, 24, 50, 66, 76, and 100 have the same median (50) as does the set of scores 49, 50, and 51 yet the distributions are quite different from each other. The median is also the appropriate choice when extreme scores are included in the sample. For example, here are the salaries for five people: $21,500, $27,600, $32,000, $18,750, and $82,000. The median is the middle-most (or the third-ranked) score, which is $27,600. The mean, however, is $36,370. Look at the large difference between these two values. Which measure do you think better represents the set of five scores and why? If you said the median, you are right. You certainly would not want an "average" ($36,370) to be larger than the second largest value in the set ($32,000). This number would not be very representative, as is the primary purpose of any measure of central tendency. From this example, one conclusion you might come to is that the median works best when a set of scores is asymmetrical or unbalanced in the extreme. It is the $82,000 data point that throws everything off here.

The mode should be your choice when the data are qualitative in nature (nominal or categorical) such as gender, hair color, ethnicity, school, or group membership. While you will not see the mode often reported in the research literature (because it may not be meaningful to average the values of nominal variables), it is the only measure of central tendency that can be used with nominal-level information.

Clearly, the mean allows us to take advantage of the most information (when available), and thereby it usually becomes the most informative measure of central tendency. When researchers can, they select variables on which this type of average can be computed.

Measures of Variability

You have just learned how a set of scores can be represented by different types of averages. But the average is not enough to fully describe a set of scores. There is another important quality or characteristic that describes the amount of variability or dispersion in a set of scores.

Variability is the degree of spread or dispersion that characterizes a group of scores and is the degree to which a set of scores differs from some measure of central tendency, most often the mean. For example, the set of scores 1, 3, 5, 7, and 9 (which has a mean of 5) has a higher degree of variability than the set of scores 3, 4, 5, 6, and 7, which has the same mean. The first set is simply more "spread out" than the second. There are several measures of variability, each of which will be covered in turn.

The Range

The **range** is the difference between the highest and the lowest scores in a distribution. It is the simplest and most direct measure of how disperse a set of scores is.

For example, for a set of scores such as

31 33 35 38 40 40 41 41 41 42 43 44 46 47 48 48 49 49 50 51

the range is 20 (or 51-31). In the reading data being used as an example of a large data set (too large to list in order here), the range for mathematics scores is 45, or 60-15. The range is a rough measure that indicates the general spread or size of the difference between extremes.

The range gives you a quick estimate of the variability in a distribution.

The Standard Deviation

The **standard deviation** is the most commonly used measure of variability. The standard deviation is the average amount that each of the individual scores varies from the mean of the set of scores. The larger the standard deviation, the more variable the set of scores is. If all the scores in a sample are identical, such as 10, 10, 10, and 10, then there is no variability, and the standard deviation is 0.

The formula for computing the standard deviation is

$$s = \sqrt{\frac{\sum (X - \bar{X})^2}{n - 1}}$$

where s = standard deviation
$\sum$ = summation sign
X = raw score
$\bar{X}$ = mean of the distribution
n = sample size

To compute the standard deviation, follow these steps shown in Table 7.4. We will be computing the standard deviation for the following set of 10 scores

13 14 15 12 13 14 13 16 15 9

1. List all the original scores, and compute the mean (which is 13.4).
2. Subtract the mean from each individual score (13.4), and place these values in the column titled "Deviation from the Mean." Notice that the sum of all these deviations (about the mean) is 0.

Remember when the standard deviation was defined as the average amount of deviation? You might want to know why you just do not stop here since an average has been computed. It is because this average is always 0 (more about this in a moment). So to get rid of the zero value, each deviation is squared.

	Original Scores	Deviation from the Mean	Squared Deviation
	13	-.4	.26
	14	0.6	.36
	15	1.6	2.56
	12	-1.4	1.96
	13	-.04	.16
	14	.6	.36
	13	-0.4	.16
	16	2.6	6.76
	15	1.6	2.56
	9	-4.4	19.36
Sum	134	0	34.4
Average	13.4	0	
		Standard Deviation	1.96
		Variance	3.82

Table 7.4 Computing the standard deviation.

3. Square each of the deviations and place them in the column labeled "Squared Deviations."
4. Sum the squared deviations (the total should be 34.4).
5. Divide the sum of the squared deviations (34.4) by the number of observations minus 1 (which is 9 in the example) to get 3.82.

You divide by 9 rather than 10 since you want to err on the side of being conservative and artificially increase the value of this descriptive statistic. As you may notice, as the sample size increases (say, from 10 to 100), the adjustment of subtracting 1 from the denominator makes increasingly little difference between the biased (with the full sample size as the denominator) and the unbiased (with the sample size minus 1 in the denominator) values.

6. Take the square root of the value from Step 5 (3.82), and the standard deviation is 1.96. The symbol for the standard deviation is s.

The deviations about the mean always add up to 0.

Aren't you dying to know why the square root is used? Because you want to get back to the values as originally listed, and you had to square them back in Step 3 (to get rid of the negative deviations, otherwise they would add up to 0 and every standard deviation would be 0!).

Some of the numbers you get on the way to computing the standard deviation are very interesting. Look at the sum of the deviation about the mean. Do you know why it is (and always is) 0? Because the mean (from which each of the scores is subtracted) represents the point about which the sum of the deviations always equals 0. If the sum of this column is not 0, then either the mean is incorrectly computed or the subtracted values are incorrect.

Another measure of variability that you often see in research reports is the variance, which is the square of the standard deviation. The variance is everything in the formula for the standard deviation except for the square root. Just as the variance is the square of the standard deviation, the square root of the variance is the standard deviation. The symbol for variance is s^2.

For the set of 200 reading and math competency scores that have been used as an example, the standard deviation for reading is 7.22 and for math is 10.02. The variance for reading is 52.13 and for math is 100.40. You can confirm these values later in Appendix A, where the use of SPSS is demonstrated.

Understanding Distributions

While several measures of central tendency and variability have been covered, you need only two to get a very good picture of a distribution's qualities: the mean and the standard deviation. With these two descriptive statistics, you can fully understand the distribution and what it means.

The Normal, or Bell-Shaped, Curve

You have seen the shape in Figure 7.4. It is most commonly referred to as a normal, or bell-shaped, curve. It is the shape that represents how variables (such as height and weight) are distributed and has some very interesting characteristics:

- The mean, the median, and the mode are all the same value (represented by the point at which the vertical line crosses the X axis).
- It is symmetrical about its midpoint, which means that the left and right halves of the curve are mirror images.

The two halves of a normal curve mirror each other.

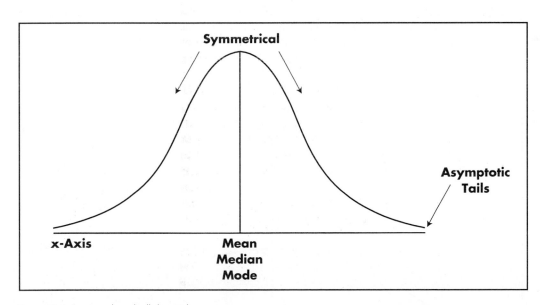

Figure 7.4 A normal, or bell-shaped, curve.

- The tails of the curve get closer and closer to the X axis, but never touch it. That is, the curve is *asymptotic*.

In fact, many inferential statistics (which you will learn about in the next chapter) are based on the assumption that population distributions of variables from which samples are selected are normal in shape.

OK, so here is this nicely shaped theoretical curve (since no real curve is quite as pretty in reality), but how can it be used to help you understand what individual scores mean?

Let's begin with the role that the mean and the standard deviation play in defining the characteristics of the normal curve and then move on to the concept of standard scores.

The Mean and the Standard Deviation

To begin with, curves can differ markedly in their appearance. For example, you can see how the two curves in Figure 7.5 differ in their mean scores but not in their variability. On the other hand the two curves in Figure 7.6 differ in their variability but have the same mean.

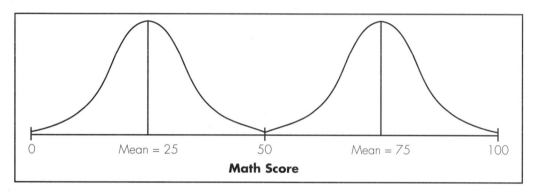

Figure 7.5 Two distributions of scores that differ in their mean score but not in their variability.

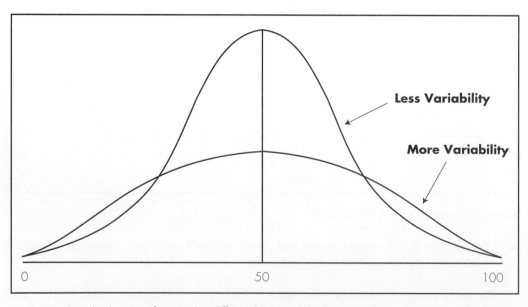

Figure 7.6 Two distributions of scores that differ in their variability but not in their mean.

Exploring Research

Regardless of their shape or the location of the mean along the X axis, some other things (besides those three qualities listed above) hold true for all normal distributions. These are as follows:

The distance between the mean of the distribution and one unit of standard deviation to the left or the right of the mean (no matter what the value of the standard deviation) always takes into account approximately 34% (really 34.12%) of the area beneath the normal curve as shown in Figure 7.7. If the mean for math for all 200 students is 47.37 and the standard deviation is 10.02, then 34% of all the scores in the distribution fall between the values of 47.37 and 57.39 (the mean plus 1 standard deviation) and another 34% fall between the values of 37.35 (the mean minus 1 standard deviation) and 47.37.

No matter what the mean or variance, if a distribution is normal, 1 standard deviation above or below the mean always incorporates 34% of the scores.

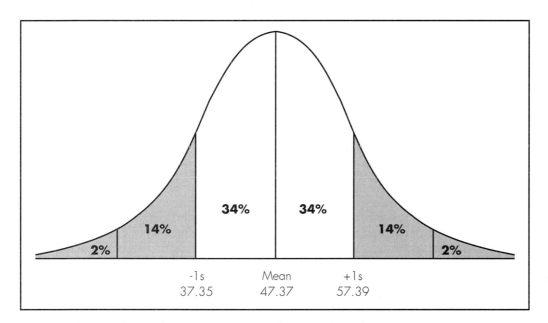

Figure 7.7 The normal curve showing percentages and areas underneath.

This is pretty neat once you consider that the 34% number is *independent* of the actual value of the mean or standard deviation. This 34% is 34% because of the shape of the curve, not the value of any of its members or measures of central tendency or variability. If you actually drew a normal curve on a piece of cardboard and cut out the area between the mean and +1 or -1 standard deviation and weigh it, it would tip the scale at exactly 34% of the weight of the entire piece of cardboard you cut out.

You can see that the curve is symmetrical. Thus, in a normal distribution 68% of all the scores fall between the values represented by 1 standard deviation below the mean and 1 standard deviation above the mean.

In our example, this means that 68% of the scores fall between the values of 37.35 and 57.39 (as you see in Figure 7.7). What about the other 32%? Good question. Those scores fall above (to the right of) 1 standard deviation above the mean and below (to the left of) 1 standard deviation below the mean, in the shaded part of the curve you see in Figure 7.7. More precisely, you can see how different percentages of scores fall within different boundaries. Since the curve slopes, and the amount of area decreases as you move further away from the mean, it is no surprise that the likelihood that a score will fall more toward the extremes of the distribution is less than the likelihood it will fall toward the middle.

Computing and Using z scores

You have seen in several places in this chapter how distributions differ from one another primarily as a function of the values of the mean and standard deviation. To make sense of information obtained from different distributions, a method needs to be used that takes these differences into account. Welcome to standard scores.

Standard scores are scores that have the same reference point and the same standard deviation. The type of standard score that you will see most frequently in the literature is called a **z score** and is the result of dividing the amount that an individual score deviates from the mean by the standard deviation, using the following formula:

$$z = \frac{(X - \bar{X})}{s}$$

Standard scores allow us to compare scores from one distribution with scores from another.

where z = z score
X = raw score
$\bar{X}$ = mean
s = standard deviation

For example, if the standard deviation is 10, and the raw score is 110, and the mean of the distribution of scores is 100, then the z score is

$$z = \frac{(110 - 100)}{10} = +1.0$$

Table 7.5 shows the original raw scores plus the z scores for the set of 10 mathematics test scores that appeared in Table 7.4. Any raw score above the mean will have a positive z score, and any raw score below the mean will have a negative z score. For example, a raw score of 13 has the equivalent z score of -0.2, which would be located slightly below the mean of 13.4. A score right on the mean has a z score equal to 0. A score that is one standard deviation above the mean (15.36) has a z score equal to 1, and so forth.

Original Score	X-$\bar{X}$	z-score [X-$\bar{X}$/s]
13	-.4	-.2
14	.6	.31
15	1.6	.82
12	-1.4	-.71
13	-.4	-.2
14	.6	.31
13	-.4	-.2
16	2.6	1.33
15	1.6	.82
9	-4.4	-2.24
Mean = 13.4		
s=1.96		

Table 7.5 Computing z scores from raw scores.

The most valuable use of these standard scores is to compare scores from distributions that are different from one another. A simple example is shown in Table 7.6. The average math score in Sara's class was 90 and the standard deviation was 2. She received a score of 92, for a z score of 1. In Micah's class, the average score was the same and he received the same absolute score as Sara, but the standard deviation was twice as great (4), making his z score (92-90/4), or 0.5. You can see that although they received the same raw score, Sara's score is located "above" Micah's score, indicating that she outperformed him when the same standard was used. Why did she outperform him? Relative to the rest of the members of the class, she scored higher. There was less spread in her class, indicating that the same absolute score (which both kids received) situated them in a different place within each distribution.

This is why raw scores should not be just added together and the averages compared. Instead, z scores (or some other type of standard score) should be used as the basis for comparison when scores from different distributions are being considered.

	Class Mean	Class s	Test Score	z score
Sara	90	2	92	1
Micah	90	4	92	.5

Table 7.6. Comparing z scores and raw scores.

What z Scores *Really* Mean

You already know that a z score represents a particular location along the X axis. For example, in a distribution with a mean of 100 and a standard deviation of 10, a z score of 1 represents the raw score 110. Likewise, different z scores correspond to different locations along the X axis of the normal curve. Since you already know the percent of area that falls between certain points along the X axis (see Figure 7.7) such statements as the following are true:

- 84% of all the scores fall below a z score of +1.0 (the 50% that fall below the mean plus the 34% that fall between the mean plus 1 z score).
- 16% of all the scores fall above a z score of +1.0 (since the total area has to equal 100%, and 84% fall below a z score of +1.0).

These types of statements can be made about the relationship between z scores at any point along the distribution, given a knowledge of the corresponding area that is incorporated between points along the axis. For example, using special tables, one could determine that in any normal distribution of 50 scores, the number of scores that would fall between 1.5 and 2.5 standard deviations above the mean is about 3 scores, or 6% of the total.

These numbers are expressed as percentages, which can be considered a statement of probability as well. In other words, the likelihood that someone will score between 1.5 and 2.5 standard deviations is .06, or 6 out of 100. Likewise, the probability that someone will score above the mean is .50, or 50%. In the next chapter

z scores' values are associated with the likelihood that a score will show up in a distribution.

this idea of assigning a value (in this case a percent or a probability) to an outcome (in this case a score) is discussed as part of the role of inference in the research process.

Some people really like to collect data, and others find it tedious and boring. One thing that everyone agrees on: It is hard work. All the work pays off when you begin to assemble the data into a body of information that makes sense. You collect the data then organize them, then apply some of the fundamental descriptive tools talked about in this chapter to begin to make sense of them. You are not finished by any means, but at least you have some idea where your data are going.

Exercises

1. You are in charge of a project that is investigating the effects of gender differences (male versus female) on the reading scores of first-, third-, and fifth-graders in three different school districts. Design a data collection form that takes into account the independent and dependent variables.
   - gender
   - school district

   Be sure you provide space on the form for important information such as the initials of the person who collected the form, date of data collection, identifying number for the participant, and any other comments that need to be made.

2. The mean of a sample of 10 scores is 100, and the standard deviation is 5. For the following raw scores, compute the z score.
   a. 101
   b. 112
   c. 97

   For the following z scores, work backwards to compute the corresponding raw score.
   a. -0.5
   b. 1.1
   c. 2.12

   Why would you want to work with z scores rather than raw scores? What is the primary purpose of standard scores?

3. For the following set of 10 scores, compute the range, the standard deviation, and the variance.

   $$5, 7, 3, 4, 5, 6, 7, 2, 5, 3$$

4. Claire and Noah are wonderful students. The results of their math and science tests were as follows:

	Math Test	Science Test
Claire's score	87	92
Noah's score	78	95
Class mean	68	84
Class standard deviation	8.5	11.5

   a. What are the standard scores (z scores) for Claire and Noah in math?
   b. If a larger z score means a "better" score, who received the higher grade and on what test?
   c. Who is the overall better student?

5. If someone receives a z score of 0, how well did he or she do in comparison with other students in the group?

6. Compute the mean and the median for the following group of scores.

$$1, 2, 3, 4, 10$$

   a. In this case why is the median a more useful average than the mean?
   b. Why wouldn't you use the mode as an average?

7. When the average income of Americans is reported in the media, do you think that the mean, median, or mode is used?

8. Roll a pair of dice, and record the results after each of 10 rolls. Do some totals occur more than others? Do you think your distribution of scores is typical? If you plotted the results, would you have a shape close to a normal curve?

9. One IQ test has a mean of 100 and a standard deviation of 15. What percentage of children would have an IQ of 115 or over when given this test?

10. What are the three types of measures of central tendency? Define each measure.

11. Determine the mean, the median, and the mode for the follow groups.

Group 1	Group 2
1	3
1	2
1	10
4	3
3	7
5	5

Want to Know More?

Further Readings

Christensen, L. B. (1994). *Experimental methodology*. Boston, MA: Allyn & Bacon.
> Provides an introduction to the basic principles of psychological research and the research process.

Freedman, D., Pisani, R., & Purves, R. (1978). *Statistics*. New York: Norton.
> An excellent nontechnical introduction to descriptive statistics, inferential statistics, and correlations. Takes great pains to present the information in words, charts, and tables and to avoid the use of statistical jargon.

Garnham, A., & Oakhill, J. (1994). *Thinking and Reasoning*. Oxford, England: Basil Blackwell Inc.
> Covers a wide range of research on all aspects of thinking and reasoning.

Gullo, D. F. (1995). *Understanding assessment and evaluation in early childhood education*. New York: Teachers' College Press.
> Covers assessment issues in the field of early childhood. Discusses test scores, percentiles, and methods to compare individual performance on various testing instruments.

Oostrerhof, A. C. (1987). Obtaining intended weights when combining students' scores. NCME instructional module. *Educational Measurement: Issues and Practice, 6,* 29-37.
> Describes a method for weighting measures of student achievement. Standard deviation methods are explained and given priority attention in this method.

Other Readings of Interest

Adler, I. (1957). *Magic house of numbers*. London: Dobson Books.
> A set of puzzles, games, and brain teasers which actually, honestly, really (I promise) makes manipulating numbers fun.

Boyd, R. D., Welge, P., Sexton, D., & Miller, J. S. (1989). Concurrent validity of the Battelle developmental inventory: Relationship with Bayley scales in young children with known or suspected disabilities. *Journal of Early Intervention, 13(1),* 14-23.
> Looks at correlations between the Battelle and the Bayley in assessing infants with known or suspected disabilities.

Huizenga, J. (1992). *Cold fusion: The scientific fiasco of the century*. Rochester, NY: University of Rochester Press.
> Describes the events preceding and following the 1989 announcement that two American physicists had accomplished cold fusion. Excitement was short lived when other scientists were unable to replicate the experiments, and the validity of the original data was questioned. Serves as a reminder that numbers only have meaning if they represent some truth.

Paulos, J. A. (1988). *Innumeracy*. New York: Hill and Wang.
> An interesting collection of essays concerning why so little is known about mathematics. Includes discussions of probability, innumeracy (or ignorance of how to use mathematics), and statistics.

Vetere, A., & Gale, A. (1987). *Ecological studies of family life*. Chichester, England: Wiley.
> An example of how research can quantify data on subjective issues such as family life by use of activities and other observable behaviors.

CHAPTER

8

EIGHT

Introducing Inferential Statistics

What You'll Learn About in this Chapter

- Why the inferential process is important to research
- The role that chance plays in any scientific endeavor
- What statistical significance is, and why it is important
- What Type I and Type II errors are, and their importance
- The steps in completing a test of statistical significance
- Some of the basic types of statistical tests, and how they are used
- A bit about multivariate statistics and its application
- A bit more about factor analysis and its application
- The difference between significance and meaningfulness
- The use of meta-analysis in behavioral and social science research

Understanding measures of central tendency, variability, and the working of the normal curve provides the tools to describe the characteristics of a sample. These tools are also an excellent foundation to help you make informed decisions about how accurately the data you collect reflect the validity of the hypothesis you are testing.

Once you have described a sample of data, as you learned to do in chapter 7, the next step is to learn how this descriptive information can be used to infer from the smaller sample on which the data were collected to the larger population from which the data were originally selected.

Inferential Statistics

Where descriptive statistics are used to describe a sample's characteristics, **inferential statistics** are used to infer something about the population from which the sample was drawn based on the characteristics of the sample. At several points throughout the first half of this book, I have emphasized that one hallmark of good scientific research is choosing a sample in such a way that it is representative of the population from which it was selected. The more representative it is, the more trusting one can be of the results based on information gleaned from the sample. The whole notion of inference is based on the assumption that you can accurately select a sample in such a way as to maximize this representativeness. The process then becomes an inferential one, where you infer from the smaller sample to the larger population based on the results of tests (and experiments) conducted using the sample.

How Inference Works

Let's go through the steps of a research project and see how the process of inference might work.

For example, a researcher wants to examine whether a significant difference exists between male and female adolescents in the way they solve moral dilemmas. Reviewing the general steps of the research process discussed in chapter 1, here is a sequence of how things might happen.

1. The researcher selects representative samples of both males and females in such a way that the samples represent the populations from which they are drawn.
2. Each adolescent is administered a test to assess his or her level of moral development.
3. The mean score for the group of males is compared with the mean score for the group of females using some statistical test.
4. A conclusion is reached as to whether or not the difference between the scores is the result of *chance* (meaning some factor other than gender is responsible for the difference) or the result of "true" differences between the two groups.
5. A conclusion is reached as to the role that gender plays in moral development in the population from which the sample was originally drawn. In other words, an inference, based on the results of an analysis of the sample data, is made about the population.

The Role of Chance

In fact, if *nothing* else is known about the relationship between the variables involved, **chance** is always the most attractive explanation for any relationship that might exist. For example, before you eliminate all the possible causes for any differences in moral development between the two groups of adolescents, the one explanation that is most attractive is that, if the groups do differ, it is because of chance. What is chance? It is the occurrence of variability that cannot be accounted for by any of the variables that you are studying. That is why you cannot begin with the assumption that any difference you observe between males and females is due to gender differences. There is no evidence to support such an assumption.

Chance is initially the most attractive explanation for any outcome.

Your primary role as a scientist is to *reduce the degree that chance might play in understanding the relationship between variables*. This is done primarily by controlling the various sources of variance (causes of differences such as previous experience, age, and so forth) that might exist.

You will learn more about how to control for various sources of error (or competing explanations for your outcomes) in chapter 10. For now, let's move on to understanding the rationale behind how one can look at a relatively small sample of observations and make an inference to a much larger population. The technique (and the underlying rationale) is truly fascinating and is the basis for much of the everyday reporting of scientific results. Just think of the precision that professional poll takers incorporate into their selection of a sample of about 1,200 adults who represent more than 160 million adults!

The Central Limit Theorem

The absolutely critical link between the results you get from the sample and being able to generalize these results to the population is the assumption that repeated sampling from the population will result in a set of scores that are representative of the population. If this is not the case, then many (if not all) tests of inferential statistics cannot be applied.

The central limit theorem is the basis for inferential statistics.

Remember the question posed earlier, "How does one know if the population distribution from which a sample is selected is normal?" The answer is that you don't, because you can never actually examine or evaluate the characteristics of the entire population. And what is more, in a sense you should not even care (horrors!) because of the **central limit theorem**, which dictates that *regardless of the shape of the population (be it normal or not), the means of all the samples selected from the population will be normally distributed!* This means that even if a population of scores is shaped like a U (the exact opposite of a bell-shaped curve), if you select a number of samples of size 30 or larger from that population, the means of those samples will be normally distributed. You will see this in a moment, but sit back for a second and ponder what this observation really means in the application of these principles to the real research world, where the true shape of the distribution of population scores is not normal, or bell shaped.

Most important, it means that nothing about the distribution of scores within the population need be known to generalize results from a sample to the population. That is pretty heavy duty, but you can see that if this were not the case, it would be very difficult, if not impossible, to infer from a sample to the population from which it was drawn.

One of the keys to the successful operation of this theorem is that the sample size be greater than 30. If the sample size is less than 30, you may need to apply nonparametric or distribution-free (meaning not "normal curve") statistics.

An Example of the Central Limit Theorem

Table 8.1 shows a population of 100 values ranging from 1 to 5, and Figure 8.1 shows a graph of their distribution (score by frequency). The mean of the entire population is

1	5	5	2	5
2	3	2	5	1
1	5	2	1	1
4	4	5	1	1
1	5	5	5	1
1	3	5	1	1
4	5	4	1	4
1	3	1	4	5
5	2	5	5	5
1	1	5	3	5
2	5	2	2	1
5	2	5	5	1
5	5	5	5	1
2	4	2	2	1
1	1	1	1	2
4	4	3	4	5
1	1	4	5	1
5	4	1	5	4
3	4	4	1	5
1	1	2	2	5

Table 8.1 A population of 100 scores, which is a minipopulation. You can see what the distribution of these scores looks like if you chart the values of the scores (ranging from 1 to 5) by the number of times the score occurs.

3.0. As you can see, the distribution is U-shaped. In the real world the entire population can never be directly observed (otherwise why be interested in inference?), but for illustrative purposes let's have some faith and assume it is possible.

A sample of 10 scores from this population is selected (at random), and the mean is computed. Its value (Mean 1), is 4. Now another sample is selected (Mean 2) and so on, until the means of 30 different samples of size 10 are selected. These 30 means (rounded off) are listed in Table 8.2. Once these means are plotted (as if they were a distribution of scores) the distribution approaches normality, as shown in Figure 8.2. Thus, from a population whose scores were distributed in a way opposite (that is, U-shaped, Figure 8.1) to what normal curves usually look like, a normal distribution of values can be generated. And "the mean of all the means" (the average of the 30 different sample means) is quite close (2.76) to the mean of the original population (remember it was 3.00?) from which they were drawn. A coincidence? Nope. Amazing! Nope. Just the power of the central limit theorem.

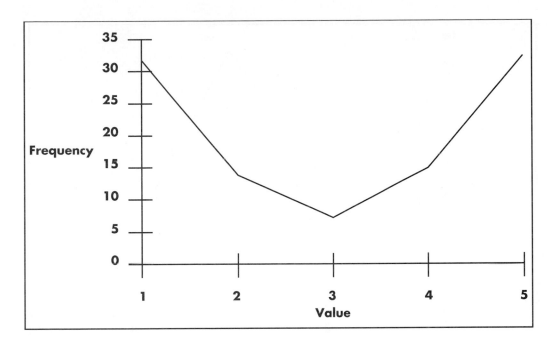

Figure 8.1 A graph of 100 data points.

4	3	3
1	2	5
3	3	3
2	3	3
3	2	4
3	2	2
1	3	4
3	1	3
4	3	3
3	2	2

Table 8.2 The 30 means, each generated from a sample of size 10.

This theorem is important stuff. It illustrates how powerful inferential statistics can be in allowing decisions to be based on the characteristics of a normal curve when indeed the population from which the sample was drawn *is not normal*. This fact alone provides enormous flexibility and in many ways is the cornerstone of the experimental method. Without the power to infer, the entire population would have to be tested, an unreasonable and impractical task.

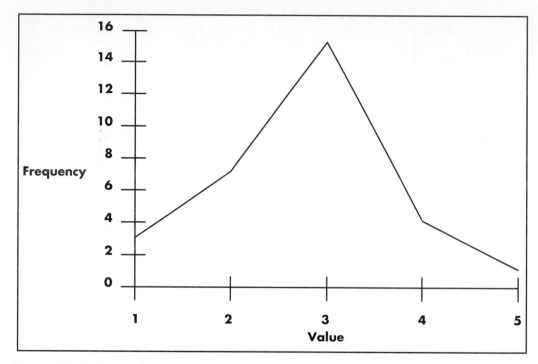

Figure 8.2 A distribution of means.

The Idea of Statistical Significance

Because sampling is imperfect (in that you can never select a sample of subjects that exactly matches the profile of those in the population), some error (sampling error) is introduced into the sampling process. In addition, because hypotheses cannot be directly tested on populations (since that is simply impractical; populations are too big), inferences may not be perfect either. Also, inferences just might be plain old wrong in concluding that two groups are different from each other (which the sample data might show) when in reality (which is the condition that really exists in the population) they are not.

For example, let's say a researcher is interested in seeing whether there is a difference in the academic achievement of children who participated in a preschool program and of children who did not participate. The null hypothesis is that the two groups are equal to each other on some measure of achievement.

The research hypothesis is that the mean score for the group of children who participated in the program is higher than the mean score for the group of children who did not participate in the program.

As a good researcher, your job is to show (as best you can) that any differences that exist between the two groups are due *only* to the effects of the preschool experience and no other factor or combination of factors. Through a variety of techniques described in chapter 10, you control or eliminate all the possible sources of difference such as the influence of parents' education, number of children in the family, and so on. Once these other potential explanatory variables are removed, the only remaining alternative explanation for differences is the effect of the preschool experience itself! But can you be absolutely sure? No, you cannot. Why? Because you are not sure that you are testing a sample that ideally fits the profile of the population. And if that is not the case, perhaps there is some room for error.

By concluding that the differences in test scores are due to differences in treatment (but considering that you are basing these conclusions on an examination of a sample and not the population itself), you accept some risk. This degree of risk is in effect the level of (drum roll, please) statistical significance at which you are willing to operate.

Statistical significance is the degree of risk that you are willing to take that you will reject a null hypothesis when it is actually true. For our example above, the null says that there is *no* difference between the two groups (remember, the null is always a statement of equality). In your data, however, you did find a difference. That is, given the evidence you have so far, group membership seems to have an effect on achievement scores. Maybe in reality, however, there is no difference, and, if you reject the null you stated, you make an error. The risk you take in making this kind of error (or the level of significance) is also known as a **Type I error**.

The level of significance has certain values associated with it. The conventional levels of .01 and .05 to assign that degree of risk of error have been used. For example, if the level of significance is .01 it means that on any one test of the null hypothesis, there is a 1% chance you will reject it when the null is true (and conclude that there is a group difference) when there really is no group difference. If the level of significance is .05, it means that on any one test of the null hypothesis, there is a 5% chance you will reject it when the null is true (and conclude that there is a group difference) when there really is no group difference. Notice that the level of significance is associated with an independent test of the null, and it is not appropriate to say that "On 100 tests of the null hypothesis, I will only make an error on five."

In a research report, statistical significance is usually represented as p < .05, read as "the probability of observing that outcome is less than .05," often expressed in a report or journal article simply as "significant at the .05 level."

There is another kind of error you can make, which along with the Type I error is shown in Table 8.3. A **Type II error** is when you inadvertently accept a false null hypothesis. For example, there really are differences between the populations represented by the sample groups, but you mistakenly conclude there are not.

A Type I error and level of statistical significance are the same things.

Type II errors can be decreased by increasing sample size.

If You	When It Is	You Are
reject the null hypothesis	true	making a Type I error
reject the null hypothesis	false	correct
accept the null hypothesis	false	making a Type II error
accept the null hypothesis	true	correct

Table 8.3 The types of errors you can make when working with a null hypothesis.

Ideally, you want to minimize both Type I and Type II errors, but it is not always easy or under your control. You have complete control over the Type I error level or the amount of risk that you are willing to take (since you actually set the level itself). Type II errors are not as directly controlled but instead are related to factors such as sample size. Type II errors are particularly sensitive to the number of subjects in a sample, and as that number increases Type II error decreases. In other words, as the sample characteristics more closely match that of the population (achieved by increasing the sample size), the likelihood that you will accept a false null hypothesis decreases as well.

Tests of Significance

What inferential statistics does best is allow decisions to be made about populations based on the information about samples. One of the most useful tools for doing this is a test of statistical significance that can be applied to different types of situations, depending on the nature of the question being asked and the form of the null hypothesis.

For example, do you want to look at the difference between two groups, such as whether boys score significantly differently than girls on some test? Or the relationship between two variables, such as number of children in a family and average score on intelligence tests? The two cases call for different approaches, but both will result in a test of the null hypothesis using a specific test of statistical significance.

How a Test of Significance Works

Tests of significance begin with the starting point, the null hypothesis.

Tests of significance are based on the fact that each type of null hypothesis (such as $H_o : \mu_1 = \mu_2$, representing no difference between the means of two samples) has associated with it a particular type of statistic. The statistic has associated with it a distribution of values used to compare what your sample data reveal and what you would expect to obtain by chance. Once again, chance is the most plausible of all explanations if you have no evidence to indicate otherwise.

Here are the general steps one takes in the application of a statistical test to any null hypothesis.

1. *Statement of the null hypothesis.* Do you remember that the null hypothesis is a statement of equality? The null hypothesis is the "true" state of affairs given no other information on which to make a judgment. For example, if you know nothing about the relationship between long-term memory and daily practice, you assume they are unrelated. That might not be what you want to test as a hypothesis, but it is always the starting point.
2. *Establishing the level of risk (or the level of significance or Type I error) associated with the null hypothesis.* With any research hypothesis comes a certain degree of risk of Type I error. The smaller this error is (such as .01 compared with .05), the less risk you are willing to take. No test of an hypothesis is completely risk-free because you never really know the "true" relationship between variables.
3. *Selection of the appropriate test statistic.* Each null hypothesis has associated with it a particular test statistic. You can learn what test is related to what type of question in more detail than we offer here in the Statistics 1 and Statistics 2 classes offered at your school.

4. *Computation of the test statistic value (called the obtained value).* The obtained value is the result of a specific statistical test. For example, there are test statistics for the significance of the difference between the averages of two groups, for the significance of the difference of a correlation coefficient from 0, and for the significance of the difference between two proportions.

5. *Determination of the value needed for rejection of the null hypothesis using the appropriate table of critical values for the particular statistic.* Each test statistic (along with group size and the risk you are willing to take) has a critical value associated with it. This is the minimum value you would expect the test statistic to yield if the null hypothesis is indeed false.

6. *Comparison of the obtained value to the critical value.* This is the crucial step. Here the value you obtained from the test statistic (the one you computed) is compared with the value (the critical value) you would expect to find by chance alone.

7. *If the obtained value is more extreme than the critical value, the null hypothesis cannot be accepted.* That is, the null hypothesis's statement of equality (reflecting chance) is not the most attractive explanation for differences that were found. Here is where the real beauty of the inferential method shines through. Only if your obtained value is more extreme than chance (meaning that the result of the test statistic is not a result of some chance fluctuation) can you say that any differences you obtained are not due to chance and that the equality stated by the null hypothesis is not the most attractive explanation for any differences you might have found. Instead, the differences must be due to the treatment.

8. *If the obtained value does not exceed the critical value, the null hypothesis is the most attractive explanation.* If you cannot show that the difference you obtained is due to something other than chance (such as the treatment), then the difference must be due to chance or something you have no control over. In other words, the null is the best explanation.

<aside>The proof of the pudding in the test of any hypothesis is the comparison of the critical and obtained values.</aside>

Let's go through these steps in the context of an example of how one test of significance can be applied.

t-Test for Independent Means

The t-test for independent means is an inferential test of the significance of the difference between two means based on two independent, unrelated groups. These are two different groups, such as males and females or those who received a treatment and those who did not.

<aside>Means can be independent of one another when they are from two different groups.</aside>

Chuamshemg Chenn and Harold Stevenson (1989) examined cultural differences among 3,500 elementary school children and their parents and teachers in Beijing (China), Chicago, Minneapolis, Sendai (Japan), and Taipei. One of the research hypotheses associated with this large set of studies was that the amount of homework done (as estimated by the mothers of the children) changed over the four-year period of the study from 1980 to 1984.

The eight steps just described (using this study as an example) are as follows:

1. *Statement of the null hypothesis.* In this case the null hypothesis is; there is no difference between the average amount of time spent on homework in 1980 and the amount of time spent on homework in 1984. Using symbols, it is stated as

$$H_o: \mu_{1980} = \mu_{1984}$$

where H_0 represents the null hypothesis
  μ_{1980} = the population average for 1980 homework levels
  μ_{1984} = the population average for 1984 homework levels

Remember that since null hypotheses always refer to populations, parameters like μ are used to represent the mean rather than $\overline{X}$.

2. *Establishing the level of risk (or the level of significance or Type I error) associated with the null hypothesis.* It is conventional to assign a value of .05 or .01. In this case, the value of .05 was used.
3. *Selection of the appropriate test statistic.* The appropriate test statistic for this null hypothesis is the t-test between independent means. The means are independent because they are averages computed from different groups.
4. *Computation of the test statistic (or the obtained value).* In this study, the value of the test statistic for the comparison of 320 mothers' estimates of the amount of time spent on homework in 1980 and 1984 was 2.00. This was the result of applying the formula mentioned in Step 3. This value was taken directly from the journal article.
5. *Determination of the value (called the critical value)* needed for rejection of the null hypothesis using the appropriate table of critical values for the particular statistic. In order to determine the critical value, a table for that particular statistic has to be consulted. Table 8.4 shows you a portion from such a table.

Degrees of Freedom	Critical Value for Rejection of the Null Hypothesis at the .05 Level of Significance	Critical Value for Rejection of the Null Hypothesis at the .01 Level of Significance
40	2.021	2.704
60	2.000	2.660
120	1.960	2.617

Table 8.4 A partial table of critical values used in testing of a t-value for the difference between the averages of two independent groups. Notice that as the sample size increases, the critical value decreases.

To determine the critical value that a test statistic needs to reach significance, you need to know two things: the level of significance at which the research hypothesis is being tested (.05 in this case) and the degrees of freedom, a reflection of the size of the sample (320 in this case). You need to know the sample size since the critical value changes as sample size changes. Can you figure out why? It is because as the sample size increases it becomes more like the population, and the difference you need between the obtained and the critical value for rejection of the null hypothesis decreases.

Look at Table 8.4 and use this information to determine the critical value. Read down the column labeled **degrees of freedom** until you get as close to 320 as possible (which is 120). Now read over to the column for the .05 level of significance. Because you did not hypothesize any direction to the difference, this is a *two-tailed*, or *nondirectional*, test. At the juncture of 120 degrees of freedom and the .05 level, you can see that the critical value of 1.960 is needed for rejection of the null.

Degrees of freedom help us define the critical value of the test statistic.

Exploring Research

This is the t-value that you would expect by chance alone, given the sample size and the level of significance at which you want to test the research hypothesis.

6. *Comparison of the obtained and critical values.* Here, the two values of interest are the obtained value (t = 2.00) and the critical value (t = 1.96)
7. *If the obtained value is more extreme than the critical value, the null hypothesis cannot be accepted.* That is, this statement of equality (reflecting chance) is not the most attractive explanation for any differences that were found. In this case, the obtained value is greater than the critical value. In other words, the likelihood that this t-value would result from chance alone is less than .05 (or 5 out of 100) on any one test of the null hypothesis. The conclusion based on the sample data, then, is there is a difference in the average number of minutes spent on homework between 1980 and 1984. What is the nature of the difference? An examination of the means (252 minutes per week in 1980 compared with 305 minutes per week in 1984) shows that homework levels increased, a result consistent with the research hypothesis mentioned earlier.
8. *If the obtained value does not exceed the critical value, the null hypothesis is the most attractive explanation.* In this case, the obtained value exceeded the critical value. The null is not the most attractive or tenable explanation for differences.

So, What Does $t_{(120)} = 5.43$, $p < .01$ Really Mean?

As you become more familiar with journal articles and how they are written, you will soon recognize a statement that goes something like this.

The results were significant at the .01 level ($t_{(120)} = 5.43$, $p < .01$).

The words are clear enough, but what do the parts mean?

- The *t* represents the type of statistical test, which in this case is a t-test.
- The (120) represents the number of degrees of freedom.
- The 5.43 is the obtained value, or the value which resulted from applying the t-test to the results of the study.
- The *p* represents probability.
- The .01 represents the level of significance or Type I error rate.

Once you have some experience reading these expressions through your exposure to completed studies and journal articles, you will find it very easy to quickly glance at the numbers and recognize what they mean. You will find for the most part that this format is standard, with the value of these elements changing (such as *F* for an *F*-test, or .05 for a different level of significance) but not their meaning.

Some Other Tests of Significance

As you have already learned, there are different tests of significance that can be applied to different types of questions. In the previous example, the appropriate test of significance examined the difference between the averages of two groups that were unrelated or independent of each other. Let's look at other common tests of statistical significance. Keep in mind that there are well over 100 different tests that can be applied. Table 8.5 shows you a sample of some of these with the associated research question, the null hypothesis, and the appropriate statistical test.

The purpose of the following examples is to acquaint you with some of the most frequently used tests that you are likely to encounter in your reading of the research literature. Once again, if you want to know more about these tests, you should consider taking the first- and second-level statistics courses that your department offers.

Looking at Differences Between Groups

You have just seen an example of applying a statistical test to examine the difference between the average of two groups when the measurements in each of the groups are unrelated to each other; that is, the measurements are independent.

The Question	The Null Hypothesis	The Statistical Test
Group Differences		
Is there a difference between the means of two unrelated groups?	$H_o: \mu_{group1} = \mu_{group2}$	t-test for independent samples
Is there a difference between the means of two related groups?	$H_o: \mu_{group1a} = \mu_{group1b}$	t-test for dependent samples
Is there an overall difference between three or more means?	$H_o: \mu_{group1} = \mu_{group2} = \mu_{group3}$	analysis of variance (or F-test)
Group Relationships		
Is there a relationship between the scores of two groups?	$H_o: \rho_{xy} = 0$	t-test for the significance of the correlation coefficient
Is there a difference between two correlations coefficients?	$H_o: \rho_{xy} = \rho_{xz}$	t-test for the significance of the difference between correlation coefficients.

Table 8.5 What null hypotheses do for a living! For almost any research question you want to ask that is based on sample data, there is a corresponding null hypothesis.

Group averages can be dependent when the averages are from the same group.

Another common situation is where the groups are related to each other. For example, what if you are interested in seeing what changes, if any, occurred throughout the school year on reading competency scores for the same group of children? You could give the competency test in September and then give it again in June. The null hypothesis would be that there is no difference in the scores between the two testings. Since the scores for the two testings are dependent on each other or correlated and since the same pupils are taking both tests, the t-test for independent means is not appropriate. Instead, *a t-test for dependent or correlated means* is the appropriate statistical test. The primary difference between these two procedures is

Exploring Research

that the test for dependent means takes into account the degree that the two sets of scores are related to each other.

For example, the mean score for 28 boys on the fall reading test was 76.8 with a standard deviation of 6.5. The mean score for the same boys on the spring reading test was 82.4 with a standard deviation of 7.8. Is there a significant difference between the two testings? Let's follow the same set of steps identified earlier.

1. Statement of the null hypothesis.

$$H_o{:}\mu_f = \mu_s$$

2. Establishing the level of risk (or the level of significance or Type I error) associated with the null hypothesis. The value of .01 will be used.
3. Selection of the appropriate test statistic. The appropriate test statistic for this null hypothesis is the t-test between dependent means. The means are dependent because they are averages based on the performance of the same groups.
4. Computation of the test statistic value, which is

$$t = 2.581$$

5. Determination of the value needed for rejection of the null hypothesis. Using the values in Table 8.6, the critical value is determined just as was done for a test of independent means. That is because the same test statistic is being used. The number of degrees of freedom is $n - 1$ (27) where n equals the number of pairs of observations, which in this case is 28. $n - 1$, and not n, is used since we want a conservative estimate of the population value, so we intentionally underestimate the size of the sample (27 versus 28).

	Level of Significance for a Directional or One-Tailed test			
	.05	.025	.01	.005
Degrees of Freedom	Level of Significance for a Non-Directional or Two-Tailed test			
	.10	.05	.02	.01
26	1.706	2.056	2.479	2.779
27	1.703	2.052	2.473	2.771
28	1.701	2.048	2.467	2.763
29	1.699	2.045	2.462	2.756
30	1.697	2.042	2.457	2.750

Table 8.6 Another partial table of critical values. You can see that the same type of information is contained in this table as you saw in Table 8.4, but now it applies to pairs of observations.

Given this information and a .01 level of significance, the critical value needed for rejection of the null hypothesis for a two-tailed test is 2.771.

6. If the obtained value is more extreme than the critical value, the null hypothesis cannot be accepted. That is, this statement of equality (reflecting chance) is not the most attractive explanation for any differences that were found. In this case, the obtained value of 1.671 (I made this up!) does not exceed the critical value of 2.771, so we move on to the next step.

7. If the obtained value does not exceed the critical value, the null hypothesis is the most attractive explanation. The observation based on the sample data is not extreme enough to reject the null hypothesis and conclude that there is a significant difference between the two testings. The null hypothesis that there is no difference between the two groups is the most attractive explanation. Any difference that was observed (76.8 versus 87.4) is due to sampling error.

Looking at Relationships Between Groups

In chapter 9, you will learn about a descriptive statistic called the correlation coefficient (also mentioned in chapter 5), a mathematical index of the relationship between two variables. If you know nothing about two variables, say you call them X and Y, what would you expect the relationship between them to be by chance alone? Since you have no reason to believe they are related, you have to assume that the relationship is 0. That is exactly what you would expect if chance were the only factor operating and if these two variables shared nothing in common.

The test of significance of a correlation is whether the value of the coefficient, and hence the relationship between the variables, is significantly different from a value of 0. The null hypothesis is

$$\rho_{xy} = 0$$

If the correlation value is different from 0, it does not necessarily mean that the relationship is due to something other than chance.

For example, let's assume that you want to test the research hypothesis (at the .01 level) that the relationship between math and reading scores (where the correlation coefficient equals .13, or $r_{xy} = .13$) is different from 0.

The value for this test statistic is a distribution of t-scores. Once that t-value is computed you go to the same table that was consulted for the various statistical tests where t-scores are involved.

If the null hypothesis cannot be rejected, in effect you are saying that there is no relationship between the two variables. If there is no significance (or "real" relationship between X and Y), then how can any correlation at all (such as .13) be different from 0? Simple. It is *sampling error*. Indeed, the value of .13 is not the true value that you would find in the population from which the sample was drawn but only a function of inaccurate or less than precise sampling. Sampling error is that ever present threat, and one of your jobs is to separate differences due to sampling error from differences due to true differences or relationships in the sample being examined.

Working with More Than One Dependent Variable

The research question you are asking may demand that you assess more than one dependent variable. In this case, there are at least two techniques that are more

Multivariate analysis of variance (or MANOVA) is an advanced technique that examines whether group differences occur on more than one dependent variable. In many ways MANOVA resembles a series of simple t-tests between groups. The major difference between the two techniques is that MANOVA takes into account the relationship between the dependent variables. In other words, if the dependent variables are closely related to each other, it would be difficult to tell whether a difference on dependent variable 1 is not as much the result of differences on dependent variable 2. MANOVA separates the unique contribution that each dependent variable makes to understanding group differences so that if there is a difference on dependent variable 1 it is not mingled with any difference on variable 2.

There are a variety of sophisticated techniques for testing the significance of more than one dependent variable simultaneously.

The fact that dependent variables can be related to one another makes several pairwise t-tests a serious threat to a sound study. For example, let's say that you are testing the differences between the experimental and the control group on variables named comprehension, memory, recall, and speed of reading. As you might suspect, these variables are all related to one another. So, a t-test between differences on speed of reading between groups may show up to be significant, but the real reason behind the difference is that speed of reading is very closely linked to comprehension, and that is where the real difference lies.

Because of the interrelated nature of these variables, the true Type I or alpha error is not .01 or .05 but rather

$$1 - (1 - a)^k$$

where   a = Type I error rate, and
          k = the number of variables.

In this case, with three variables, the true Type I error is $1 - (1 - .05)^3$, or .14, which is certainly different from the assumed .05. In other words, multiple t-tests are risky since you artificially inflate the level of the Type I error you think you are dealing with. The solution? Use some type of technique that controls for these relationships between dependent variables which initially is MANOVA, followed by some type of post-hoc procedures that compare means to one another and controls the level of Type I error.

Factor analysis is another advanced technique that allows the researcher to reduce the number of variables that represent a particular construct and then use what are called factor scores as dependent variables. The more related variables are to one another, the fewer factors are needed to represent the entire *matrix* of variables.

For example, let's say you are studying the effects of knowledge expectant parents have of their coming child's sex on the parents' perceptions of the child's personality. A factor analysis groups similar variables together so that several variables can represent a particular construct. These groups, or *factors*, are each then named by the researchers. The big strength of factor analysis is that it allows researchers to examine sets of variables and see how closely they are related to each other. For example, rather than dealing with the variables eye contact, touching, and verbalizing, you can deal with the one construct called attachment.

Significance Versus Meaningfulness

What an interesting situation for the researcher when discovering that the results of an experiment indeed are statistically significant. Even though you may be at the

Results might be
significant, but that does
not mean that they are
meaningful.

start of your career, you probably have heard scuttlebutt around your department and from other students that the absolutely most desirable outcome of any research is that "the results are significant."

What your colleagues mean by this, and what statistical significance really means, may be two different things. What they mean is that the research was a *technical success*, since the null hypothesis is not a reasonable explanation for what was observed. Now if your experimental design and other considerations were taken well care of, statistically significant results are unquestionably the first step toward making a contribution to the literature in your field. However, the presence and importance of statistical significance must be kept in perspective.

For example, let's take the case where a very large sample of illiterate adults (say, 10,000) are divided into two groups. One group receives intensive training to read using computers, and the other receives intensive training to read using classroom teaching. The average score for Group 1 (who learned in the classroom) is 75.6 on a reading test, the dependent variable. The average score on the reading test for Group 2 (who learned using the computer) is 75.7. The amount of variance in both groups is about equal. As you can see, the difference in score is only *one-10th* of 1 point (75.6 versus 75.7), yet when a t-test for the significance between independent means is applied, the results are significant at the .01 level, indicating that computers work better than classroom teaching. In other words, the role of chance is minimized. The difference of .01 is indeed statistically significant, but is it meaningful? Does the improvement in test scores (by such a small margin) provide sufficient rationale for the $300,000 it costs to equip the program with computers? Or is the difference negligible enough that it can be ignored, even if it is statistically significant?

Here is another example. Since the larger the sample, the more closely it approximates the characteristics of the population, you often need a very small correlation between two variables for statistical significance when the size of the sample is substantial. For 100 pairs of scores, a correlation between X and Y of .20 is significant at the .05 level. The square of this correlation coefficient (or the *coefficient of determination* as an indicator of how powerful the correlation is) explains only 4% (or .2 squared) of the variance! That means that 96% of the variance goes unexplained or unaccounted for. Given a statistically significant relationship and one that is not occurring by chance alone, that is a lot of explaining to do! In fact, if samples are large enough, any difference between them will be significant.

From these two examples, here are some conclusions about the importance of statistical significance.

First, statistical significance in and of itself is not very meaningful unless the study that is conducted has a sound conceptual base that lends some meaning to the significance of the outcome.

Second, statistical significance cannot be interpreted independently of the context within which it occurs. If you are the superintendent in a school system, are you willing to retain children in Grade 1 if the retention program significantly raises their standardized test scores by one-half point (not one-half the standard score)?

Finally, while statistical significance is important as a concept, it is not the end-all and certainly should not be the only goal of scientific research. That is the reason why we set out to *test* hypotheses rather than *prove* them. If our study is designed correctly, then even null results tell you something very important. If a particular treatment does not work, it is important information that others need to know about. If your study is designed well, then you should know why the treatment does not work, and the next person down the line can design his or her study taking into account the valuable information you provided.

Meta-Analysis

You have heard this one before. One of the most important characteristics of good science is that results can be replicated. For example, if you successfully used a certain technique to teach illiterate adults how to read, you would like to think that the same technique can be used in similar circumstances with a similar population, and the results will be the same.

But what of the case where there are 10 or 50 or even 100 studies on the same phenomenon where different numbers of subjects are used, in different settings, and even different treatments or programs? The only thing these studies have in common is the use of the same outcome or dependent variable, be it reading, cognitive ability, age at onset of senile dementia, or any one of thousands of dependent variables. How does one make sense of this collection of findings? Can they be combined, even though the research that produced them differed from one another on many important factors such as sample size and selection, treatment variables, and so forth?

The answer is a qualified "yes." Through the use of **meta-analysis**, a relatively new technique, the findings from a variety of studies that have the same dependent variable can be compared. Before you see an example how meta-analysis works, be sure you understand that the "same dependent variable" does not necessarily mean that the identical instrument is used across studies. Rather, the same *conceptual* variable is measured (such as intelligence or aggression or achievement). If one is interested in studying a particular component of personality, a variety of instruments such as the 16 Personality Factor Questionnaire or the Minnesota Multiphasic Personality Inventory could be used and the results from these studies "combined" in a meta-analysis.

The term meta-analysis was coined in 1976 by Gene Glass. He meant it to represent an approach toward summarizing the results of individual experiments. It is an attempt to integrate a wide and diverse body of information about a particular phenomenon. Keep in mind that the data for a meta-analytic study and analysis come from experiments that have already been conducted, not new data that yet need to be collected and then analyzed. In effect, a good part of the work is already done.

Meta-analysis is a technique for looking at the general trends in differences between many different groups across many different studies.

How Meta-Analytic Studies Are Done

Here is an example of a meta-analysis conducted on the efficacy of early intervention programs (Castro and Mastropieri, 1988). There are basically four steps in a conventional meta-analysis, with lots of variation as to how these steps are carried out.

First, as many studies as possible or as representative a group of studies as possible on a particular phenomenon are collected. Castro and Mastropieri used many of the techniques and sources described in chapter 3 to find what studies had been done, including *Dissertation Abstracts*, *ERIC*, and *Psychological Abstracts*. They also sent letters to every researcher they recognized as having published in this area or participated in some type of early intervention program. Castro and Mastropieri settled on 74 studies, each one investigating the effectiveness of early intervention programs on preschoolers (ages birth through 5 years) who had a handicap.

Second, the results of the studies need to be converted to some common metric so that they can be compared to one another. This only makes sense, since it would otherwise be a waste of time to try to compare unlike things. The metric used in many meta-analytic studies is called the *effect size*. This value is derived through a comparison of the observed differences between the results for the experimental group (or the one that received the intervention) and the control group (the group that did not receive the intervention) as measured in some standard unit. The larger the effect size, the larger the difference between the two groups. The use of the standard unit allows comparisons between different groups and outcomes, the heart of the meta-analytic technique.

In a meta-analytic study, the effect size becomes the dependent variable. The independent variable is the factor that was manipulated, be it type of intervention, age of children, and so forth. In the Castro and Mastropieri study, there was a total of 215 experimental-control group comparisons and a total of 215 effect sizes from the 74 studies that were reviewed.

Third, the researchers develop a system to code the various dimensions of the study including a description of the subjects, type of intervention used, research design selected, type of outcome measured, and conclusions reached by the authors of the study. These factors are then used in an examination of the effect sizes computed in Step 2.

Finally, a variety of descriptive and correlational techniques are used to examine the outcomes of the studies as a whole. The researcher looks for a trend or a substantial commonality in the direction of the outcomes across the factors that were identified and coded as described in the previous two steps. In the Castro and Mastropieri study, the researchers concluded that early intervention programs do result in "moderately large immediate benefits for handicapped populations." These benefits seem to apply to outcomes such as IQ scores, motor, language, and academic achievement. Efficacy of treatment was not found on other variables such as social competence, self-concept, and family relationships.

Here is another example to show you the scope of these kinds of studies. A classic study examined a classic question: Does psychotherapy work? Smith and Glass (1977) conducted a meta-analysis of more than 375 studies, which yielded a total of 833 effects. These 833 effects represented more than 25,000 cases of experimental and control subjects (those who did and did not receive psychotherapy). An examination of the effects' sizes yielded strong and convincing differences between those groups of participants who participated in therapy and those who did not. On the other hand, there were no differences between types of therapy (such as behavioral or psychoanalytic).

What is really so hot about this meta-analytic technique? One thing: Meta-analytic studies do what good science does. They organize data and help us understand what they mean. Imagine a list of 375 studies with the results of each study listed in an adjacent column and how difficult it would be to reach any generalizable and valid conclusion. To make matters even more confusing, let's say that some of the studies used very young children, others used infants, some examined social skills, others intelligence, and so on. It could be a mishmash of outcomes. Meta-analysis reduces the mishmash to something understandable.

This chapter was a brief introduction to the world of inferential statistics and how the concept of inference can provide some very powerful decision-making tools. In the last two chapters you learned a great deal about collecting data and then examining them for patterns, differences, and relationships. You are now ready to explore the first of several models of design used in research methods; non-experimental research methods.

Exercises

1. Why is chance initially the most attractive explanation for the differences observed between two groups?

2. A researcher analyzed the results of an experiment and found that the obtained t-value (on a test of independent means) was 1.29 with a total of 25 children in Group 1 and 30 children in Group 2. Use a table of critical values and discuss whether the null hypothesis can or cannot be rejected.

3. How can the results of a study be statistically significant but not meaningful?

4. How does the central limit theorem work, and why is it so important to the use of inferential statistics?

5. From the following set of scores, select a random sample of 10 scores. Now do this four more times until you have a total of five separate samples of size 10.

5	1	5	5	5
1	5	1	1	1
4	5	5	5	4
2	4	2	4	4
1	2	4	5	4
2	2	3	2	3

   a. What is the mean of the entire population?
   b. What is mean of the means?
   c. How can the central limit theorem be used to explain why the answers to a. and b. above are so close?
   d. How does this example illustrate the power of the central limit theorem?

6. What does the term "statistically significant" mean?

7. .Explain why a research scientist does not set out to prove a hypothesis.

8. As a researcher you are interested in the effect of infant day care on the security of attachment which develops between infant and caregiver. You suspect that infants in day care will be insecurely attached at 11 months after being in day care from 2 months of age when compared to infants not attending day care but taken care of at home by their principal caregiver. What are the general steps you would take to test your hypothesis?

9. What is the difference between a Type I and a Type II error?

10. As a researcher you are interested in investigating the effectiveness of a new reading curriculum. You plan to do this by monitoring the progress in reading of a single group of 10th-graders using the curriculum once each quarter. Which statistical test would be most appropriate, and why?
    a. t-test for independent means
    b. t-test for dependent means
    c. analysis of variance

11. What is a meta-analysis, and why is it important as a research tool?

Want to Know More?

Further Readings

Harcum, E. R. (1990). Deficiency of education concerning the methodological issues in accepting null hypotheses. *Contemporary Educational Psychology, 15(3)*, 199-211.
>Examines the disparity between methodology and empirical research literature to suggest a cause for the casual acceptance of null hypotheses simply because obtained differences are not statistically significant.

Maleske, R. T. (1995). *Foundations for gathering and interpreting behavioral data: An introduction to statistics*. Pacific Grove, CA: Brooks and Cole Publishing.
>Targeted for the reader who wants to gain a fundamental understanding of the total process of gathering and interpreting behavioral data. Addresses the issues and concepts involved in this process.

Schmidt, F. L. (1993). What do data really mean? Research findings, meta-analysis and cumulative knowledge in psychology. *American Psychologist, 47*, 1173-1181.
>Discusses how important it is to build a base of knowledge and then how meta-analyses can help understand trends and patterns within that body of understanding.

Readings of Other Interest

Hernstein, R. J., & Murray, C. (1994). *The bell curve: Intelligence and class structure in American life*. New York: The Free Press.
>Controversial book that investigates the differences in intellectual capacity among people and groups and what those differences mean for America's future.

Williams, F., Larose, R., and Frost, F. (1981). *Children, television and sex role stereotyping*. New York: Praeger.
>Review of research on how television affects young children's sex roles or self-images. Gives a synopsis of the research and provides ideas for further questions.

Nonexperimental Research Methods

What You'll Learn About in this Chapter

- How historical research is conducted, and how it differs from other methods
- What primary and secondary sources of data are, and how they are used
- What authenticity and accuracy of a historical study are, and why they are important
- How internal and external criticism are used in evaluating historical research
- What survey research is, and what are some of its advantages and disadvantages
- The kinds of questions developmental research answers
- The advantages and disadvantages of the longitudinal and cross-sectional method
- The importance and use of follow-up studies
- The purpose and use of correlational research
- How to compute and interpret a correlation coefficient

In some ways, your work on the first eight chapters of *Exploring Research* has been done to prepare you for the next three, all of which deal with particular types of research designs or research methods. In this chapter, you will learn about non-experimental research methods which are ways of looking at research questions without the direct manipulation of a variable.

For example, if you wanted to understand how the use of drugs to treat mental illness has developed over the past 100 years, you would be using historical sources. Similarly, if you want to know the frequency with which punishment is used in different levels of prison security, you would be collecting relevant information to answer that question. You would not be manipulating any variable (such as placing different programs in a high or low punishment group). For the prison question you would be describing an outcome, and you would be doing descriptive research.

This chapter focuses on historical and descriptive research questions, how they are asked, and how they are answered. You will also learn about questions of a correlational nature that look at the association between variables and the important distinction between association (two things being related since they share something in common) and causality (one thing causing another).

Historical Research

The past offers important insight into the future.

Just by reading the preface of Thomas Jordan's *Victorian Childhood* (1987), you can get at least one clue about how different historical research is from the types of experimental research you usually see in the journals representing social and behavioral sciences. His thanks to libraries at the University of Missouri, Church of Jesus Christ of Latter-day Saints, Washington University, the Library of Congress, the British Library, the Royal Society of Health, the Reform Club, and the Royal Statistical Society indicate their contribution of data in one form or another to his book, which focuses on the children of the Victorian era. These data, be they 150-year-old records of children's heights or what percent of children under 15 years of age worked in the textile mills (about 14%), were his "subjects," and what he did with them exemplifies the focus of our discussion about historical research.

Victorian Childhood is organized into nine chapters, each focusing on a separate theme such as cities, work, life and death, learning and advocacy, and reform. Jordan consulted especially interesting sources of data to support conclusions about the way children were raised and treated during this period in England. The data are not just this or that article from a journal by another scholar. Jordan often went to primary sources (be patient, you will learn more about what they are in a moment) that you might not have imagined existed, let alone have known they were accessible.

Just look at some of the materials he used:

- Data from the records of ships that regularly transported boy "felons" from England to Australia.
- Poems reflecting attitudes about children and the roles of parents such as

   The Baby

   If baby holds his hands,
   And asks by sounds and sign
   For what you're eating at your meals,
   Tho' mother's heart inclines

To give him what he wants,
Remember, he can't chew;
And solid food is bad for him,
Tho' very good for you.

- Newspaper classified ads, such as the one from the September 14, 1817, *Morning Chronicle* advertising care and education for "YOUNG LADIES," who will be "treated with the tenderest attention, be constantly under her immediate inspection, and form in every respect. . . ." and instructed in "History, Geography, Writing, Arithmetic, and Needle Works. . . ." all for 30 guineas a year.
- The number of Sunday schools open from 1801 through 1851 by denomination (there were at least 11).

It is clear that Jordan did his homework. He looked here and there and everywhere to find what he needed to present as complete a picture as possible of what it was like to be a child during that period. Like any other good scientist, he collected data (of a wide variety from a wide variety of sources) and organized this information in a way that allows the reader to reach some conclusions that would go unnoticed without his efforts.

Doing Historical Research

Historical research (or **historiography**) in the social and behavioral sciences is sometimes given second class status unfairly. People often cannot decide whether such research should be placed in the social sciences or in the humanities, and it often ends up within each domain (history of education, history of physics, etc.) and not having a home of its own. It is certainly a social science because historians collect and analyze data as does any social scientist. On the other hand, it is a humanity as well, because historians (or anyone doing historical research) also examine the role that individuals play in social institutions such as the school and the family. Further, because few behavioral and social scientists are ever taught about historical research and its associated methodology, few actually do research in that area or are even familiar with the appropriate methodology. For the most part, it is people called "historians" who are interested in such topics as the history of day care or educational reform or the origins of psychoanalysis or one of hundreds of other interesting topics and who end up making the important contributions.

Understanding the historical nature of a phenomenon is often as important as understanding the phenomenon itself. Why? For the simple reason that you cannot fully evaluate or appreciate the advances that are made in science (be it developmental psychology or particle physics) without some understanding of the *context* within which these developments occurred.

For example, the graying of the American population that has occurred over the past 50 years is an historical event that has prompted increased interest in gerontology as a field of study. Similarly, understanding the customs and conditions of the Victorian era and late 19th century Vienna (when Sigmund Freud began the development of his theory of psychoanalysis) provides insights that help us to understand and to appreciate more about Freud's theory than we otherwise would.

It is not just idle talk when you hear the quote, "Those who cannot remember the past are condemned to repeat it." It is true and another reason why you should have an understanding of the historical method as part of your arsenal of research skills.

Historiography is another term for historical research.

The Steps in Historical Research

Although the data for historical research may look different, many steps in the process are similar to more traditional research models.

Although you may have never thought it to be the case, conducting historical research is in many ways very similar to conducting any of the other types of research already mentioned in *Exploring Research*.

While the data or the basic information may differ markedly, the historical researcher proceeds with many of the same steps as a researcher using any other method. Let's take a look at each of these six different steps.

First, *historical researchers define a topic or a problem* that they wish to investigate. Historical research is unlimited in scope since it is a constant interchange between events of the present day and events of the past. All of the past is the historians' database, a vast collection of documents and ideas, much of them difficult to find and more difficult to verify. Like detectives, historical researchers search through everything from ships' logs to church birth registers to find who is related to whom and what role this or that person might have played in the community. It is from an inspection (which might be just simple reading or a discussion with a colleague) of this legacy of information that ideas for further explorations often begin.

This step is much like any other researcher's mental effort, which usually results from a personal interest in a particular area. For example, one might be interested in the history of educational reform and specifically in the notion of the origin of laws requiring children to go to school.

Second, to whatever extent possible, the *researcher formulates an hypothesis*, which more often is expressed as a question. For example, the question might be, "When, how, and why did school become mandatory for children under the age of 16?" While posing hypotheses in a nondeclarative form is something not usually done in scientific studies, historical research demands that a different set of rules be adopted. Some of the criteria for a good hypothesis discussed in chapter 2 are applicable to historical research (such as an hypothesis being an educated guess) but others are not (such as looking for statistical relationships between variables).

Data for historical research are often rich in detail and difficult to find.

Third, as with any other research endeavor, one has to *utilize a variety of sources to gather data*. As you will shortly see, these sources differ quite markedly from those you may be used to. While interviewing can be a source of data in almost any type of research, the analysis of written documents and the culling of records and such is usually the province of the historical researcher.

Fourth, evidence needs to be evaluated both for its *authenticity* as well as for its *accuracy*. More about these later in this chapter.

Fifth, *data need to be synthesized or integrated* to provide a coherent body of information. This is similar to steps that you may have taken when you reviewed the literature in the preparation of a proposal, but here you are integrating outcomes and looking for trends and patterns that eventually might suggest further questions worth asking.

Finally, as with any other research project, you will need to *interpret the results* in light of the argument you originally made for why this topic is worth pursuing and in light of the question that you asked when the research began. Your skill as an interpreter will have a great deal to do with how well prepared you are for understanding the results of your data collection. For example, the more you know about the economic, political, and social climate of the late 19th and early 20th centuries, the more comprehensively you will be able to understand how, why, and when mandatory school attendance became the rule rather than the exception.

Sources of Historical Data

Historians usually rely on two different types of data, primary sources and secondary sources. They each play a particular role in conducting historical research and are equally valuable.

Primary Sources of Historical Data

Primary sources of historical data are *original* artifacts, documents, interviews and records of eyewitnesses, oral histories, diaries, and school records that are original in nature. For example, if you wanted to know how Japanese families adjusted to internment during World War II, the child you interview from such a family would be a primary source. So would a diary kept by an adult of his or her experiences.

Primary sources are the direct outcomes of an event or an experience that is recorded without there necessarily being any intent by the historian for later use of the reference. Such sources might be a newsreel shown in a movie theater 50 years ago or a record of the number of people who received psychotherapy in 1952 or the minutes from a school board meeting. If you were an historian, the only thing that would prevent you from forming a very accurate picture of what it was like to be at that school board meeting is the fact that you are viewing someone else's perspective through the minutes. Still, you are as close to being there as it may be possible to get.

Table 9.1 summarizes some important primary sources of data.

Primary sources can yield otherwise unobtainable information.

Secondary Sources of Historical Data

While primary sources are firsthand accounts of events, **secondary sources** of historical data are secondhand or at least once removed from the original event, such as a summary of important statistics, a list of important primary sources, and a newspaper column based on an eyewitness account (the account itself would be a primary source). These sources give accounts as witnessed by others, such as a bystander, but not witnessed directly by the source. And just like the children's game Telephone, something often gets lost in the translation.

The most important consideration when using secondary sources is how much can you trust the original source of the data. For example, a reanalysis of Sir Cyril Burt's 100-year-old data on twins led several scientists to conclude that the data were falsified. A great deal of what was known (and was believed to be true) about the nature of intelligence, for example, was based on the initial analysis.

Secondary sources are more readily available but not as rich in detail as primary sources.

Primary or Secondary Sources: Which Ones to Shoot For?

It would be an ideal world for the historian if primary sources were always available, but that is often not the case. As with so many other situations in the research world, the ideal (such as the perfect sample) is just not attainable. Instead, one has to settle for what is best, which may be a secondary source.

Category	Example
Documents	minutes of meetings contracts deeds wills permits photographs lists bills films catalogues maps newspaper accounts (if first person narrative) diaries graduation records
Oral Histories	spoken or recorded accounts of events court transcripts
Remains Remnants and Relics	tools food religious artifacts clothing buildings equipment books scrolls

Table 9.1 A list of some primary sources of historical data. Can you imagine all the work it takes to locate some of these sources?

Given that both types of sources may be equally useful (and trustworthy), researchers should not place any implicit value on one over the other, since they both provide important information. For example, you would have a difficult time interviewing the teachers who taught in the Victorian England that Jordan described, but you may very well get a good idea of what happened during the school day by reading a letter from a parent to the principal. Good historians do not bemoan the lack of primary sources or whether this or that potentially important letter is missing. Instead, they make the best of what is available.

Here is another example. For those of you interested in child development, there is an incredible repository of manuscripts and visual materials at Antioch College in Yellow Springs, Ohio, where both types of source can be found. There, the *Society for Research in Child Development* has stored (and continues to solicit) thousands of primary and secondary sources relating to children and their families, often contributed by the scientists who originally conducted the work. Some of the materials they have available are

- correspondence between researchers about a particular topic,
- personal letters that include information about ideas and progress toward a particular goal,

- drafts of what would later be important research papers,
- original data that can be used and analyzed with new techniques by other people interested in the same area,
- films of research studies, such as those detailing the growth and development of young children compiled by "ages and stages" Dr. Arnold Gesell, and
- programs and schedules from hundreds of meetings of professional societies that focus on children.

Authenticity and Accuracy

Nonetheless, just as researchers who use achievement tests as a source of data have to be sure that the test is reliable and valid, so historians need to establish the value of the data from primary and secondary sources that underlie their arguments. As do others, historiographers need to adopt a critical and evaluative attitude toward the information they collect. Otherwise, the inaccurate primary document of today (perhaps a forgery) becomes another historian's source of information tomorrow. The cycle repeats itself, and one's primary source becomes another's secondary source, and the whole database becomes increasingly contaminated with unauthentic information.

The evaluation of primary and secondary data is accomplished through the application of two separate criteria: **authenticity** (also known as external criticism) and **accuracy** (also known as internal criticism).

External Criticism as a Criterion

External criticism as applied to historical data is concerned with the *authenticity* of the data. Basically, this criterion asks whether the data are genuine and trustworthy, or are they fake? Were they written when claimed? By the person who signed them? And found where left? These are only some of the questions that must be asked before the data can be trusted.

Authenticity is another name for validity.

The authenticity of a document or some other primary source is sometimes easy to establish and other times next to impossible. The age and quality of particular inks can be examined to date a document. Types of writing styles, printing techniques, composition of paper, use of language, and general knowledge are all indicators of when (and even how) a document was prepared. The one thing the historiographer needs to look for is consistency. Do all the pieces fit together as in a jigsaw puzzle, or are there important outliers that just do not fit in, raising doubts? And of what value can any work be if the data upon which it is based are questionable?

For example, the presence of ancient coins in the same containers as the famous Dead Sea scrolls lent additional evidence that the scrolls were as old as suspected. The coins and some very sophisticated forensic tests, such as carbon dating, led to the conclusion that the scrolls were about 2,500 years old (at this writing).

The beginning historian does not have the training or the techniques available to do analyses nearly as sophisticated, so you more or less have to base your decisions about authenticity on several pieces of evidence and make a judgment about the usefulness of the data. Even if you do not have the tools, you must make sure you have exhausted every possibility to establish the authenticity of your data. Otherwise, your research efforts may be for naught.

Internal Criticism as a Criterion

Accuracy is another name for trustworthiness.

A second evaluative criterion is **internal criticism,** which is concerned with *accuracy,* or how trustworthy the source is as a true reflection of what happened. Do the numbers from the 1890 survey of how many children were in school seem plausible? Are parents' reports of adolescent mood swings during the 1950s an accurate reflection of the child's real behavior?

One way to determine the level of accuracy is to have an expert examine documents or relics and lend her or his opinion that it is an accurate reflection of what events were like during the period under investigation.

The Limitations of Historical Research

There is no question that historical research comes with some significant shortcomings when compared with other methods of doing research in the social and behavioral sciences.

Limitations in generalizability are one of the main drawbacks to historical research.

First, since the availability of data is always limited by factors that are not under the control of the researcher, *results will likely be limited in their generalizability*. If all you have to go on is correspondence, with nothing to verify whether events really happened, you cannot take much from those findings and apply it to another time or setting. In fact, historians often have to settle for what they can get to study a particular topic, rather than the ideal.

Second, *the data of historical research are often questioned because they are primarily derived from the observations of others*, be they letters, books, or works of art. Those schooled in the belief that firsthand observation (tests, tasks, etc.) yields information that has the most potential for understanding behavior may be right in part, but that is no reason to ignore the other type of data that history presents.

Third, historical research is often *a long and arduous task that can include hundreds if not thousands of hours* poring over documents (if you can locate them!), looking for clues and hints wherever they can be found to support your hypotheses.

Fourth, since some of the criteria that would normally be applied to empirical research include such things as the reliability and validity of the instruments used, in historical research other, *less rigorous (but more comprehensive) criteria are used to evaluate measurement tools*.

Descriptive Research

While several factors distinguish different types of research from one another, probably the most important factor is the type of question that you want to answer. If you are conducting historical research, you are trying to understand events that occurred in the past and how they might relate to current events. You generate questions or hypotheses, collect data, and continue as you would if you were conducting any type of research.

Descriptive research describes the current state of some phenomenon.

Descriptive research, on the other hand, is different. The purpose of descriptive research is to *describe the current state of affairs at the time of the study*. For example, if you want to know how many teachers use a particular teaching method, you could ask a group of students to complete a questionnaire, thereby measuring the outcome as it occurs. If you wanted to know if there were differences in particular types of words among 3-, 5-, and 7-year-olds, you would *describe* those differences within a descriptive or developmental framework.

As with historical research, the most significant difference between descriptive research and causal comparative or experimental research (mentioned in chapter 1 and discussed in detail in the next chapter) is that descriptive research does not include a treatment or a control group. You are not trying to show the influence of any variable upon another. In other words, all you are doing for the reader of your research is painting a picture. When someone reads your report that includes one of the several descriptive methods that will be discussed, she or he should be able to see the larger picture of what occurred. While there may be room for why, that question is more often left to a more experimental approach.

While there are many different types of descriptive research, the focus of this discussion will be

- case studies or in-depth studies of individual people or organizations,
- developmental studies where changes or differences in development are studied, and
- correlational studies, where relationships between variables are described.

Case Studies

There once was a child named Genie who was isolated from human companionship for the majority of her early years (Curtiss, 1977). When at last she was discovered and released at age 14, she provided psychologists a bounty of information about the effects of delayed speech on language development.

Psychologists and linguists studied her language development through the use of a **case study.** A case study is a method used to study an individual or an institution in a unique setting or situation in as intense and as detailed a manner as possible. The word *unique* here is critical since the researcher is as interested in the existing conditions surrounding the person as much as the person himself or herself. It is the quality of uniqueness that sets this person (and this case) apart from others.

You may have heard the term *case study* used before. The case study idea represents a major part of the methodology that physicians use to collect and disseminate information. *The Journal of the American Medical Association* (published weekly by the American Medical Association) regularly offers case studies of individuals whose conditions are so unusual that their symptoms and treatment demand special attention, and information about their cases needs to be disseminated.

It was the physician turned psychologist Sigmund Freud who pioneered the use of the case study in the development of his psychoanalytic theory of personality development. His famous patient, Anna O., and his detailed observations about her condition led to the use of free association as a method in the treatment of hysteria and other conditions. There is also the work of Jean Marc Itard, one of the first "special educators," and his case study description of the wild boy of Aveyron, the basis for the popular movie *The Wild Child*.

Case studies are not limited to people. The Harvard Business School makes a regular practice of including case studies of businesses that fail or succeed as a staple of its graduate students' diet of materials to study. Investigating one case, under the microscope so to speak, allows students to review the steps that were taken and better understand the mechanics of how a business might be affected by a variety of factors. Similarly, families, schools, gangs, and social organizations are all fair game for the case study approach.

Case studies are highly detailed, often personal descriptions.

Case studies take a great
deal of time but can yield
a great deal of detail
and insight.

For example, the well-known description of an experimental school, *Summerhill* (Neill, 1960), is an elaborate and detailed case study of a unique English school based on the idea of an "open" education. A similar, more recent work is Tracey Kidder's *Among School Children*, a narrative case study of a fifth-grade teacher and her activities over the course of a school year. Partly because of the skill of these writers and partly because of the case study nature of the books, the reader gets an intimate look into the life of the two different types of school. And we should not forget the author Jonathan Kozol, who in his books *Rachael and Her Children*, *Savage Inequalities*, and *Amazing Grace*, let the larger social community know about how poor schools, homelessness, and poverty affect individual children and families.

Some Pluses for the Case Study Method

Case studies are a unique way of capturing information about human behavior for a variety of reasons.

First, case studies focus on only one individual or one thing (be it, for example, a person or a school district), which allows for *very close examination and scrutiny and the collection of a great deal of detailed data*. It is for these reasons that case studies have always been popular as a method used in clinical settings.

Second, case studies *encourage the use of several different techniques to get the necessary information* ranging from personal observations to interviews of others who might know the focus of the case study to schools' or doctors' records regarding health and other matters.

Third, *there is simply no way to get a richer account of what is occurring* than through a case study. This was exactly what Freud did in his early work. He certainly could not have used a questionnaire to inquire about his patients' dreams, nor could he think to reach his level of analysis through the use of anything other than intensive scrutiny of the most seemingly minor details concerning the way the mind functions. These data helped contribute to his extraordinary insight into the functioning of the human mind and the first accepted stage theory of human development.

Fourth, while case studies do not necessarily result in hypotheses being tested, *they suggest directions for further study*.

Some Minuses for the Case Study Method

Case studies are limited
in their generalizability.

While the case study method has provided some very important information (which probably could not have been revealed any other way), it does have its shortcomings.

First, as with everything else, *what you see is not always what you get*. The case study might appear to be easy to do (only one subject, one school, one classroom, one office, one family, etc., to find), but in fact it is the most time-consuming research method imaginable. You need to collect data in a wide variety of settings and sources, under a wide variety of conditions, and you rarely have the choice as to these settings and conditions. If the child you are observing stays in the room rather than goes out for recess, so do you.

Second, *the notes you record in your log or journal may accurately reflect reality (or what you observe), but they may not*. Everyone comes to any situation with a bias, and researchers must try not to let that bias interfere with the data collection and interpretation process. A step in the right direction here is recognizing that you are biased (as am I or as your best friend is) so you can be sure that the conclusions you draw are not based on a biased reality.

212

Third, *what case studies provide in depth, they lose in breadth*. While extremely focused, they are not nearly as comprehensive as other research methods. As a result, case studies are for you only if you want to complete an in-depth study of one type of phenomenon.

Fourth, *do not even think about trying to establish any cause-and-effect links between what you see and what you think might be responsible for the outcomes*. While you might want to speculate, there is nothing in the case study approach that allows you to reach such conclusions. Not only is there insufficient data (an *n* of 1) to conclude that a cause-effect relationship exists, but, most important, studying causal relationships is not the purpose of the method. If you want to study causal relationships, you will need to use tools that are popularly accepted to do such.

Finally, by the very nature of case studies, *the generalizability of the findings is limited*. Although you might be able to learn about another child or another institution like the one your case study is based on, it is not wise to conclude that because the focus of the study is similar, the findings might be as well.

Some scientists believe that case studies will never result in ground-breaking basic research (which is not their purpose in any case). Case studies do, however, reveal a diversity and richness of human behavior that is simply not accessible through any other method.

Survey Research

The best application of sampling theory and practice can probably be found in survey research. Survey researchers attempt to study directly the characteristics of populations through the use of surveys. Perhaps the type of survey that you are most familiar with is the ones done around election time. In those, relatively small samples of potential voters (about 1,200) are questioned about their presidential voting intentions. Much to the credit of the survey designers, the results are often very close to the actual outcomes following the election.

Survey research, also called sample surveys, examines the frequency and relationships between psychological and sociological variables and taps into constructs such as attitudes, beliefs, prejudice, preference, and opinion. For example, a sample survey could be used to assess

- parents' attitudes toward the use of punishment in the schools,
- neighborhood residents' attitudes towards new parking restrictions,
- adolescents' perceptions of curfew enforcement, and
- use of drugs in high schools.

The Interview

The basic tool used in survey research is the interview. **Interviews** (or oral questionnaires) can take the form of the most informal question-and-answer session on the street to a highly structured and detailed interaction. In fact, many of the points that were listed for questionnaires apply to interviews as well. For example, although you need not be concerned about the physical format of the questions in an interview (since the respondent never sees them), you do need to care about such issues as transitions between sections, being sensitive to the type of information you are requesting, and being objective and straightforward.

Most interviews begin with what is called **face-sheet information.** It is the neutral information about the respondent such as age, living arrangements, number of children, income, sex, and educational level. Such information helps the interviewer accomplish several things.

First, it helps establish a rapport between the interviewer and the interviewee. Such questions as "Where did you go to college?" or "How many children do you have?" are nonthreatening.

Second, it establishes a set of data that characterizes the person being interviewed. Those data can prove invaluable in the analysis of the main focus on the interview that is to come later on in the survey.

There are two general types of questions that interviews contain. **Structured** or **closed-ended questions** have a clear and apparent focus and a clearly called for answer. They are clear to the interviewer as well as the interviewee. Such questions as "At what age did you start smoking?" and "How many times have you visited this store?" call for explicit answers. On the other hand, **unstructured** or **open-ended questions** allow the interviewee to elaborate upon responses. Such questions as "Why were you opposed to the Persian Gulf War?" or "How would you address the issue of teenage pregnancy?" allow for a more broad response by the interviewee. In both cases, the interviewer can follow up with additional questions.

Interviews can be especially helpful if you want to get at information that might otherwise be difficult to come by, including firsthand knowledge of people's feelings and perceptions. For example, in a study by Smith and Shepard (1988), interviews with teachers and parents were part of a multifaceted approach to understanding kindergarten readiness and retention. In this study, interviewing was combined with other techniques such as in-class observations and the analysis of important documents. These researchers put the interview results to good use when they examined these outcomes in light of other information they collected throughout the study.

On the positive side, interviews offer great flexibility in letting you go in any direction (within the scope of the project) with the questions. You can also note the interviewee's nonverbal behavior, the setting, and other information that might prove valuable. Another advantage of interviews is that you can set the general tone and agenda at your own convenience (to a point, of course).

But there is a downside to interviews as well. They take time, and time is expensive. Interviews of 10 people could take 20 to 30 hours including travel time and such. Also, with less anonymity than, say, a questionnaire, respondents might be reluctant to come forward as honestly as they might otherwise. Other disadvantages are your own biases and the lack of a standardized set of questions. A good interviewer will probe deeply for additional information, perhaps of a different type than another interviewer, who started with the same questions, would seek. Although asking follow-up questions is an excellent practice, what do you do about the interview where probing did not lead to the same information, nor hence, to the same results?

Developing an Interview

The development of an interview begins much as does any proposal for a research project. Your first step is to *state the purpose of the interview* by taking into account your goals for the project. Then, as before, you review the relevant literature to find out what has been done in the past and whether other interview studies have been conducted. You may even find the actual interview that has been used and be able to use parts of that in your own research. This is a very common practice when researchers use the same interview, say, 10 years later to look for changes in trends.

Second, *select a sample that is appropriate for your study both in characteristics and size*. If you want to know about feelings regarding racial unrest, you cannot ask only white citizens but need to address all minorities as well. Similarly, even if interviews take lots of time and effort, you cannot skimp on sample size thinking that what you lose in sample size can be made up in richness and detail. It does not work that way.

Next, *the questions need to be developed*. As you know by now, questions, be they structured or unstructured, need to be clear and to the point without any hidden agenda, no double negatives, no 75-cent words that cannot be understood, and so forth. One of the best ways to find out how good your interview is, is by field-testing it. Use it with people who have the same characteristics as the intended audience. Listen to their feedback and make whatever changes you find necessary.

After the interview form is (more or less) finished, it is time to *train the interviewers*. Most of the traits you want in an interviewer are obvious: polite, neatly dressed, an uncontroversial appearance, and responsible enough to get to the interview site on time. These qualities, however, are often not enough. Interviewers need to learn how to go beyond the question should the need arise. For example, if you are asking questions about racial strife, the respondent might mention

> *"Yes, I sometimes feel as if I am being discriminated against."*

For you not to ask "Why?" and to follow up on the respondent's answer will result in the loss of potentially valuable and interesting information. The best way to train is to have an experienced interviewer watch the trainees interview a practice respondent and then provide feedback.

Finally, it is time for the actual interviews. *Leave plenty of time*, and go to it. Do not be shy, but do not be too aggressive either.

Test your interview form so changes can be made before you go out in the field.

The Ten Commandments of Interviewing

If you have worked hard at getting ready for the interview, you should not encounter any major problems. Nonetheless, there are certain things you should keep in mind to make your interview run a bit more smoothly and be more useful later, when it comes time to examine the results of your efforts.

With that in mind, here are the 10 commandments of interviewing (drum roll, please). Keep in mind that many, if not all of these, could also be classified as interviewer effects, where it is behavior on the part of the interviewer that can significantly affect the outcome.

1. Do not begin the interview cold. Warm up with some conversation about everything from the weather to the World Series (especially if there is a game that night and you know the interviewee is a fan). Use anything you can to break the ice and warm up the interaction. If you are offered coffee, accept (and then do not drink all of it if you don't want to). If you do not like coffee, politely refuse or ask for a substitute.
2. Remember that you are there to get information. Stay on task and use a printed set of questions to help you.
3. Be direct. Know your questions well enough so you do not have to constantly refer to your sheet, but do not give the appearance that you are being casual or uninterested.
4. Dress appropriately. Take out five of your six earrings if you feel wearing six would put respondents off.

5. Find a quiet place to do the interview where you and the interviewee will not be distracted. When you make the appointment for the interview, decide where this place will be. If a location proposed is not acceptable (such as "in the snack bar"), then suggest another (such as the lounge in the library). Call the day before your interview to confirm your visit. You will be amazed at how many interviewees forget!

6. If your interviewee does not give you a satisfactory answer the first time you ask a question, rephrase it. Continue to rephrase it in part or in whole until you get closer and closer to what you believe you need.

7. You may want to use a tape recorder so that you can review responses later. If you do, you should be aware of several things. First, be sure to ask permission to tape before you begin. Second, the tape recorder should not be a crutch. Do not let the tape run without your taking notes and getting all the information you can while the interview is going on.

8. Make the interviewee feel like an important part of an important project and not just someone taking a test. Most people like to talk about things if they are given the chance. Tell them you recognize how valuable their time is and how much you appreciate their participation. Be sure to promise them a copy of the results!

9. You become a good interviewer the same way you get to Carnegie Hall: practice, practice, practice. Your first interview, like everyone else's, is full of apprehension and doubt. As you do more of these, your increased confidence and mastery of the questions will produce a smoother job that results in more useful information.

10. Thank the interviewee, and ask if he or she has any questions.

Other Types of Surveys

Have you ever been at home during the dinner hour and the phone rings, and the person on the other end of the line wants to know how often you ride the bus, recycle your newspaper, use a computer, or rent a car?

Those calls represent one of several types of survey research, all of which are descriptive in nature. Besides interviews, the primary survey research method, and telephone surveys, there are panels or focus groups (where a small group of respondents is interviewed and reinterviewed) and mail questionnaires.

How to Do Survey Research

Survey research starts out with a general plan, called a flow plan, of what activities will occur when. The plan begins with the objective of the study, leads into the various methods that may be used to collect the data, and finishes with a final report and summary of the findings.

Clarifying the Objectives

The first step is to be clear what the objectives of the survey research are. For example, let's say that a researcher is asked by a small school system to study attitudes toward the use of punishment in the public schools. As part of her plan, she needs to consider the nature of the question being asked. Is the concern over the effectiveness of punishment? The way punishment is administered? The type of punishment (physical or other)?

Defining the nature of the objectives may require some preliminary interviewing of respondents who might be interviewed in depth later in the project. One of the primary goals in this step of the project is to define the variables, such as punishment and attitudes, that are to be studied. Both of those terms, fairly vague by themselves, need further clarification and definition if the questions eventually asked by the researcher are to yield information of any importance.

Identifying a Sample

After the objectives have been specified, the next step is in the definition of a sampling plan and getting a sample of individuals who will participate in the study. Will all teachers and parents be included? Probably not, since they would be too large a sample, and it would be inefficient to survey such a large group. But how to fairly represent the community?

Back to chapter 4! How about taking a stratified random sample of three parents from each grade from four schools in the district? And a random sample of administrators from each of two administrative levels, building and central administration? If children are involved, the researcher may want to devise a plan that takes into account how frequently these children have been punished and for what reason. Having only children who are rarely punished or only children who are always punished would skew the characteristics of the sample and the results.

Defining a Method

Now that the objectives and the sampling plan is clear, exactly what will happen during the interview or panel study? Here are some of the questions that a researcher may be concerned about.

Will the questions be primarily open ended or closed, or a combination of both? How will each question sample content, opinions, or attitudes?

How will the sample of respondents be defined? Will it include parents or teachers or administrators or all three? How about students?

How will the data be collected? Will interviews be used? Mail surveys?

What types of questions will be asked? What factual information will be included?

These questions will be answered, in part, by the types of information the researcher needs to meet the objectives defined early in the project.

Coding and Scoring

Survey research can result in anything from lengthy responses that have to be analyzed to a simple *yes* or *no* response, depending on the format and the content of the question. Once the data are collected, the researcher needs to code them (1 = male, 2 = female, for example) and then score the responses in an organized fashion that lend themselves to easy tabulation.

A simple example is shown in Fig 9.1. Here is a breakdown of parents who regularly use physical punishment and those who do not and the judgments of both groups as to effectiveness of physical punishment.

Some type of analysis of the frequencies of these responses can be done to answer the question about parents' attitudes towards punishment.

	Physical punishment is cruel and ineffective	Physical punishment is harsh and not necessary	Physical punishment can work under certain conditions	Physical punishment is a useful deterrent for poor behavior	Physical punishment is the most effective method for dealing with poor behavior
Parents who use punishment	12	14	15	23	32
Parents who don't use punishment	46	13	14	7	6

Figure 9.1 The number of parents who reacted to statements about physical punishment.

The Validity of Survey Data

Collecting survey data is hard work. It means constantly seeking subjects and dealing with lots of extraneous sources of variance that are hard to control. It is somewhat of a surprise, however, how relatively easy it is to establish the validity of such data. For example, if a person is interviewed, one way to establish the validity of the data is to seek an alternative source for confirmation. Public records are easy to check to confirm such facts as age and party affiliation. Respondents can even be interviewed again to confirm the veracity of what they said the first time. There is no reason people could not lie twice, but a good researcher is aware of that possibility and tries to confirm factual information that might be important to the study's purpose.

Evaluating Survey Research

Like all research methods, survey research has its ups and downs.

Some ups? First, survey research allows the researcher to get a very broad picture of whatever is being studied. If sampling is done properly, it is not hard to generalize to millions of people as is done on a regular basis with campaign polling and such. Along with such powers to generalize comes a big savings in money and time.

Second, survey research is efficient in that the data collection part of the study is finished after one contact is made with respondents and the information is collected. Also, minimal facilities are required. In some cases, just a clipboard and a questionnaire is enough to collect data.

Third, if done properly and with minimal sampling error, surveys can yield remarkably accurate results.

The downs can be serious ones. Most important are sources of bias, of which there are two types, that can arise during interviews and questionnaires. **Interviewer bias** occurs when the interviewer subtly biases the respondent to respond in one way or another. This bias might take place, for example, if the interviewer encourages (even in the most inadvertent fashion) approval or disapproval of a response by a smile, a frown, looking away, or other action. On the other hand, the person being interviewed might respond with a bias since he or she may not want to give anything other than *socially acceptable responses*. After all, how many will respond with a definite "yes!" to the question, "Do you beat your spouse?" These bias threats have to be guarded against by carefully training interviewers to be objective, by assuring that questions are neither leading nor putting respondents in a position where few alternatives are open.

Another problem with survey research is that people may not respond, as in the case of a mail survey. What is the big deal? Simply that the people who do not respond might constitute a qualitatively distinct group from those who do. Therefore, findings based on those who do respond will be different than if the entire group had been considered.

Developmental Research

The province of the developmental psychologist (and of many educators, pediatricians, anthropologists, and others) is to understand changes that occur throughout the process of development, from conception through death. To do this, two basic research methods have evolved over the past 100 years to describe changes or differences in behavior within a framework of different ages or stages across the life span. Let's take a look at each type, discuss an example, and then talk about their relative advantages and disadvantages.

The developmental method examines changes over time.

The Longitudinal Method

The **longitudinal method** assesses changes in behavior in one group of subjects at more than one point in time. In other words, if you were to test a group of 30-year-olds in 1960, then test the same group again in 1965 (when they were 35 years old) and again in 1970 (when they were 40 years old) and so on (as you see in Figure 9.2), you would be conducting a longitudinal study. The dashed line in Figure 9.2 illustrates the design for a longitudinal study where the same group of study participants born in 1930 is tested five successive times at five-year intervals.

		Year of Testing				
		1960	1965	1970	1975	1980
	1940	20	25	30	35	40
	1935	25	30	35	40	45
Year of Birth (cohort)	1930	30	35	40	45	50
	1925	35	40	45	50	55
	1920	40	45	50	55	60

Age appears in italics   Cross-sectional   Longitudinal

Figure 9.2 Here you can see both a longitudinal and cross-sectional design giving the year subjects were born, when they were tested, and their age. The solid line indicates a cross-sectional study and the dotted line indicates a longitudinal study.

Longitudinal studies are conducted to examine *age changes* over an extended period of time. For example, Singer and others (1984) conducted a longitudinal study of television, imagination, and aggression. The purpose of the study was to examine television viewing within a family setting and the possible influences that such viewing might have on the social interaction patterns of the family.

They did this by testing various waves (or groups) of children, beginning in 1977 through 1982, with a final group of 84 children available at the end of the experiment. Parents were asked to keep a daily log of their children's television viewing, and researchers interviewed parents, analyzed school reports and measures of intelligence, interviewed the children, and obtained other information.

There are clear advantages to the longitudinal method. Most important, it allows for the study of development over an extended period of time. What is more, because the same people are studied at more than one point in time, the subjects act as their own controls. In other words, any one person always brings the same (his or her own) background (genetic, ethnic, or otherwise) and experiences to the testing situation. This type of design is very powerful since intra-individual variability is minimized.

There are some significant disadvantages as well. First, these types of studies are very expensive to conduct. Not only is it costly to keep track of people over a long period of time, but staff and overhead costs increase from year to year. That is one reason relatively few longitudinal designs are started today, compared with many years ago, when some of the classics began. One of these, the Terman study of gifted children, began in the 1920s and continues today.

Another disadvantage of longitudinal designs is that people drop out of experiments (often called mortality). While you could assume that this dropout rate is random, there is often some concern that this dropout is systematic. This means that a particular type of person might drop out, thereby leaving the remaining sample substantively different in characteristics and qualities from the original sample.

The Cross-Sectional Method

Whereas the longitudinal method examines one group of people repeatedly over time, the **cross-sectional method** examines several groups of people at one point in time. In other words (as you can see in Figure 9.2), if you examined *age differences* in 30-, 35-, 40-, 45-, and 50-year-olds (all born in different years) in the year 1970, you would be conducting a cross-sectional study. The cross-sectional method is used to examine age differences rather than age changes, as done using the longitudinal method.

Cross-sectional studies
provide information
about age differences.

For example, to find out whom children of different ages ask for different types of advice when confronted with different types of problems, Wintre and others (1988) used the cross-sectional method. They looked at 24 males and 24 females aged 8, 11, 14, and 17 years, and presented them three hypothetical problems. Researchers asked the children to select a familiar adult, an adult expert, a familiar peer, or a peer expert as a consultant. Here, the researchers were examining age differences (not changes), and by selecting different age groups and evaluating their responses at the same point in time, the researchers' goal was accomplished.

As with the longitudinal approach, the cross-sectional approach has its advantages and disadvantages.

It is much less expensive than the longitudinal method, since testing takes place over a limited time period. Because the time period for testing is short, dropout is minimized. People tend to be located in the same place for a sufficient amount of time to complete the project. Disadvantages? The most serious is the lack of comparability of groups, since the only thing they differ on is age. And as you will see in a moment, age is not a very useful independent variable.

Table 9.2 shows you a comparison of the advantages and disadvantages of longitudinal and cross-sectional research strategies.

Using Follow-Up Studies

The information in Table 9.2 gives you a pretty good idea as to the benefits and shortcomings of each of these methods. The decision as to which one you want to use depends on such factors as the amount of resources available, time constraints, and, of course, the question you are asking.

	Advantages	Disadvantages
Cross Sectional	Inexpensive	Lack of comparability of groups
	Short time span	Gives no idea as to the direction of change that a group might take
	Low dropout rate	Examines people of the same *chronological* age who may be of different *maturational* ages
	Requires no long term administration or cooperation between staff and subjects	Tells us nothing about the continuity of development on a person-by-person case
Longitudinal	Extensive detail on the process of development	Expensive
	High comparability of groups	Potential for high dropout rate
	Allows for the study of continuity between widely differing ages	
	Allows for modified cause and effect speculation about the relationship between variables	

Table 9.2 A comparison of cross-sectional and longitudinal research designs showing the advantages and disadvantages.

It is usually impractical for any type of longitudinal study to be completed as part of your undergraduate and graduate school experience since the time span for collection of data is usually too long. But **follow-up studies** are highly feasible, where data that have already been collected can be used as a basis for collecting additional data.

For example, look at a classic study of 25 infants reared in an orphanage where they received good basic care but very little human attention and affection. Harold Skeels (1942) had 13 of these infants transferred from the orphanage to an institution for mentally retarded women, where the children were "adopted" by the women. He found that the children who were reared in the institution for women

Follow-up studies can help us answer development questions without some of the expense and time required by a longitudinal study.

and received stimulation scored 28 points higher on IQ tests than those children who were left in the orphanage. The follow-up part of the study was conducted by Skeels 21 years later (the results of the follow-up were published in 1966 by Skeels), when he examined whether there were any long-lasting effects of the different care that the groups of children had received. Much to his delight, he found that all infants who had been part of the experimental group (those who had been transferred) were self-supporting, 11 were married, and nine of those had children. Sadly, one-third of those children who did not receive any special experiences were still in institutions as adults, and only a few of the children who had remained in the orphanage were leading normal adult lives. Skeels did not follow these subjects throughout their lives, but he did conduct a follow-up study that provided information of a longitudinal nature.

The Role of Age in Studying Development

Age describes development but does not explain it.

Age is a funny variable and one that people become very dependent on to help explain changes observed in a large variety of human behaviors. For example, while it might be convenient to describe changes in the way children use words at different ages as a function of age, it is probably more accurate if these changes are understood in terms of changes in cognitive complexity, experience, and the ability to manipulate symbols.

In other words, age has *descriptive* value but not necessarily any *explanatory* value. Although age can describe what is happening, age alone cannot tell us why. Don Baer (1970) summarizes this observation in a very persuasive article, "An Age Irrelevant Concept of Development." He argues that experience, not age, is the driving force behind the differences observed in development, and that studying these experiences is much more fruitful than studying behavior as a function of chronological or maturational age.

These observations and general concerns about the utility of age have led to additional types of developmental designs besides the longitudinal and cross-sectional methods described above. Some of these new techniques take into account such variables as when the behavior is measured, called *time of measurement effects*, and *cohort (or group) effects*. Take a basic cross-sectional study that examines groups of people born in different years and tested on the same date. If you find differences between the groups (or age differences), how do you know that the differences are not due to the year in which they were born, rather than their age? How could birth date contribute to such differences? Easy. What if one group of people was born before the discovery of a drug or technique or even a cultural event that makes learning easier or harder? Take, for example, children born before and after "Sesame Street," the intensive, preparatory cognitive enrichment program on public television. Watching that program might very well have an impact on language skills. In this case, cohort (year of birth) and age, may be *confounded* (a great word!). Confounding occurs when two variables (such as date of birth and age) explain the same thing (differences in language skills), and you cannot separate the effects of the two.

Another example of confounding occurred with age and the time that the measurement took place in a study conducted by Nesselroade and Baltes (1974). They examined personality changes in adolescence and found declines with age in measures of superego strength, anxiety, and achievement. While one might want to attribute those changes to age, these scientists also found that regardless of the child's age over the three-year examination period (some went from 13 to 15 years while others went from 16 to 18 years), the decline in scores was the same. The change in age evidently was irrelevant. What was relevant, however, was the "cultural moment" when the behaviors were assessed. This is an example of an historical influence. Whatever was going on during the time of testing seemed to affect children's scores regardless of their age.

Although developmental studies that use maturational or chronological age as the major dependent variable can do a good job of *describing* change over time, be cautious that other factors, such as those pointed out in the Nesselroade and Baltes study, are not attractive as sources of explanation as well.

Correlational Research

Correlational research describes the linear relationship between two or more variables without any hint of attributing the effect of one variable on another. As a descriptive technique, it is very powerful since this method indicates whether variables (such as number of hours of studying and test score) share something in common with each other. If they do, the two are correlated (or co-related with one another).

You might remember that in chapter 5 the correlation coefficient was used to estimate the reliability of a test. The same measure is used here, again in a descriptive sense. For example, correlations are used as the standard measure to assess the relationship between degree of family relatedness (twins, cousins, unrelated, etc.) and similarity of intelligence test scores. The higher the correlation, the higher the degree of relatedness. In such a case, you would expect that twins raised in the same home to have more similar IQ scores (they share more in common) than twins raised in different homes. And they do! Twins reared apart share only the same genetic endowment, while twins reared in the same home share both hereditary and environmental backgrounds.

Correlational studies look for relationships between variables.

The Relationship Between Variables

The most frequent measure of relationships is the correlation coefficient. A **correlation coefficient** is a numerical index reflecting the relationship between two variables. It is expressed as a number between -1.00 and +1.00, and it increases in strength as the amount of variance that one variable shares with another increases. That is, the more two things have in common (like identical twins), the more strongly related they will be to each other (which only makes sense). If you share common interests with someone, it is more likely that your activities will be related than if you compared yourself with someone with whom you have nothing in common.

For example, you are more likely to find a stronger relationship between scores on a manual dexterity test and a test of eye-hand coordination than between a manual dexterity test and a person's height. Similarly, you would expect the correlation between reading and mathematics scores to be stronger than that between reading and physical strength. This is because performances on reading and math tests share something in common with each other (intellectual and problem-solving skills, for example) than a reading test and, say, weight lifting performance.

Correlations can be *direct* or *positive,* meaning that as one variable changes in value the other changes in the same direction, such as the relationship between the number of hours you study and your grade on an exam. The more you study, the better your grade. Likewise, the less you study, the worse your grade. Notice that the word *positive* is sometimes interpreted as being synonymous with good. Not so here.

Correlations can also reflect an *indirect* or *negative* relationship, meaning that as one variable changes in value in one direction, the other changes in the opposite direction, such as the relationship between the speed at which you go through multiple choice items and your score on the test. The faster you go (in general), the lower your score. The slower you go, the higher your score. Do not interpret this to mean that if you slow down you will be smarter. Things do not work like that, further exemplifying why correlations are not causal. What it means is that for a specific set of students, the correlation between test-taking time and total score is negative. Since it is a group statistic, it is difficult to conclude anything about any one individual's performance and impossible to attribute causality. More about that later.

Interestingly, the important quality of a correlation coefficient is not its sign, but its absolute value. A correlation of -.78 is stronger than a correlation of +.68, just as a correlation of +.56 is weaker than a correlation of -.60.

What Correlation Coefficients Look Like

The most frequently used measure of relationships is the *Pearson product moment correlation,* represented by the small letter r followed by symbols representing the variables being correlated. The symbol r_{xy} represents a correlation between the variable x and the variable y. For a correlation to be computed, you must have a pair of scores (such as a reading and a math score) for each subject in the group you are working with.

As you just read, correlations can range between -1.00 and +1.00 and can take on any value between those two extremes. For example, look at Figure 9.3, where there are four sets of data (A, B, C, and D) represented by an accompanying scattergram for each of the sets. A **scattergram** is a plot of the scores in pairs. In Set A, the correlation is +.70. (You will see how to compute that value in a moment).

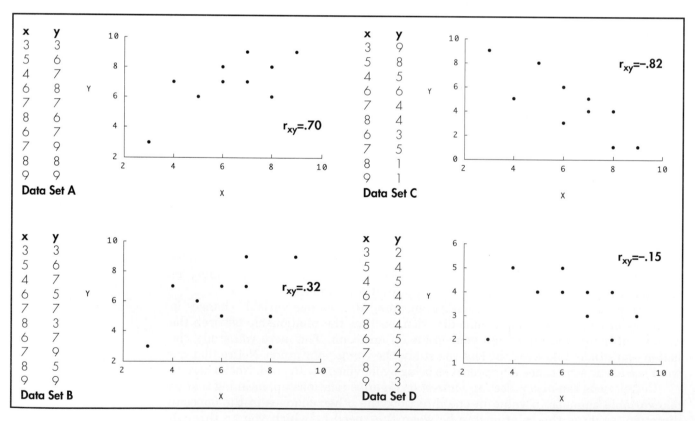

Figure 9.3 Looking at different scattergrams and correlations.

To draw a scattergram, follow these steps:

1. Using graph paper, set up an x (horizontal) and y (vertical) pair of axes.
2. Indicate which variable from the pair will be x and which will be y.
3. For Subject 1, enter the coordinates for the x and y values. In this example (Data Set A in Figure 9.2), the x score is 3 and the y score is 3, so a data point corresponding to (3,3) was entered.
4. Repeat Step 3 for all the data points, and you will see the scattergram as shown in Figure 9.2 for Data Set A.

Now look at Data Set B, where the correlation is only .32, which is substantially weaker than .70. You can see that the stronger correlation (Set A) is characterized in the following ways.

■ The data points group themselves closer and closer along a straight line as the correlation increases in strength.
■ As the slope of this grouping approaches a 45-degree angle, the correlation becomes stronger.

The data in Set A show a high positive correlation while the data in Set B show a much lower one. The data in Set C show a high negative correlation (-.82), and just as with a high positive correlation the coordinates that represent the intersection of two data points align themselves along a diagonal (in this case from the upper lefthand corner to the lower right, approaching a 45-degree angle). The last data set, Set D, shows very little relationship (r_{xy} = -.15) between the x and the y variables, and the accompanying plot of the coordinates reveals a weak pattern. In other words, a line drawn through these points would be almost flat or horizontal.

In summary, the stronger the formation of a pattern and the more the pattern aligns itself in a 45-degree angle (either from the lower lefthand corner of the graph to the upper right for positive correlations, or from the upper lefthand corner of the graph to the lower righthand corner for negative correlations), the stronger the visual evidence of the existence of a relationship between two variables.

Computing the Pearson Correlation Coefficient

The easiest manual way to compute the correlation between two variables is through the use of the raw score method. The formula for r_{xy} (with the subscript xy representing the correlation between x and y) is

The Pearson coefficient is the most frequently used type of correlation.

$$r_{xy} = \frac{\Sigma(X-\bar{X})(Y-\bar{Y})}{\sqrt{[\Sigma(X-\bar{X})^2][\Sigma(Y-\bar{Y})^2]}}$$

where: r_{xy} = the correlation coefficient
X = an individual's score on the x variable
Y = an individual's score on the y variable
$\bar{X}$ = sample mean for the x variable
$\bar{Y}$ = sample mean for the y variable

Let's look at a simple example where the correlation coefficient is computed from Data Set C shown in Figure 9.3. The mean for variable x is 6.3 and the mean for variable y is 4.6. Here is what the finished equation looks like.

$$r_{xy} = \frac{-37}{\sqrt{(32.1)(62.4)}}$$

Try it yourself and see if you can get the same answer ($r_{xy} = -.82$).

The correlation is the expression of the relationship between the variables of x and y, shown as r_{xy}. What happens if you have more than two variables? Then you have more than one correlation coefficient. In general, if you have n variables, then you will have "n taken two at a time" pairs of relationships. In Table 9.3, you can see a correlation matrix, or a table revealing the pairwise correlations between three variables (grade, reading score, and mathematics score). Each of the three correlation coefficients was computed using the same formula as described above.

	Grade	Reading	Math
Grade	1.000		
Reading	0.321	1.000	
Math	-0.039	0.605	1.000

Table 9.3 The correlations of grade, reading score, and mathematics score.

You might notice that the diagonal of the matrix is filled with 1.000's since the correlation of anything with itself is always 1. Also, the coefficients to the right of the diagonal and to its left form a mirror image. That is, if you filled in the correlations for the other "half" of the matrix (above the diagonal of 1.000's in Table 9.3), the same values would be repeated.

Interpreting the Correlation Coefficient

The correlation coefficient is an interesting index. It reflects the degree of relationship between variables, but it is relatively difficult to interpret as it stands. However, there are two ways you can interpret these general indicators of relationships.

The first is the "eyeball" method, where correlations of a certain value are associated with a certain nominal degree of relationship such that

Correlations between...	are said to be
.8 and 1.0	very strong
.6 and .8	strong
.4 and .6	moderate
.2 and .4	weak
.0 and .2	very weak

Remember: Do not be fooled by these numbers. Even the weakest correlation (such as .1) can be statistically significant if the sample upon which it is based is large enough and sufficiently approaches the size of the population. You read about the significance versus meaningfulness distinction in the last chapter.

A sounder method for interpreting the correlation coefficient is to square its value and compute the **coefficient of determination**. This value, r_{xy}^2 is the amount of variance that is accounted for in one variable by the other. In other words, it allows you to estimate the amount of variance that can be accounted for in one variable by examining the amount of variance in another variable. So if the correlation between two variables is .40, then the coefficient of determination is .16. Sixteen percent (16%) of the variance in one variable can be explained by the variance in the other variable. By logic, 84% of the variance is unexplained. This portion of unexplained variance is often referred to as the **coefficient of alienation**.

The coefficient of determination is the square of the correlation coefficient.

An interesting comparison is to see how the amount of variance explained in the relationship between two variables changes as the correlation gets stronger.

In Table 9.4 you can see the simple correlation coefficient (Column A) and the coefficient of determination (Column B). Look at the change in the amount of variance accounted for as the value of the correlation coefficient increases. For example, if the correlation is increased from .4 to .5, the increase in the amount of variance accounted for is 9%. But if the correlation is increased a similar amount (say, from .6 to .7), then the increase in the amount of variance accounted for is 13%. The increase in the variance explained is not linear. The higher the correlation, the larger the "jump" in explained variance.

r_{xy}	r_{xy}^2	Change in variance accounted for
.1	1%	-
.2	4%	3%
.3	9%	5%
.4	16%	7%
.5	25%	9%
.6	36%	11%
.7	49%	13%
.8	64%	15%
.9	81%	17%
1.0	100%	19%

Table 9.4 Differences in the amount of variance accounted for as a function of different values of the correlation coefficient. The amount of explained variance increases as the correlation increases.

Is a nonexperimental design for you? That is not really the question that should be asked. Rather, does your subject of interest demand that you use the tools suggested by the historical or descriptive method? As emphasized before, the question that is asked determines the way it is answered. If you want to investigate how the Oklahoma settlers of the 1930s raised their children or how child rearing has changed, historiography may be for you! And what does the descriptive method offer?

It provides an account of an event, often in such detail that it serves as a springboard for other questions to be asked and answered. Case studies, developmental research, and correlational studies describe a particular phenomenon in a way that communicates the overall picture of whatever is being studied. Although these methods do not allow the luxury of implying any cause-and-effect relationship between variables, their use provides the tools needed to answer questions that are otherwise unanswerable.

Exercises

1. What is the primary purpose of historical research?

2. What are some of the most important differences in the methods that historical researchers use when compared with more traditional (experimental) researchers in the social and behavioral sciences?

3. Write a one-paragraph description of a historical research study that you would like to complete. Answer the following questions:
   a. How would you establish the authenticity of your sources?
   b. How would you establish the accuracy of your sources?

4. Write a null and a research hypothesis for a longitudinal and a cross-sectional study. Provide examples of studies where you would want to look at age changes versus age differences.

5. Rank the following correlation coefficients in order of their strength from strongest to weakest.
   a. .21
   b. -.67
   c. .53
   d. -.01
   e. .78

6. What is wrong with the following argument? The relationship between the numbers of hours you study is directly related to how well you do on school tests. Therefore, if you do not do well on a test, it means that you did not study enough.

7. What are some of the problems with using age as a dependent variable, and how can they be addressed?

8. Indicate what type of correlation each of the following relationships describes: positive, negative, or no relationship.
   a. As A increases, B increases in value.
   b. As A increases, B decreases in value.
   c. As A decreases in value, B does not change.
   d. As A decreases, B increases in value.

9. Tell whether the following hypotheses are correlational in nature.
   a. There are no differences in cognitive ability between preschoolers in private day care settings and preschoolers who do not attend day care.
   b. There is a relationship between parents' education, socioeconomic status, and children's achievement in math.
   c. There is no relationship between the rate of violent crime in New York and socioeconomic status.
   d. Parent education does not increase a child's performance on a math achievement test.
   e. Over time, there are differences in discipline policies used in rural and urban schools.

10. What is the purpose of descriptive research?

11. What is the difference between the cross-sectional method and the longitudinal method? Identify two advantages and two disadvantages of each method.

12. Which of the following statements about correlation coefficients are true?
    a. Correlations can be positive.
    b. Correlations can be negative.
    c. Correlations reflect causation.
    d. Correlations measure the relationship between two variables.

Want to Know More?

Further Readings

Huck, S. W., Cormier, W. H., & Bounds, W. G. Jr. (1990). *Reading statistics and research*. New York: Harper Collins.
> Intended for individuals whose primary interest is in understanding the research of others. Presents quite a nice introductory chapter on single case design.

Leventhal, G., & Ontell, M. (1989). A descriptive demographic and personality study of second-generation Jewish Holocaust survivors. *Psychological Reports, 64*, 1063-1073.
> Illustrates a descriptive study format and procedures. Details behaviors observed in the Jewish survivors and further defines behaviors by categorizing individuals by parts of the country they inhabited.

Maleske, R. T. (1995). *Foundations for gathering and interpreting behavioral data: An introduction to statistics*. Pacific Grove, CA: Brookes Cole Publishing.
> Targeted to the reader who wants to gain a fundamental understanding of the total process of gathering and interpreting behavioral data and addresses the issues and concepts involved in this process.

McCall, R. B., & Kagan, J. (1994). *Fundamental statistics for behavioral sciences* (6th ed.). Fort Worth, TX: Harcourt Brace College Publishers.
> Provides an in-depth view of descriptive statistics, inferential statistics, correlational statistics, and issues in research design.

Merriam, S. B. (1989). Contributions of qualitative research to adult education. *Adult Education Quarterly, 39*, 161-168.
> Defines qualitative research and lists its potential for contributions for the future of adult education. Also lists new concepts now introduced in the adult education field, such as enrollment economy and self-directed learning.

Sears, R. R. (1975). *Your ancients revisited: A history of child development*. Chicago: University of Chicago Press.
> A monograph written by a well-known developmental psychologist about the history of childhood and the study of it in the United States over the past 100 years.

Readings of Other Interest

Boyd, R. D., Welge, P., Sexton, D., & Miller, J. S. (1989). Concurrent validity of the Battelle developmental inventory: Relationship with Bayley scales in young children with known or suspected disabilities. *Journal of Early Intervention, 13(1)*, 14-23.
> Looks at correlations between the Battelle and the Bayley in assessing infants with known or suspected disabilities.

Brazelton, T. B. (1969). *Infants and mothers: Differences in development*. New York: Dell.
> A descriptive history through observation of the different developmental stages from birth. Illustrates four different temperaments and how the temperaments somewhat affect different development changes in this longitudinal history.

Kosinsiki, J. (1976). *The painted bird*. Boston: Houghton Mifflin.

   A child's book that reviews the brutal aspects of World War II through the eyes of a Polish child. A different type of example of descriptive history research.

Moore, J. W., Biddle, B., & Gagne, E. (1973). A system for increasing the probability of teacher control of their teaching behavior. *Educational Technology, 13(10)*, 44-47.

   Investigated scientific problem solving methods of hypothesis testing in order to solve classroom problems for teachers.

Rayl, A. J., & Gunther, C. (1989). *Beatles '64: A hard day's night in America*. New York: Doubleday.

   A description of the activities in the middle 1960s of the Beatles and news such as John F. Kennedy's assassination. Also connects historical events to the Beatles' songs and activities.

Yalom, I. D. (1989). *Love's executioner and other tales of psychotherapy*. New York: Basic Books.

   A superb example of the use of a case study to describe techniques, patient feelings, and more. Yalom has written 10 compassionate case studies of different patients.

CHAPTER

10

TEN

Experimental Research Methods

What You'll Learn About in this Chapter

- The importance and role of experimental designs
- The importance of randomization in the experimental method
- The role of chance in the experimental method
- The principles of experimental design
- The concepts of internal and external validity, and the role they play in the experimental method
- Threats to internal and external validity, and how they can be controlled
- How to control extraneous sources of variability

What scientists try to do best is find out why things happen. They go to all kinds of lengths trying to establish, for example, why some children are more active than others, why some adults are more successful, or where differences between attitudes come from. The methods and models described in this chapter can go a long way toward understanding such phenomena.

One tool that can assist in understanding these differences is the **experimental method**. Unlike any of the other methods discussed so far in *Exploring Research*, the experimental method tests for the presence of a *distinct cause and effect*. This means that once this method is used the judgment can be made that A does cause B to happen or that A does not cause B to happen. Other methods, such as historical and descriptive models, do not offer us that luxury. Although they can be used to uncover relationships between variables, there is no way that a causal relationship can be established. Why? It is by virtue of the experimental method, which allows for the control of potential sources of differences (or variance), that the following can be said: One factor is related to another in such a way that changes in that factor are causally related to changes in the other.

For example, the simplest experimental design would be where two groups of subjects are randomly selected from a population and one group (labeled the **experimental group**) receives a treatment, and the other group (labeled the **control group**) receives no treatment. At the end of the experiment, both groups are tested to see if there is a difference on their test scores. Assuming (and this is the big assumption) that the two groups were equivalent from the start of the experiment, any observed difference at the end of the experiment must be due to the treatment. That is what experimental design, in one form or another, is all about.

When done correctly, experimental designs can provide a tremendous amount of power and control over understanding the causal relationships between variables. Its use is, to a significant extent, responsible for a good deal of the understanding scientists have about psychological and social processes.

Experimental Designs

There are a variety of types of experimental designs. In this section you will find a description of the set that Donald Campbell and Julian Stanley made famous in their 1963 monograph (*Experimental and Quasi-Experimental Design for Research on Teaching*) that helped revolutionize the way people plan and carry out their research projects. They identified three general categories of research design: pre-experimental designs, true experimental designs, and quasi-experimental designs. Quasi-experimental designs are also referred to as causal-comparative designs. This chapter will discuss the pre-experimental and true experimental designs, and in the next chapter you will learn about quasi-experimental design.

The major way that these various types of experimental designs differ from one another is the degree to which they impose control on the variables being studied, with the pre-experimental method having the least amount of control, the true experimental method having the most, and the quasi-experimental method being somewhere in the middle. The more control, the easier it is to attribute a cause-and-effect sequence of events.

Another way these pre-, true and quasi-experimental designs differ from one another is the degree of randomness that enters into the design. You already know that the word *random* implies an equal and independent chance of being selected, but that definition and concept can be applied beyond the selection of subjects from a population to form a sample to the concept's importance in experimental design.

Actually, there are different steps that need to be taken to ensure the quality of true randomness in the best of all experimental designs.

The experimental method is the way to establish cause-and-effect relationships.

Quasi-experimental designs are also referred to as causal-comparative designs.

The point at which random assignment enters the process distinguishes different experimental designs from one another.

The first is one you know most about, the random selection of subjects from a population to form a sample. This is the first procedure you would undertake in an experiment. Now you have a sample.

Second, you want to randomly assign subjects to different groups. You want to make sure, for example, that subjects assigned to Group 1 had an equal chance of being assigned to Group 2.

Finally (if you did what Steps 1 and 2 prescribe above), you have two groups that you assume are quite equivalent to each other. Now you need to decide which of the two groups will receive the treatment or, if you have five groups, which treatment each group will receive. In the same way that you used a table of random numbers in the past, you just assign (at random) different treatments to the groups.

Following these three steps you can ensure that the subjects are randomly selected from a population and randomly assigned to groups, and which group receives which treatment is decided at random as well.

Table 10.1 summarizes some of the primary differences between pre-experimental, quasi-experimental and true experimental designs. Even though we save our discussion of quasi-experimental designs for the next chapter, we are including it here so you can see a comparison of all designs types. Notice that many of these differences focus on the process of randomization of selection procedures, subjects, and assignment.

	Pre-Experimental Designs	Quasi-Experimental Design	True Experimental Designs
Presence of a control group?	In some cases, but usually not	Yes	Yes
Random selection of subjects from a population?	No	Yes, but restricted in pre-assigned groups	Yes
Random assignment of subjects to groups?	No	No	Yes
Random assignment of treatment to groups?	No	When possible	Yes
Degree of control over extraneous variables	Low	Some	High

Table 10.1 Differences between pre-experimental, true experimental, and quasi-experimental designs.

Pre-Experimental Designs

Pre-experimental designs are not characterized by random selection of participants from a population, nor do they include a control group. Without either of these, the power of the research to uncover the causal nature of the relationship between independent and dependent variables is greatly reduced, and almost eliminated. These designs have little or no control over extraneous variables that might be responsible for outcomes other than what the researcher intended.

Pre-experimental designs have no random assignment of subjects or conditions.

For example, a parent uses an old family remedy (wearing garlic around the neck!) to ward off the evil spirits associated with a child's cold. Lo and behold, it works! This is the weakest type of experimental conclusion to reach since there is virtually no comparison to show that the garlic worked better than anything else or better than nothing at all for that matter. The child, of course, might have gotten better on his or her own. There is simply no control over other factors that might cause the observed outcome (such as the cold virus running its course).

In research terms, this type of study is called a **one-shot case study design** and looks like this:

Group 1   Treatment   Post-test

As you can see, a group is exposed to some type of treatment and then tested.

What shortcomings might you notice about this one-shot case study type of pre-experimental design? First, there is no attempt at randomization. Of what use might the pre-experimental design such as this one-shot case study be? Not much for experimental work or for establishing cause-and-effect relationships, but acceptable if you are speculating about factors that occurred at an earlier time and their effect on later behavior.

Another pre-experimental design, called the **one-group pretest post-test design** is represented by the following:

Group 1   Pretest   Treatment   Post-test

For example, a researcher is interested in studying how effective Method A is in increasing muscle strength. He or she follows these steps in the completion of the experiment:

1. Advertises for volunteers for the experiment.
2. Administers a pretest to measure strength.
3. Exposes the subjects to the hypothesized strength increasing treatment.
4. Administers the post-test.

The important comparisons are between the pretest and post-test scores for each subject. The primary problem with this type of design is that there is no control group, and without any control group how can the researcher tell that any difference observed between the pre- and post-test scores is a function of the treatment or a function of some other factors? What if 50% of the sample did not get enough sleep prior to the post-test? Or if they participated in another study designed to increase strength as well? These factors, rather than the specific treatment, might be responsible for differences in strength.

True Experimental Designs

True experimental designs control selection of subjects, assignment to groups, and assignment of treatments.

True experimental designs include all the steps in selecting and assigning subjects in a random fashion, plus a control group, thereby lending a stronger argument for a cause-and-effect relationship. One of the reasons these designs are so powerful is that they all have random selection and assignment of treatments and to groups.

For example, let's look at one of the most popular of these designs, the **pretest post-test control group design**, which looks like this:

Group 1   Pretest   Treatment   Post-Test
Group 2   Pretest   No Treatment   Post-Test

The steps that are followed using this design are

1. Randomly assign the subjects to the experimental or the control group.
2. Pretest each group on the dependent variable.
3. Apply the treatment to the experimental group. The control group does not receive the treatment.
4. Post-test both the experimental and the control group on the dependent variable (in another form or format if necessary).

The assumption here, and you are probably on to this, is that since the subjects are randomly assigned to either the control or the experimental group, they are equivalent at the beginning of the experiment. Any differences observed at the end of the experiment must be due to the treatment since all other explanations are accounted for.

Pretest post-test control group designs are not limited to two groups either. For example, let's say that a researcher wants to examine the effects of different literacy programs on how well adults learn to read. One treatment might be instruction five days a week and another might be instruction three days a week. The third group would be a control group, whose members do not receive any instruction.

The experimental design would look something like this:

Group 1	Pretest	5 days/week	Post-test
Group 2	Pretest	3 days/week	Post-test
Group 3	Pretest	No treatment	Post-test

The number of treatment groups does not really make any difference as long as there is a control group. There is an important difference as to the nature of the control group. In some cases, the control group might receive no treatment whatsoever, while in others, the control group might just receive a different type of treatment. The difference between the role of a control group is a reflection of the type of question that was originally asked.

If the control group does not receive any treatment, then the obvious question is whether the treatment is effective when compared with no treatment at all. If the treatment group is compared with another group receiving treatment, then the question becomes, which of the two is the more effective. A somewhat fine distinction, but it is an important one to remember when you are thinking about how to structure your experiment.

Here is another true experimental design that is very popular: the **post-test only control group design**. This one looks like this:

| Group 1 | Treatment | Post-test |
| Group 2 | No Treatment | Post-test |

The most apparent characteristic here is that there is no pretest for either the control or the experimental group. The rationale for this approach is that if you randomly select and assign people to groups, there is no need for a pretest. They are already equivalent anyway, right? The answer is "yes," when you have a sufficiently large sample (at least 30 or so in each group). Another reason to use the post-test only design as compared with the pretest post-test design is when it is not convenient or it is impossible to administer a pretest. Under these conditions, you can go with the post-only design.

There are basically two disadvantages, however, of using only a post-test. First, if the randomization procedures were not effective, then groups might not be equivalent to begin with. Second, you cannot use the pretest to assign people to other

The Solomon four group is extremely useful, but expensive and time-consuming to use.

experimental groups such as high or low on some variable. These disadvantages might not be of much consequence, yet they are important to consider in any case.

The last true experimental design is kind of the granddaddy of them all, the **Solomon four group design** as shown here:

Group 1 (Experimental)	Pretest	Treatment	Post-test
Group 2 (Control)	Pretest	No Treatment	Post-test
Group 3 (Control)	No Pretest	Treatment	Post-test
Group 4 (Control)	No Pretest	No Treatment	Post-test

There are four groups in this design, one experimental (which receives the treatment) and three control groups, one of which receives the treatment as well.

What is most interesting and most useful about this design is the many types of comparisons that can be made to determine what factors might be responsible for certain types of outcomes. For example, let's say that you are interested in determining the effects of the treatment but you also want to know if the very act of taking a pretest changes final scores as well. For the effectiveness of the treatment, you could compare the experimental group with Group 2 since the only thing that differs between them is the inclusion of a treatment. For a test of the influence of the pretest on later outcomes, a comparison of Group 1 and Group 3 will provide the information you need. The only difference is that one Group received the pretest, while Group 3 did not. You can make all kinds of other comparisons as well. For example, the effect of the treatment on groups that did not receive the pretest (but the treatment) would result in a comparison of Group 3 and Group 4.

So why doesn't everyone who does true experimental research use this type of design? One good reason: time. While the Solomon four group experimental design is very effective for separating out factors responsible for differences in the dependent variable, it is a time-consuming design to execute. You have to arrange for four groups, randomly selected and assigned, three control and one experimental conditions, and lots of testing. Time and money "ain't" what they used to be, so for many researchers this kind of design is impractical.

Internal and External Validity and Experimental Design

The different types of experimental designs that have already been mentioned in this chapter were outlined in the seminal work by Campbell and Stanley. They realized that it was not enough just to come up with different designs, but what was also needed was a way to evaluate these designs. What outside criteria might one use to judge the usefulness of these different ways of approaching a problem?

Their decision? Use the criteria of internal and external validity; both measure how well the design does what it should.

Internal validity is synonymous with control.

Internal validity is the quality of an experimental design such that the results obtained are due to the manipulation of the independent variable. For example, if you can show that a treatment works to increase withdrawn children's social skills, and if that treatment is the only apparent cause for the change, the design (and the experiment) is said to be internally valid. If there are several different explanations for the outcomes of an experiment, the experiment does not have internal validity.

External validity is synonymous with generalizability.

External validity is the quality of an experimental design such that the results can be generalized from the original sample to another sample and then by extension to the population from which the sample originated. For example, if you can apply the treatment for increasing withdrawn children's social skills to another group of withdrawn children, the design (and the experiment) is said to have external validity.

But not all designs and not all experiments have acceptable levels of internal and external validity for a variety of different reasons, which Campbell and Stanley call *threats to internal and external validity*. Once you understand what these threats are, you will be able to see which experimental designs are preferable and why.

Threats to Internal Validity

The following is a brief explanation of those threats to internal validity that lessen the likelihood that the results of the experiment are due to the manipulation of the independent variable. Good scientists try to reduce these threats.

Good research controls threats to internal validity.

History

Many experiments take place over an extended period of time, and other events can occur outside of the experiment that might affect its outcome. These other events might offer a more potent explanation for the differences observed between groups than the original treatment.

For example, a researcher wants to study the effect of two different diets on hyperactive children's school behavior. Without the researcher's knowledge, some of the parents of the children in the experimental group have contacted their child's teacher, and together they have started an at-home program to reduce troublesome school behaviors. If there was a difference in school behavior for the kids on the diet plan, how would one know that it was not due to the teacher-parent collaboration? That outside influence (the teacher and parent activity) is an example of **history** as a threat to internal validity since the outside of school activity, and not diet, might account for any observed difference.

Maturation

Maturation can be defined as changes due to biological or psychological forces. These changes might overshadow those that are the result of a treatment.

For example, a researcher is studying the effects of a year-long training program on increasing the strength of school-aged children. At the end of the program she evaluates the children's strength and finds that the average strength score has increased over the year's time. Her conclusion? The program worked. Correct? Maybe. But as attractive as that explanation is, by the very nature of physical development children's strength increases with age or maturation.

Abracadabra! It was not the treatment but Mother Nature that helped the children walk as they got older. That is maturation.

Selection

The basis of any experiment is the **selection** of subjects as participants. Selection is a threat to the internal validity of an experiment when the selection process is not random but instead contains a systematic bias that might make the participating groups different from each other.

For example, a researcher wants to determine how extended after school care affects family cohesion. As part of the experiment, the researcher forms an experimental group (those families whose children are in extended care) and a control group (those families whose children are not in extended care). Since the families were not randomly selected or assigned to treatments, there is no way to tell if they were equivalent to each other. The group of extended-care children might come from families with a positive or negative attitude toward the program before it even begins, thereby biasing the outcomes.

Testing

As with many of these threats, control testing by using a control group.

In many psychological experiments, a pretest is part of the experiment. When the pretest affects performance on later measures (such as a post-test), **testing** can be a threat to internal validity.

For example, a researcher pretests a group of subjects on their eighth-grade math skills, and then teaches them (the treatment) a new way to solve simple equations. The post-test is administered, and there is an increase in correct answers. Given this information, one does not know whether the increase is due to learning a new way to solve the simple equations or to the learning that might have taken place as the result of the pretest. The experience with the pretest alone might make them "test wise," and their performance reflects that, rather than the effectiveness of the treatment.

Instrumentation

When the scoring of an instrument itself is affected, any change in the scores might be due to the scoring procedure rather than to the effects of the treatment.

For example, a researcher is using an essay test to judge the effectiveness of a writing skills program. There is little doubt that when he grades the 100th examination, a different set of criteria will be used than when he graded the first one. Even if the criteria do not change, simple fatigue is likely to cloud the scorer's judgment and result in differences due to **instrumentation** and not the actual effects of the program.

Regression

This is a really fascinating (and often misunderstood) threat. The world of probability is built in such a way that placement on either extreme of a continuum (such as a very high or low score), will result in scores that regress toward the mean on a subsequent testing (using the same test). In other words, when children score very high or very low on some measure, you can expect their subsequent scores to move toward the mean, rather than away from it. This is true only if their original placement (in the extreme) resulted from their score on the test. If you do not already realize it, regression occurs because of the unreliability of the test and the measurement error that is introduced, placing people more in the extremes than they probably belong.

Given the lower likelihood that someone will end up in the extreme part of a distribution (be it high or low), the odds are higher that on additional testings, they will score in an area more central to the distribution. And for high or low scorers, moving towards the center of the distribution means moving toward the mean, which is what regression is all about.

For example, a teacher of children with severe physical handicaps designs a project to increase their self-care skills and pretests the group using anecdotal information in September before the program begins. In June, she tests them again and finds that their skills have increased. One solid argument that could be made is that the increase was due to **regression** and not to anything the teacher did. That is, children who were extreme to begin with (on the self-care skills test) would move toward the average score (and be less extreme) if nothing happened. The change takes place through regression alone and may have nothing to do with the treatment.

Mortality

One of the real-world issues in research is that subjects are sometimes difficult to find for follow-up studies. When this happens, the researcher must ask whether the composition of the group after people had left is basically the same as before subjects dropped out. **Mortality** is a threat to the internal validity of an experiment when those who drop out change the nature of the group itself.

For example, research with very young infants is fascinating but often frustrating. They usually arrive either sleeping or crying or ready to eat but rarely ready to "play," and many have to be sent home and rescheduled or even dropped from the experiment. Those who are dropped may indeed be substantively different from those who remain, making the final sample of subjects no longer equivalent to the initial sample and raising questions about the effectiveness of the treatment on this different sample. Another word for mortality is *attrition*.

Mortality is an even more serious problem in long-term research projects.

Threats to External Validity

Just as there are threats to the internal validity of a design, so there are threats to the external validity. Once again, external validity is not concerned with whether the manipulation of the independent variable had any effect on the dependent variable (that is the provence of internal validity), but whether the results of an experiment are generalizable to another setting. Here are the threats to external validity, complete with definitions and examples. As with threats to internal validity, good scientists try to reduce the threat these pose as well.

Multiple Treatment Interference

A set of subjects might receive an "unintended" treatment in addition to the intended treatment, thereby decreasing the generalizability of the results to another setting where the unintended treatment may not be available.

For example, let's say that a group of nursing home residents is learning how to be more assertive, and one of the nursing aides picks up on the program and does a little "teaching" of his or her own. The results of the experiment would not be easily generalized to nursing home residents in another setting, hence not generalizable, because the other settings may or may not have an aide that is as aggressive.

Reactive Arrangements

The Hawthorne effect shows how researchers must consider the subject's knowledge of the experimenter's purpose.

In the Hawthorne manufacturing plant in Chicago, Illinois, researchers set out some 50 years ago to measure the effects of changing certain environmental cues, lighting and working hours, on work production. The problem was that the participants in the study knew about the researcher's intent. Even when the lighting was worse and the working hours longer, production increased for the experimental group. Why? Because the workers received special attention from the researchers. The extra attention resulted in changes in productivity; lighting and work hour conditions were found to be secondary in importance. Unless subjects were studied within other settings (which would defeat the intent of the experiment), the external validity would be low, as would the generalizability.

Incidentally, the threat to external validity, called reactive arrangements, is also sometimes called, you guessed it, the Hawthorne effect.

Experimenter Effects

Another threat to external validity involves researchers. Imagine an experiment to reduce the anxiety associated with a visit to the dentist. (Yikes!) What if the person conducting the desensitization training unintentionally winces each time the dentist's drill starts up. The results of such a training program cannot be generalized to another setting since the other setting would require a trainer who would behave in a similar fashion. Otherwise, the nature of the experience is changed. In other words, the training program might not be as effective without the trainer's emotional expressions, and hence the results of the training program might not be generalizable since the person conducting the training is not part of the program.

Pretest Sensitization

You have already seen how pretests can inform people about what is to come and affect their later scores, thereby decreasing the internal validity of a study. In a similar fashion, the presence of a pretest can change the nature of the treatment, so that the treatment applied in another setting is less or more effective without the presence of the pretest. To make things equivalent and maximize generalizability to other settings, the pretest would have to be part of the treatment, which, by definition, would change the nature of the treatment and the experiment's purpose.

Increasing Internal and External Validity

First, internal validity. It is no secret how you can maximize the internal validity of an experiment: Randomly select subjects from a population, randomly assign them to groups, and use a control group. In almost every design where these characteristics are present, most threats will be eliminated. Let's take the example of children with severe physical handicaps and the project that begins in September to increase self-care skills. If a group that does not receive the program (the control group) is included, then the assumption is that both the control and the experimental groups

Table 10.2 Threats to internal and external validity of an experiment. Although any of these can be the death blow to an experiment, the simple addition of a control group often can eliminate the threat.

	Design ↓ / Threat →	History	Maturation	Selection	Testing	Instrumentation	Regression	Mortality	Multiple Treatment Interference	Reactive Arrangements	Experimenter Effects	Pretest Sensitization
Pre-experimental Designs	One-Shot Case Study	-	-	-				-			-	
	One-Group Pretest Post-test Design	-	-	+	-	-	?	+		?	-	-
True Experimental Designs	Pre-test Post-test Control Group Design	+	+	+	+	+	+	+		?	?	-
	Post-test Only Control Group Design	+	+	+	+	+	+	+		?	?	+
	Solomon Four Group Design	+	+	+	+	+	+	+		?	?	+

Notes:

+   The threat is accounted for.

?   Depending upon the setting and the circumstance, the threats might be accounted for.

-   The threats are not accounted for.

A blank means the threat is not relevant.

The most effective way to increase external validity is through the use of a control group.

will progress or regress equally, so any difference one sees at the end of the year must be due to the self-care program.

Similarly, if the groups are equivalent to begin with (ensured through randomization), changes are due to the treatment and not to the lack of equivalence at the beginning of the experiment.

The inclusion of a control group and the use of randomization similarly takes care of the other threats such as testing, mortality, and maturation. Assuming that groups are equal to start with and exposed to similar circumstances and experiences, the only differences between them would be a function of the treatment, right?

Ensuring external validity is a somewhat different story since it is tied less tightly to the design than to the behavior of the people conducting the experiment. For example, the only way to ensure that experimenter effects are not a threat to the external validity of the experiment is to be sure that the researcher who administers the treatment acts in a way that does not interfere. In the example of desensitizing anxious dental patients, you want to be sure the trainer does not have any real problems with the dentist's office setting.

Where most threats to internal validity are taken care of by the experiment's design, most threats to external validity need to be taken care of by the designer of the experiment.

Table 10.2 summarizes threats to the internal and external validity of the designs that are discussed in this chapter and how well each design compensates for each threat.

Internal or External Validity: A Trade-Off?

This might be a situation where you can have your cake and eat it too as long as you do not make a pig out of yourself!

An experiment can have both internal and external validity, but the two need to be balanced.

An experiment can be both internally and externally valid, but with some degree of caution and balance. For example, internal validity in some ways is synonymous with control. The higher the internal validity, the more confident you can be that what you did (manipulate the independent variable) is responsible for the outcomes you observe. But if there is too much control (such as very exacting experimental procedures with a very specifically defined sample of subjects), the results of the experiment might be difficult to generalize (hence lower external validity) to any other setting. This is true since the degree of control might be impossible to replicate, to say nothing of how difficult it might be to find a sample that is similar to the one that was originally used.

The answer? Use your judgment. Strive to conduct your experiments in such a way as to ensure a moderate degree of internal validity by controlling extraneous sources of variance through randomization and a control group. Ditto for external validity. Unless you can generalize to other groups, the value of your research (depending upon its purpose) may be limited.

Controlling Extraneous Variables

All this talk about extraneous variables! Just what are they? Extraneous variables are factors that can decrease the internal validity of a study. They are variables that, if not accounted for in some way, can confound the results. As you read in chapter 9, results are confounded when you cannot separate the effects that different factors might have on some outcome. For example, a researcher is studying the effects of school breakfasts on attendance. Parents who are more highly motivated might get their children to school for the breakfasts, which might make the difference between those who attend and those who do not. The breakfast, per se, might have nothing to do with any group difference. In this case, the treatment (the breakfast) is confounded with parents' motivation.

Almost everywhere you look in experimental research, there are variables that have the potential to confound the results. These muddy the waters in a scientist's attempt to understand just what factors cause what outcomes. The solution to this problem? There are several. The general question becomes *Which variables need to be worried about and which can be assumed to be unimportant?* For the variables that are of concern, what can be done to minimize the effect they might have on the outcomes of the experiment?

First, you can choose to ignore any variable that is unrelated to the dependent variable being measured. For example, if attendance is the primary dependent variable and offering school lunch is the primary independent variable, can factors such as gender of the child, gender of the teacher, class size, or parents' age be important? They may be. The only way you can tell is through a review of the literature and the development of some sound conceptual argument as to why the teacher's gender is or is not related to the child's attendance. For the most part, if you cannot make an argument why a variable is related to the outcome you are studying, it is probably best ignored.

Second, it is through the use of randomization that the effects of many different potential sources of variance can be controlled. Most important, randomization helps to ensure that the experimental and control groups are equivalent on a variety of different characteristics. In the example used above, randomly assigning children to the eat breakfast or not eat breakfast groups would ensure that parental motivation would be an equally likely influence for both groups and, therefore, not be very attractive as an explanation for any observed difference.

Variables of no importance should be ignored.

Randomization is, once again, a terrific way to control for unwanted variance.

Matching

Random assignment of subjects to groups is a good way to ensure that there will be equivalence, in general, between groups. The occasion may arise, however, when a researcher wants to make sure that the two groups are matched on a particular attribute, trait, or characteristic. For example, in the school breakfast program study, if parental influence is a concern and if the researcher does not think that random assignment will take care of the potential problem, matching is a technique that can be used.

Matching of subjects simply means that for every occurrence of an individual with a score of X in the experimental group, the researcher would make sure there is a person in the control group with a similar score. In general, the rule you want to remember is that the variable on which subjects is matched needs to be strongly related to the dependent variable of interest; otherwise matching does not make much sense. Since this is the general rule, it comes as no surprise to you that the first step in the matching process is to get a measure of the variable to be matched on before group assignment takes place. These scores are then ranked, and the pairs that are close together are selected. One subject from each pair is placed in each group, and the experiment continues.

What researchers are doing when they follow this strategy is stacking the cards in their favor to ensure that some important and potentially strong influences are not having an undue effect on the results of the study. This is a simple and effective way of ensuring this.

But as you might suspect, there is a downside to matching as well. Matching can be expensive and time-consuming, and you might not be able to find a match for all

Matching can be an effective way of equalizing groups.

individuals! Suppose one set of parents is extremely highly motivated and the next most motivated set of parents is far down on the scale. Can you match those sets? It is doubtful. You probably have to exclude the extreme scoring parents or find another with a similarly high score to whom those parents can be matched.

Use of Homogeneous Groups

One of the best ways to ensure that extraneous variables will not be a factor is to use a homogeneous population, or one whose members are very much alike, from which to select a sample. In this way, most sources of differences (such as racial or ethnic backgrounds, education, political attitude, etc.) might automatically be controlled for. Once again, it is really important for the groups to be homogeneous only on those factors that might affect their scores on the dependent variable.

ANCOVA

A final technique is a fairly sophisticated device called analysis of covariance, or ANCOVA. This statistical tool equalizes any initial differences that might exist. For example, let's say you are studying whether a specialized exercise program increases running speed. Since you know that running speed is somewhat related to strength, you want to make sure the participants in the program are equal in strength. Let's say you try to match subjects but discover there is too wide a diversity to ensure that matching will equalize the groups. Instead, you use analysis of covariance, or ANCOVA.

Analysis of covariance, on its simplest level, subtracts the influence of the relationship between the covariate (which in this case is strength) and the dependent variable (which in this case is speed) from the effect of one treatment. In other words, ANCOVA adjusts final speed scores to reflect where people started as far as strength is concerned. It is like playing golf with a handicap of a certain number of strokes. Handicapping helps to equalize unequals. ANCOVA is an especially useful technique in quasi-experimental or causal-comparative designs when you cannot easily randomly assign people to groups, but you have information concerning variables that are related to the final outcome and on which people do differ.

Want to find out if A (almost) causes B? Experimental methods are the peaches, the max, the top of the line. They provide a degree of control that is difficult to approach by using any of the other methods discussed so far in Exploring Research. *The milestone work of Campbell and Stanley identified the various threats to these designs and provided tools to evaluate the internal and external validity of various pre-experimental and experimental designs. Through such techniques as matching, the use of homogeneous groups, and some statistical techniques, you can have a good deal of confidence that the difference between groups is the result of the manipulation of the independent variable rather than some other source of differences. If cause and effect is the order of the day, you came to the right place when you came to this chapter.*

Exercises

1. Define each of the following threats to external validity, and provide an example of how each one might be a factor in an experiment.
   a. Pretest sensitization
   b. Reactive arrangements

2. Why is a balance between external and internal validity necessary for acceptable research?

3. A set of children with emotional handicaps is placed in a special program to improve the quality of their social interactions based on their extreme test scores. At the end of the program, the average increase in the quality of their interactions is 57%. What threat to internal validity negates the value of this finding, and what can you do to remedy the situation?

4. List the steps you would go through to ensure that two groups participating in a study of attitude toward divorce are equally matched.

5. Write an abstract that describes a study where regression is a threat to the internal validity of the study. Be sure that you describe what steps the researcher might take to account for regression as a threat.

6. What are the ethical considerations for assigning first-graders to different experimental learning groups? Does it affect your ethical concerns if the assignment is random?

7. What are some examples of pre-experimental research you see in the real world?

8. What are some benefits of using pretests?

9. What are the threats to external validity? How could each threat affect you as a researcher? Come up with a research example for each threat to external validity. What are some methods to increase internal validity?

Want to Know More?

Further Readings

Christensen, L. B. (1994). *Experimental methodology*. Boston: Allyn & Bacon.
> Provides an introduction to the basic principles of psychological research and the research process.

G. (1990). The Hawthorne Effect: A fresh examination. *Educational Studies, 16*, 261-267.
> Fascinating paper questioning whether or not the Hawthorne effect even exists as it has been described for more than 50 years. Questions a formerly basic tenet of experimental concerns and reminds us that everything deserves re-examination every now and then

Pettit, G. S., Bates, J. E., & Dodge, K. E. (1993). Family interaction patterns and children's conduct problems at home and school: A longitudinal perspective. *School Psychology Review, 22(3)*, 403-422.
> Examines the predictive associations among family interaction patterns, comparing internalizing and externalizing behavior problems.

Readings of Other Interest

Taylor, S. E. (1989). *Positive illusions*. New York: Basic Books.
> An examination of how the world is viewed because of our wishful thinking instead of our knowledge of reality. Illustrates a descriptive way to correlate factors as to which relate to a main hypothesis and which do not.

Utts, J. (1988). Successful replication versus statistical significance. *Journal of Parapsychology, 54(4)*, 305-320.
> Addresses the issues surrounding the suggestion that replication in parapsychology may be equated with the achievement of statistical significance.

Quasi-Experimental Research: A Close Cousin to Experimental Research

What You'll Learn About in this Chapter

- The difference between experimental and causal-comparative designs
- How quasi-experimental designs differ from pre-experimental and true experimental designs
- How quasi-experimental designs differ from one another
- The use of single-subject designs in experiments
- How single-subject designs are evaluated

In chapter 10, you read about how an experimental design can be used to investigate the cause and effect relationship that might exist between two variables. Another type of research design also attempts to establish a cause-and-effect relationship but does not have the particular strength or power of the traditional experimental method. In this chapter, you will explore the quasi-experimental method as an alternative to the experimental designs you have already learned about. Although the quasi-experimental method may not have the power, it is the preferred design when important cultural and ethical issues are introduced into the decision making process as to design choice. More about this last point in a moment.

The Quasi-Experimental Method

The **quasi-experimental method** differs from pre-experimental and experimental methods in one very important way.

In quasi-experimental research, the hypothesized cause of differences you might observe between groups has already occurred. For example, if you looked at differences between males and females on verbal ability, the possible cause of differences in verbal ability (the independent variable, gender) has already "occurred." In other words, *group assignment has already taken place.*

You had no control over who would be in each group since sex is predetermined, as is age, ethnicity, hair color, and hundreds of other variables. In other words, there is a *preassignment* to groups based on some characteristics of the group. When you use the experimental method (as described in chapter 10), you may have an infinite range of values of the independent variable from which to select. When you use the quasi-experimental method, you do not, nor does anyone else. The values of the independent variable are simply there to begin with, such as in the case of gender (male and female), race (Caucasian, Asian, etc.), age (under 18, and 18 or over), and illness (history of heart disease and no heart disease).

This preassignment to groups (or treatments) introduces the major shortcoming of the quasi-experimental method when compared with the classic experimental method: less power in understanding the cause for any differences that might be observed in the dependent variable. For example, if differences are found between males and females on verbal ability, your conclusion that the difference is due to gender differences might be correct, but conceptually the argument is left wanting. To what can this difference between the sexes be attributed? The way they were treated when younger? The experiences and opportunities they did or did not have? Hormonal differences that affect brain development? These are only three classes of factors that could explain the difference. To fully understand the nature of the differences, however, these other factors would need attention.

So, when does quasi-experimental come in handy, and when is it preferred? In spite of the doubts just raised, the quasi-experimental method is essential for one reason. It allows for the exploration of topics that otherwise could not be explored because of ethical, moral, and practical concerns. Just look at some of the following research topics, and try to think how you would understand their origins:

- differences in the personalities of abused versus nonabused children
- the effects of malnutrition on infants
- the effects of maternal cocaine use during the third trimester of pregnancy on neonatal (newborn) behavior
- differences in intellectual capacity between old people placed in nursing homes and those living with their spouses in their own homes

The list goes on and on. Can you spot the reason why quasi-experimental is preferred over the experimental method in these instances? It is staring you right in the face; all these examples include "treatments" or placement into groups that would be unethical for a researcher to arrange artificially. Placing one child in Group A (which receives reading help) or Group B (which does not) is one thing, but could you justify depriving a pregnant woman of sufficient nutrition to examine the effects on the child or moving an elderly person into a nursing home to see the effects of the move on intellectual ability? Never. Quasi-experimental studies allow a look at the effects of such variables *after the fact*, which is why they are also referred to as *ex-post facto* (or after the fact) *research*.

As you shall see, quasi-experimental designs allow for the random assignment of people to groups such as when you select 50 of 500 males to make up Group A. You cannot, however, randomly assign "treatments" to groups (they are already assigned), the major shortcoming.

In terms of control and internal validity, quasi-experimental studies have a higher level of internal validity than pre-experimental designs (which you remember are missing a control group) but not as much as true experimental designs (which you remember have both a control group and random assignment of treatments to groups). Also, quasi-experimental designs can have substantial levels of external validity, perhaps as high as true experimental designs.

Quasi-Experimental Designs

The most desirable characteristics of any good research design are the random selection and assignment of subjects and the use of a control group. They are desirable because they ensure that groups will be equivalent to one another before the treatment is applied.

In some cases, however, randomization is simply impractical or impossible, and the use of a control group is impossible or too expensive or unreasonable. For example, you cannot randomly decide which expectant parents will have boys and which will have girls. Nor can you decide which children will attend preschool and which will not. Designs where it is impossible to randomly assign participants to all groups are called quasi-experimental designs because they are not truly experimental. The argument about cause and effect relationships in quasi-experimental designs is simply not as strong as in true experimental designs.

In this section of the chapter you will read about some of the most commonly used quasi-experimental designs.

The Nonequivalent Control Group Design

The **nonequivalent control group design** is one of the most often used quasi-experimental designs, especially when it is impossible or difficult to randomly assign subjects to groups. For example, in an educational setting children cannot be rearranged very easily into different classes, but you would like to be able to use them as part of a sample. Here's what the nonequivalent control group design looks like:

| Group 1 | Pretest | Treatment | Post-test |
| Group 2 | Pretest | No Treatment | Post-test |

The first thing you may notice is how similar the design is to the pretest post-test control group design that was discussed in chapter 10, except that there is no random selection or assignment. The researcher uses intact groups, such as nursing home residents, children in a classroom, or factory workers. This situation immediately decreases the power of the design to establish a causal relationship since there are doubts about the equivalence of the groups before the experiment begins. That is why it is called a nonequivalent design.

The most serious threat to the internal validity of this design is selection, since the groups might initially differ on characteristics that may be related to the dependent variable. With the inclusion of a pretest, you can compare pretest scores and see if the groups are equivalent. If they are (that is, if there is no significant difference between them), you should have less (but still some) concern about their equivalence. Statistically, differences can be worked with using such techniques as analysis of covariance. But even if you can statistically equalize initial differences on the pretest, that does not mean that there are not other factors (that randomization could take care of) that can still pose a threat to the internal validity of the experiment.

For example, let's assume that you are studying the effect of different antibigotry programs in junior high school. Since you cannot easily assign children to different groups (since they cannot be taken out of their home classrooms), you will use Program 1 in a certain classroom and Program 2 in another classroom. These intact groups are not equivalent. Even if you use some statistical method to make them so (such as a pretest that assesses bias), you are still not likely to account for other differences such as the ethnicity of the children or past experiences or attitudes, all factors that could better (but not entirely) be taken care of through randomization.

The **nonequivalent control group design** is the most frequently used design when randomization is not possible. It works because there is some control over the influence of extraneous variables (through the use of the control group). Some equivalence of groups, while not assured, is at least approachable.

The Static Group Comparison

What if you cannot randomize and cannot administer a pretest? Then your choice of designs should be the **static group comparison**, which looks like this:

Group 1	Treatment	Post-test
Group 2		Post-test

This design is similar to the nonequivalent control group design, except there is no pretest. Under what conditions might you need the nonequivalent design? For whatever reason, there may not be time to administer a pretest or it might be too expensive or the sample might not be available before the treatment begins. These are just some of the examples of why the static group comparison design might be appropriate.

Problems with this design? A bunch. There is little control of the major threats to internal validity, such as selection and mortality. As far as external validity, all the threats (multiple treatment interference, reactive arrangements of setting, and experimenter effects) remain as well. For example, let's say you are testing a treatment for nursing home residents to increase their social interaction with other residents. You are using three different nursing homes and have to use the same treatment (one of two treatment groups and one control group) for each of the homes. If you find a difference in social skills after the treatment, how do you know the difference is not due to differences that existed before the experiment began? You do not. And having no pretest information, you cannot determine that as well.

Threat →	History	Maturation	Selection	Testing	Instrumentation	Regression	Mortality	Multiple Treatment Interference	Reactive Arrangements	Experimenter Effects	Pretest Sensitization
The Nonequivalent Control Group Design	+	+	+	+	+	?	+		?	?	-
The Static Group Comparison	+	?	-	+	+	+	-			-	

Notes:
+ The threat is accounted for.
? Depending upon the setting and the circumstance, the threats might be accounted for.
- The threats are not accounted for.
A blank means the threat is not relevant.

Table 11.1 Threats to the internal and external validity of some quasi-experimental designs.

Why would you want to use this design? When you have no other choice, and that is an important lesson to be learned about any of these less than optimal designs. They are used when circumstances prevent the use of true experimental designs and the results of such experiments are interpreted within the framework of those limitations.

A summary of the threats to the internal and external validity of quasi-experimental designs and how they are (or in these cases are not) met is shown in Table 11.1.

Single-Subject Design

The experimental method, as described throughout the last chapter, is the most common way of testing whether cause-and-effect relationships exist. It is not, however, the only way.

Single-subject designs allow in-depth examination of specific behaviors.

There is an entirely different approach to understanding cause-and-effect differences that does not look at groups but, rather, at individuals. **Single-subject research designs** are quite common to fields such as behavior analysis, but they are useful in almost any setting where a researcher wants to know the effects of manipulating an independent variable on the behavior of one individual. In fact, it is safe to say that while group designs (such as those discussed by Campbell and Stanley) focus on one or more behaviors across many individuals, single-subject designs focus on one individual across many behaviors (of a similar type). The goal, however, is the same: to determine the effects of an independent variable on behavior.

It is not just the method that is different here but the entire view of behavior and what is important to examine when conducting research. Single-subject design is very much rooted in the behavioral view of development, where changes in behavior are seen as a function of its consequences. This school of thought, made popular by the animal studies of B. F. Skinner, has helped provide substance to an entirely different view about the whys of behavior as well as the way behavior should be studied. No better or worse than the group method, the single-subject method goes about answering the important question of causality in a unique and creative fashion.

The basic method in a single-subject experiment is to:

1. Measure a behavior before the treatment.
2. Apply a treatment.
3. Withdraw the treatment (called a reversal).

The assumption is that if the behavior changes as a result of the treatment, when the treatment is withdrawn, the behavior will return to its pretreatment levels. Therefore, if a researcher were interested in increasing the level of verbal behavior of a particularly withdrawn child in a class, he or she would do the following:

1. Measure the rate of verbal behavior every 5 minutes each hour for a period of 10 days. The researcher assumes this measurement scheme will result in a representative sampling of the child's verbal behavior.

This first step is called the **baseline** since it is this measure against which the researcher will compare the results of the treatment to see if the verbal behavior increases.

2. Implement the treatment. Each time the child exhibits some verbal behavior, it is reinforced by strong verbal praise on the part of the teacher. Over a period of 10 days, the same type of record is kept.

3. As a final test of whether the treatment was effective, the verbal praise is withdrawn, and the verbal behavior is once again measured.

A graph of what this experimental design might look like is shown in Figure 11.1. You can see that the frequency of the behavior decreased when the treatment was applied and that it increased when the treatment was withdrawn.

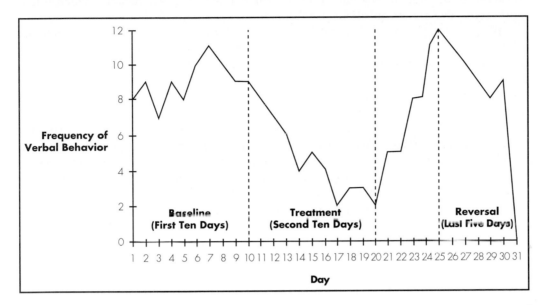

Figure 11.1 A simple ABA design, consisting of the establishment of a baseline, treatment, and measurement.

In single-subject design terminology, the baseline is labeled A and the treatment B. In the example that you just read, the design would be an ABA design. As you might expect, a whole variety of designs use the A and B conditions, such as the most simple AB design where a baseline is established and a treatment implemented. Then there is a set of ABAB designs where there are alternating baseline and treatment conditions as well.

ABAB designs allow for the reapplication of an effective treatment.

The primary advantage of the ABAB design over the AB and the ABA design is that the ABAB design reduces concern about the ethical issue of introducing what is a potential correcting treatment (B), and then measuring only the effects of the withdrawal of the treatment. The ABAB design seeks to reintroduce the treatment and get the behavior back to where it was as the result of the first attempt at applying the treatment. For example, if the child who had a low rate of verbal behavior were left in that situation, some questions might be raised as to whether this was an ethical decision. When it is easy to use an ABAB design and once again show the effectiveness of a treatment, why not make that choice and use that design?

Evaluating Single-Subject Designs

You can apply the same criteria of internal and external validity as measures of the trustworthiness to single-subject designs as you did to other designs.

Single-subject designs
can be evaluated using
many of the same criteria
as other designs.

Most single-subject designs of the ABA and ABAB type have sufficient internal validity. They demonstrate that by the manipulation of the independent variable (its presentation or withdrawal), a behavior will or will not change. Thus, what one observes is the result of what one did, the primary criterion for internal validity to be present.

External validity, or generalizability, is another story. Some critics of single-subject design would claim that such experiments have limited generalizability since you cannot generalize beyond the results with a single subject. As you might expect, those critics are usually the ones that use the traditional group designs which reflect a different view of how questions are formed.

What these critics overlook is that traditional group designs also have problems with generalizability. In particular, many experiments do not have random assignment of groups, and their generalizability to another setting is often a bit of a stretch and a small leap of faith.

The way, of course, that you increase generalizability is by eliminating the threats discussed earlier in this chapter and making your experiment as "naturally" occurring as possible, so that the results can easily be applied to another setting. The way that the results of a single-subject design can be generalized depends on the extent to which the results of a single-subject experiment can be replicated, given identical or slightly varied conditions. For example, if the girl in our experiment was in fourth grade, would a single-subject experiment with a fifth-grader and the same exact procedures increase the generalizability of the results so that one could talk about the independent variable and the experiment as having external validity? Probably so. And with more replications of varying kinds, the more this external validity will be increased.

This is the last chapter in the book that will discuss different types of experimental design. Now that you have the basics about how to design and carry out and experiment, the most important next step is learning about how to share the results of all your hard work. To do this, we turn to chapters 12 and 13, which cover writing a research proposal and writing a research report.

Exercises

1. Single-subject research is quite different from group experimental research. How do they differ, and under what conditions would you want to use a single-subject design?

2. When are quasi-experimental studies appropriate?

3. Based on the following independent variables, which ones are appropriate for a quasi-experimental design and why?
   blood type
   reading group
   level of abuse
   math strategy
   deprivation of food

4. In what way does quasi-experimental design differ from experimental design?

5. What are some examples of quasi-experimental research questions?

Want to Know More?

Further Readings

Kasdin, A. (1982). *Single case research designs: Methods for clinical applied settings*. New York: Oxford University Press.
> A detailed discussion of the rationale behind the use of single-subject designs accompanied by a description of how different types of single-subject designs are used in clinical areas such as in the treatment of abnormal behaviors.

Keppel, G. (1991). *Design and analysis: A researcher's handbook* (3rd ed.). Englewood Cliffs, NJ: Prentice Hall Inc.
> Provides the basic information needed to design meaningful experiments and analyze data in behavioral, social, and biological sciences.

Maleske, R. T. (1995). *Foundations for gathering and interpreting behavioral data: An introduction to statistics*. Pacific Grove, CA: Brooks and Cole Publishing.
> Targeted to the reader who wants to gain a fundamental understanding of the total process of gathering and interpreting behavioral data. Addresses the issues and concepts involved in this process.

Readings of Other Interest

Kerlinger, F. N. (1986). *Foundations of behavioral research* (3rd ed.). New York: Holt, Rinehart & Winston.
> Primarily conceptual and theoretical in approach, but does not avoid numbers and statistics! A very thorough book on research. However, does not cover single subject design.

Kozol, J. (1991). *Savage inequalities: Children in America's schools*. New York: Crown Publishers.
> Provides astonishing stories of children's lives and the inequalities with which they are faced, case by case. Award winning book on the inequality of schools.

Radford, J. (1990). *Child prodigies and exceptional early achievers*. New York: Free Press.
> A fascinating book that raises interesting questions about studying people and their behavior "after the fact," which in this case is after they have been identified as prodigies.

Exploring Research

Writing a Research Proposal

What You'll Learn About in this Chapter

■ Only one thing: How to Write a Proposal

If one of the requirements for this class is to write a research proposal, you have come to the right place. This chapter will lead you through the considerations you need to take into account when completing a proposal. Even if you are not required to write a proposal for class, stick around anyway. What you learn here will be helpful in your research endeavors since you will learn what distinguishes acceptable proposals from unacceptable ones. You will also learn of the importance of framing a question in a logical and clear way so it is easier to answer.

Writing a proposal is not an easy task for anyone, and it may be especially difficult if you have not done one before or if you have not done much writing. The job takes diligence, commitment, and lots of hard work. But all the hard work is well worth it. You will end up with a product of which you can be proud, and that is only the beginning. If you actually follow through and complete the proposed research, you will be making a significant contribution to your field. With those good words of encouragement, here are the major steps in the completion of a proposal, beginning with what a proposal looks like.

The Format of a Research Proposal

Knowing how to organize and present a proposal is an important part of the research craft. The very act of putting thoughts down on paper will help you to clarify your research interests and to be sure that you are saying what you mean. Remember the fellow on the television commercial who would say, "Pay me now or pay me later?" The more work and thought you put into your proposal, the easier it will be to complete the research later on.

With this in mind, here is a basic outline of what should be contained in a research proposal and a few comments on each of these sections. Keep in mind that proposals can be organized differently.

I.   Introduction
    A.   The problem statement
    B.   A rationale for the research
        1.   Statement of the research objectives
    C.   Hypothesis
    D.   Definitions of terms
    E.   Summary including a restatement of the problem
II. A (brief) review of the relevant literature
    A.   The importance of the question being asked
    B.   The current status of the topic
    C.   The relationship between literature and problem statement
    D.   Summary including a restatement of the relationships between the important variables under consideration and how these relationships are important to the hypothesis proposed in the introduction.
III. Method
    A.   Participants including a description and selection procedures
    B.   Research design
    C.   Data collection plans
        1.   Operational definition of all variables
        2.   Reliability and validity of instruments
        3.   Results of pilot studies
    D.   Proposed analysis of the data
    E.   Results of the data
IV. Implications and limitations

V. Appendices
   A. Copies of instruments that will be used
   B. Results of pilot studies (actual data)
   C. Human experimentation approval
   D. Participant permission form
   E. Time line

If you have looked at someone else's thesis or dissertations, you might notice that this outline is organized around the same general sequence of chapter titles: introduction, review of literature, methodology, results, and discussion. Since this is only a proposal, the last two sections cannot present the analysis of the real data or discuss the findings. Instead, the proposal simply talks about the implications and limitations of the study and the last part (V) contains all the important appendices.

A quick guideline as to what a proposal should contain is the first three sections of the finished proposal: introduction, review of literature, and method. The rest of the material (implications and such) should be included at your own discretion and based on the wishes of your adviser or professor. Keep in mind that the first three sections may be a lot to ask. You will have to gather that information anyway, however, and doing it before you collect your data will give you just that much more confidence in your research as well as a very good start.

Being Neat

While your words are important, the way your proposal appears is, too. While what you say is more important than how you say it, there is a good deal of truth to Marshall McLuhan's statement that the medium is the message. With that in mind, here are some simple and straightforward tips about proposal preparation. If you have any doubts about presentation (and if you don't have any other class guidelines), follow the guidelines set forth in the Publication Manual of American Psychological Association (1994). You will see an example of that format in chapter 13.

- All pages should be typed with 1-inch margins on top, bottom, left, and right. This leaves sufficient room for comments.
- All pages should be double-spaced.
- All written materials should be proofread. This does not imply just using a spell-checker. These marvels only check your typing skills (to, two, or too?) and not really your spelling or how well you use words. So, proofread your paper twice— once for content, and once for spelling and grammatical errors.
- The final document should be stapled together, with no fancy covers or bindings (too expensive and unnecessary).
- All pages should be numbered with a running head and a page number like this:

Cognitive style and gender differences/Your Name   *15*

As for the format of the contents, you cannot go wrong following the example that you will see in chapter 13, which is written using the guidelines for manuscript presentation followed by the American Psychological Association. There are some differences between what you are reading here and what you will see in chapter 13, but nothing major. For example, APA guidelines do not require the author's name on pages because the review for journals is "blind." Your professor, however, needs your name on each page.

Evaluating the Studies You Read

When you begin to go through research articles in preparation for writing a proposal (or just to learn more about the research process), you want to be sure that you can read, understand, and evaluate the content.

As a beginning researcher there is no question that you might not be ready to take on the "big boys" and start evaluating and criticizing the work of well-known researchers, right? Wrong! Even if you are relatively naive about the research process and inexperienced, you can still read and critically evaluate research articles. Even the most sophisticated research should be written in a way that is clear and understandable. Finally, even if you cannot answer all the questions listed below to your satisfaction at this point, they provide a great starting place for learning more. As you gain more experience, the answers will appear.

So what makes good research? Researchers Hall, Ward, and Comer (1988) asked that very question about 128 already published research articles. Among a survey of research experts, they found the following shortcomings (in order of appearance) to be the most pressing criticisms:

- The data collection procedure was not carefully controlled.
- There were weaknesses in the design or plan of the research.
- The limitations of the study were not stated.
- The research design did not address the question being asked by the research.
- The method of selecting participants was not appropriate.
- The results of the study were not clearly presented.
- The wrong methods were used to analyze the information collected.
- The article was not clearly written.
- The assumptions on which the study was based are unclear.
- The methods used to conduct the study were not clearly described or not described at all.

Quite a series of pits to fall into. To help you avoid the worst of them, here is a set of questions you might want to ask about any research article.

Criteria for Judging a Research Study

The Review of Previous Research

1. How closely is the literature reviewed in the study related to previous literature?
2. Is the review recent? Are there any outstanding references you know of that were left out?

The Problem and Purpose

3. Can you understand the statement of the problem?
4. Is the purpose of the study clearly stated?
5. Does the purpose seem to be tied to the literature that is reviewed?

6. Is the objective of the study clearly stated?
7. Is there a conceptual rationale to which the hypotheses are grounded?
8. Is there a rationale for why the study is an important one to do?

The Hypothesis

9. Are the research hypotheses clearly stated?
10. Are the research hypotheses explicitly stated?
11. Do the hypotheses state a clear association between variables?
12. Are the hypotheses grounded in theory or in a review and presentation of relevant literature?
13. Are the hypotheses testable?

The Method

14. Are both the independent and dependent variables clearly defined?
15. Are the definition and description of the variables complete?
16. Is it clear how the study was conducted?

The Sample

17. Was the sample selected in such a way that you think it is representative of the population?
18. Is it clear where the sample comes from and how it was selected?
19. How similar are the subjects in the study to those that have been used in other, similar studies?

Results and Discussion

20. Does the author relate the results to the review of literature?
21. Are the results related to the hypothesis?
22. Is the discussion of the results consistent with the results?
23. Does the discussion provide closure to the initial hypothesis that the author presents?

References

24. Is the list of references current?
25. Are they consistent in their format?
26. Are the references complete?
27. Does the list of references reflect some of the most important reference sources in the field?
28. Does each reference cited in the body of the paper appear in the reference list?

29. Is it clearly written and understandable?
30. Is the language biased (non-sexist and relatively culture free)?
31. What are the strengths and weaknesses of the research?
32. What are the primary implications of the research?
33. What would you do to improve the research?

Planning the Actual Research

You are well on your way to formulating good, workable hypotheses, and you now know at least how to start reviewing the literature and making sense out of the hundreds of resources available. But what you may not know, especially if you have never participated in any kind of research endeavor, is how much time it will take you to go from the very first visit to the library to your final examination or submission of the finished research report. That is what you will learn here.

While you still have plenty to learn about the research process, now is a good time to get a feel for the other activities you will have to undertake in order to complete your research project. It is also good to get a sense of how much time they might take.

First the activities. Table 12.1 shows you an example of a checklist of activities you have to complete on your way to completing your proposal (or research). The activities are grouped by the general headings previously discussed.

OK, now for computing how much time it will take. One effective way to do this is to estimate how much time each individual activity (writing the literature review, collecting data, etc.) will take you, using some standard measure such as days, considering that sometimes things go

- just as planned,
- not as well as planned, and
- not well at all (which usually is the rule, rather than the exception).

Now take the average of these values. To be more precise, let's break work days into 4-hour chunks (for a.m. and p.m.) and call each chunk 1 unit of time. There are then 10 units of time in one week.

For example, let's look at *Search through primary sources* (as part of the literature review) and estimate that it will take you

- four days, or 8 time units, if things go great,
- six days, or 12 units, if things do not go exactly as planned, and
- a whopping eight days, or 16 units, if things do not go well at all.

Once you have these estimates, just average them for the activity, and you will have a singular estimate of how long any one activity should take, such as

$$(8 + 12 + 16)/3 = 12 \text{ units}$$

or 6 days, which is about one very full week's work (if you work on Saturday or Sunday).

If you want to be even more precise, weight the estimates. For example, let's say that you anticipate having lots of trouble finding a sample, and at best you can expect things to go only OK. Writing the descriptive section, though, should be a snap. Then weight the "not as well as planned" estimate two or three times as much as the others.

	Activity	Estimate when things go just as planned	Estimate when things don't go as well as planned	Estimate when things go not at all as well as planned
Checklist for Planning Proposal Writing and Research Activities				
Within each cell, enter the estimates of how many units (or half days) each activity will take. If you are writing a prposal, consider only proposal-related activities. If you are actually going to be writing the proposal and conducting the research, consider all the activities. Be fair to yourself and be reasonable. Do not set up such high expectations they cannot be met or give yourself so much time you never finish!				
Introduction	• Search general sources and come up with an idea • Formulate a research question • Present a preliminary hypothesis	_____	_____	_____
Review the literature	• Search through secondary sources • Search through primary sources • Reconsider the literature and state the research hypothesis	_____	_____	_____
Methodology	• Identify and describe the independent variables • Identify and describe the independent variables • Field test the dependent variables • Create data entry forms • Locate a suitable sample • Pilot test the research hypothesis • Distribute permission forms • Collect data	_____	_____	_____
Results	• Analyze the data • Report the results using tables and graphs when necessary	_____	_____	_____
Discussion	• Review the nature and the purpose of the research • Refer to the results in light of the research • Draw the appropriate conclusion about the confirmation or refutation of the research hypothesis • Discuss limitations of the study • Discuss implications of the study • Discuss future directions	_____	_____	_____

Table 12.1 There is no substitute for planning, and the more time you spend now in planning, the less time you will need to spend later.

These estimates can be computed for all the activities you see in Table 12.1 and then added together to get an estimate for the overall activity. Keep in mind that *everything* takes longer than you initially think. So even for your most optimistic estimate, be generous.

Selecting a Dependent Variable

You have read at several places in *Exploring Research* how important it is to select a dependent variable or an outcome measure with a great deal of care. It is the link between all the hard preparation and thinking you did and the actual behavior you want to measure. Even if you have a terrific idea for a research project and your hypothesis is right on target, a poorly chosen dependent variable will result in disaster.

Here are nine things to remember when selecting such a variable. Use them as a checklist when you search through previous studies to find what you need.

- Try to find measures that have been used before. This lends them credibility and allows you to support your choice by citing previous uses in other research studies.
- Be sure the validity of the measure has been established. Simply put, you just do not want to select dependent variables whose validity either has not yet been established or is low. Doing so will raise too many questions about the integrity of your entire study. Remember, you can find out if a test has been shown to be valid through a review of other studies where the test has been used or through an examination of any manuals that come along with the test or assessment tool.
- Be sure the reliability of the measure has been established. Just as with validity, you know how crucial reliability is as a characteristic of a useful dependent variable.
- If the test requires special training, consider the time and the commitment it will take to learn how to use it. We are not talking about simply reading the instructions and practicing administration of a test. We are talking about intense training such as that required for the administration of intelligence and several personality scales.
- Be sure you can get a sample of the test before you make any decision about whether you will use it. You might have read about it in a previous study, but until you examine its guidelines on the population it is intended for, requirements for administration, costs, and so on, you should not make any final decision. You can usually get a sample packet either at no cost or minimal cost from the test developer or publisher (although you may need a letter from your adviser since several test companies will not send materials to anyone who requests it).
- If you will need them, be sure that norms are available. Some tests do not require the use of norms, but if your intention is to compare the performance of different samples with scores from a more general population, you have to be sure and have something to compare it with. As you will see later, norms are especially important for norm-referenced tests.
- Be sure you get the latest version of the test. Publishers are always changing test materials, whether a repackaging of the materials or a change in the actual normative or reliability and validity data. Just ask the simple question, "Is this the latest version available?"
- The test needs to be appropriate for the age group you are working with. If a test measures something at age 10, it does not mean it will be equally reliable and valid at age 20, or even that it will measure the same underlying construct or behavior at that age. Look for other forms of the same test or another test that measures the same construct for the intended age group.

- Finally, look for reviews of the test in various journals and reference sources such as *Tests in Print* (Mitchell, 1983), which lists hundreds of tests on everything, and *Mental Measurement Yearbook* (Conoley and Kramer, 1989). Both these publications contain extensive information about different types of tests including everything from administration procedures to costs to critical reviews of the tests by outside experts. Look at these critical reviews before you decide to adopt an instrument.

Reviewing a Test

Here is more about selecting dependent variables (or screening measures for assignment to groups as independent variables). At best, with all things going in your favor, it is difficult to find exactly the test you want to use to diagnose, evaluate, look for effects, or use as a placement tool, and so on. The dependent variable you select may not even be a *test* in the formal sense of the word. But if it is, you need to be concerned about lots of different characteristics and qualities of the instrument.

With that in mind, here is an outline of criteria you should consider that would allow you to compare and contrast various tests. For each test you want to consider, complete the outline to the extent possible and then use this information to make a decision. Be sure to weigh each of the criteria accordingly as well. For example, while a test might be just right as far as its design and purpose, if it is prohibitively expensive or if you need special training (which you do not have) to administer it, it is not likely that you will be able to use it.

Basic Information

1. Name of the test:
2. Date of publication:
3. Test author(s):
4. Publisher:
5. Cost of all needed test materials:
6. Cost of sample packet:

General Test Information

7. Purpose of the test as stated by author(s):
8. Purpose of the test as used in other studies:
9. Age levels included:
10. Grades included:
11. Special populations included:
12. Method of administration (individual or group):
13. Method of scoring (manual or computer):
14. Administration time:
15. Ease of administration:
16. Ease of scoring:
17. Amount of training required for administration:
18. Adequacy of test manual and other materials:

Design and Appearance

19. Clear and straightforward directions:
20. Design and production satisfactory:
21. Arrangement of items on page:
22. Ease of reading:

Reliability

23. Reliability data provided:
24. Type of reliability established (test-retest, parallel forms, etc.):
25. Independent studies used to establish reliability:

Validity

26. Validity data provided:
27. Type of validity established:
28. Independent studies used to establish validity:

Norms

29. Norms available:
30. Description of norm groups:
31. How norm groups were selected:
32. Appropriateness of norm groups to your purpose:

Evaluation

33. How used in the past:
34. Summary of outside review(s):
35. Other evaluative information:

Selecting a Sample

Many researchers feel there is nothing more important than selecting a sample that accurately reflects the characteristics of the population they are interested in studying. Yet, sample selection can sometimes be a risky business, with all kinds of questions needing to be answered before you can make any moves toward the sample selection process. Here is a list of factors to keep in mind.

■ Think of yourself trying to find a suitable pool of candidates from which to select a sample, and multiply the number of other people trying to do the same thing in your community by 100. That is a small estimate of how many people in every university community are looking for a sample to include in their study. Where can you look? Try some of the following:

> Church and synagogue groups
> Boy and Girl Scouts
> Retirement homes and villages
> Preschools
> Singles clubs
> Special interest and hobby groups
> Fraternal organizations

Remember, you do not want to select any group that is organized for a particular reason if that reason is even remotely related to what you are studying. You would not select, for example, members from the Elks Club and study loyalty or friendship, just as you would not select parents who send their kids to private schools for a survey on attitudes toward supporting public education, unless the selection of such samples is an important part of your sampling plan.

- Approach candidates with an absolutely crystal clear idea of what you want to do, how you want to do it, and what they will get in return (a free workshop, the results of the study, or anything else you think might be of benefit to them).
- Similar to our last point, the population must match the characteristics of those groups you want to study. It might go without saying (we will say it here anyway), but selecting a sample from a poorly identified population is the first major error in sample selection. If you want to study preschoolers, you cannot study first-graders just because the two groups are close in age. The preschool and the first-grade experience are substantially different from each other.
- The type of research you do will depend on the type and size of sample you need. For example, if you are doing case study descriptive research, which involves intense and long interviews and has limited generalizability (which is not one of the purposes of the method), you will need very few subjects in your sample. If you are doing a group differences study, you will need at least 30 for each group.
- A highly reliable test will yield more accurate results than a homemade essay exam. The less reliable and valid your instruments, the larger the sample size you will need to get an accurate picture of what you want.
- Consider the amount of financial resources at your disposal. The more money (and resources in general) you have, the more subjects you can test. Remember, the larger the sample (up to a point) the better since larger samples come closer to approximating the population of which they are a part.
- The number of variables you are studying and the number of groups you are using will affect the sample selection process. If you are simply looking at the difference in verbal skills between males and females, you can get away with 25 to 30 in each group. If you add age (5- and 10-year-olds) and social class (high and low), you are up to six different possible combinations (such as 5-year-old females of high social class) and up to 6 x 30, or 180, subjects for an adequate sample size.

Data Collection and Analysis

If you are following the various steps in this chapter, you probably have completed, plan on completing, or can do the following:

- You understand the format of a research proposal.
- You have chosen a problem of some significance in your field and specified what the variables of interest (both dependent and independent) will be.
- You have located measures of the dependent variable that are both reliable and valid.

Now you are ready to begin the data analysis stage.

In chapters 7 and 8, you learned how to use some basic statistical tools to describe the characteristics of the data you collect during the early stages of your research.

At this point in your proposal, you want to address the following tasks and be sure that they are completed before you move on.

1. The development of a data collection form to help you with organization and accuracy.
2. Specification of which types of descriptive statistics you will use to describe the variables you are examining. At what level of measurement do they fall, and what level of measurement—nominal, ordinal, interval, or ratio—would best reflect what you are trying to say?
3. Identification of the other kinds of information you need to present in this initial analysis of what your data look like. Maybe you need demographic information such as the gender of the participants, their age, social class, or political affiliation. Even if this information is not directly related to the question you are asking, it does not hurt to collect it at this point anyway. You might find later on that you want to go back and look at some of the other information, and you will be glad you collected it. This does not mean that the demographic questionnaire you use is 10 pages long and contains more than 1,000 questions. It means that within reason, you collect information related to, but not bearing directly upon, your main question.
4. Pilot data collection, so that you can practice the simple descriptive and inferential statistics discussed in chapters 7 and 8. Treat the analysis as if it were the real thing and go through each and every step that you plan to go through for the final data analysis. This way you will know exactly what you do and do not understand and can get help when necessary. Do the data analysis both by hand using the formulas in this chapter as well as by using SPSS, which is discussed in Appendix A.

Selecting an Inferential Statistic

It does not matter who you are. Selecting an inferential test is always a task that takes some care. When you are first starting out, as you are, the choice can be downright intimidating.

You can learn about some of the most common situations (using the flow chart shown in Figure 12.1) such as testing the difference between the means of two or more groups and looking at relationships between groups. In both cases, the same principles of testing for the significance of an outcome apply.

Now, do not think for a minute that (a) you can substitute a chart like this for a basic statistics course, or that (b) this is a statistics course. Instead, this chart is some simple help to guide you toward a correct selection. You got a little bit of the *why* about inference in chapter 8, but to get all of the *why*, enroll in that Statistics 1 class and make your adviser happy.

Protecting Human Subjects

As you learned in chapter 2, most organizations that sponsor research (such as universities) have some kind of committee that regularly reviews research proposals to ensure that humans (and animals) are not in any danger should they participate.

Before investigators begin their work and as part of the proposal process, a form like the one you saw in Figure 2.4 is completed and attached to the proposal. The committee reviews the information and either approves the project (and indicates that human subjects are not in danger) or tries its best to work with the investigator to change the proposed methods so that things go as planned.

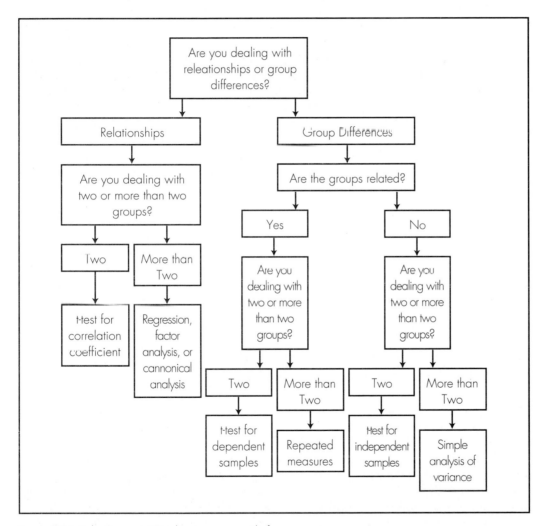

Figure 12.1 Selecting a statistical test—an example for comparing groups.

When it comes time to write a proposal, here is the quote you want to paste over your desk:

Pay me now or pay me later.

And that is the truth. Successful scientists will tell you that if you start out with a clear and well thought through question, then the rest of your proposal as well as the execution of your research will fall into place. On the other hand, if your initial question is unclear, you will find yourself floundering and not able to focus on the real issue. Work on writing your proposal every day, read it over, let it sit for a while, have a friend or colleague glance at it and offer suggestions, write some more, let it sit some more...Get the message? Practice and work hard, and you will be well rewarded.

Exercises

1. Go to the library, and select a journal article that represents work in your field of interest. Apply each of the criteria that we specified in this chapter (see the section titled "Criteria for Judging a Research Study"). To make this exercise even more interesting, work on the task with a colleague, or select the same journal article as a colleague and compare your results.

2. Complete the human experimentation form you saw in Figure 2.4. If you are working on a research project, include the real information. If not, include hypothetical information.

CHAPTER 13 THIRTEEN

Writing A Research Manuscript

What You'll Learn About in this Chapter

- About the American Psychological Association's *Publication Manual* and guidelines for manuscript preparation
- The different parts of a manuscript, and how they should be prepared
- Formatting the manuscript in the correct fashion

One day, if you work real hard, you may have the opportunity to submit a manuscript of your own or with a coauthor to a real-live journal. Then, if you have lived right, the manuscript may even be accepted, and won't you be proud!

There are many ways to organize a manuscript, and most journals require that manuscripts be submitted according to specific guidelines. In the social and behavioral sciences, the American Psychological Association's *Publication Manual* is this standard. This chapter is all about preparing a manuscript for submission according to those guidelines. While there is no substitute for buying this manual (it is about $17, but your department or adviser probably has one), this chapter will provide the basics of how a manuscript should be organized, formatted, and mechanically prepared.

And to help you out, there is an example of a manuscript prepared in the correct fashion. The manuscript was completed by my colleague, Professor Steven Lee, and his students at the University of Kansas, and I appreciate his letting me use it in *Exploring Research*. After some general guidelines about manuscript preparation, you will see Dr. Lee's manuscript, annotated with tips and hints. Just follow along.

What a Manuscript Looks Like

Like a book, a report, or any document that contains information, a research manuscript consists of different parts. Here is an outline of these parts and the order in which they are to be assembled. A description of what each contains will follow.

- Title Page
- Abstract
- Text
- References
- Appendixes
- Author Notes
- Footnotes
- Tables
- Figure Captions
- Figures

This 10-part organization is fairly simple. Here is a brief description of the function of each part and what each contains.

Title Page

The title page is the first thing the reader sees when considering the manuscript. It should contain information that is as clear and to the point as is possible. The title itself should be able to stand alone, convey the importance of the idea, and communicate the content of the manuscript. The title page is removed by the journal editor when the manuscript is sent out for review so the reviewer does not know who authored the manuscript.

The most important reason why the title should be concise and explanatory is that these titles are often used as the basis for index entries of the kind that were discussed in chapter 3. If the title of a manuscript does not clearly reflect the content, a person who wants to use an index to find a study on a certain subject could easily miss the important work that has been done.

As you can see in the sample manuscript, the title page consists of the following components:

- a running head for the publication
- the title of the manuscript
- a byline, or the authors listed in order of their contribution (and not necessarily alphabetical order) along with institutional affiliation (for each author if appropriate)

The running head appears on every page of the manuscript along with the page number and is used to identify the manuscript (since there is no other identifying information on the manuscript). Many are reviewed without knowledge of the author (or authors), so something has to be used for identification. The running head should be short and, as you will see, appear on each page.

The Abstract

The abstract is a summary of the contents of the manuscript. It provides enough information for the reader to learn the purpose and the results of the research being reported and does so in a concise and forthright fashion. No extras, no frills—just the facts—and in less than 960 characters. It should include the following specific information:

- a one sentence statement of the purpose
- a description of the participants used in the research including the number, their age, gender, ethnicity, special conditions, and other identifying characteristics
- the results
- any conclusions being offered

The abstract should not be indented, should be titled "Abstract" in upper and lower case letters centered at the top of the page, and include numerals as digits (such as *3*) instead of words (such as *three*) to save space. The page should be numbered 2.

The Text

The first page of the text begins with the title of the manuscript centered, with the first letter of each word capitalized (except for articles such as *a*, and *an* and prepositions such as *for*). The introduction, unlike other sections in the manuscript, is not labeled explicitly as such. Rather, it just begins after the manuscript title. The introduction provides a framework for the problem that is being studied and a context for the statement of the purpose of the study being reported.

A good introduction orients the reader as to the importance of the problem by providing sufficient background material. This is not the place for an extensive historical review of the important literature. It should mention only the most important works that have been done and illuminate the important studies that have been done in the area. Basically, your goal is to provide the reader with sufficient information to understand and appreciate the importance and scope of the problem.

Once the problem under study is stated and explained (and the stage is set), it is time to end the introduction with a clear statement of what will actually be done in the study. Some writers also include a statement of the hypothesis. That is what Professor Lee does when he states (on page 289) "it is the purpose of this study to replicate the recently established link...," followed by the hypothesis being tested, "it is hypothesized that both preservice and practicing teachers may be influenced...."

The Method

The method section of the manuscript describes how the study was conducted. This information is reported in sufficient detail so that any one can refer to this section and duplicate the study exactly as it was originally done.

Since there are many different components to the method section, which vary from manuscript to manuscript, there are different subheadings used as well. The most general are participants, instruments, and data analysis.

Participants

The participants section describes the participants in great detail answering questions such as who participated in the study, how the participants were selected, and how many were there. In addition, the *who* is further described by providing information on gender, ethnicity, location, age, marital status, and other possibly important descriptors. Which descriptors should be included? Whatever ones you think have some bearing on the nature of the study. For example, there are few studies using human participants where gender would not be important to report, while there are few where reporting height would be important.

In some cases, it is easier to compile a table of participant characteristics as is done in Table 1 of the Lee manuscript.

Instruments

The instruments section focuses on the apparatus, tests, and other devices used to measure behavior. The text in this section usually describes each of the instruments being used, information about the administration of the instrument, and reliability and validity data if they exist. For example, in the sample manuscript you will find information about the *Home Experience Survey*.

Sometimes the procedures used in the experiment, such as the administration of various tests and the like, are included in a description of the instrumentation. Other times, there is a separate section titled "Procedure."

Data Analysis

The last part of the method section, often named "Data Analysis," tells the reader what statistical techniques were used to analyze the data. This is not the place for a presentation of the actual results of the analysis, but for only information about how the analysis was done. It would specify which variables were used in the analysis and, if necessary, a rationale for why these particular procedures were selected. For example, in the "Origins" manuscript, factor analysis and multiple regression were the primary tools used to analyze the data.

The Results

Here is the author's opportunity to report the actual results of the study, including numbers, numbers, and more numbers. As you can see, Professor Lee uses lots of tables (such as Tables 3, 4, and 5) to visually present the results, but he also provides a verbal description through the results section. Because the manuscript reports the results of more than one study, the contents are organized by Study 1 and Study 2. Within each of these subheadings, Lee and his coauthors describe the sample, method, and results. By separating the studies, he keeps the purpose and results of each clear and easier for the reader to understand than if all the information was combined.

Discussion

Here is where the author of the manuscript is free to explore important relationships among what has been done in the past, the purpose of the study, the stated hypothesis, and the results of the current study. Now it is time for an evaluation of what has been done and a "measuring up" to see if the reported results fit the researcher's expectations.

Here is an opportunity for the researcher to sum up the purpose and findings reported in the manuscript. It is here that you will find any statement as to what contribution might have been made by the current research and how well the original question was answered. The discussion section is also the place where the implications and limitations of the current study are discussed as are suggestions for future research.

References

The references are a list of sources that were consulted during the course of the research and the writing of the manuscript. References can be anything from a book to a personal communication, and all references have to be entered in the reference list in a particular format which you will learn about later in this chapter.

Appendixes

An appendix usually contains information that is not essential for understanding the content of the manuscript but is important for getting a thorough picture of what happened. Usually, an appendix will contain original data or drawings.

Author Notes

Author notes include any ancillary material that is important to understanding the content of the manuscript but does not belong in any of the previous sections.

Footnotes

Footnotes are used to elaborate upon references or some other technical point concerning the content of the manuscript.

Tables

Tables are text arranged in columns or rows, most often used in the results section.

Figure Captions

A figure caption identifies each of the figures with a number and a title.

Figures

Here is where the actual figures for the manuscript are physically placed.

Nuts and Bolts

The content of a research manuscript is by far the most important part of the presentation. The format, however, takes on some importance as well, especially since most journals review hundreds of manuscripts each year. Standardization of some kind helps streamline the process.

So, here goes, a miniguide to some of the most important format rules to keep in mind.

1. Make sure that your type on the paper is readable. An old ribbon with a dot matrix printer will not produce readable copy. If you can, print the manuscript using a laser printer.
2. All lines, including the heading, must be double spaced.
3. Leave 1 inch for a margin on the left, right, top, and bottom of the page.
4. Pages are numbered as follows:

    - The title page is a separate page, numbered 1.
    - The abstract is a separate page, numbered 2.
    - The text starts on a separate page, numbered 3.
    - The references, appendixes, author notes, footnotes, tables, figure captions, and figures all start on separate pages, and the pages are continuously numbered.

5. The first line of each paragraph must be indented five spaces.
6. Headings are to be typed as follows. Here is an example of three different levels of headings which is sufficient for most papers.

Format	**Level**
Centered Uppercase and Lowercase	First
Flush Left Uppercase and Lowercase and Underlined	Second
Indented, Uppercase and Lowercase Underlined.	Third
(note the period at the end)	

For example, here are three levels of headings from the Lee paper.

Origins of Teachers' Selection
of Aversive Interventions (Level 1)

Preactive Planning and Classroom Management (Level 2)
Past Disciplinary Experiences (Level 2)
The Present Study (Level 2)

Study 1 (Level 1)

Method (Level 2)
    Participants. (Level 3)
    Instruments. (Level 3)

7. Place one space after all commas(,) semicolons (;), and periods (.).
8. Do not indent the abstract.
9. Tables and figures are each numbered consecutively and labeled as Table 1, Figure 5, and referred to in the text as Table 1 or Figure 1 (for example).
10. Start the list of references on a new page. Here are some sample formats for common types of references. The underlining is used to tell the typesetter to place the characters in italics, as you can see has been done in the references for *Exploring Research*.

A Journal Article Reference

    Strupp, H. H. (1986). Psychotherapy: Research, practice, and public policy (How to avoid dead ends). American Psychologist, 41, 120-130.

A Book Reference

    Sagan, C. (1979). Dragons of Eden. New York: Random House.

An Edited Book Reference

    Datan, N., & Ginsberg, L. H. (Eds.) (1975). Life Span Developmental Psychology: Normative Life Crises. New York: Academic Press.

A Book Chapter Reference

Loeb, M. B. (1975). Adaptation and survival: New meanings in old age. In N. Datan & L. H. Ginsberg (Eds.), <u>Life Span Developmental Psychology: Normative Life Crises.</u> New York: Academic Press.

A Magazine Article Reference

Snarely, J. (1987, June). A question of morality. <u>Psychology Today, 21,</u> 6-7.

That is it for preparing a manuscript according to APA guidelines and Exploring Research *as well. I sincerely hope you enjoyed using the book as much as I have enjoyed writing it. My best wishes for success in all the years to come.*

Title → Origins of Teachers' Selection of Aversive Interventions

Authors → Steven W. Lee, Melissa D. Forinash, & Glenna Weis

Institutional → University of Kansas
Affiliation

The title is to the point and tells the reader the focus of the manuscript.

ORIGINS OF AVERSIVE INTERVENTIONS

Running head (all capitals)

No indent
↓

Abstract

This paper presents two studies examining the origins of teachers' selection and use of aversive consequences. Reports of past discipline experiences of teachers from both the home and school environment served as predictors of the nature of their selection of intervention for a hypothetical classroom case scenario. The major findings of this study included: a) preservice teachers' experience with aversive consequences at home and school were not predictive of their utilization of aversive techniques, and (b) practicing teachers' experiences with <u>restrictions</u> at home were significantly predictive of their selection of more aversive interventions. These findings are discussed in relation to the literature on the effect of prior beliefs on teacher behaviors as well as the research on reflective teaching and preactive planning. Limitations of the studies and directions for future research are discussed.

Brief & concise abstract (this one is 133 words), all one paragraph

The purpose of this paper and the major findings are reported in the abstract. Sometimes the sample size is reported.

Level 1 →
heading
Origins of Teachers' Selection
of Aversive Interventions
Title

*Margin should
be 1.5 inches*

Indent 5 spaces

Introduction →
begins here
Over the past 10 to 15 years, increasing emphasis has been
given to teacher reflection as a key element in good teaching
2 spaces ↓
(Porter and Brophy, 1988). Even though teacher reflection was
identified as critical to a teacher's repertoire by Dewey as
early as 1904, recent research into the components of teachers'
thinking and behavior has led to the conclusion that reflection
or inquiry (Tom, 1985) is an essential element for good teaching
(Porter and Brophy). As Posner (1993) points out, "Experience
with no reflection is shallow and at best and leads to
superficial knowledge" (p. 21).

*The
introduction
provides a
background
for the reader
to understand
the context in
which the
study
appears.*

*Manuscript
is printed
cleanly and
clearly*
Definitions of teacher reflection has been elusive (Tom,
1988) and complex (Roth, 1989). For Posner (1993), "reflective
teachers actively, persistently, and carefully consider and
reconsider beliefs and practices" (p. 20) against the assumptions
that support them. The reflective process seems to involve a
large array of cognitive and behavioral functions including:
frequent questioning of actions, hypothesizing about problems and
potential actions to be taken, evaluation of teaching procedures,
and perspective taking, to name a few (Roth). One critical
element of the reflective teaching process seems to be planning
(Shavelson, 1983; Porter and Brophy, 1988; Rudney and Guillaume,
1989-90; Bullough, 1989; Froyen, 1993; Posner).

*All text is
double spaced*

*Earlier
citations
provide some
history of the
topic*

*Margin should be
1.5 inches*

Porter and Brophy (1988) have proposed a model, shown in Figure 1, which illustrates possible relationships between teacher reflection and preactive planning which was developed from studies done at the Institute for Research on Teaching (IRT) at Michigan State University. This hypothetical model cogently shows that preactive planning is influenced by numerous sources including teacher reflection. For example, Porter and Brophy proposed that teacher preactive planning may be affected by student characteristics, external factors (e.g., school policies, administrators, etc.), and teachers' knowledge base which includes content knowledge, pedagogy, professional education and personal experiences at home and school as a child.

Previous research, theory, and models are all important as a foundation for the current research.

Level 2 → *heading*

Preactive Planning and Classroom Management

While preactive planning seems to play an important role in the delivery of lesson content, numerous scholars have argued that preactive planning is important for all aspects of teaching including classroom management and student discipline (Borko and Niles, 1985; Brophy, 1986; Sugai and Fabre, 1987; Maclennan, 1987; Frisby, 1991; Charles, 1992; Lee, 1992; Froyen, 1993). The recent interest in classroom management planning is not surprising given the large percentage of teacher time spent on these kinds of activities (Gump, 1957), and the value associated with preactive planning (Zahorik, 1970; Clark, 1983; Shavelson, 1983; Borko and Niles).

The writer uses subheadings to further focus the introduction on the topic.

However, even with formal planning teachers must be flexible enough to revise their plans on the basis of a myriad of day-to-day influences (Clark, 1983; Kaplan, 1992; Lee, 1992). This is especially true in relation to managing student behaviors and classroom procedures. Therefore, it seems reasonable to assume that teachers' daily classroom behaviors will result from a combination of reflection and preactive planning (written, mental, or both), and intuitive or "reflexive" actions directed toward students (Kaplan, 1992). Reflective versus reflexive teacher actions may be viewed as a continuum of complete and fully planned actions to impulsive reactions to student behavior.

Level 2 → heading

Reflective and Reflexive Teaching and Past Experiences

While it has already been posited from Porter and Brophy's (1988) model that teachers' past experiences play a role in the reflective-planning process, it seems logical that past experiences may play a more significant role in reflexive teaching behavior (Rosen, 1968; Kaplan, 1992). For example, since inexperienced or preservice teachers have few true teaching experiences to draw from (knowledge), they may be more likely to act as they recall their parent or teachers might have reacted to a similar situation. Even experienced teachers may be more likely to respond reflexively to an unexpected classroom situation based on their childhood experiences.

Relatively little is known about how childhood experiences at home and school influence teachers' planning or choices for classroom interventions (Kaplan, 1992), although numerous authors theorize that these past experiences do affect teachers' classroom behavior (Rosen, 1968; Porter and Brophy, 1988; Hollingsworth, 1989; Kaplan; Posner, 1993). Perhaps among the strongest or long-lasting of influences on children is their

More sub-headings are used to define other important areas that are related to important facets of the study.

Earlier citations are used to help support the writer's ideas and arguments.

experiences with aversive consequences, encompassing everything from reprimands to corporal punishment (Lennox, 1982; Rust and Kinnard, 1983; Zaidi, Knutson, and Mehm, 1989). With these concepts in mind, this study sought to examine the relationship between teachers' selection of aversive consequences and their childhood experiences with the same.

Level 2 → heading

Past Disciplinary Experiences

Although the notion of a cycle of abuse has received virtually axiomatic support from a theoretical basis (Zaidi, Knutson, and Mehm, 1989), evaluation of the empirical evidence that has been collected on the topic has led to the conclusion that while being maltreated as a child puts one at risk for becoming abusive as an adult, the link between the two points is far from direct and definitely not inevitable. In fact, the best estimate of the rate of intergenerational transmission is considered to be approximately 30% (Kaufman and Zigler, 1987). However, the research that has been conducted within this area has admittedly yielded highly inconsistent findings, thus leaving the hypothesized existence of such a relationship as an area worthy of further consideration. It is within the framework of this research base, therefore, that the notion of teachers' experiences with punishment impacts their choice of discipline strategies was originally derived. However, the basis for the inclusion of this component in the proposed model has recently been substantiated by research that has directly examined this relationship.

Dr. Lee further focuses the main point of the paper by exploring past disciplinary practices.

In his effort to determine why teachers use corporal punishment in the classroom, Lennox (1982), in an unpublished dissertation, found that the best predictor of the use of corporal punishment was how often teachers had been spanked as children and or paddled in school. Teachers who had been spanked rarely or never as children almost never spanked their students. Likewise, Rust and Kinnard (1983) have found that teachers who employ corporal punishment at an individual level tend to be teachers who were physically punished as children. Furthermore, support for the supposition that preservice teachers' home experiences with punishment serve as an originating source of their use of punitive techniques in the classroom has likewise been demonstrated by Kaplan (1992) as he found that "disciplinary experiences in the families of origin are predictive of the strategies they select for classroom management" (p. 263). Hence, the implication that such a relationship exists is not only theoretically grounded but empirically grounded as well, although research within this area is admittedly limited. Although no empirical evidence was found to support the inclusion of teachers' punitive experiences with peers and other adults as factors associated with their utilization of punitive disciplinary strategies, these factors have been included in the proposed model based upon the assumption that the repercussions of such experiences as children may emerge in adulthood as a function of modeling as set forth by Bandura (1977).

Level 2 →
heading

The Present Study

In light of the scarcity of research that exists regarding the influence that teachers' past experiences have on their use of disciplinary strategies in the classroom, it is the purpose of this study to replicate the recently established link between such experiences and the use of punitive strategies in the classroom (Kaplan, 1992). This study also serves to extend Kaplan's study by examining the possible effect of past school

The introduction ends with a summary of what's already been presented, as well as a statement of the study's purpose.

experiences on teachers' choice of interventions.

As previously mentioned, it is hypothesized that both preservice and practicing teachers may be influenced by their previous experiences with aversive consequences as a child and that it seems likely that these previous experiences would more likely affect preservice teachers due to their lack of teaching practice rather than experienced teachers who have had the benefit of on the job experience. Therefore, Study 1 was designed to explore the nature of childhood (home and school) experiences with aversive consequences in preservice teachers and their resultant selection of (aversive vs. non-aversive) intervention choices. Study 2 extended the research to practicing teachers to examine the degree to which childhood aversive consequences influenced their choice of intervention.

The end of the introduction also can include a statement of the hypothesis.

Here Dr. Lee distinguishes between the purposes of the two studies.

*Level 1 →
heading*   Study 1

Study #1 and Study #2 both have their own section in the manuscript.

*Level 2 →
heading*   Method

*Level 3 →
heading*   Participants.

The participants were 131 undergraduate education majors from the University of Kansas. Demographic information about the sample can be seen in Table 1. All participants were volunteers and agreed to participate after signing an informed consent form.

_____

Insert Table 1 about here   ← *References to where Table 1 should appear*

_____

*Level 3 →
heading*   Instruments.   *Underlined text will be italicized in publication*
↓

The Home Experiences Survey (HES) developed by Kaplan (1992) was utilized as a means of assessing the frequency and intensity of punishing experiences in the home that an adult could remember

It's important to describe what instruments are used and how they are used to measure what they are supposed to.

from his/her childhood. The survey consists of 20 items covering such disciplinary practices as "grounding," loss of privileges, verbal reprimands, corporal punishment, explanation of rules, parental praise and criticism, and parental demands for total obedience. The items were empirically developed from the most frequent responses obtained from undergraduate students over a period of months when asked to list those punitive and nonpunitive disciplinary practices they had directly observed and vicariously observed while growing up (Kaplan, 1992). Each item was ranked by the participants on the following five point Likert scale:

1. Never (not even once)

2. Very Rarely (only once or twice that I can recall)

3. Occasionally (more than just once or twice, but probably not more than 4 or 5 times during all of my years at home)

4. Pretty Often (often enough to remember this as a common experience in my family)

5. Very Often (so common I couldn't even begin to guess how often I experienced this)

This instrument has yielded test-retest item reliabilities ranging from .48 to .81 over a two week period and from .75 to .91 over a five week period (Kaplan, 1992). The Home Experiences Survey can be seen in Appendix A.

Reliability data, when available, is reported.

The School Experiences Survey (SES Part 1), developed by Lee, Weis, and Forinash (1991) was employed to assess the frequency and intensity of punishing experiences in school that an adult could recall from his/her childhood. This survey consists of two parts with 20 items each which are identical to those of the Home Experiences Survey with the exception of changes in wording to account for experiences within the school environment rather than the home environment.

Part 1, Personal Experience, assesses the preservice teacher's direct or personal experiences with punishment as a student, and Part 2, Observed Experience, assesses the preservice teacher's indirect or observed experiences with punishment as a student (i.e., witnessing the punishment of other students). The areas assessed by this survey consist of loss of privileges, physical punishment, verbal punishment, teacher demands for total obedience, explanation of rules, praise, and restrictions. The same five point Likert scale utilized with the Home Experiences Survey was utilized with this survey as well. Test-retest item reliabilities associated with Part 1 of the School Experiences Survey have been found to range from .39 to .82 over a two week period and test-retest item reliabilities ranging from .37 to .80 were found for Part 2 of the survey. Test-retest item reliabilities for all instruments used in this study can be seen in Table 2, and the School Experiences Survey can be seen in Appendix B.

Insert Table 2 about here   ← *References to where Table 2 should appear*

A one page case scenario (see below) was used to assess preservice teacher's choice of intervention strategies. Special attention was given to the wording of the scenario to avoid conveying the impression that "Charlie" was seeking attention, disrupting the class, being defiant, or behaving in an aggressive or destructive manner (Kaplan, 1992).

Charlie, a first-grader, is described by his teacher as "lost in space." Ms. Potts reports that she needs to tell him repeatedly that he has "this assignment" or "that worksheet" to finish within a given time limit. If left alone, he reportedly "spaces out," toying with objects in his desk, staring out the window, or even getting up to wander around the room. Ms. Potts says that if she reminds him to get busy he willingly returns to the task at hand. Unfortunately, within a few moments after leaving him to work independently, Charlie "spaces out" again. Ms. Potts is becoming concerned because Charlie is falling farther and farther behind, and the other children are beginning to laugh at him when she reminds him to "get busy." Besides, she has 29 other children to attend to and can't stay by Charlie's side all day.

Level 3 → heading

Procedure.

In Session 1, each participant completed the Home Experiences Survey (Kaplan, 1992) and the School Experience Survey (Lee, Weis, and Forinash, 1991). No standard order of administration was used. Two to three weeks later in Session 2, the same participants again completed the above mentioned questionnaires. In addition, each participant responded to the same case scenario of a hypothetical student with learning and behavioral problems. Standard instructions were used for all questionnaire administrations. For the case scenario, respondents were asked to design an intervention program that would result in a more independent Charlie. Respondents were also asked to consider antecedents and consequences in their intervention program.

The Procedure section discusses the exact steps that were taken so someone else can replicate the study.

Level 3 → heading

Data Analysis.

The participants' choices of intervention for the case scenario were evaluated in accordance with three types of interventions, rewarding, neutral, and aversive, and were subsequently categorized by three independent raters into one of the following categories:

1. Rewarding Interventions only

2. Rewarding and Neutral Interventions only

3. Neutral Interventions only

4. Rewarding and Aversive Interventions

5. Neutral and Aversive Interventions

6. Aversive Interventions

Definition of rewarding, neutral, and punishing interventions are shown in Table 3. Correlations between the independent ratings of the case scenarios to measure interrater reliability were obtained.

These independent ratings of the case scenarios yielded interrater reliabilities ranging from .78 to .95 suggesting that the interventions were reliably rated in accordance with the six intervention categories utilized in Table 3. The average ratings showed the highest degree of consensus and were used in all subsequent data analysis.

———————————————

Insert Table 3 about here   ← *References to where Table 3 should appear*

———————————————

A factor analysis of the Home Experiences Survey and the School Experiences Survey, Parts 1 and 2, was conducted to identify the latent structure of the questionnaires. A stepwise multiple regression was conducted using the derived factor scores as the independent variables predicting the average case scenario ratings which served as the dependent variables.

Different types of hypotheses require different types of analysis. Here both factor analysis and multiple regression are used.

Level 1 → heading   Results

Level 2 → heading   <u>Study 1</u>

The descriptive statistics for the preservice sample are shown in Table 4 for the items from the <u>Home Experiences Survey</u> and the <u>School Experiences Surveys, Part 1 and 2</u>. It can be seen that in general the preservice sample noted few aversive conscquences either at home or at school. In fact, their parents' and teachers' demonstrations of approval and praise was commonplace.

The results section presents the analysis of the actual data in the research.

Insert Table 4 about here   *← References to where Table 4 should appear*

A principal component, factor analysis, was performed on each of the scales. The resultant factors, factor names, factor loadings, and items are shown in Table 5. All factor loadings resulted from a varimax rotation to clarify the factor structure. For all scales only those factors with eigenvalues of greater than 1.0 were retained.

Insert Table 5 about here   *← References to where Table 5 should appear*

As can be seen in Table 5, four factors were extracted from the <u>Home Experiences Survey</u>. Factor I was identified as techniques that involved using rules, explaining rules, and use of praise. Items that clustered on Factor II involved restrictive punishments (e.g., grounded, sent to room). Factor III items involved physical punishment (e.g., spanked, hit), and on Factor

The results are not only presented in tables but are also described in the text.

IV verbal punishment items clustered together.

The factor analysis of the <u>School Experiences Survey—Part 1</u> identified five factors total, with three factors (Physical Punishment; Rules, Explain and Praise; and Restrictions) that were quite similar to those obtained on the <u>Home Experiences Survey</u>. However, Factors III and IV emerged indicating a different combination of items denoting lost privileges and total obedience to authority.

The analysis of the <u>School Experiences Survey—Part 2</u> also identified five total factors with the factors Rules, Explain and Praise, and Physical Punishment found within this scale. The remaining items of this scale clustered together indicating Verbal Punishment, Total Obedience, and Lost Privileges factors.

A stepwise multiple regression was completed using the factor scores of each of the scales as independent variables predicting the average case scenario ratings. For the preservice teachers, none of the factors significantly predicted their intervention selection for the case scenarios.

Level 1 →
heading

Study 2

Level 2 →
heading

Method

Level 3 →
heading

Participants.

The participants were 46 primary teachers representing five schools (K-5) in a small school district located in Kansas City, Kansas. Further demographic information of the participating teachers is presented in Table 6.

The participants are described in as much detail as necessary.

_____

Insert Table 6 about here

← *References to where Table 6 should appear*

_____

Level 3 →
heading

Instruments.

The Home Experiences Survey developed by Kaplan (1992) was utilized as a means of assessing the frequency and intensity of aversive interventions in the home that an adult could remember from his/her childhood. The factor analysis conducted in Study 1 identified four factors underlying the survey including Rules, Explain and Praise; Restrictions; Physical Punishment; and Verbal Punishment. Each item was ranked by the participants identically as in Study 1. Test-retest item reliabilities were reported in Study 1.

The School Experiences Survey developed by Lee, Weis, and Forinash (1991) was employed to assess the frequency and intensity of aversive interventions in school that an adult could recall from his/her childhood.

Part 1, Personal Experience, assesses the teacher's direct or personal experiences with aversive consequences as a student and Part 2, Observed Experience, assesses the teacher's indirect or observed experiences with aversive interventions as a student (e.g., witnessing the punishment of other students). Factor analysis conducted in Study 1 identified five factors comprising Part 1 of the survey including Physical Punishment, Rules, Explain and Praise, Lost Privileges, Total Obedience, and Restrictions. The five factors comprising Part 2 consist of Verbal Punishment, Rules, Explain and Praise, Physical Punishment, Total Obedience, and Lost Privileges. The same five point Likert scale utilized with the Home Experiences Survey in Study 1 was utilized with this survey. Test-retest item reliabilities associated with Part 1 of the School Experiences

All the important types of reliability are noted. Here, test-retest reliability is reported.

<u>Survey</u> were reported in Study 1 and were not examined in this sample.

The identical one page case scenario from Study 1 was used to assess teacher's choice of intervention strategies.

<u>Procedure.</u>

Participant participation was attained following weekly staff meetings at each of the schools. After being provided a description regarding the purpose of the study and the expectations of participation, teachers volunteered to participate. The same administration procedures utilized in Study 1 were utilized in Study 2.

<u>Data Analysis.</u>

The data analysis was completed in an identical way as in Study 1. Correlations conducted on the independent rating of the case scenarios yielded inter-rater reliabilities ranging from .93 to .98 suggesting that the interventions were reliably rated in accordance with the six intervention categories utilized. Because the average ratings showed the highest degree of consensus, they were used in all subsequent data analysis.

In accordance with the factor structure previously demonstrated with both the <u>Home Experiences Survey</u> and the <u>School Experiences Survey</u> from Study 1, a stepwise multiple regression was conducted using the derived factor scores as the independent variables predicting the average case scenario ratings which served as the dependent variables.

Results

<u>Study 2</u>

The descriptive statistics for the practicing teacher sample are shown in Table 7 for the items from the <u>Home Experiences </u>

Survey and the School Experiences Survey, Parts 1 and 2. The practicing teachers also experienced few aversive consequences as a group, but they witnessed more restrictions (e.g., timeout/grounded or lost privileges) than they personally experienced either at home or at school. For the practicing teachers, praise and approval were experienced quite often.

Insert Table 7 about here ← *References to where Table 7 should appear*

Using the same factors identified in Study 1, a stepwise multiple regression was performed using the factor scores on each of the scales as independent variables predicting the case scenario ratings for the practicing teachers. Two factors were predictive of the case scenario ratings, and accounted for approximately 30% of variance in the teacher's selections of interventions for the case scenario. Table 8 shows the results of this analysis.

Insert Table 8 about here ← *References to where Table 8 should appear*

Factor II (Restrictions) from the Home Experiences Survey and Factor III (Lost Privileges) from the School Experiences Survey, Part 1, were significantly related to the teachers' case scenario ratings and in total accounted for approximately 30% of the variance. No other factors significantly predicted the teacher's case scenario interventions (including those from the School Experiences Survey, Part 2).

Level 1 heading → Discussion

The purpose of this investigation was to replicate and

extend Kaplan's (1992) study to determine if past home <u>and</u> school disciplinary experiences significantly impact teachers' and preservice teachers' choice of intervention strategies for misbehavior in the classroom. Regarding past home experiences, those classified as "Restrictions" were significantly predictive of teachers' choice of punishing intervention strategies. In other words, the loss of privileges for misbehavior, restrictions in interactions with friends, grounding, confinement to one's room, and the imposition of punishment before the explanation of rule infraction experienced as a child significantly contributed to the selection of a punishing intervention when faced with a misbehavior problem as a teacher. However, for the preservice teachers, past experiences with punishment in the home or at school did not significantly predict a more punishing intervention choice.

School experiences classified as "Loss of Privileges" were significantly predictive of practicing teachers' choice of punishing interventions. It should be noted that the "Lost Privileges" factor on the <u>School Experiences Survey</u>, Part 1, shares the "lost privileges" item with the Factor II (Restrictions) of the <u>Home Experiences Survey</u> which was also significantly related to the selection of punishing intervention by the teachers. Combining these results it would appear that those teachers who had experienced restrictive punishments (e.g., grounded, sent to room, lost privileges, restrictive punishments) at home, at school, or at both significantly selected more punishing interventions for the child in the case scenario than those who did not.

The Discussion section provides a format for the writer to speculate about the findings, propose implications and explain limitations. It's also a time to talk about future directions for new research.

Several explanations may be advanced regarding the finding that preservice teachers experiences with punishment did not carry over to their selection of interventions, while it did with the practicing teachers. It is postulated that practicing teachers simply select more punishing techniques than preservice teachers. However, this hypothesis was not borne out in these data as the interventions selected by preservice teachers were relatively more punishing than the practicing teachers (see descriptive statistics in Tables 5 and 7).

Another plausible hypothesis for these results is that working in a school in a potentially conflictual situation with young people serves as a stimulus for remembering and use of restrictive interventions that these teachers had experienced as children. Since preservice teachers have not as yet practiced their profession, they have no stimulus for use of restrictive discipline techniques that may have been used with them as children. Therefore, it may be that the preservice teachers will use more punishing interventions (than those reported here) when they actually are out teaching than they would for a hypothetical situation in a college context.

In regard to understanding why restrictions and loss of privileges are significantly predictive of intervention selection, it is hypothesized that these punishments were considered to be more reasonable and rational than verbal and physical punishments that were unrelated to the misbehavior. As a result, these types of punishing techniques were selected for use.

The finding that experiences with physical punishments were not significantly predictive of intervention selection is

In the description, the author tries to explain how well the findings support the hypothesis.

inconsistent with Kaplan's (1992) study as he reported that
"individuals selecting punitive strategies were significantly
more likely to report higher instances of a variety of
punishments including being screamed at, being spanked with
objects such as belts, being bruised by spanking, and being
punished physically after the age of 12" (p. 263). This
inconsistency, however, is of little surprise considering the
fact that the link between being a victim of even severe abuse
and becoming an abusive adult has yet to be consistently
established. As was previously noted, at best, the rate of
intergenerational transmission of abuse may reach 30% (Kaufman
and Zigler, 1987). Thus, while the effects of physical punishment
may lead to post traumatic stress disorder, reduced self-esteem,
humiliation, and increased aggressive behavior (Hyman and Wise,
1979; Hyman, 1987), and thus, such management techniques may be
deemed as inappropriate and undesirable, they do not seem to
necessarily propel one to perpetuate the often proposed cycle of
punishment through the subsequent employment of such techniques
in the classroom.

Only 30% of the total variance in intervention selection was
accounted for by past experiences with discipline thus leaving
70% unaccounted for in this investigation. Once again this
finding is not surprising if one adheres to the proposed model
which posits that training, student/problem characteristics,
personal, school, and community variables also impact teachers'
choice of intervention in the classroom. Clearly, while one's
past experiences with discipline do seem to have an impact upon
intervention selection, it serves as only one variable among
many. Although the degree of impact associated with each such

variable has yet to be ascertained, the picture clearly being painted is one of a complex web of variables that influence teachers' responses to student misbehavior in the classroom. It is also interesting to note that only those school experiences that are direct and personal in nature seem to significantly impact the teachers' selection of punishing interventions, as compared to those experiences in which one is simply an observer which do not seem to significantly impact adult actions regarding intervention.

Placing great emphasis upon past disciplinary experiences in attempts to understand the dynamics influencing a teacher's selection of intervention seems rather inappropriate in light of the current findings. This may be perceived as good news for teacher training institutions suggesting that one's past does not serve as unalterable constraints to adoption of appropriate management techniques. Although one may be influenced to a slight degree by his or her past experiences with punitive and nonpunitive measures, there are perhaps many other variables which are more amenable to change ultimately impacting their management of behavior in the classroom.

Future research addressing the interaction of the variables presented in the proposed model is warranted. Furthermore, research on the role that past disciplinary experiences play in intervention selection needs to be conducted with a larger, more heterogeneous teacher population. The small and rather limited sample of practicing teachers from Midwestern, suburban schools utilized in Study 2 leads one to question the generalizability of these results to a larger, more diverse population.

Another limitation of this study was the lack of punishing

Here the author discusses possibilities for future research.

backgrounds of both the preservice and practicing teachers. Neither group experienced much punishment and the entire group of practicing teachers report never being spanked or hit in school. This is not congruent with Pross (1988), and one must wonder whether a sample of teachers that had experienced more punishment at home or in school would have yielded different results. The next logical step would be to select different samples from various settings to find teachers with a more extensive punishment history and examine their responses to a case scenario.

Here the author discusses possible limitations of the study.

The inclusion of multiple case scenarios, presented in various formats (e.g., video, role play) may serve to enhance the stability of new findings. In addition to the utilization of case scenarios, the examination of teacher's actual responses to misbehavior in the classroom is needed to validate the assumption that how a teacher responds to a simulated discipline problem is congruent with his or her response to actual problems occurring within a classroom environment.

References begin → 1

Book reference
↓

Level 1 heading → References

on page 1

Bandura, A. (1977). <u>Social learning theory.</u> Englewood Cliffs, N.J: Prentice-Hall.

Journal →
article reference

Borko, H., & Niles, J. A. (1985). <u>How should I teach it?</u>. New York: Macmillan.

Brophy, J. (1986). Teacher influences on student achievement. <u>American Psychologist</u>, <u>41</u>, 1069-1077.

Bullough, R. V. (1989). Teacher education and teacher reflectivity. <u>Journal of Teacher Education</u>, <u>40</u>, 15-21.

Charles, C. M. (1992). <u>Building classroom discipline: From models to practice</u>. New York: Longman.

Clark, C. M. (1983). Research on teacher planning: An inventory of the knowledge base. In D.C. Smith (Ed.). <u>Essential knowledge for beginning teachers</u>. Washington, D.C.: American Association of Colleges for Teacher Education.

Frisby, C.L. (1991). A teacher in-service model for problem-solving in classroom discipline: Suggestions for the school psychologist. <u>School Psychology Quarterly</u>, <u>5</u>, 211-230.

Froyen, L.A. (1993). <u>Classroom management: The reflective teacher leader</u>. New York: Macmillan.

Report →
reference

Gump, P. (1967). <u>The classroom behavior setting: Its nature and relation to student behavior</u>. (Report No. BR-5-0334). Washington, D.C.: Office of Education, Bureau of Research. (ERIC Document Reproduction Service No. EDO 15515).

Hollingsworth, S. (1989). Prior beliefs and cognitive change in learning to teach. <u>American Educational Research Journal</u>, <u>26</u>, 160-189.

Chapter →
reference

Hyman, I.A. (1987). Psychological correlates of corporal punishment. In M.R. Brassard, R. Germain, & Hart (Eds.),

References list the sources the author consulted in doing the research and writing the manuscript.

Double-spaced

Psychological maltreatment of children and youth (pp. 59-68). New

York: Pergamon Press.

Kaplan, C. (1992). Teachers' punishment histories and their

selection of disciplinary strategies. Contemporary Educational

Psychology, 17, 258-265.

Hyman, I.A., & Wise, J. (1979). Corporal punishment in American

education. Philadelphia: Temple University Press.

Kaufman, J., & Zigler, E. (1987). Do abused children become

abusive parents? American Journal of Orthopsychiatry, 57, 186-

191.

Professional → Lee, S.W. (1992, April). The Flex Model Classroom Management

paper reference Planning System. Paper presented at the meeting of the

National Association of School Psychologists, Nashville, TN.

Unpublished

manuscript → Lee, S.W., Weis, G., & Forinash, M.D. (1991). School Experiences

reference Survey. Unpublished manuscript.

Lennox, N. (1982). Teacher use of corporal punishment as a

function of modeling behavior. Ph.D. dissertation, Temple

University.

Maclennan, S. (1987). Integrating lesson planning and classroom

management. English Language Teaching Journal, 41, 193-197.

Porter, A.C., & Brophy, J. (1988). Synthesis of research on good

teaching: Insights from the work of the Institute for Research

on Teaching. Educational Leadership, 45, 74-85.

Posner, G.J. (1993). Field experience: A guide to reflective

teaching (3rd. Ed.). New York: Longman.

Pross, M.N. (1988). To paddle or not to paddle. Learning, 17, 42-

49.

Rosen, J.L. (1968). Personality and first-year teachers

relationships with children. The School Review, 76, 294-311.

Roth, R.A. (1989). Preparing the reflective practitioner: Transforming the apprentice through the dialectic. <u>Journal of Teacher Education</u>, <u>40</u>, 31-35.

Rudney, C.L., & Guillaume, A.M. (1989). Reflective teaching for student teachers. <u>The Teacher Educator</u>, <u>25</u>, 13-20.

Rust, J.O., & Kinnard, K.Q. (1983). Personality characteristics of the users of corporal punishment in the schools. <u>Journal of School Psychology</u>, <u>21</u>, 91-105.

Shavelson, R.J. (1983). Review of research on teachers' pedagogical judgments, plans and decisions. <u>The Elementary School Journal</u>, <u>83</u>, 392-413.

Sugai, G., & Fabre, T.R. (1987). The behavior teaching plan: A model for developing and implementing behavior change programs. <u>Education and Treatment of Children</u>, <u>10</u>, 279-290.

Tom, A.R. (1985). Inquiring into inquiry oriented teacher education. <u>Journal of Teacher Education</u>, <u>36</u>, 35-44.

Zaidi, L.Y., Knutson, J.F., & Mehm, J.G. (1989). Transgenerational patterns of abusive parenting: Analog and clinical tests. <u>Aggressive Behavior</u>, <u>15</u>, 137-152.

Zahorik, J.A. (1970). The effect of planning on teaching. <u>The Elementary School Journal</u>, <u>70</u>, 143-151.

All figures have captions on separate pages   Figure Caption

<u>Figure 1.</u> Model of factors influencing teachers' instruction of their students in particular content

[Reprinted from Porter and Brophy (1988) with permission]

Table 1 ← *Tables are numbered and placed in the order in which they are mentioned*

<u>Demographic characteristics of the preservice teacher sample</u> (N=131).

↑
Tables titles are underlined

<u>Sex</u>	<u>% of Sample</u>	<u>Area</u>	<u>% of Sample</u>
Male	18	Primary	51
Female	82	Secondary	35
		Primary & Sec	2
		SPED	1
		Unspecified	11

<u>Ed. Emphasis</u>	<u>% of Sample</u>	<u>Ethnicity</u>	<u>% of Sample</u>
Gen. Ed.	31	White N/H	93
Math	13	Black	3
PE	3	Am. Indian	1
English	16	Hispanic	1
Social Science	11	Other	2
Science	6		
Psychology	3	<u>Home School</u>	<u>% of Sample</u>
Music	1	Rural	6
Foreign Lang	3	Sm. Town	33
Special Ed	7	Suburb	48
Other	6	Urban	13

<u>Age</u>

$\overline{X}$ = 22.3 years
SD = 5.4

Table 2

<u>Test-retest item reliabilities for the Home and School Experiences</u>
<u>Surveys</u> (N=131).

Home Experiences Survey Retest Reliabilities	School Exp. (Part one-Pers.) Survey Retest Reliabilities	School Exp. (Part two-Obs) Survey Retest Reliabilities
#1 - .66	#1 - .65	#1 - .57
#2 - .76	#2 - .35	#2 - .37
#3 - .52	#3 - .51	#3 - .59
#4 - .50	#4 - .49	#4 - .51
#5 - .56	#5 - .51	#5 - .42
#6 - .75	#6 - .68	#6 - .69
#7 - .63	#7 - .55	#7 - .55
#8 - .67	#8 - .53	#8 - .46
#9 - .68	#9 - .47	#9 - .51
#10 - .48	#10 - .57	#10 - .80
#11 - .82	#11 - .58	#11 - .63
#12 - .67	#12 - .66	#12 - .66
#13 - .65	#13 - .48	#13 - .74
#14 - .81	#14 - .48	#14 - .43
#15 - .81	#15 - .72	#15 - .58
#16 - .80	#16 - .54	#16 - .75
#17 - .81	#17 - .82	#17 - .63
#18 - .66	#18 - .59	#18 - .52
#19 - .54	#19 - .44	#19 - .49
#20 - .62	#20 - .39	#20 - .57

Table 3

Rating scale and interrated reliabilities for rating of the case scenarios.

Rating Scale Used for Scoring Case Scenario

Definitions

Rewarding Interventions—Teacher techniques, methods, or strategies whose purpose is to reward, with the potential for increasing, a student's behavior. Examples include stickers, food rewards, praise, etc.

Neutral Interventions—Teacher techniques, methods, or strategies whose purpose is to change a student's behavior through organizational approaches or teacher monitoring that are not clearly rewarding or aversive in nature. Examples include parent conferences, proximity control, etc.

Punishing interventions—Teacher techniques, methods, or strategies whose purpose is to reduce or to eliminate a student's problem behavior. Examples include reprimands, striking at student, exclusion, etc.

Rating Categories

1 — Rewarding Interventions only
2 — Rewarding & Neutral Interventions
3 — Neutral Interventions only
4 — Rewarding & Punishing Interventions
5 — Neutral & Punishing Interventions
6 — Punishing Interventions only

Interrater Reliabilities for the Case Scenario

	Rater 1	Rater 2	Rater 3	Avg. Rating
Rater 1	1.0			
Rater 2	.90	1.0		
Rater 3	.78	.79	1.0	
Avg. Ratings	.95	.95	.91	1.0

Table 4

Descriptive Statistics of the items on the Home Experiences Survey (HES) and the School Experiences Survey, Part 1 (SES-1) and 2 (SES-2) for the Preservice sample (N=131).

Item #	HES Item Descriptions*	HES Mean	SD	SES-1 Mean	SD	SES-2 Mean	SD
1	Absolute obedience	3.17	1.13	3.31	.94	3.51	.95
2	Explanations	3.87	1.00	3.62	.98	3.46	.89
3	Restricted from friends	2.89	1.05	2.65	1.03	3.02	1.00
4	Lost privileges	3.47	1.01	3.22	1.02	3.68	.86
5	Punished first	2.21	1.28	2.26	1.18	2.46	1.00
6	Cursed at me	2.11	1.15	1.20	.58	1.50	.73
7	Sent to room	3.10	1.08	2.16	1.06	3.02	1.14
8	Explained rules	3.58	1.33	3.50	1.12	3.58	.82
9	Willing to listen	3.50	1.10	3.10	.98	3.04	.86
10	Approval	4.14	.91	4.06	.81	3.99	.84
11	Spanked	2.82	1.20	1.20	.73	1.43	.79
12	Hit-bruises	1.43	.94	1.04	.36	1.16	.59
13	Praised	4.30	.95	4.18	.82	4.12	.83
14	Spanked-object	1.85	1.16	1.14	.54	1.34	.85
15	Grounded	2.82	1.28	2.43	1.15	3.60	.88
16	Screamed at me	2.83	1.19	1.71	.82	2.23	.97
17	Physical punishment	1.42	.94	1.12	.51	1.30	.77
18	Criticized	2.74	1.08	2.34	.95	2.74	.93
19	No question parents	2.40	1.16	2.54	.99	2.79	.92
20	Understand effect	3.62	1.01	3.23	1.11	3.5	.86

*HES items were slightly altered to fit the school setting for the SES-1 and the SES-2.

Table 5

Factors for the Home Experiences Survey, School Experiences Survey Parts 1 and 2.

Home Experiences Survey	School Experiences Survey (Part 1)	School Experiences Survey (Part 2)

Home Experiences Survey

Factor I (Rules Explain & Praise)

Item #	Factor Loading
1-Obedience	-.508
2-Explain	-.734
8-Explain rules	.753
9-Listen	.754
10-Approval	.631
13-Praise	.509
19-No question	-.629
20-Beh effect	.779

Factor II (Restrictions)

Item #	
3-Restrictions	.691
4-Lost privileges	.864
5-Punished first	.517
7-Sent to room	.615
15-Grounded	.706

Factor III (Physical Punishment)

Item #	
11-Spanked-hand	.604
12-Hit	.785
14-Spanked-obj	.711
17-Phy punish	.624

Factor IV (Verbal Punishment)

Item #	
6-Cursed	.764
16-Screamed	.551
18-Criticized	.552

School Experiences Survey (Part 1)

Factor I (Physical Punishment)

Item #	Factor Loading
6-Cursed	.569
11-Spanked-hand	.745
12-Hit	.766
14-Spanked-obj	.856
17-Phy punish	.907

Factor II (Rules Explain & Praise)

Item #	
2-Explain	.697
8-Explain rules	.771
9-Listen	.666
10-Approval	.780
13-Praise	.750
20-Beh effect	.755

Factor III (Lost Privileges)

Item #	
3-No friends	.756
4-Lost privileges	.725

Factor IV (Total Obedience)

Item #	
1-Total obedience	.802
19-No question	.715

Factor V (Restrictions)

Item #	
7-Time out	.710
15-Restrictions	.737
18-Criticized	.551

School Experiences Survey (Part 2)

Factor I (Verbal Punishment)

Item #	Factor Loading
5-Immd Punish	.471
6-Cursed	.720
15-Screamed	.666
17-Criticized	.496

Factor II (Rules Explain & Praise)

Item #	
2-Explain	.832
8-Listen	.604
9-Approval	.808
12-Praise	.738
19-Understand	.761
20-Rsns for rules	.771

Factor III (Physical Punishment)

Item #	
10-Spanked-hard	.704
11-Hit	.667
13-Spanked-obj	.808
16-Phy punish	.779

Factor IV (Total Obedience)

Item #	
1-Obedience	.808
18-No question	.534

Factor V (Lost Privileges)

Item #	
3-No friends	.773
4-Lost privileges	.643
7-Time out	.447

Table 6

<u>Demographic characteristics of the practicing teacher sample</u>
(N=46).

<u>Sex</u>	<u>% of Sample</u>	<u>Religious Affiliation</u>	<u>% of Sample</u>
Male	98	Methodist	22
Female	2	Protestant	20
		Catholic	18
<u>Current Grade Teaching</u>		Christian	9
Kindergarten	4	Lutheran	7
1st	22	Presbyterian	4
2nd	22	RLDS	2
3rd	13	Nazarene	2
4th	4	Baptist	0
5th	9	Other	16
K-5 Special Ed.	17		
K-5 Music	4	<u>Length of Past Teaching Experiences</u>	
1-5 Rem.Mth. & Rgd.	4	<u>(in years)</u>	<u>% of Sample</u>
		Less than 3	16
<u>Mean Number of Students</u> = 22*		3-6	16
		6-9	16
<u>Mean Age of Teachers</u> = 38		9-12	7
		12-15	5
<u>Home Location</u>	<u>% of Sample</u>	15-18	14
Suburban	82	18-21	9
Urban	11	21-24	2
Rural	7	24-27	11
		27+	5

*Excluding total number of students assigned to each music
teacher.

Table 7

<u>Descriptive statistics of the items on the Home Experiences</u>
<u>Survey (HES) and the School Experiences Survey, Part 1 (SES-1)</u>
<u>and 2 (SES-2) for the practicing teacher sample</u> (N=46).

Item #	HES Item Descriptions*	HES Mean	SD	SES-1 Mean	SD	SES-2 Mean	SD
1	Absolute obedience	3.64	1.15	3.64	.99	3.72	1.00
2	Explanations	3.89	.92	2.67	1.11	3.41	1.00
3	Restricted from friends	2.28	1.15	1.86	.97	2.76	1.02
4	Lost privileges	3.07	1.23	2.42	1.05	3.80	.93
5	Punished first	2.27	1.27	2.12	.97	2.80	1.13
6	Cursed at me	1.44	.83	1.07	.33	1.20	.62
7	Sent to room	2.39	1.31	1.5	.85	2.74	1.29
8	Explained rules	3.24	1.48	3.14	1.21	3.46	1.07
9	Willing to listen	3.52	1.13	2.47	.94	2.65	.92
10	Approval	4.15	1.10	3.98	.95	3.83	1.17
11	Spanked	2.87	1.06	1.09	.36	1.52	.96
12	Hit-bruises	1.34	.65	1.00	0	1.13	.45
13	Praised	4.24	.83	4.11	1.03	4.13	1.00
14	Spanked-object	1.74	1.06	1.00	0	1.37	.88
15	Grounded	2.24	1.30	1.84	1.12	3.67	1.17
16	Screamed at me	2.13	1.11	1.43	.87	2.46	1.11
17	Physical punishment	1.29	.59	1.02	.15	1.30	.63
18	Criticized	2.53	1.14	1.98	.93	2.98	1.02
19	No question parents	2.64	1.23	2.48	1.02	3.17	.93
20	Understand effect	3.63	1.04	3.16	1.07	3.30	.99

*HES items were slightly altered to fit the school setting for the
SES-1 and the SES-2.

Table 8

<u>Stepwise multiple regression of past home and school factors that significantly predicted practicing teachers' selection of punishing interventions.</u>

<u>Step</u>	<u>Factors</u>	<u>Dfs</u>	<u>R</u>	$\underline{R^2}$
1	<u>Home Experiences Survey</u> Restrictions	1, 35	.35	.12
2	<u>School Experiences Survey</u> Part 1-Loss of Privileges	2, 34	.55	.30

APPENDIX

A

An Introduction to SPSS 7.0

You are probably familiar with other Windows applications, and you will find that many SPSS features operate exactly the same as those in other applications. You know about dragging, clicking, double-clicking, and working with windows. If you do not, you can refer to one of the many Prentice-Hall books that can help. Keep in mind that SPSS 7.0 is designed to work with the Windows 95 operating system and will not work with any earlier version of Windows. SPSS 7.0 takes advantage of Windows 95's special architecture as well as other features such as shortcuts, right-clicking, and multitasking. We will assume that you are familiar with Windows, file management, and the most simple of Windows skills, such as using the mouse.

This appendix is an introduction to SPSS and shows you just some of the things it can do. For a more complete treatment see *Using SPSS for Windows* (either the Windows 95 or Macintosh version) by Samuel B. Green, Neil J. Salkind and Terri Akey, both published by Prentice Hall. Throughout the examples in this appendix, we will use the sample data set shown in Appendix B. You are welcome to enter that data manually, or have your professor contact me and I will e-mail or post a copy of the file to him or her.

Starting SPSS

Like other Windows 95 based applications, SPSS is organized on the Start menu. This group was created when you first installed SPSS. To start SPSS, follow these steps.

1.   Click **Start**, then point to **Programs**.
2.   Place the mouse pointer on the SPSS group icon, then click SPSS. When you do this, you will see the SPSS opening screen as shown in Figure A.1.

When you first open SPSS, you will be in the **Data Editor**. This is where you enter data that you want to analyze. If you think the Data Editor is similar to a spreadsheet in form and function, you are right. In form, certainly, since it consists of rows and columns just like Excel, Lotus 1-2-3, and Quattro Pro. The columns represent variables, and the rows represent cases. In function as well, the Data Editor is much like a spreadsheet. Values that are entered can be transformed, sorted, rearranged, and more.

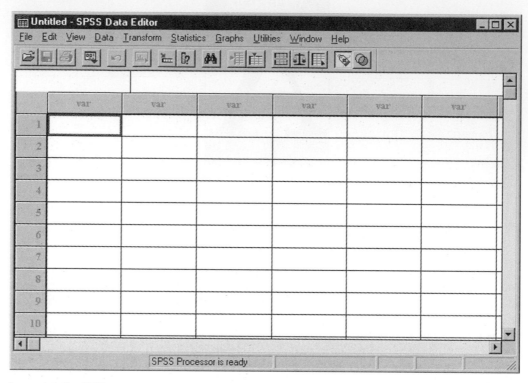

Figure A.1 The SPSS opening screen.

The SPSS Toolbar and Status Bar

The use of the **Toolbar**, the set of icons that are underneath the menus, can greatly facilitate your SPSS activities. If you want to know what an icon on the Toolbar does, just place the mouse pointer on it, and you will see a brief discussion of its function. Here is what each tool does.

Title	What it does
Open File	Opens an already created file.
Save	Saves a new or already created file.
Print	Prints a file.
Dialog Recall	Recalls a category of dialog boxes.
Undo/Redo	Undoes a change in formatting or data entry.
GoTo Chart	Goes to a name chart.
GoTo Case	Goes to a numbered case.
Variables	Provides information about a variable.
Find	Finds a record.
Insert Case	Inserts a case in the data file.
Insert Variable	Inserts a new variable into the data file.
Split File	Splits a file along some defined variable.
Weight Cases	Weights cases.
Select Cases	Selects a set of cases using a certain criterion.
Value Labels	Turns labels on and off.
Use Sets	Creates sets of variables.

Exploring Research

The **Status Bar**, located at the bottom of the SPSS window, is another useful on screen tool. Here, you can see a one line report as to what activity SPSS is currently involved in. Messages such as "SPSS processor ready," tells you that SPSS is ready for your directions or input of data. Or, "Running Means..." tells you that SPSS is in the middle of the procedure named Means.

Using SPSS Help

If you need help, you have come to the right place. SPSS offers help that is only a few mouse clicks away, and it is especially useful when you are in the middle of data file and need information about an SPSS feature. **SPSS Help** is so comprehensive that even if you are a new SPSS user, it can show you the way.

You can get help in SPSS by pressing the F1 function key or using the Help menu you see in Figure A.2.

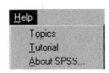

Figure A.2 The SPSS Help menu.

As you can see, there are three options on the Help menu. **Topics** gives you a list of topics for which you can get help. **Tutorial** offers you a short tutorial on all aspects of using SPSS. **About SPSS** tells you the version of SPSS that you are currently using.

Using the F1 Function Key

Any time you need help on any feature of SPSS, there is a quick and easy way to get it. Press the F1 function key while you are working in a dialog box, for example, and you will see the Help dialog box shown in Figure A.3.

The Contents Tab describes the major headings for help. Double-clicking on any one heading provides a list of possible topics that you might want to consult for the help you need. For example, if you want help on the Output Navigator and how to edit output, you would follow these steps.

1. Press **F1**.
2. Click the **Contents tab**.
3. Double-click **Output management**, and you will see a list of topics within that general content area.
4. Double-click the topic labeled **Editing Output**.

Using the Topics Index

The Index in SPSS Help provides an alphabetical listing of help topics. To find help on a particular topic, follow these steps. For example, here is how you would use the Index option to find help on computing the mean of a set of numbers.

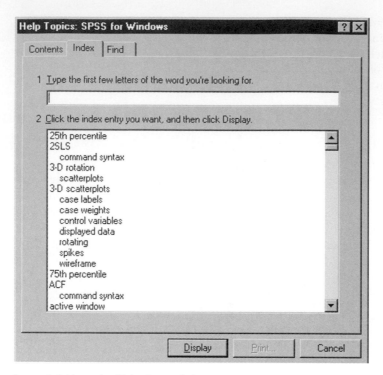

Figure A.3 Using the F1 key to get help.

1. Click **Help**, then click **Topics**.
2. Click the **Index tab**.
3. Type **mean**. As you enter the letters of the term on which you need help, SPSS Help immediately tries to identify the topic listing. Double-clicking on the index entry *mean* or clicking the Display button produces the help that you are looking for.

Using Help Options

Once you find help on what you want (such as information about the mean), you can click on the Options button in the Help window and perform a variety of tasks such as annotating the help screen so you can add your own information to what help already exists, copy the help contents to the Clipboard, print out the contents of the help menu, change the fonts of the help contents, change the position of help on the screen, and change colors. In a Help window, you can also click How To and have SPSS walk you through the steps of the procedure.

Using Find

What if you cannot find a term in the Index, but you need help anyway? The Find option in the Help dialog box you see in Figure A.3 allows you to enter any words that may be part of a help screen. SPSS then searches for the word, rather than just presenting help on a topic. In effect, you are searching all the words in all the topics.

SPSS Find is very sensitive to what words you enter. For example, the word mean is general and will turn up lots of references. The word *Mean*, however, is more specific and the word *MEAN* even more so (since that is the specific procedure in

SPSS syntax language). So if you know exactly what you want, you can be specific, but be careful since it can be at the expense of missing what you are looking for if you are not sure of what you want.

A Brief Tour of SPSS

Sit back and enjoy a brief tour of what SPSS can do. Nothing fancy here. Just some simple descriptions of data, a test of significance, and a graph or two. What we are trying to show you is how easy it is to use SPSS. Then we will show you how to perform some of these operations.

Opening a File

You can enter your own data to create a new SPSS data file, use an existing file, or even import data from such applications as Microsoft Excel into SPSS. Any way you do it, you need to have data to work with. In Figure A.4 the data contained in Appendix B is shown.

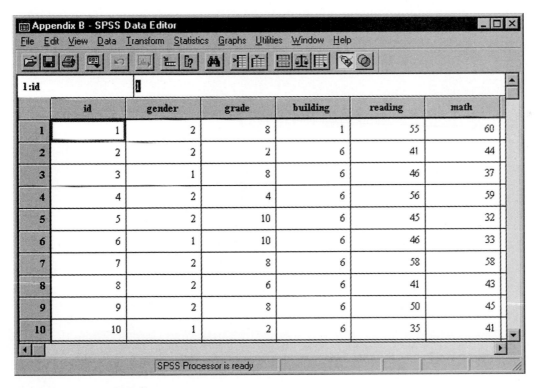

	id	gender	grade	building	reading	math
1	1	2	8	1	55	60
2	2	2	2	6	41	44
3	3	1	8	6	46	37
4	4	2	4	6	56	59
5	5	2	10	6	45	32
6	6	1	10	6	46	33
7	7	2	8	6	58	58
8	8	2	6	6	41	43
9	9	2	8	6	50	45
10	10	1	2	6	35	41

Figure A.4 An open SPSS file.

A Simple Table and Graph

Now it is time to get to the reason why we are using SPSS in the first place, the various analytical tools that are available.

First, let's say we want to know the general distribution of males and females. That is all, just a count of how many males and how many females are in the total sample we are working with. We also want to create a simple bar graph of the distribution.

In Figure A.5, you will see the output that provides exactly the information we asked for which was the frequency of the number of males and females. We used the Frequencies option on the Summarize (under the main menu Statistics) to compute these values, and then told SPSS all we wanted was the mean.

GENDER

		Frequency	Percent	Valid Percent	Cumulative Percent
Valid	1	95	47.5	47.5	47.5
	2	105	52.5	52.5	100.0
	Total	200	100.0	100.0	
Total		200	100.0		

Figure A.5 The results of a simple descriptive analysis.

Then we used the Graph option to create a simple bar graph of the frequency, as you see in Figure A.6.

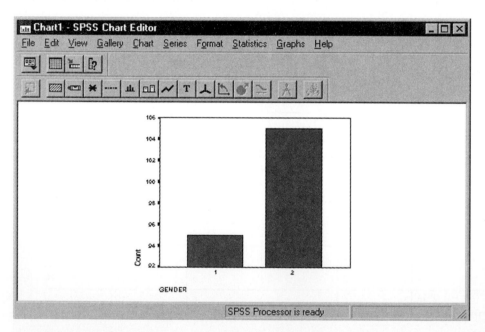

Figure A.6 A simple bar graph.

A Simple Analysis

Let's see if males and females differ in their average reading scores. This is a simple analysis requiring a t-test for independent samples. The procedure is a comparison between the mean of the group of males and the mean for the group of females.

In Figure A.7 you can see a partial summary of the results of the t-test. Notice that now the listing in the left pane of the Output Navigator shows the Frequencies, Graph, and T-Test procedures listed. To see any part of the output, all we need do is click on that element. Almost always when SPSS produces an Output window, you will have to scroll to see the entire output.

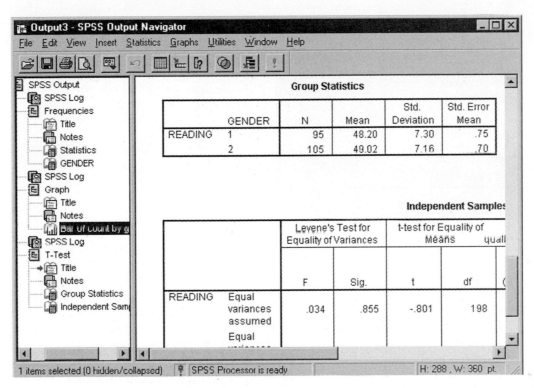

Figure A.7 The results of an independent samples t-test.

Creating and Editing a Data File

As a hands-on exercise, let's create the beginning of the data file you see in Appendix B. You should have a new Data Editor window open.

Defining Variables

SPSS cannot work unless variables are defined. You can have SPSS define the variables for you, or you can do the defining yourself, thereby having much more control over the way things look and work. SPSS will automatically name the first variable *var00001* once it is defined. If you defined a variable in row 1, column 5, then SPSS would name the variable *var00005* and also number the other columns sequentially. But you can also define variables, assigning a name of your choice.

Custom Defining Variables

When it comes to getting started with a new data file, custom defining variables should be your choice since it allows for much greater flexibility.

To define a variable name, follow these steps. We will start in a new data window. You can follow along and enter data in your own file if you wish.

1. Highlight the column you wish to represent the variable.
2. Click **Data**, then click **Define Variable**. When you do this, you will see the **Define Variable dialog box** as shown in Figure A.8.

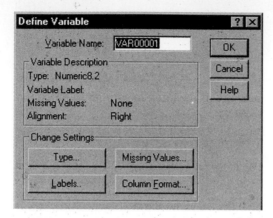

Figure A.8 The Define Variable dialog box.

As you can see, SPSS will automatically assign the name *var00001* in the Variable Name text box.

3. Enter a name for the variable. In our example, we are going to use ID (variable 1 in the data set in Appendix B). Remember that the name you assign to a variable must follow the rules of DOS, such as no more than eight characters.
4. Click **OK**, and the first variable is defined.

Defining Variable Labels

If you click the Labels button in the Define Variable dialog box, you see the **Define Labels: id** dialog box as shown in Figure A.9.

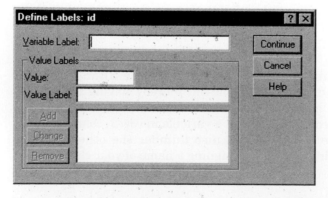

Figure A.9 The Define Labels dialog box.

Why would you want to change the label of a variable? You probably already know that, in general, it makes more sense to work with numbers than with "string" or alphanumeric variables in an analysis. In other words, values such as 1 for male and 2 for female provide more information than entering the actual text that describes the label of the gender.

It sure is a lot easier, though, to look at a data file and see words rather than numbers. Just think about the difference between data files with numbers representing various levels (such as 1 and 2) of a variable and with the actual values (such as male and female)? The Labels option in the Define Variable dialog box allows you to enter values in the cell but what you will see are value labels.

Changing Variable Labels

To assign or change a variable label, follow these steps. Here, we will label males as 1 and females as 2.

1. Click the second column in the Data Editor window.
2. Click **Data**, then click **Define Variable**.
3. Click **Labels**.
4. Enter a name (gender) for the variable in the Variable Label text box. Remember the eight character limit.
5. Enter a value for the variable. This value, such as 1 or 2, is what will appear in the data file window.
6. Enter the value label for the value. In the example shown in Figure A.10, you can see that male is being entered as a value of 1.

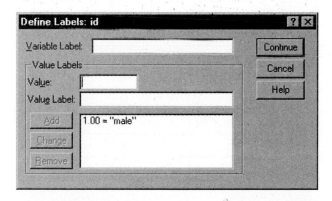

Figure A.10 Assigning a value label in the Define Labels dialog box.

7. Click **Add**.
8. Click **Continue**. Now define the value 2 as female. When you finish your business in the Define Variable dialog box, click **OK**, and the new labels will take effect.

Continue to define all six variables labeled as ID, Gender, Grade, Building, Reading, and Math. Gender is the only variable where labels will be used.

Entering Data

Entering data into the Data Editor window and creating a data file is simple: Place the cross-hair shaped cursor in the cell where you want to enter data, click, and type.

Let's enter data for the first case like this.

1. Place the cursor in row 1, column 1.
2. Click once. The cell borders of the individual cell in the data file will be outlined.
3. Enter the value 001 for id. SPSS will enter the value 1.00 since the default format is two decimal places. The cell in the Data Editor that is highlighted and shows the value in the information bar is the **active cell**.
4. Press the **Tab** key to move to the next variable in the current case. You can also press the → key. If you want to move to the next cell in the column, press the Enter key.
5. Press the Tab key to move to the column labeled Gender.
6. Type **2** and press Enter. Notice that, if you assigned labels for gender, the value is still 2, but it appears as *female* in the Data Editor window.
7. Continue entering data in the Data Editor until the first 10 cases of the data in Appendix B are entered as shown in Figure A.11.

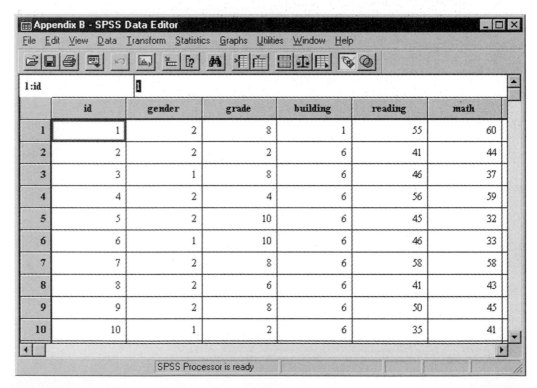

Figure A.11 The first 10 cases of Appendix B.

If you make an error, just backspace and retype your entry.

Saving a Data File

This is the easiest operation of all, but it may be the most important. As you know from your experience with other applications, saving the files that you create is essential. First, saving allows you to recall the file to work on at a later point in time. Second, it allows you to back up files. Finally, you can always save a file under a new name and use the copy for a purpose other than that for which the original was intended.

Exploring Research

How often should you save? You should get in the habit of saving after every set amount of work or number of minutes. One general rule is to save as often as necessary so that you can re-create any work you might happen to lose between saves. Every time you finish a case or every 15 minutes (whichever comes first) is a good guideline.

In order to save the data document that is currently active (which is the data you entered and you see in Figure A.11), follow these steps.

1. Click **File**, then click **Save**. When you do this, you will see the **Save Data As** dialog box as shown in Figure A.12.

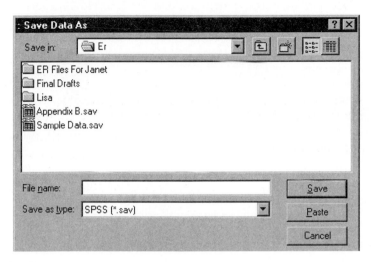

Figure A.12 The Save Data As dialog box.

2. Select the directory in which you want to save the data. If you are saving to a hard drive and you are working in a computer lab, be sure you have permission. If you are saving to a floppy disk, select Drive A or Drive B.
3. Enter the file name you want to use in the File Name text box to save the data that has been entered. Notice that the *.sav* extension is already there. In Figure A.11, we named the file Sample Data.
4. Click **OK**.

The data you entered will then be saved as a data file, and the name of the file will appear in the title bar of the Data Editor window. The next time you select Save Data from the File menu, you will not see the Save Data As dialog box. SPSS will just save the changes under the name you originally assigned to the data file. And remember, SPSS will save the data in the active directory. In most cases, that will be the same directory which contains SPSS, a situation you may or may not want.

Opening a Data File

Once a file is saved, you have to open or retrieve it when you want to use it again. The steps are simple.

1. Click **File**, then click **Open**. You will see the **Open Data File** dialog box.
2. Find the data file you want to open, and highlight it.
3. Click **OK**.

A quick way to find and open an SPSS file is by clicking on its name at the bottom of the File menu. SPSS lists the most recently used files there.

Printing and Exiting an SPSS Data File

Here comes information on the last thing you will do once a data file is created. Once you have created the data file you want or completed any type of analysis or chart, you probably will want to print out a hard copy for safekeeping or for inclusion in a report or paper. Then, when your SPSS document is printed and you want to stop working, it is time to exit SPSS.

Printing with SPSS

Printing is almost as important a process as editing and saving data files. If you cannot print, you have nothing to take away from your work session. You can export data from an SPSS file to another application, but getting a hard copy directly from SPSS is often more timely and more important.

Printing an SPSS Data File

It is simple to print, either an entire data file or a selection from one.

1. Be sure that the data file you want to print is the active window.
2. Click **File**, then click **Print**. When you do this, you will see the **Print** dialog box shown in Figure A.13.
3. Click **OK**, and whatever is active will print.

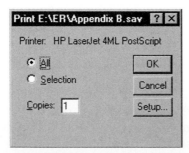

Figure A.13 The Print dialog box.

As you can see, you can choose to print the entire document or a specific selection (which you will have already made in the Data Editor window) and to increase the number of copies from 1 to 99 (that is the limit).

Printing a Selection from an SPSS Data File

Printing a selection from a data file follows exactly the steps that we listed above for printing a data file, except that in the **Data Editor** window, you select what you want to print, and click on the **Selection** option in the Print dialog box. The steps go like this.

1. Be sure that the data you want to print is selected (using the techniques we discussed in the last lesson).
2. Click **File**, then click **Print**, or click the Print icon on the Toolbar.
3. Click **Selection** in the Print dialog box.
4. Click **OK**, and whatever you selected will be printed.

Exiting SPSS

To exit SPSS, follow these steps.

1. Click **File**, then click **Exit SPSS**. SPSS will be sure that you get the chance to save any unsaved or edited windows and will then close.

Creating an SPSS Chart

A picture is worth a thousand words, and SPSS offers you just the features to create charts that bring the results of your analyses to life. In this lesson, we will go through the steps to create several different types of charts and provide examples of different charts. Then, we will show you how to modify a chart, including adding a chart title, labels to axes, modifying scales, working with patterns, fonts, and more.

Creating a Simple Chart

The one thing that all charts have in common is that they are based on data. While you may import data to create a chart, in this example we will use the data from Appendix B to create a line chart of reading scores by grade.

Creating a Line Chart

The steps for creating any chart are basically the same. You first enter the data you want to use in the chart, select the type of chart you want from the Chart menu, define how the chart should appear, and then click OK. Here are the steps we followed to create the chart you see in Figure A.14.

1. Enter the data you want to use to create the chart.
2. Click **Graphs**, then click **Line**. When you do this, you will see the **Line Charts** dialog box you see in Figure A.15.
3. Click **Simple**.
4. Click **Summaries for Groups of Cases**.
5. Click **Define**. When you do this, you will see the **Define Simple Line: Summaries for Groups of Cases** dialog box.
6. Click **Reading**, and then click Other summary information, then click ▶.
7. Click Grade, then click ▶ in the Category Axis area indicating that the grade variable is used as the category or X axis variable.
8. Click **OK**, and you see the results of the chart in Figure A.16.

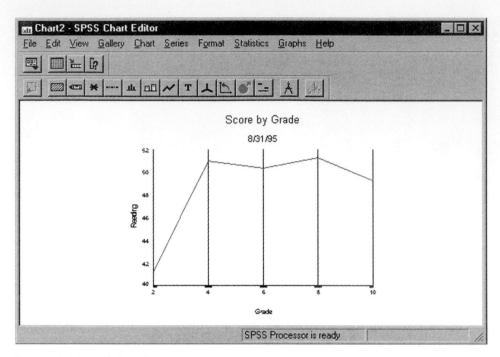

Figure A.14 A simple line chart.

Figure A.15 The Line Charts dialog box.

What you see in Figure A.16 is a chart in the Output Navigator. You cannot see the entire chart in this window, and it is necessary to take one more step to see the entire chart and be able to modify it if you so choose.

9. Double-click on the chart, then click the maximize button. You will see the entire chart in Figure A.14 in the **Chart Editor** window.

    This is the default chart with no additions, changes, or edits. We will get to that next.

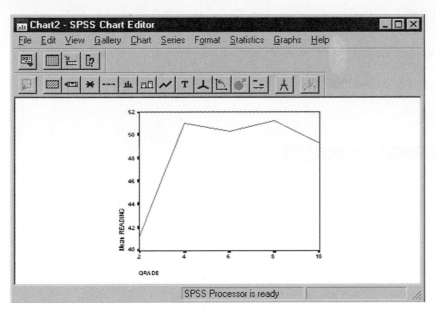

Figure A.16 The line chart in the Output Navigator window.

Saving a Chart

A chart is only one component of the Output Navigator window. A chart is part of the output generated when you perform some type of analysis. The chart is not a separate entity that stands by itself, and it cannot be saved as such in the Output Navigator. To save a chart, you need to save the contents of the Output Navigator. Follow these steps to do that.

1. In the Chart Editor window, click **Close**.
2. Click **File** in the Output Navigator window, then click **Save**.
3. Provide a name for the Output Navigator window.
4. Click **OK**. The Output Navigator is saved under the name that you provide with an *.spo* extension.

Enhancing SPSS Charts

Once you create a chart as we showed you in the last section, you can finish the job by editing the chart to reflect exactly what you want to say. Color, shapes, scales, fonts, and more can be worked with. We will be working with the line chart that was first shown to you in Figure A.14.

Modifying a Chart

The first step with the modification of any chart is to double-click on the chart in the right pane of the Output Navigator, and then click the maximize button on the Application title bar to expand the Chart Editor.

Working with Titles and Subtitles

Our first task is to enter the title and a subtitle on the chart you see in Figure A.14.

1. Click **Chart**, then click **Title**. When you do this, you will see the **Titles** dialog box as shown in Figure A.17.

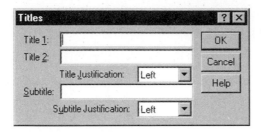

Figure A.17 The Titles dialog box.

2. Type **Score by Grade** in the Title 1 section.
3. Press the Tab key.
4. Type **8/31/95** in the Title 2 section.
5. Click **Center** from the drop-down menus for justification of the title and subtitle.
6. Click **OK**.

The title and subtitle should appear on the chart. If you want to edit a title or a subtitle, just be sure that the chart is active, then select Title from the Chart menu.

Working with Fonts

Now it is time to work with the font used to represent any of the text in the chart. You can do this one of two ways, with each way using the same dialog box.

1. Select the area of the chart containing the font you want to change. When you select text, it appears with a solid line around it.
2. To select a new font and size, you can either select Text from the Format menu or click on the Text button. When you do either of these steps, you will see the **Text Styles** dialog box shown in Figure A.18.

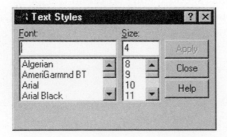

Figure A.18 The Text Styles dialog box.

3. Select the font and size you want to use.
4. Click Apply, and the font will change in the chart.

In Figure A.19, the font size was changed to 14 point for the title and 12 point for the subtitle. You cannot highlight more than one text area at a time, so you have to highlight each one and then select the font you want to use.

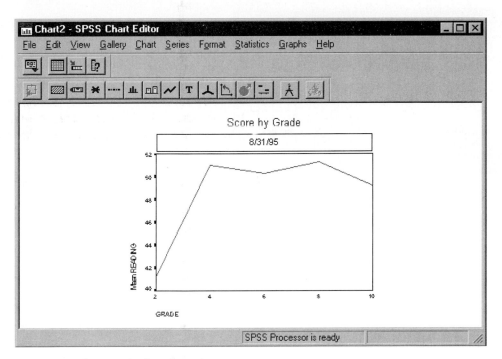

Figure A.19 Changing the font of graph text.

Working with Frames

SPSS, by default, places a frame around the top and right side of the chart, an inside frame. If you want, it can also place a frame around the entire chart, called an outside frame. To include or exclude an inner or outer frame, select the option (Inner Frame or Outer Frame or both) from the Chart menu. You can see how the inner frame was removed making for a less cluttered appearance as shown in Figure A.14.

Working with Axes

The X and Y axes provide the calibration for the independent (usually the X axis) variable and the dependent (usually the Y axis) variable. SPSS names the Y axis the **Scale axis** and the X axis the **Category axis**. Each of these axes can be modified in a variety of ways. To modify either axis, double-click on the title of the axis.

How to Modify the Scale (Y) axis.

For example, to modify the Y axis, follow these steps.

1. Double-click on the label of the axis. When you do this, you will see the **Scale Axis** dialog box as shown in Figure A.20.

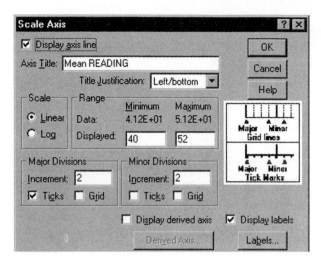

Figure A.20 The Scale Axis dialog box.

2. Select the options you want from the Scale Axis dialog box. We did the following:
   - changed the label MEAN reading to Reading.
   - centered the axis title

We could have done several other things, such as changing the range of the scale (which is 40 to 80 based on data values of 45 and 72) and working with major divisions and minor divisions.

Working with the Category (X) Axis

Working with the X axis is no more difficult than working with the Y axis.
Here is how the X axis was modified.

1. Double-click on the label of the X axis. The Category Axis dialog box opens. It is very similar to the Scale Axis dialog box you see in Figure A.20.
2. Select the options you want from the Category Axis dialog box. We did the following:
   - centered the axis title
   - included a grid for the major divisions

Describing Data

Now you have some idea about how data files are created in SPSS. Let's move on to some examples of simple analysis.

Frequencies and Crosstab Tables

Frequencies simply compute the number of times that a particular value occurs. Crosstabs allow you to compute the number of times that a value occurs when categorized by one or more dimension such as gender and age. Both frequencies and crosstabs are often reported first in research reports since they give the reader an overview of what the data looks like. To compute frequencies, follow these steps.

1. Click **Statistics**, point to **Summarize**, then click **Frequencies**. When you do this, you will see the **Frequencies** dialog box as shown in Figure A.21.

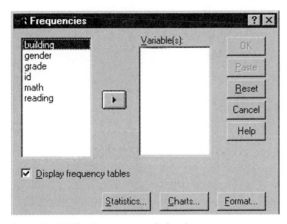

Figure A.21 The Frequencies dialog box.

Click the variables for which you want frequencies computed. In this case, they are reading and math.

2. Click **math**, then click ▶ to place it in the Variable(s) box.
3. Click **reading** if it is not already highlighted, then click ▶ to place it in the Variable(s) box.
4. Click **Statistics**. You will see the **Frequencies: Statistics** dialog box as shown in Figure A.22.

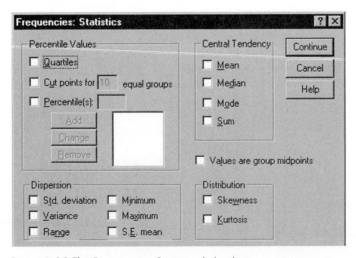

Figure A.22 The Frequencies: Statistics dialog box.

5. In the Dispersion area click **Std. deviation**.
6. Under the Central Tendency area click **Mean**.
7. Click **Continue**.
8. Click **OK**.

The output consists of a listing of the frequency of each value for total reading and math, plus summary statistics (mean and standard deviation) for reading and math.

Describing and Exploring Data

Here, we will use various options on the Summarize menu to compute simple descriptive statistics.

How to Compute Descriptive Statistics

To use the Descriptive option, follow these steps.

1. Click **Statistics**, point to **Summarize**, then Click **Descriptive**. When you do this, you will see the **Descriptive** dialog box shown in Figure A.23.

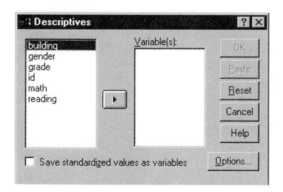

Figure A.23 The Descriptive dialog box.

2. Click **reading** if not already selected, then click ▶ to place the variable in the Variable(s) box.
3. Click **math** if not already selected, then click ▶ to place the variable in the Variable(s) box.
4. Click **Options**, and you will see the **Options** dialog box as shown in Figure A.24.
5. Click the descriptive statistics you want to compute. In this example, we will compute the mean, standard deviation, a maximum, and a minimum and arrange them in alphabetical order.
6. Click **Continue**, then click **OK**. The results of the descriptive analysis are shown in Figure A.25.

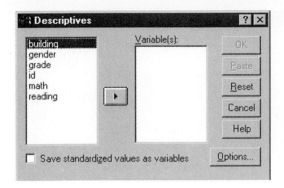

Figure A.24 The Options dialog box.

Descriptive Statistics

	N	Minimum	Maximum	Mean	Std. Deviation
MATH	200	15	60	47.37	10.02
READING	200	27	60	48.63	7.22
Valid N (listwise)	200				

Figure A.25 The results of the descriptive analysis.

Applying the Independent Samples T-Test

Independent t-tests are used to analyze data from a number of types of studies, including experimental, quasi-experimental, and field studies such as those shown in the following example where we test the hypothesis that there are differences between males and females in reading.

How to Conduct an Independent T-Test

To conduct an independent t-test, follow these steps.

1. Click **Statistics**, click **Compare Means**, then click **Independent-Samples T Test**. When you do this, you will see the **Independent-Samples T Test** dialog box as shown in Figure A.26.

   On the lefthand side of the dialog box you see a listing of all the variables that an be used in the analysis. What you now need to do is define the test and the grouping variable.

2. Click **reading**, then click ▶ to move it to the Test Variables(s) area.
3. Click **gender**, then click ▶ to move it to the Grouping Variable area.
4. Click **Define Groups**.
5. In the Group 1 box, type **1**.
6. In the Group 2 box, type **2**.
7. Click **Continue**.
8. Click **OK**.

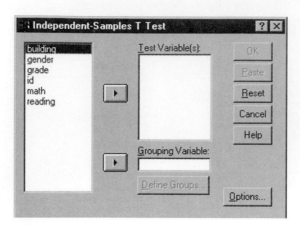

Figure A.26 The Independent-Samples T Test dialog box.

The output contains the means and standard deviations for each variable, plus the results of the t-test as shown in Figure A.27.

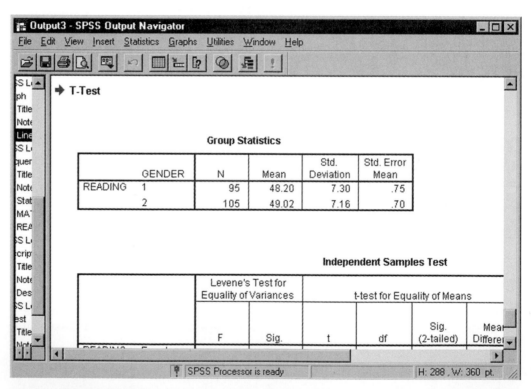

Group Statistics

	GENDER	N	Mean	Std. Deviation	Std. Error Mean
READING	1	95	48.20	7.30	.75
	2	105	49.02	7.16	.70

Independent Samples Test

	Levene's Test for Equality of Variances		t-test for Equality of Means			
	F	Sig.	t	df	Sig. (2-tailed)	Mean Differe

Figure A.27 Results of the t-test.

We have just given you the briefest of introductions to SPSS, but if you are motivated you can certainly learn a lot more on your own by just exploring while using the data in Appendix B.

APPENDIX

B

Sample Data Set

ID	Gender	Grade	Building	Reading Score	Mathematics Score
001	2	8	1	55	60
002	2	2	6	41	44
003	1	8	6	46	37
004	2	4	6	56	59
005	2	10	6	45	32
006	1	10	6	46	33
007	2	8	6	58	58
008	2	6	6	41	43
009	2	8	6	50	45
010	1	2	6	35	41
011	1	4	6	56	58
012	1	6	1	47	33
013	1	2	6	43	44
014	2	2	6	44	39
015	1	6	6	48	37
016	1	8	6	50	51
017	2	4	6	48	54
018	1	2	6	45	44
019	2	6	6	58	59
020	1	4	6	57	53
021	2	6	4	32	36
022	2	4	6	60	60
023	1	4	6	57	52
024	2	2	6	40	42
025	1	2	6	44	44
026	2	6	6	58	60
027	2	2	6	43	44
028	1	8	6	47	53
029	1	10	3	55	49
030	1	2	6	40	44
031	2	6	6	50	55
032	2	8	6	51	58
033	2	2	6	44	43

ID	Gender	Grade	Building	Reading Score	Mathematics Score
034	2	8	6	56	59
035	1	4	6	45	43
036	1	8	6	57	54
037	1	10	6	58	59
038	1	10	6	47	20
039	2	4	6	48	43
040	1	2	5	31	34
041	1	8	6	60	59
042	1	8	6	41	42
043	1	10	6	54	55
044	1	10	6	56	57
045	2	6	6	56	57
046	1	6	6	48	46
047	2	2	6	43	40
048	1	6	6	58	60
049	1	6	6	45	47
050	1	6	6	50	56
051	2	10	6	51	41
052	2	6	6	50	45
053	2	8	6	54	54
054	1	8	4	38	22
055	1	4	6	53	51
056	2	4	2	53	47
057	2	2	6	42	45
058	1	2	6	43	41
059	2	6	6	57	57
060	2	2	6	38	45
061	2	6	6	56	57
062	2	10	6	50	44
063	1	6	5	53	56
064	1	2	6	41	41
065	2	4	6	48	53
066	1	4	4	39	45
067	1	2	6	44	39
068	2	6	6	55	58
069	2	4	6	50	57
070	1	8	6	31	31
071	2	8	6	59	57
072	1	6	6	51	50
073	2	2	6	44	43
074	2	8	6	52	40
075	1	8	6	58	59
076	2	8	6	42	48
077	2	8	6	51	49
078	1	10	6	58	59
079	1	2	6	43	38
080	1	4	6	55	58
081	2	10	6	58	57
082	2	10	6	49	23
083	1	2	6	33	35

ID	Gender	Grade	Building	Reading Score	Mathematics Score
084	2	6	6	53	39
085	2	6	6	56	60
086	2	10	6	54	53
087	1	4	6	49	54
088	1	8	6	58	56
089	1	6	6	48	51
090	1	2	6	43	40
091	2	4	6	52	43
092	1	6	6	58	57
093	2	2	6	45	45
094	2	4	6	49	55
095	2	4	6	55	55
096	1	4	6	54	54
097	2	10	6	53	41
098	1	4	6	53	53
099	2	2	6	41	41
100	1	6	6	51	56
101	1	10	4	48	30
102	2	4	6	57	57
103	2	4	6	56	59
104	2	6	6	57	60
105	2	10	6	56	45
106	2	2	6	37	45
107	1	8	6	47	39
108	2	4	6	56	51
109	2	2	6	42	44
110	1	8	6	55	59
111	2	6	6	52	56
112	1	8	6	58	60
113	2	6	5	54	53
114	1	2	6	39	29
115	1	10	6	49	45
116	2	10	6	47	40
117	1	8	6	54	53
118	1	4	6	51	54
119	2	8	4	55	48
120	1	4	6	49	53
121	1	2	6	45	44
122	2	2	3	42	42
123	2	4	6	42	46
124	2	4	6	49	43
125	1	8	6	56	59
126	1	2	6	40	43
127	2	4	6	55	60
128	2	10	6	54	58
129	2	6	6	47	50
130	2	6	6	56	58
131	2	4	3	43	38
132	2	6	6	41	45
133	1	8	6	47	57

ID	Gender	Grade	Building	Reading Score	Mathematics Score
134	1	6	6	55	55
135	2	2	6	41	44
136	1	10	6	47	29
137	2	8	6	52	37
138	1	4	6	51	48
139	1	6	6	59	59
140	1	8	6	36	47
141	1	4	6	53	58
142	2	2	6	37	37
143	1	6	6	49	55
144	2	8	6	55	57
145	2	10	6	40	47
146	2	10	6	53	56
147	2	4	6	57	59
148	1	2	6	45	44
149	2	4	6	56	57
150	1	4	6	46	50
151	1	8	6	48	36
152	2	6	6	43	41
153	2	6	6	51	54
154	2	8	6	41	52
155	1	4	4	41	30
156	2	2	6	45	42
157	2	10	4	39	19
158	2	6	6	57	59
159	1	8	4	58	59
160	2	4	6	52	48
161	2	10	6	27	18
162	1	2	6	40	43
163	1	10	6	41	15
164	1	6	6	51	53
165	1	6	4	39	52
166	2	6	6	58	60
167	2	2	6	42	41
168	2	6	6	52	51
169	1	10	6	41	39
170	2	6	6	38	23
171	2	10	6	55	59
172	2	6	6	59	59
173	1	10	6	31	31
174	2	6	6	50	55
175	1	8	6	59	59
176	1	10	4	49	19
177	1	2	6	36	37
178	2	10	6	54	50
179	1	10	6	46	41
180	2	4	6	35	38
181	2	6	6	45	57
182	2	6	4	40	31
183	1	10	6	54	47

ID	Gender	Grade	Building	Reading Score	Mathematics Score
184	1	8	6	57	52
185	2	2	6	41	42
186	1	10	6	52	47
187	1	10	6	55	57
188	2	8	6	36	33
189	2	6	6	39	43
190	1	2	6	45	45
191	2	6	6	49	42
192	2	6	6	51	51
193	2	8	6	55	43
194	1	2	4	38	33
195	1	10	6	50	45
196	1	8	6	55	59
197	2	8	6	58	53
198	1	8	6	52	54
199	2	8	6	52	48
200	1	6	6	42	53

Gender Grade Reading Homework
Score

APPENDIX

C

Answers to Exercises

A note to the Students:

Lots of questions that are asked at the end of chapters are specific to you and your needs as a beginning researcher and have no right or wrong answer. Some of these questions have answers such as "Answers will vary" or "Library Assignment", not too creative, but you get the point. They're included to give you an opportunity to think about different topics and issues.

Chapter 1

1. This is an exploratory exercise and answers will vary.

2. This is an exploratory exercise and answers will vary.

3. This is an exploratory exercise and answers will vary.

4. This is an exploratory exercise and answers will vary.

5. A correlation between variables only indicates an association, not a cause and effect relationship. It is always possible in correlational research for other variables to be the true cause of the effect. For instance, strength may be the result of differences in nutrition and exercise, not age. Even if one variable does affect the other, a correlational study can never reveal which is the cause and which is the effect.

6. Definitions of science often include some of these elements:
    a system for seeking knowledge,
    a measurement process or component,
    a research activity, and
    asking questions within the framework of a theory.

    A physical scientist is more likely to work within a tightly structured theory and may believe more strongly in the objective nature of truth.

7. This is an exploratory exercise and answers will vary.

8. Among many correct answers, the value of generating new questions, checking the results of others, and increasing the likelihood that results did not occur by chance. Also, a replication helps clarify the equivocal nature of certain findings, where several different studies may report results that are opposite or contradictory to one another.

9. Good research is based on the work of others, can be replicated, is generalizable, is based on some logical rationale and tied to theory, is doable, generates new questions or is cyclical in nature, is incremental and is an apolitical activity that should be undertaken for the betterment of society.

10. Attending day care during preschool and primary grade school years has a positive impact on children's social interactions with peers.

11. Historical research relates to events that have occurred in the past to current events. It addresses the nature of events that have happened in the past.

   Correlational research provides an indication as to how two or more things are related to one another, or how well a specific outcome might be predicted by one or more pieces of information.

   Quasi-Experimental (or Post-Hoc) research takes place after the assignment of participants to groups. Therefore the researcher has a high degree of control, but not the highest degree of control over the cause of whatever effects are being examined.

Chapter 2

1. a. The independent variables are the individuals in the sample (children) and the type of fitness program. The dependent variable is strength.
   b. The independent variables are the various "stop-smoking" programs. The dependent variable is the number of cigarettes smoked each day.
   c. The independent variable is the various methods used to teach the material. The dependent variable is the measure used to assess student learning of the material, such as a comprehensive final exam.

2. The null hypothesis is always a statement of equality since, without any other knowledge, the researcher assumes that the starting point for investigating a relationship is that groups are equal. The research hypothesis can take on many forms since there are so many different questions that can be asked if one assumes that the null hypothesis is not the most attractive explanation for any observed differences.

3. Null Hypothesis: Attitudes toward work and family will be the same for middle-aged men who have children than for those who do not.

   Research Hypothesis: The attitudes toward work and family will differ between middle-aged men who have children and those who do not.

4. This is an exploratory exercise and answers will vary.

5. What does not "work" (or is not significant) is as important a contribution as being aware of what does. It is information that provides a perspective on the other side of the coin.

6. Level of measurement always depends on how something is measured. Keep that in mind.

   Lew's hair color (C)
   age in years (V)
   number of windows in your residence (C)
   a late-model car (C)
   the current time of day (C)
   number of correct answers on this week's quiz (V)
   signers of the Declaration of Independence (C)
   name of the fifth girl in the third row (C)
   today's date (C)
   number of words remembered (V)

7. This is an exploratory exercise and answers will vary.

8. A good hypothesis is stated in declarative form and posits an expected relationship between variables. Good hypotheses reflect the theory and literature upon which they are based and are brief, to the point, and testable.

9. A good scientist must be familiar with the research done in his or her topic of interest. By reading and evaluating research articles, the scientist can observe what has already been done, how similar studies were designed, and most importantly, lend a rationale to the relationship implied between factors the scientist believes to be important in the study.

10. Any three of the following five are acceptable:
    1. must be stated in a declarative form
    2. posits a relationship between variables
    3. reflects a theory or a body of literature on which they are based
    4. should be brief and to the point
    5. should be testable

11. 1. All research is voluntary and an individual should not be forced to participate in a research study.
    2. An individual should be able to remain anonymous when he or she participates in a study. No one should know the names of the participants with the exception of the principal investigator.

    One should also not invade a person's private space to observe behavior or collect data.

Chapter 3

Questions 1 through 9 are library activities and answers will depend upon individual student's selections and interests.

9. Here's a recommended sequence of steps, although yours can vary as long as you address the general topics.
   a. Read other literature reviews to see what has already been done on your topic.
   b. Develop a theme or a unified thought to tie together your review.
   c. Systematically organize your materials and thoughts. This can be done through index cards, a computer system, or note taking or any combination of techniques.
   d. Make an outline of your topic and work from it.
   e. Create logical bridges between the different areas of the literature review.
   f. Write several drafts. Keep trying to refine your writing through lots of practice.

10. The review of the literature serves to set the stage for the research question you are going to ask. The purpose of a literature review is to examine literature in areas related to your topic and present a rationale for your study. Reviews of literature also summarize important empirical results that have a direct bearing on the question you are asking. Finally, literature reviews build logical bridges between related and not so related areas of research that are pertinent to your research idea.

11. a. Are there gender differences in the process of adolescent development of independence?
    b. Does this process start at different ages for males and females?
    c. What are important factors in the development of independence for males versus females?
    d. What role do family variables such as parenting style play in the development of independence?
    e. What role do peer groups play in the development of independence?

12. This is an exploratory exercise and answers will vary.

13. A research question is not a declarative statement like a hypothesis, but a clearly stated expression of interest and intent.

Chapter 4

1. a. Define the population from which I want to draw a sample; in this case, high school students.
   b. Compose a list of all the high school students.
   c. Assign each individual high school student a number.
   d. Decide upon some criterion not related to the study to select individuals for the sample, such as a table of random numbers.

2. The numbers in the table appear in random order and are unrelated to any characteristics of the population from which the sample is being drawn.

3. Probability sampling is a strategy used when the likelihood of any member of the population being selected is known. For example, if there are 300 centers playing college basketball out of 2000 players in all, the odds of selecting one center as part of the sample is 300/2000 or .15. In a nonprobability sampling strategy, the likelihood of selecting any one member from the population is unknown. For example, if we do not know how many mothers consume alcohol during their

pregnancy, we cannot compute the likelihood of any one being selected. The advantages of a probability strategy is that selection is based on chance factors, thus eliminating determination by nonsystematic and random rules and increasing the chance that the sample will represent the population well. The main advantage of a nonprobability strategy of sampling is that it is relatively convenient and inexpensive as well as ensures some degree of representativeness in the population. However, the disadvantage is that the results may be questionable with regard to representativeness since the true probability was never known.

4. The easiest way to reduce sampling error is to use good selection procedures and increase the size of the sample.

    There is an inverse relationship between sampling error and the generalizability of the results of the study. As sampling error increases the generalizability decreases and vice versa because sampling error is the degree of variability in the sample. If it is large, the implication is that the population is diverse which means that the results are not very generalizable. If the sample size is increased, sampling error will decrease because as the sample gets larger it approaches the size and representativeness of the actual population which includes some of the diversity that elevates sampling error.

5. Since the number of individuals are unequal to begin with in the population, in order to select a representative sample where N=150, one might use a stratified sampling strategy with two variables stratified. If 150 children will be selected from a population of 10,000, this represents 1.5%. This percentage is to be multiplied by the percentages representative of nonwhites, whites, single and dual parent families in the population of 10,000. For example, there are 5,700 single parent children, and the sample of 150 should include 85.5 children from single parent families (1.5% X 5,700). In the sample of 150 children using this strategy, 64.5 of the children have dual parent families, 45 are nonwhite and 105 are white.

6. You expect there to be an even distribution of males and females in the sample because there is an even number of males and females in the population.

7. When a sample is too small, it may not represent the population well, which adds to the error of your study. This can be overcome by taking a larger sample, but if the sample is too large one is sure to find significant differences among groups which may not be "truth."

    This is due to the power and nature of statistical inference. For this reason using too large a sample might be uneconomical and self-defeating.

8. Use the formula:

    Where s is the standard deviation, t is the value with a minimum of 30 subjects in each group, and D is the estimated difference between groups, N is computed to be 180. Thus, 180 subjects will be needed in each group to yield the estimated difference above.

9. a. It is not economical
    b. The researcher is not taking advantage of the power of inference

10. Cluster sampling should be used when the population consists of units rather than individuals, while simple random sampling should be used when the population's members or individuals are similar to one another.

11. It is a lack of fit between the sample and the population or the difference between the characteristics of the population from which the sample was selected. A good researcher wants to reduce sampling error and have a sample that is representative of the population.

    This is important in order to have research results that can be effectively generalized back to the population. If a sampling error is too large the results can only be effectively generalized to the population from which the sample was taken, and even then, without a great deal of confidence.

Chapter 5

1. a.   interval
   b.   nominal
   c.   interval or ratio
   d.   ratio
   e.   interval
   f.   nominal
   g.   ratio
   h.   nominal
   i.   interval
   j.   ordinal

2. a.   t
   b.   m
   c.   m
   d.   m
   e.   t

3. Test-retest. The same test is given at two points in time to the same group of individuals. The two sets of scores are correlated with each other to measure consistency over time.

   Parallel forms. Two different tests made from the same general pool of possible questions are given to one group of people.

   Internal consistency. One test is designed so that the items are unidimensional in nature.

4. Content validity and one way to establish it is to have experts in the area of history examine the questions and pass on their appropriateness for inclusion in the test.

5. Answers might include ACT, SAT, GRE, and (perhaps) intelligence tests.

6. Level of measurement is the scale representing a hierarchy of precision on which a variable is assessed.

7. a. Nominal - Gender
   b. Ordinal - place/rank in a competition
   c. Interval - Intelligence test scores
   d. Ratio - Age

8. A test can be reliable without being valid but a test cannot be valid without first being reliable.

Chapter 6

1. a. Discrimination score = .37
      Difficulty score = .28
   b. Discrimination score = -.08
      Difficulty score = .21

2. Here are some samples of Likert scale items with both positive and negative direction.
   a. It is stealing to borrow something without returning it.
      SA A N D SD
      1 2 3 4 5
   b. There should be stiff legal penalties for stealing.
      SA A N D SD
      1 2 3 4 5
   c. Stealing is not a "hard" crime like murder.
      SD D N A SA
      1 2 3 4 5
   d. Religious groups that cut off someone's hand for stealing are justified.
      SA A N D SD
      1 2 3 4 5
   e. It is okay to steal food if you are starving.
      SD D N A SA
      1 2 3 4 5

3. This is an exploratory exercise and answers will vary.

4. Questionnaires are paper and pencil tasks that consist of a set of structured, focused questions. They are time-saving because they are self administered. Questionnaires can be used to survey large geographic areas, and are cheaper than interviews to conduct. It may be possible to obtain more truthful information because anonymity is assured. A disadvantage of questionnaires, however, is that large mail-outs of surveys may have low return rates. A small percentage of people that receive them will return them.

   Interviews are useful to gain hard to come by information. The format of an interview allows for greater individuality and flexibility in the direction of the data collection. Using an interview format also allows you to note other interesting information such as nonverbal behavior, and the setting that may have an impact on the data being collected. The disadvantage to conducting interviews as a measurement technique is cost and time. Interviews are costly and take a long time to conduct.

5. a. This item has a moderate difficulty level. Approximately half the students answered it correctly. However, the negative discrimination score indicates that most of the lower third of students answered it correctly, while the upper one third did not. It discriminates between the upper and lower thirds of the group, but not in the "right" direction.
   b. This item has a high difficulty index; almost everyone answered it correctly. This item also does not discriminate very well between the upper one third and lower one third of the class.

6. a. Questions that are clear and not too personal.
   b. Coverage in a clear concise manner.
   c. Interesting questions.

7. a. If you keep it anonymous individuals will be more willing to be truthful.
   b. You can survey a larger geographic area by using the mail.
   c. Questionnaires are cheaper than using personal interviews.

Chapter 7

1. Your form will probably look different from others; just be sure it contains the important information.

2. a. .2
   b. 2.4
   c. -.6

   a. 97.5
   b. 105.5
   c 110.6

   Z-scores allow us to compare performances on tests which use different scoring systems. They indicate where a score falls on the normal curve associated with a particular test.

3. range = 5, mean = 4.7, sd = 1.703

4. a. For math:
         Claire's z-score = 2.235
         Noah's z-score =1.18
      For science:
         Claire's z-score = .70
         Noah's z-score = .96
   b. The best performance overall is Claire on the math test.
   c. Based on z-scores alone, Claire is the better student overall.

5. A z-score of 0 indicates performance exactly at the mean, and if normally distributed, the student did better than 50% of the other students.

6. Mean = 4
   Median = 3
   a. The score of 10 is so far away from most of the other scores that the mean is not representative. The median is insensitive to extreme scores.

b. There are five modes in this distribution. No score appears more frequently than others.

7. Because the few mega-millionaires would make the mean far above what most people earn, the median is usually reported as the average income.

8. This is an exploratory exercise and answers will vary.

9. 16%

10. The mean is the average of all of the scores. The median is the middle score. The mode is the most frequently seen score.

11. Mean (Group 1) = 2.5   Mean (Group 2) = 5
    Median (Group 1) = 2   Median (Group 2) = 4
    Mode (Group 1) = 1   Mode (Group 2) = 3

Chapter 8

1. When you begin studying the variables that you think are responsible for any observation including differences, you have no evidence to support such assumptions. The only explanation that you can choose that is not presumptuous is that the differences are due to chance.

2. The null hypothesis cannot be rejected. According to the table of critical values, with 60 (closest to 53) degrees of freedom at .05 and .01, in order to reject the null hypothesis the t value must be greater than or equal to 2.000 or 2.660, respectively.

3. Statistical significance means that the findings indicate that the null hypothesis is not the best explanation for the observed differences. It is possible that even if the findings are significant, they may not be meaningful for a variety of reasons. First, even if the treatment from which change is implied produces significant changes, are the changes large enough to warrant spending taxpayer money, investing millions, etc., to produce?

   Secondly, significant findings may not be meaningful in another context. It seems prudent to assess significant findings in the arena of a cost/benefit analysis in order to determine meaningfulness.

4. The central limit theorem posits that regardless of how a characteristic is distributed in the population, through repeated sampling a normal distribution of scores will represent the population. This is the critical link in inferential statistics because while it would not be possible to ever truly know how the distribution is shaped in the population, the central limit theorem allows the researcher to generalize back to the population distribution. Without it the researcher would be heavily restricted in generalizing back to the population.

5. a. Mean of the entire population = 3.23
   b. Mean of all five means computed = 3.16
   c. The central limit theorem explains why these "means of the means" is so close to the mean of all 30 scores because the theorem says that repeated

will produce a normal distribution of means whether they are normally distributed in the population or not. By taking the mean of the means and it being so close to the mean of all the scores, it is implied that the means are normally distributed about the true mean of the population.

d. This example illustrates the power of the central limit theorem when it comes to making inferences from samples to populations because it reveals how the researcher need not know the true state of affairs existing in the population in order to make generalizations to it from the findings generated from a sample.

6. To say that findings are statistically significant is saying that the observed differences between groups are due to factors other than chance, primarily a treatment effect. The researcher sets a level on the odds of observing a value and once it is equalled or surpassed the findings are considered statistically significant.

7. When the null hypothesis is rejected because the critical value equals or surpasses the value needed for rejection, the research hypothesis may be accepted as a likely alternative to account for the observed group differences. The research hypothesis can never be proven because what is being tested is the null hypothesis.

8. 1. Statement of the null hypothesis: There will be no differences in attachment between infants attending day care and those taken care of at home up to 11 months.
   2. Level of risk: $p < .05$.
   3. Selection of test statistic: t-test for independent means.
   4. Computation of test statistic value.
   5. Determine the value needed to reject the null hypothesis using an appropriate table of critical values for t test statistic.
   6. Compare the obtained value with the critical value.
   7. Either fail to accept or accept the null hypothesis based on comparison of critical value with obtained value.
   8. Draw conclusions based on the most attractive explanation. For example, if the critical value was not surpassed, then the most attractive explanation for any differences in attachment between day care infants and infants cared for at home is chance factors. On the other hand, if the critical value was equalled or surpassed, the null hypothesis can be rejected and the research hypothesis can be accepted as a possible explanation for the differences in attachment.

9. a. no
   b. yes
   c. yes
   d. n
   e. no

10. To describe a phenomenon as it occurs or is occurring.

11. Cross sectional studies examine age difference while longitudinal studies examine age changes.

12. a. T
    b. T
    c. F
    d. T

Chapter 9

1. The purpose of historical research is to examine trends of phenomena over time and to relate these trends to each other or to current events.

2. Several differences exist between historical research and other types of research. Historical researchers use the past in the form of documents and people for data collection. Historical research is not concerned with the statistical relationship between variables. Historical data is gathered from two major sources; primary sources such as original artifacts, documents, interviews, and records, and secondary sources such as summary statistics and newspaper clippings. Data must be evaluated for authenticity and accuracy, rather than reliability and validity. Historical data is integrated and synthesized into historical trends.

3. This is a library assignment and answers will vary.

4. A cross-sectional null hypothesis would be: There are no differences between groups of 12, 16, and 22 year olds in levels of moral reasoning. A longitudinal null hypothesis would be: Moral reasoning does not change over time.

   A study that looks at age changes would be whether early aggressive behavior in preschool predicts aggression in adulthood. A study that examines age differences would be one that answers the question "Do children at different ages exhibit different television viewing preferences?"

5. .78, -.67, .53, .21, -.01

6. The fault with this argument is that there is no reason to think that a relationship between two variables is causal. One does not necessarily cause the other. There may be other factors that contribute to the relationship between study time and test performance. One cannot assume from the information that lack of study time causes poor performance without controlling for other important variables, such as amount of sleep, test anxiety, and the style of the teacher.

7. Age as a variable provides descriptive information about what is occurring; however, age is unable to explain why something occurs. Experience, not age, explains developmental differences. Techniques, such as time of measurement effects, are concerned with determining when behaviors occur, not simply age.

8. a. positive
   b. negative
   c. no relationship
   d. negative

9. a. no
   b. yes
   c. yes
   d. no
   e. no

10. The purpose of descriptive research is to assess the current status of a set of things, people, events or constructs. It provides a descriptive account of

phenomena and often serves as a catalyst for other research ideas. Descriptive research simply describes phenomenon, it does not explain or attribute cause and effect relationships to variables.

11. Cross-sectional research examines age differences while longitudinal research examines age changes. The advantages of the cross-sectional method is that it is inexpensive and takes a short time span. The disadvantages is that there is a lack of comparability of groups and it provides no ideas as to the direction of change that a group might take. One of the advantages of longitudinal is the extensive detail on the process of development and the high comparability of groups. The disadvantages are that this method is expensive and has a potential for a high dropout rate.

12. A, b, and d are true.

Chapter 10

1. Pretest-sensitization—Subjects increase or decrease performance because of exposure to a pretest. One example would be a pretest to measure levels of self-esteem in young people which might awaken thoughts which had not surfaced before. The new thought patterns could affect performance during treatment.

   Reactive arrangements—Simply knowing that one is being observed affects performance. In many experiments, subjects are not told the true nature of the study until its conclusion.

2. Results should be both attributable to the hypothesized cause and generalizable to other populations.

3. Regression is a threat. The children were placed in the extreme due to the measurement error associated with the instrument and on subsequent testings, the likelihood is high that the scores will become less extreme - that is, approach the mean.

4. Some steps could be:
   Random assignment of subjects to groups.
   Random assignment of groups to treatments.
   Relevant variables on which to match might be:
       gender
       parental income
       parental level of education

5. One possible abstract would be as follows.

   A researcher wishes to measure the effect of a new memory enhancing drug on the intelligence of rats as measured by the speed at which they learn a new maze. She chooses the ten slowest, or "dumbest," rats out of a group of 100, administers the drug to them, and is pleased to see that their learning speed has increased.

6. This is an exploratory exercise and answers will vary.

7. Answers might include superstitions, unproven betting systems, and behaviors meant to bring good luck.

8. Answers might include a comparison with posttest allows for a measure of change and establishing a criterion for equalizing initial differences.

9. a. Multiple treatment inference—Subjects may receive an additional treatment besides the intended treatment which decreases the researcher's ability to generalize results to other settings in which the additional treatment may not be available.
   b. Reactive arrangements—If subjects know about the researcher's intent, they may act differently, thus reducing the generalizability of the study.
   c. Experimental effects—If the experimenter becomes actively involved in the research, he can become a treatment variable. This would reduce the generalizability of the study.
   d. Pretest Sensitization—When the researcher informs subjects about what is to come or what is expected and it affects their later scores and decreases the internal validity.

Chapter 11

1. Group design generally measures one behavior over a group of individuals, while single subject design measures one individual over a group of behaviors. Single subject design is best when there is a limited availability of subjects, or the condition being studied is rare or unique.

2. Quasi-experimental research is conducted when the independent variables cannot be manipulated experimentally because of ethical or natural limitations. Examples might include the effect of different parenting styles, differences in salary based on gender, or a nation's gross national product as a function of employment rate.

3. Blood type, level of abuse, and food deprivation must be studied using the quasi-experimental method since participants are already assigned to "treatments".

4. In quasi-experimental design the differences you might observe between the groups has already occurred. Whereas in experimental design you control the assignment of groups

5. a. How does gender affect assertiveness?
   b. Does religion influence career choice?
   c. Does ethnic race affect age of marriage?

References

American Psychological Association (1992). *Ethical principles of psychologists and code of conduct, 47,* 1597-1611. Washington, D.C.: Author.

American Psychological Association (1994). *Publication Manual of the American Psychological Association.* Washington, D.C.: Author.

Baer, D. (1970). An age irrelevant concept of development. *Merrill-Palmer Quarterly, 16,* 238-245.

Burton, N., & Jones, L. (1982). Recent trends in achievement levels of black and white youth. *Educational Researcher, 11,* 10-14.

Campbell, D. T. & Stanley, J. (1963). Experimental and quasi experimental design for research on teaching. In N.L. Gage (Ed.), *Handbook of Research on Teaching.* New York: Macmillan, 171-246.

Castro, G., & Mastropieri, M. A. (1988). The efficacy of early intervention programs: A meta-analysis. *Exceptional Children, 52,* 417-424.

Chen, C., & Stevenson, H. (1989). Homework: A cross-cultural examination. *Child Development, 60,* 551-561.

Conoley, J. C., & Kramer, J. J. (Eds.). (1989). *The 10th mental measurements yearbook.* Lincoln, NE: Buros Institute of Mental Measurements.

Csikszentmihalyi, M., & Larson, R. (1987). Validity and reliability of the experience-sampling method. *Journal of Nervous and Mental Diseases, 175,* 526-536.

Curtiss, S. (1977). *Genie: A psycholinguistic study of a modern day "wild child."* New York: Academic Press.

Duckett, E., & Richards, M. (1989). *Maternal employment and young adolescents' daily experiences in single-mother families.* Paper presented at the Society for Research in Child Development, Kansas City, MO.

Fleming, A. S., Klein, E., & Corter, C. (1992). The effects of a social support group on depression, maternal attitudes, and behavior in new mothers. *Journal of Child Psychology and Psychiatry, 33,* 685-698.

Gardner, H. (1983). *Frames of mind: The theory of multiple intelligence*. New York: Basic Books.

Glaser, R. (1963). Instructional technology and the measurement of learning outcomes. *American Psychologist, 18*, 519-521.

Hanson, S. L., & Ginsburg, A. L. (1988). Gaining ground: Values and high school success. *American Educational Research Association, 25*, 334-365.

Jordan, T. E. (1987). *Victorian childhood: Themes and variations*. New York: State University of New York Press.

Kaufman, A. S., & Kaufman, N. L. (1983). Kaufman assessment battery for children. Circle Pines, MN: American Guidance Service.

Kidder, T. (1989). *Among school children*. New York: Random House.

Krohn, E. J., Lamp, R. E., & Phelps, C. G. (1988). Validity of the K-ABC for a black preschool population. *Psychology in the Schools, 25*, 15-21.

Lampl, M., Veldhuis, M. L., & Johnson, M. L. (1992). Saltation and stasis: A model of human growth. *Science, 258*, 801-803.

Likert, R. (1932) A technique for the measurement of attitudes. *Archives of Psychology, No. 140*.

Mitchell, J. V. (Ed.). (1983). *Tests in print III: An index to tests, test reviews, and the literature on specific tests*. Lincoln, NE: Buros Institute of Mental Measurements.

Neill, A. S. (1960). *Summerhill*. New York: Hart.

Nesselroade, J., & Baltes, P. (1974). Adolescent personality development and historical change: 1970-1972. *Monographs of the Society for Research in Child Development, No. 39*.

Ottenbacher, K. (1995). An examination of reliabilty in developmental research. *Developmental and Behavioral Pediatrics, 16*, 177-182.

Peretti, P.O., & Majecen, K.G. (1992) Emotional abuse among the elderly: Affecting behavior variables. *Social Behavior And Personality, 19*, 255-261.

Radin, N., & Harold-Goldsmith, R. (1989). The involvement of selected unemployed and employed men with their children. *Child Development, 60*, 454-459.

Singer, J. L., Singer, D. G., & Rapaczynski, W. (1984). Children's imagination as predicted by family patterns and television viewing: A longitudinal study. *Genetic Psychology Monographs, 110*, 43-69.

Skeels, H. M. (1942). A study of the effects of differential stimulation on mentally retarded children: A follow-up report. *American Journal of Mental Deficiency, 46*, 340-350.

Skeels, H. M. (1966). Adult status of children with contrasting early life experiences: A follow-up study. *Monographs of the Society for Research in Child Development, 31,* 340-350.

Smith, M. L., & Glass, G. (1977, September). Meta-analysis of psychotherapy: Outcome studies. *American Psychologist, 39,* 752-760.

Smith, M. L., & Shepard, L. A. (1988). Kindergarten readiness and retention: A qualitative study of teachers' beliefs and practices. *American Educational Research Association, 25,* 307-333.

Solomon, D., Watson, M., Deluccci, K., Schaps, E., & Battistich, K. A. (1988). Enhancing children's prosocial behavior in the classroom. *American Educational Research Journal, 25,* 527-554.

Stevens, S. S. (1951). Mathcmatics, measurement, and psychophysics. In S.S. Stevens (Ed.), *Handbook of experimental psychology.* New York: Wiley.

Terman, L. (1925). Mental and physical traits of a thousand children. In L. M. Terman (Ed.), *Genetic studies of genius.* Stanford, CA: Stanford University Press.

Terrance, L., & Johnson, M. (1978). Ratings of educational and psychological journals. *Educational Researcher, 19,* 8-10.

Thurstone, L. L. & Chave, E. J. (1929). *The measurement of attitudes.* Chicago: The University of Chicago Press.

Vaughn, B., Lefever, G., Seifer, R., & Barglow, P. (1989). Attachment behavior, attachment security, and temperament during infancy. *Child Development, 60,* 728-737.

Vellman, P. F., & Wilkinson, L. (1993). Nominal, ordinal, interval, and ratio typologies are misleading. *The American Statistician, 47,* 6572.

Wigfield, A., & Eccles, J. (1989). Text anxiety in elementary and secondary school students. *Educational Psychologist, 24,* 159-183.

Wintre, M. G., Hocks, R., McVey, G., & Fox, J. (1988). Age and sex differences in choice of consultant for various types of problems. *Child Development, 59,* 1046-1055.

Glossary

A

abstract — A brief summary of a journal article that appears before the actual article or as a collection of abstracts.

accuracy — A measure of how trustworthy and accurate a historical data source is.

achievement test — A test used to measure knowledge in a specific content area, such as math or reading.

applied research — Research that has an immediate application.

attitude test — A test that assesses an individual's feelings or preferences about objects, events, and people.

authenticity — Genuineness of historical data sources.

average — A measure of central tendency represented as the mean, median, or mode.

B

baseline — Level of behavior associated with a subject before an experiment begins.

basic research — Pure research that while adding to the base of information in a field has no immediate application.

browser — A software tool that is used to tour and work with the World Wide Web.

C

case study—A descriptive research method used to study an individual in a unique setting or situation in an intense manner.

causal-comparative research—Research where subjects are assigned to groups based on a characteristic beyond the control of the experimenter, such as sex or age. It is also another name for post hoc or quasi-experimental research.

central limit theorem—The theorem in inferential statistics that states that regardless of the shape of the population distribution, repeated samples from it will produce means that are normally distributed.

chance—The unassuming explanation for differences between groups that implies the differences are accounted for by variables other than those being studied.

choice status—A sociometric index that indicates how well an individual is doing in a particular group.

closed-end question—A question that has a clear and apparent focus and a clearly called for answer. Same as a structured question.

cluster sampling—A probability sampling procedure where units of subjects are selected rather than the subjects themselves.

coding—Using numbers to represent data.

coefficient of alienation—The amount of variance that is unaccounted for in the relationship between variables.

coefficient of determination—The squared correlation coefficient, which indicates the amount of variance in one variable that is accounted for by the other.

communications software—Software that directs a modem how to transfer information from one computer to another.

concurrent validity—A type of criterion validity.

construct validity—The extent to which a test truly measures a proposed psychological ability or skill and is related to an underlying theory or model of behavior.

content validity—The extent to which a test fairly represents the universe of all possible questions that might be asked.

continuous recording—Recording behavior on a continuous basis.

control group—The group that does not receive the treatment, but may receive the other condition.

convenience sampling—A nonprobability sampling procedure where the selected sample represents a captive audience. For example, sophomore college students in an introductory psychology class.

correlation coefficient—An index of the strength of a relationship between two variables. It ranges in value from - 1.00 to + 1.00 and can be positive or negative.

correlational research—A method of research used to determine relationships between two or more variables.

criterion-referenced test—A test that measures mastery of specific definitions of performance for an individual in a particular content domain.

criterion validity—How well a test estimates (concurrent validity) or predicts (predictive validity) performance outside of the testing situation.

critical value—The tabled value at which point the null hypothesis cannot be accepted. The minimum value you would expect the test statistic to yield if the null hypothesis is true.

cross-sectional method—A method of developmental research used to examine age differences rather than age changes.

D

data collection form—A form used to record raw data and often used to facilitate entry into the computer.

data point—Each score for each individual on a test or in an experiment.

degrees of freedom—The leeway for variation a statistical value has. They help determine the critical value of the test statistic.

dependent variable—The outcome variable of research. Dependent variables are observed for effects due to the influence of another factor, the independent variable(s).

descriptive research—Research that describes a phenomenon without any attempt to determine what causes the phenomenon.

descriptive statistics—Simple measures of a distribution's central tendency and variability.

developmental research—Methods of research that examine changes over time.

difficulty index—The percentage of test takers who correctly answer a multiple choice item.

directional research hypothesis—A research hypothesis that posits an inequality between groups with direction to that difference (such as more than or less than).

discrimination index—An index that describes how well a multiple choice item differentiates between high scorers and low scorers on a test.

distribution of scores—The general shape of data that includes a mean, median, and mode.

duration recording—Recording behavior based on the amount of time it lasts.

E

electronic mail—A method of communicating over telephone lines using a modem and a computer.

error score—The part of an individual's observed score that is attributable to method or trait variance or error.

experimental group—The group that receives the treatment.

experimental method—The method used to test the cause and effect relationship between variables.

experimental research—Research that examines cause-and-effect relationships through the use of control and treatment groups.

experimenter effects—a threat to the internal validity of study where the presence of an experimenter can change the effectiveness of the treatment.

external criticism—The evaluative criterion used in historical research to establish the authenticity or validity of sources.

external validity—The extent to which the results of an experiment can be generalized.

F

face-sheet information—Information about the respondent such as age, living arrangements, number of children, income, sex, and educational level.

factor analysis—An advanced statistical technique that allows for the reduction of variables representing a particular construct and that then uses factor scores as dependent variables.

factorial design—A research design where more than one independent variable is studied in various combinations with others.

follow-up studies—Studies that use the databases of prior research as a method for the collection of additional data.

frequency recording—Recording behavior based on the incidence or frequency of the occurrence of a particular behavior.

G

general sources—General information usually available through newspapers, periodicals, or broad indexes.

generalizability—The ability to draw inferences and conclusions from data.

H

Hawthorne effect—The effect that knowledge of the experiment by the participants can have on the outcomes.

historical research—A methodology for examining how events that have occurred in the past affect events in the present and future.

historiography—Another name for historical research.

history—Uncontrolled outside influences on subjects during the course of an experiment.

home pages—A WWW location that is written in HTML and contains information about people, places, and things.

hot links—A hypertext connection between locations on the WWW.

hypothesis—An educated guess to be tested.

I

independent variable—Variables controlled by the researcher in an attempt to test the effects on some outcome, the dependent variable. Independent variables are also known as treatment variables due to their manipulation and exposure to groups and individuals at the discretion of the researcher.

index—A listing of resources, organized by topic or author.

inferential statistics—Procedures that allow inferences to be made from a sample to the population from which the sample was drawn.

institutional review board—A group of people who review research proposals for safety and consideration of participants.

instrumentation—Those conditions within a testing situation, other than the abilities of the subject, that might affect performance.

internal consistency—A measure of reliability that examines the unidimensional nature of a test.

internal criticism—An evaluative criterion used in historical research to establish the accuracy or trustworthiness of a data source.

internal validity—The accuracy in concluding that the outcome of an experiment is due to the independent variable.

Internet—A worldwide network of networks.

inter-rater reliability—Consistency of results produced by the same test given by different people.

interval level of measurement—Measurement that assigns values representing equal distances between points but that does not allow for proportional comparisons.

interval recording—Recording behavior that occurs during a particular interval of time. Also called time sampling.

interview—A method of collecting data that is similar to an oral questionnaire. An interview can be informal and flexible, or structured and focused.

interviewer bias—Bias introduced when the interviewer subtly influences the interviewee's responses.

item analysis—A process of evaluating multiple choice items by using difficulty level and the ability of the item to discriminate or differentiate between group performance.

L

level of measurement—The scale representing a hierarchy of precision on which a certain type of variable might be assessed.

Likert scale—A method used in attitude scales that requires the individual to agree or disagree to a set of statements using a five-point scale.

listserv discussion group and mailing list—An automated mailing list for receiving mail and information about a particular topic.

longitudinal method—A method of developmental research that assesses changes in behavior in one group of subjects at more than one point in time.

M

maturation—Changes due to natural development, which may threaten the internal validity of an experiment.

mean—The sum of all the scores in a distribution divided by the number of observations.

measurement—Assignment of values to objects, events, or outcomes according to rules.

measures of central tendency—Measures of central tendency represented as the mean, median, or mode.

median—The score at which 50% of the scores in the distribution fall above and 50% fall below.

meta-analysis—A procedure that allows for the examination of trends and patterns that may exist in many different groups in many different studies.

method error—The part of an individual's error score that is due to characteristics of the test or the testing situation.

mode—The most frequently occurring score.

modem—A hardware device that modulates and demodulates signals for transfer over a phone line.

mortality—a threat to the internal validity of a study based on the dropping out or removal of participants from the experiment.

multivariate analysis of variance (MANOVA)—Statistical procedures used to examine group differences that occur on more than one dependent variable.

mutual choice—In sociometric measurement, two or more individuals who choose one another.

N

Net—Another name for the Internet.

Netscape—A WWW browser.

network—A collection of computers that are connected to one another.

newsgroup—A discussion group on the Internet.

nominal level of measurement—Measurement that assigns labels that do not suggest quantity.

nondirectional research hypothesis—A research hypothesis that posits an inequality (such as a difference between groups) but that makes no suggestion of the direction of that difference (such as more than or less than).

nonprobability sampling—When the likelihood of selecting any one member of the population is unknown.

norm-referenced test—A test where the individual's performance is compared to the results of a larger group of his or her peers.

null hypothesis—A statement of equality between groups in an investigation. The null hypothesis serves as a starting point for observing the effects of the independent variable(s) on the dependent variable and as a benchmark for the comparison of chance versus significant differences between groups.

O

observed score—True score plus error score.

obtained value—The value obtained by applying a statistical test of significance.

open-ended questions—Interview questions that provide a broad opportunity for the participant to respond.

optical scanner—A special computer that reads optical scoring sheets.

optical scoring sheet—A specially printed scoring sheet that can be read and scored by computer.

ordinal level of measurement—Measurement that assigns only rank order to outcomes.

P

parallel forms reliability—The relationship of two tests made from the same pool of items.

Pearson product moment correlation coefficient—An index of the relationship between variables.

population—The entirety of some group.

post hoc—Also known as quasi-experimental research, research that is done "after the fact" or after treatments have been assigned to groups.

predictive validity—A type of criterion validity.

pre-experimental designs—Research designs that are characterized by a lack of random selection and assignment.

pretest sensitization—When the experience of taking a pretest is related to the effectiveness of the independent variable.

primary historical sources—Sources of historical data that are obtained from original sources. They include original artifacts, documents, oral histories, eyewitness accounts, and diaries.

primary sources—People or documentation that presents firsthand information.

probability sampling—The type of sampling used when the likelihood of selecting any one member of the population is known.

projective test—A personality test that asks the individual to respond to an ambiguous stimulus. It is assumed that the individual will "project" hisor her world view onto the stimulus.

proportional stratified sampling—A stratified random sampling procedure where subjects in the sample are selected in proportion to how they are represented in the population.

Q

quasi-experimental research—That is done when groups are preassigned to treatments, such as gender, social class, and neighborhood.

questionnaire—A set of structured, focused questions that employs a self-reporting, paper-and-pencil format.

quota sampling—A nonprobability sampling procedure similar to stratified random sampling in that a particular stratum is the focus; however, a specified number is set to be selected, and once that number is met no further selection occurs.

R

range—The distance between the highest and lowest score in a distribution.

ratio level of measurement—Measurement that allows for proportional comparison and a meaningful zero.

raw data—Data that is unorganized.

regression—The tendency for extreme scorers to move toward more typical levels of performance when retested.

reliability—Consistency in performance or prediction.

research—An organized process for collecting knowledge.

research design—The method and structure of an investigation chosen by the researcher to conduct data collection and analyses.

research hypothesis—A statement of inequality between groups in an investigation. Research hypotheses suggest directional or nondirectional relationships between groups.

researcher-made tests—Tests designed for a specific purpose with specific scoring and instructions for that purpose.

S

sample—A representative portion of a population.

sampling error—The magnitude of the difference between the characteristics of the sample and the characteristics of the population from which it was selected.

scattergram—A plot of scores or data points that indicates the relationship between variables.

scientific method—A set of steps that scientists follow to assure a common basis for conducting research.

secondary sources—Sources of historical data that are secondhand, such as newspaper clippings and summary statistics.

selection—A threat to the internal validity of a study based on biased selection of participants.

significance level—The type I error rate or the probability that a null hypothesis will be rejected when it is false.

simple random sampling—A sampling procedure allowing for the equal and independent chance of subjects' being selected as part of the sample.

single subject research design—Observing one subject over a variety of behaviors.

standard deviation—Average distance of each score in a distribution from the mean.

standard scores—Scores that have been derived to create a common reference point and the same standard deviation to allow for easy comparison.

standardized test—A test that has standard instructions and scoring procedures that are used for all administrations of the test.

stars—Individuals often chosen by others in sociometric measurement.

statistical significance—The degree of risk that you are willing to take that you will reject a null hypothesis when it is actually true.

stratified sampling—The process of selecting a sample that represents different groups or levels of a population.

stratified random sampling—A random sampling procedure used when subjects are known to be unequal on some variable in the population.

structured question—A question that has a clear and apparent focus and a clearly called for answer. Same as a closed-end question.

structured test—A test that contains items with fixed responses.

systematic sampling—A random sampling procedure where increments determine who becomes part of the sample; for example, every third person is selected.

T

table of random numbers—An unbiased criterion used in the selection of subjects to a sample.

telnet—A set of rules for signing on to and operating a computer at a remote site.

test—A measurement technique used to assess individual differences in various content areas.

test of significance—The application of a statistical procedure to determine if observed differences exceed the critical value indicating that chance is not the most attractive explanation.

testing—a threat to the internal validity of a study based on the sensitization of the group due to the administration of a pretest.

test-retest reliability—The stability of a test over time.

theory—A group of logically related statements that explain things that have occurred in the past and predict things that will occur in the future.

Thurstone scale—A method used in constructing attitude tests in which all of the items are assigned an attitude score. It is made up of nearly equal intervals for individuals to agree or disagree with various statements.

time sampling—Recording behavior that occurs during a particular interval of time. Also called interval recording.

trait error—The part of an individual's error score that is due to characteristics of the individual.

true score—The actual score for someone on some test.

Type I error—Same as the level of statistical significance, the level of risk you are willing to take that the null hypothesis is rejected when it is true.

Type II error The acceptance of a false null hypothesis. The probability of a Type II error's occurring can be reduced by increasing the size of the sample.

U

unstructured questions—Interview questions that provide a broad opportunity for the participant to respond. An open ended question is one such example.

URL (universal resource locator)—An address on the WWW.

USENET—The standard operating procedures for all newsgroups.

V

validity—The truthfulness or accuracy within the score of a test or interpretation of an experiment.

variability—The spread of scores in a distribution.

variable—A class of outcomes that can take on more than one value. Variables are what researchers study.

variance—A measure of the degree of dispersion or variability in a distribution of scores. The variance is the standard deviation squared.

variance—The standard deviation squared.

W

World Wide Web (or WWW)—A collection of graphically illustrated locations on the Internet.

Z

z score—A standard score based on a distribution with a mean of 0 and a standard deviation of 1.

Index

A

ABA design, 255
ABAB design, 255
Absolute zero, 116
Abstracts, 66-69
Accuracy of historical research, internal
    criticism as criterion, 209
Achievement tests, 137-143
    criterion-referenced test, 137-135
    multiple choice items, 138-143
        advantages/disadvantages of, 139-140
        distractors, 139
        item analysis of, 140-143
        structure of, 139
    norm-referenced test, 137-138
    standardized tests, 137
Advisory Committee on Human
    Experimentation, 42
Age, in developmental research, 222-223
American Doctoral Dissertations, 69
American Psychological Association (APA)
    ethical guidelines, 45
    Publication Manual, 276
Analysis of covariance (ANCOVA), to control
    extraneous variables, 246
Annual Reviews of Psychology, 62
Applied research, nature of, 15
Asymptotic curve, 173
Attitude tests
    Likert scale, 144-146
    Thurstone scale, 143-144
Authenticity in historical research, external
    criticism as criterion, 209

B

Basic research, nature of, 15
Benchmark, 28
Bookshelf, 70

C

Case studies, 211-212
    advantages/disadvantages of, 211-212
    examples of, 211
    nature of, 211

Causal-comparative research, 249-256
    groups in, 250-251
    usefulness of, 250-251
Causal correlational research, nature of, 12
Cause/effect relationships, 13-14
CD-ROM, 70
Central limit theorem, 185-188
    example of, 185-188
    sample size and, 185
Chance
    meaning of, 184
    reduction of, 184
Child Development Abstracts & Bibliography, 68
Child Development Monographs, 68
Children, informed consent, 38-39
Cluster sampling, nature of, 102
Coding data, 160-161
Coefficient of alienation, 227
Coefficient of determination, 227
Coercion, lack of, research subjects, 38
Comprehensive Dissertation Index, 69
CompuServe, 73-74
Computers
    literature review
        CD-ROM, 70-71
        on-line searches, 71-75
Confidentiality, research subjects, 40
Confounding variables, control of ANCOVA, 246
    homogenous groups, 246
    matching, 244-246
Construct validity, nature of, 126, 128
Content validity, nature of, 126-127
Control group, in experimental method, 234
Convenience sampling, nature of, 103,104
Correlational research
    correlation coefficient in, 223-227
    nature of, 12
    Pearson product moment correlation, 225-226
    relationship between variables, 223
Correlational studies, 226-227
Correlation coefficient, 223-227
    absolute value of, 226
    coefficient of determination, 227
    definition of, 223
    interpretation of, 226
    positive and negative correlations, 224
    scattergrams and, 224

Professional organizations, ethical guidelines
  American Psychological Association
    (APA), 45
  Society for Research in Child
    Development (SRCD), 45-46
Projective tests, 146
Protection from harm, research subjects, 40
Psychological Abstracts, 66
Publication of article
  acceptance/rejection rates from journals, 66
  preparation of report, 64-65
  review of article, 65
  submission to publication, 65

Q

Quasi-experimental design, 250
  nonequivalent control-group design, 251
Questionnaires,
  advantages/disadvantages of, 149
  basic assumptions of, 150-151
  cover letter, 153-154
  format of, 152-153
Quota sampling, nature of, 103

R

Random assignment, in experimental
  method, 237-238
Random sampling
  nature of, 97-100
  steps in, 97
  table of random numbers, use of, 97-100
Range, computation of, 171
Ratio level, of measurement, 116
Reactive arrangements, as threat to external
  validity, 242
Reader's Guide to Periodical Literature, The, 60
Regression, as threat to internal validity,
  240-241
Reliability, 118-125
  measurement of, 118-120
  relationship to validity, 129
  of scores, 118
  types of
    internal consistency, 124-125
    inter-rater reliability, 123-124
    parallel forms reliability, 122-123
    test-retest reliability, 122
Research
  factors for exploration, examples of, 7
  high quality, characteristics of, 3-5
  hypothesis formulation, 7-8
  model of scientific inquiry in, 6
  steps in research process, 6-10
  types of
    applied research, 15
    basic research, 15
    causal-comparative, 250
    correlational research, 12-13
    experimental, 13-14
    historical, 12
    non-experimental 10

quasi-experimental 14
Research articles
  evaluation of, 34-35
Research hypothesis
  as explicit hypothesis, 32
  nature of, 29-30
  compared to null hypothesis, 31
Research problem
  selection of, 55-56
  statement of research question from, 57
Research Related to Children, 69
Resources in Education, 67
Review
  blind review, 63
Review of Educational Research, 62
Reviews of literature, 57-69
Rorschach Test, 146

S

Sample,
  definition of, 33,96
  selection of, 33
Sampling
  nonprobability sampling
    convenience sampling, 103, 104
    quota sampling, 103, 104
    probability sampling
    cluster sampling, 102, 104
    random sampling, 97-100, 104
    stratified sampling, 101-102, 104
    systematic sampling, 100-101. 104
  sample size, estimation of, 105-107
Sampling error, 103-104
Scattergrams, 224
Science Citation Index, 69
Science Digest, 61
Science News, 61
Scientific inquiry, model of, 5
Score
  error score, 118
  observed score, 118
  true score, 118
Searching the Web 86-87
Secondary sources, 59, 62-63
  reviews of literature, 62-63
  yearbooks, 62
Selection of subjects, as threat to internal
  validity, 239-240
Significance, nature of, 33-34
Significance level, 34
Single-subject design, 254-256
  ABA design, 255
  ABAB design, 255
  evaluation of, 255-256
  method, 254
Sixteen Personality Factor Questionnaire, 146
Social Sciences Citation Index, 62
Society for Research in Child Development
  (SRCD) ethical guidelines, 45-46
Sociological Abstracts, 66
Solomon Four Group design, 238